FROM DOWN-HOME SPLIT PEA TO EXOTIC
MOONG DAHL SOUP, OLD-FASHIONED
JOHNNY CAKES TO LEMON BERRY COUSCOUS
CAKE, YOU'LL LOVE DISCOVERING THE MANY
POSSIBILITIES OF RICE, BEANS, AND GRAINS

Andrea Chesman makes it easy to prepare nutritious yet tasty meals featuring some of nature's most versatile and healthful foods. All the excitement of ethnic treats such as **Risi e Bisi** (rice and peas) joins the comfort of old-time favorites like creamy **Baked Rice Pudding** and hearty **Almost Mom's Quick Chili**. This wonderful new cookbook features:

- Mouth-watering low-fat recipes
- A detailed nutritional analysis of calories, fat grams, percentage of calories from fat, protein, fiber, calcium, and sodium for every dish
- Flavorful vegetarian recipes along with healthful variations that include salmon, shrimp, and chicken

ANDREA CHESMAN has written several cookbooks, including *Salad Suppers, Yankee Church Suppers and Potluck Dinners, Simply Healthful Skillet Suppers,* and *Simply Healthful Pasta Salads.* She lives in Vermont.

366
Delicious Ways to Cook
Rice, Beans, and Grains

ANDREA CHESMAN

A PLUME BOOK

PLUME
Published by the Penguin Group
Penguin Putnam Inc., 375 Hudson Street,
New York, New York 10014, U.S.A.
Penguin Books Ltd, 27 Wrights Lane,
London W8 5TZ, England
Penguin Books Australia Ltd Ringwood,
Victoria, Australia
Penguin Books Canada Ltd, 10 Alcorn Avenue,
Toronto, Ontario, Canada M4V 3B2
Penguin Books (N.Z.) Ltd, 182–190 Wairau Road,
Auckland 10, New Zealand

Penguin Books Ltd, Registered Offices:
Harmondsworth, Middlesex, England

First published by Plume, an imprint of Dutton Signet,
a member of Penguin Putnam Inc.

First Printing, February, 1998
20 19 18 17 16 15 14 13

Ⓟ REGISTERED TRADEMARK—MARCA REGISTRADA

LIBRARY OF CONGRESS CATALOGING-IN-PUBLICATION DATA:
Chesman, Andrea.
    366 delicious ways to cook rice, beans, and grains / Andrea Chesman.
      p.   cm.
    Includes index.
    ISBN 0-452-27654-3
    1. Cookery (Rice)   2. Cookery (Beans)   3. Cookery (Cereals)
I. Title.
TX809.R5C44   1998
641.8'1—dc21   97-24289
                                                                                           CIP

Printed in the United States of America
Set in Palatino
Designed by Leonard Telesca

To Richard,
a taster of unfailing good cheer and sensitivity.

ACKNOWLEDGMENTS

No one can undertake a work of this many recipes without enlisting the aid of numerous tasters, sharers of recipe ideas, and general supporters. My special thanks go to Richard, Rory, and Sam, who tasted day in and day out for more than a year; my sisters, Linda, Toby, and Debra, who tasted, tested, and commented; regular tasters Su White, Eric Warren, and the potters at Frog Hollow in Middlebury; the helpful folks at the Middlebury Natural Foods Co-op; Cheryl Namy Dickason, who shared her Mujdara recipe and opened my palate to the potential of lentils; M. J. Price, who shared the secret of her marvelous muffins and helped me to walk off the extra calories; Kim Kimler, who faithfully hauled away my overcooked grains and underseasoned beans to his chickens and graciously returned with fresh eggs; and the many other friends who came to dinners and parties at my house as witting and unwitting taste-testers. Finally, my deep appreciation goes to Doe Coover, who made this and other projects possible.

Contents

✦

Introduction 1

1
All About Rice, Beans, and Grains 5

2
Dips, Spreads, Starters, and Snacks 33

3
Splendid Soups 59

4
Sensational Salads 99

5
Risottos, Rice Pilafs, and More 143

6
Beans, Beans, Beans 189

7

Pasta e Fagioli   247

8

Great Grains   269

9

The Marriage of Rice and Beans, Beans and Grains   311

10

Bountiful Breakfasts   351

11

Whole-Grain Muffins, Biscuits, and Breads   385

12

Glorious Desserts   409

Index   445

Introduction

꧁

I'm not the sort of person who spends time at parties exchanging recipes. But lately I have found myself in the middle of conversations about beans and grains. Everyone wants to cook them more often, but nobody seems to have enough good recipes.

Try this one, I say. It's a Syrian dish called Mujdara (pronounced Jud-ruh). Cook up some rice in one pot, lentils in another pot. Then sauté a ton of garlic and onions, say six cloves of garlic and three large onions for a dish to serve four, until they are sweet and golden. Mix it all up and add just enough buttermilk to bind it together. Simple. Heavenly. Something you can whip up in half an hour. A dish that we eat regularly at my house.

My husband and I have a marriage made in nutrition heaven: He loves beans and I love grains. Between the two of us, we eat in a way that would make the creators of the new food pyramid beam with pride.

The 1990's food pyramid, the scientists' guide to eating well, would have us eat up to eleven servings of grains each day. To complement those grains, we are supposed to eat two to three servings from the protein group, which includes beans. The trick is not to get more than thirty percent of our calories from fat—and that means lots of beans and little or no meat.

Regardless of whether we feel compelled to eat according to the food pyramid or are strict vegetarians, it is easy to see that a diet that includes plenty of whole grains and beans can be a very healthy one. Beans and whole grains are high in fiber and low in fat and contain no cholesterol. They are also an excellent source of protein, vitamins, potassium, and calcium. A serving of about $1/2$ cup cooked beans contains between 110 and 120 calories, depending on the variety, and little or no fat. A $1/2$-cup serving of grains, depending on the grain, has about 100 calories and is low in fat.

Good intentions aside, nobody will eat beans or whole grains if they don't taste good. And nobody will want to cook them if the process is time-consuming or difficult or requires an investment in expensive kitchen equipment.

Here's my criteria for a good bean or grain recipe. First, the final dish should taste great—there's no point in cooking a meal that no one wants to eat. Second, the dish should be quick and easy to make and should not require following a recipe slavishly. (You should be able to adapt the recipe to your own taste without incurring disaster.) Finally, the dish should be quick to make, with ingredients you are likely to have on hand.

Ethnic classics dominate my collection of bean and grain recipes. These are recipes that have stood the test of time admirably and have as many variations as there are cooks. After you have made these dishes once or twice, you should be able to make them without consulting the recipe. Exact measurements are unimportant. Individual interpretations have kept these recipes alive over time.

Beans, in particular, have a bad reputation as being time-consuming to make because they must be soaked overnight and then simmered on the back of the stove for hours. Not only are there shortcuts for cooking beans, there are also a vast array of canned beans that can be used in most recipes for excellent, quick results. Those who prefer to cook everything from scratch can start with dried beans, cook them slowly, and store them in the freezer in premeasured batches.

Frances Moore Lappe, author of the classic work *Diet for a Small Planet*, had a profound impact on our understanding of nutrition when she popularized the notion of complementary proteins. The body, she argued, needs complete proteins, as are found in meat. She also explained that when you combine beans, an incomplete protein, with grains, also incomplete, you get a complete protein.

You don't have to eat your rice and beans in the same meal to remain healthy (the same day is satisfactory), but rice and beans have a strong culinary affinity—as proven by such felicitous combinations as Louisiana Red Beans and Rice, Jamaican Rice and Peas, Hoppin' John from the American South, and Cuban Black Beans and Yellow Rice. Beans also have an affinity for strong flavors: The Italians combine beans with garlic; the Mexicans combine them with chiles; and Indians combine them with ginger and heady curry spices.

Grains are even more versatile than beans. They combine well with boldly flavored ingredients to make delicious risottos and comforting pilafs. They can provide the bulk for a satisfying whole-meal summer salad or a comforting winter soup. And they can also be cooked with sweet ingredients to make pancakes, breakfast cereals, and desserts.

Not all beans and grains are created equal. Some beans are easily found in dry and canned form in the supermarket (such as black beans, cannellini, chickpeas, and red kidney beans). Some, like lentils, cook quickly and have an amazing affinity for different styles of cooking. Others, like adzuki beans, are found mainly in health food stores or Asian food markets and take some getting used to. Likewise, rice, bulgur, oats, couscous, and barley are familiar to most cooks, whereas amaranth and quinoa are sometimes hard to find and do not adapt readily to standard recipes for cereals or pilafs. In this collection the emphasis is on the familiar and easily accepted grains and beans, the foods people really like to eat, with a fair sprinkling of exotic combinations for the more adventurous.

Most of the recipes yield four to six servings. We all have different ideas of what makes a serving size. My portions are relatively generous. I expect that a dish that serves four to six will satisfy four adults as a main course. For example, a risotto complemented with salad and bread would feed four for dinner. To stretch it to serve six, I'd cook up some beans or some vegetables or add a hearty soup to the menu. The nutritional analyses that accompany the recipes are based on serving the smaller number of people (i.e., if a recipe yields four to six servings, the analysis is based on four). Where the recipe yields are given in terms of cups or a number of pieces, the nutritional analysis is based on a typical serving size or per piece.

People often ask me how I come up with new recipes. The honest answer is that there are very few truly new recipes, just inspired variations on established themes. As to how I come up with inspired variations, I think with my palate. The act of writing a recipe is an act of hunger. I think of the ingredient, rolling it around in my mind as though it were on my tongue. I envision the final dish—and feel intense hunger. This doesn't happen with an ingredient that I dislike. Although I may be able to come up with a few competent recipes for an ingredient that doesn't inspire me, my true inspirations are based upon sensual pleasure and hunger.

The recipes collected here were developed out of honest curiosity about the ingredients and a simple search for sensual pleasure. I hope you will find them as pleasurable as I do.

1
All About Rice, Beans, and Grains

❧

If you take the long view, eating enough rice, beans, and grains has been the pursuit of humans since the first cooking pot was formed. Our earliest ancestors were seed gatherers, and that includes grains and rice, which are the seeds of the grass family, and beans, the seeds of legumes. About ten thousand years ago, people discovered that it was easier to grow their own seeds than to collect them, and agriculture developed. The roaming life of the hunter-gatherer was replaced by settled life next to fields, and this in turn gave rise to all sorts of cultural activities, including writing, accountancy (bean counting), arithmetic, and the culinary arts.

The culinary arts developed intuitively. Somehow people recognized that their well-being was enhanced when they combined grains and beans. Thus, in Asia, a diet evolved rich in rice and soybeans (mainly as tofu). In the Americas, beans were combined with corn.

Though we don't think of the Western diet as evolving from a bean and cereal cuisine, beans were so important in the Middle Ages that the penalty for stealing from a bean field was death. The Old World bean (*Vicia faba*), the fava bean and its variants, originated in the Near East and was domesticated some time in the late Neolithic Period. Beans were used to cast votes in Greece, so clearly they were a commonplace item.

The New World bean (*Phaseolus vulgaris*) was brought to Europe by the Spanish some time in the sixteenth century and was fairly rapidly adopted. It is this type of bean that offers the most variety in terms of names, colors, shapes, and flavors. Some familiar New World beans include Great Northern beans, navy beans, pinto beans, red kidney beans, and cannellini (white kidney beans). Many types of beans that were once popular are no longer being grown, though a national association of heirloom seed collectors is trying to keep as many varieties in circulation as possible. Heirloom seed growers are also working to preserve nonhybrid corn types and other vegetables.

Today, as we cut down on the meat we eat in favor of a diet rich in grains and beans, we are simply returning to our earliest culinary roots. It is only recent history that has seen meat dominate the dinner plate, and we have learned the hard way that a meat-based diet brings along with it certain health problems, such as increased risk of obesity and heart disease.

A diet rich in rice, beans, and grains is healthful because these foods are naturally low in fat and high in fiber. They offer enough protein, vitamins, and minerals to sustain our bodies. And they come in so many different varieties, flavors, and textures that they can be eaten for breakfast, lunch, and dinner without provoking boredom. This book contains 366 different recipes, suited for every occasion, from snack time to formal dinner parties, from soup to dessert, from slow-cooked to nearly instant.

The key to incorporating more grains and beans into your diet is to have them available in the house for cooking. That means shopping at your local natural food store, where just about every ingredient mentioned in this cookbook can be found. While many supermarkets are responding to a consumer demand for more grains and beans, they are mostly offering pre-seasoned, precooked mixes. The fact of the matter is that for all the great size of American supermarkets, these shopping emporiums are dedicated to prepared foods. Supermarkets in this country rarely supply all the basics for a diet heavily oriented toward rice, beans, and grains. I can't find cornmeal in my local supermarket, except in the form of corn muffin mixes. Forget about finding a nice medium grind for polenta. Quinoa? Never heard of it. Adzuki beans? Forget it!

Fortunately, almost every city in this country now boasts a natural food store or food co-op where the ingredients used in this book can be found. Because natural food stores cater to a clientele who frequently cook rice, beans, and grains, their food tends to be fresher than that you might find at an all-purpose supermarket. Beans, in particular, are better when fresh, though they will keep for years.

Here is some basic information about rice, beans, and grains, including buying and cooking instructions.

All About Rice

More than a third of the world's population eats rice as their staple food. Even in the West, where wheat is considered the primary grain, most children begin their diet of solid foods with rice cereal, which is parboiled white rice that has been dried and ground into flakes that readily mix with warm milk. This is only one of the many different processes our rice may be subjected to, which includes enriching, popping, parboiling, and grinding into flour.

When rice is harvested, the grains are usually cleaned and dried. They are then milled to remove the dust and chaff as well as the husk. To make white rice, the remaining bran layer is stripped away. The bran layer is left intact for both brown and black rice.

There's plenty of evidence to suggest that rice cultivation dates back at least thirty-five hundred years, but hunters and gatherers may have been collecting wild rice grains as early as eighty-five hundred years ago. Rice cultivation spread from northeast India and northern Thailand throughout Asia and on to the Middle East, Africa, and parts of Europe. A ship bound for England blew off course to South Carolina in the seventeenth century and the grateful captain gave the governor of that colony barrels of rice, marking the beginning of rice cultivation in the Colonies. Today rice is grown on every continent except Antarctica, and there are between twenty-five hundred and forty thousand different varieties (depending on who is doing the counting).

These myriad varieties evolved in different climates and became part of different cooking traditions. In the New World, where long-grain rice grows well, we have Cajun Jambalaya, Cuban Rice and Beans, and Hoppin' John, all of which require a rice that cooks up fluffy, with well-separated grains. The starchy medium-grain rices from the Piedmont and Lombardy regions of Italy are cooked to creamy perfection in risottos, while the medium-grain rice of Valencia, Spain, gave rise to the paella for which Spain is renowned. Cooked medium-grain rice is not as dry as long-grain rice, nor as sticky as short-grain rice. Short-grain rice is preferred in many parts of Asia and is crucial to such specialties as Japanese sushi.

Any well-conceived natural food store will sell several different kinds of rice. There is a lot of variety in tastes, textures, and ideal cooking methods, so when a recipe specifies a certain kind of rice, you should make every attempt to find it. Here are some types of rice you are likely to encounter.

Glossary of Rice

Creating a list of rice types makes order out of a fairly disorderly situation. Rice may be known by its appearance, its cooking characteristics, or its brand name. For example, at my food co-op, the only short-grain rice for sale is labeled "sushi" rice.

Before the bran layer is removed, most rice is brown in color. Brown rice can be found in long-, medium-, and short-grain varieties. Brown rice has a nutty flavor and chewy texture and requires a longer cooking time (about 40 minutes) than white rice. It has twice the fiber of white rice (which isn't much: .5 g per cup of cooked rice) and is slightly more nutritious; it is slightly richer in protein, vitamin E, magnesium, potassium, and phosphorus.

Long-Grain Rice

Long-grain rice cooks up fairly dry with separate grains, which is why it is the rice of choice for most pilafs. Many of the most flavorful of the long-grain rices, such as basmati and jasmine, are known as aromatic rice because of their pronounced toasted nut or popcorn-like flavor and aroma. When you are planning to serve plain rice, without a sauce or strong seasonings, aromatic rices are a good choice. Look for both brown and white aromatic rices. Some popular types or brands of aromatic rice include Texmati, Jasmati, Wild Pecan, Popcorn, and Wehani.

Basmati Rice. Basmati translates as "something fragrant" in Hindi and this is the most well-known and appreciated of the aromatic rices. A special-occasion rice in India and Pakistan, where it is grown and aged, basmati has a spicy, flowery aroma and characteristically cooks up dry and fluffy. As it cooks, the rice kernels lengthen, in contrast to other varieties in which the rice kernels swell in width. Calmati and Texmati are American-grown rices with similar characteristics. Brown basmati rice is commonly available at natural food stores.

Black Rice. There are several different types of exotically colored blackish purple rice from Southeast Asia; the most common are Thai sweet black rice and Japonica rice. The long dark grains color the cooking water, which becomes lavender. The flavor of the cooked purple-black grains is like a cross between basmati and wild rice. The rice's sticky nature makes it ideal for desserts, and in Southeast Asia it is often cooked in coconut milk. Cook black rice as you would any long-grain brown rice, allowing about 40 minutes cooking time.

Jasmine Rice. An aromatic long-grain rice, jasmine is sometimes called

Thai fragrant rice. It is fragrantly sweet and nutty in flavor like basmati rice, but it is moister when cooked and somewhat sticky in texture.

Wehani Rice. Wehani is a brand of aromatic brown rice grown in California and marketed by Lundberg Family Farm. Its mahogany color promises a highly usual rice, but the flavor is undistinguished from other aromatic brown rices. It is available in bulk at natural food stores, as well as in expensive little boxes at supermarkets and specialty food stores.

Medium-Grain Rice

Medium-grain rices fall in between long-grain and short-grain rices in size and stickiness. The Italian rices used to make risotto, as well as certain Spanish varieties, such as Valencia, which is used to make paella, are all medium-grain rices.

Arborio Rice. The most commonly available of the medium-grain rices from Italy, Arborio grains are short and almost round. As this rice cooks, it releases starch into the cooking liquid to give it a creamy consistency, a characteristic that makes it an ideal rice for risottos and puddings.

Short-Grain Rice

Although all short-grain rices are stickier in texture that long-grain rices, they are not the same as "sticky" rice. The Japanese often prefer short-grain rice, which is easier to pick up with chopsticks, while most Chinese prefer a drier, longer grain rice. Cook as you would long-grain rice, using slightly less water.

Sticky Rice. Also known as glutinous rice, waxy rice, or sweet rice, sticky rice does have a sticky texture, but it is not sweet. Short-grain sticky rice becomes soft and gelatinous when cooked. Sticky rice is never served plain, but has many uses in Asia where it is grown.

Wild Rice

A native American grain that is related to rice, wild rice is not a rice at all, but an aquatic grass, and these days the wild rice for sale is more likely to be cultivated than wild. It cooks up firm and chewy with a grassy, almost bitter flavor.

Buying and Storing Rice

More and more space is being given over to rice at the supermarket these days, but most of this is given over to boxes of preseasoned rice mixes. I have yet to try a preseasoned rice mix that matched what I make at home. And I won't even mention costs.

You are likely to find the best rice selection at a natural food store, where you can buy in bulk, often with a choice between organic and nonorganic. At home be sure to label your storage containers. Although your nose will be able to distinguish certain aromatic rices, it is surprising how similar in appearance arborio and certain short-grain Japanese rice can look, especially when you have one and not the other on hand for comparison.

Uncooked white rice and wild rice can be stored in an airtight container at room temperature for an indefinite period of time without losing flavor or nutrients. Brown rice and other rices that have their bran layer intact contain oils that can go rancid, so it is best to store these rices in the refrigerator after a month. Rice will dry out over time, so you may have to slightly increase the amount of cooking water you use with rice that has been sitting for more than a year in the pantry.

Cooked rice can be stored in the refrigerator for up to 5 days, as long as it is in a tightly sealed container. Cooked rice can even be frozen for 6 to 8 months. Reheat leftover rice in a microwave or on top of the stove, adding a few tablespoons of water as needed.

Cooking Rice

Advice for cooking rice varies widely—and it is always delivered with the gravest authority. It is assumed that there is such a thing as "perfect rice, every time" and only one true way to achieve it. Rinse first. Never rinse. Boil. Steam. Never microwave. No wonder my mother served only instant rice when I was growing up!

The general rule that 1 cup of rice requires 2 cups of cooking liquid results in soggy, clumpy rice more often than not. I think 1 cup long-grain rice requires about $1^3/_4$ cups water. Many people find that it works to place the (long-grain) rice in the pot and fill with water about 1 inch (or one knuckle length) above the rice. Short-grain rice requires less water (about $1^1/_2$ cups per cup of rice). Given that there are so many different varieties of rice, it is important to adjust your water-to-rice ratio as needed.

It's also important to cook the rice at a gentle boil. If the water bubbles furiously, the rice will cook too quickly, leaving a hard center in the core of each grain. If it cooks too slowly, the rice will be gummy.

Rinsing Rice

Rinsing is a very controversial step in the cooking of rice. White rice that is grown and milled in the United States is usually enriched with a spray coating of vitamins. Rinsing does wash away these vitamins and perhaps some of the water-soluble vitamins in unenriched rice as well. Some writers claim that rinsing dates back to a time when rice was likely to be dirty and mixed with impurities and that today, thanks to modern milling practices, it is no longer necessary.

I rinse long-grain white rice. I have a decided preference for fluffy, almost dry rice in pilafs, stir-fries, and most recipes that call for long-grain rice, and I find rinsing helps me to achieve that fluffy consistency. The rice cooks more quickly and absorbs less water when it has been rinsed first. Rather than rinse away flavor as some writers claim, the rinsing process causes the rice to absorb less liquid, which enhances the flavor. Rinsing is never recommended for short-grain or medium-grain rice that will be made into risottos or puddings, where you want a soft, sticky texture. I don't find rinsing helpful for brown rices.

To rinse rice, place the rice in a sieve over a bowl. Run cold tap water into the rice, stirring with a spoon or rice paddle, until the rinse water runs clear. Then drain the rice well before proceeding with the recipe.

To Salt or Not to Salt

I developed a preference for unsalted rice at a Chinese restaurant, where I worked in the kitchen; however, I advise others to salt if desired for flavor. I find that leftovers are more versatile when they aren't salted because they present a completely blank slate. Also, some types of brown rice, particularly Wehani rice, cook better in unsalted water. And finally, when cooking rice in broth, salt is almost never necessary, as most broths are preseasoned with it.

A Rest Period

The flavor and texture of most rices—and most grains, for that matter—is improved with a brief rest after cooking. When all the liquid has been absorbed and the grain is tender, fluff the rice with a fork. Dry the pot lid, then crumple a clean cotton kitchen towel or paper towel and lay it on top of the rice. Cover with the dried pot lid and let stand for about 5 minutes before serving. The towel prevents condensation from forming on the lid of the pot and "raining" back down on the rice.

Cooking Methods

How you cook your rice will definitely affect its taste and texture. Rice cookers generally allow you to cook with less liquid than most stovetop methods. Boiling rice in plenty of water can yield excellent results in terms of texture, but causes the rice to lose flavor.

Electric Rice Cookers

If "perfect rice, every time" is your goal, I highly recommend the purchase of a rice cooker. Nothing could be simpler. You combine the rice and water in the correct proportions, flip a switch, and you have perfectly cooked rice in 20 to 30 minutes. Most rice cookers have a "keep warm" function that keeps the rice at a good serving temperature for up to four hours. The ease with which rice cookers work—no more split-second timing required—and the excellent results they yield could make a convert out of you. There are very few modern households in Asia that do not have a rice cooker in the kitchen—which should tell you something about how well this appliance works.

When purchasing a rice cooker, look for one with a nonstick pan (or plan to spray the pan with nonstick cooking spray before each use).

A proportion of 1 cup long-grain white rice to $1^3/_4$ cups water generally gives good results in a rice cooker. A proportion of 1 cup brown rice to $2^1/_4$ cups water will also yield good results. If you find that the brown rice is still a little too firm after all the liquid has been absorbed, add a few tablespoons of water and start cooking again. The machine will shut off when the additional water has been absorbed.

Steamed Rice

This rice is technically boiled, but it is usually called "steamed rice." Combine the cooking liquid with the rice in a covered saucepan and stir gently. Cover and bring to a rapid boil, reduce the heat to a gentle boil, and cook until the rice is tender, 12 to 15 minutes for white rice, about 40 minutes for brown rice. Do not stir. When all the liquid has been absorbed and the grain is tender, fluff the rice with a fork. Then let the rice rest for 5 minutes, as directed above.

Baked Rice

Baked rice is actually a variation of steamed rice. Combine the rice and cooking liquid in a flameproof Dutch oven or casserole, cover, and bring to a boil on top of the stove. Transfer the dish, still covered, to a preheated 400 degree oven and bake until the liquid is absorbed and the rice is tender, 15 to 18 minutes for white rice, 40 to 45 minutes for brown rice. The advantage to this method is that it is very forgiving if you leave the rice in the oven too long. Rice cooked on the stove will stick to the bottom of the pan if it is forgotten; rice cooked in the oven will merely dry out a little.

Free Boiled Rice

Some people like to cook rice like pasta, in plenty of boiling water, until it is done. I think the rice loses flavor with this method, but if you'd like to try it, bring at least 6 cups of water to a boil. Add 1 cup white rice and boil until the rice is tender, about 12 minutes. Timing is critical, so taste frequently after 10 minutes. Drain well. Some chefs like to parboil the rice this way, then finish it later with flavored liquids and herbs, and this works well.

Flavored Rice and Pilafs

When rice is first sautéed in hot oil and then cooked in broth or water flavored with herbs or spices, the rice comes out highly flavored, with each grain separate. The dish is usually called a pilaf or *pilau*. The proportion of rice to liquid is the same as for steamed rice.

I use both homemade and canned broths or stocks in my pilaf. You will find recipes for vegetable, mushroom, and chicken broths in Chapter 3, and these can be used in many recipes. I have taste-tested a lot of canned vegetable and chicken broths as well as dry bouillon mixes and have found only one satisfactory national brand of vegetarian broth for pilafs: Westrae Natural UnChicken Broth. In most commercial vegetarian products usually one flavor—carrot or tomato—dominates. I think Campbell's Healthy Request Chicken Broth also is an excellent product for both soups and pilafs, and I always have a few cans on hand for the sake of convenience. I urge you to conduct your own taste-tests to find a broth you consider acceptable.

Risottos

Like pilaf, risotto starts with rice that is sautéed in hot butter or oil and the cooking liquid is usually a flavored broth. But here the similarity ends. With a risotto the broth is added slowly and the rice grains are constantly stirred to achieve a creamy consistency. A risotto generates its own sauce. Depending on the amount of liquid added, a risotto can be rather dry or very soupy, but it should never be undercooked so that there is a hard core to each grain. Neither should it be overcooked; each grain should be separate, suspended in a creamy sauce, not soft and mushy.

All About Beans

Beans—or rather, legumes—are a part of every known cuisine and have been eaten for at least eight thousand years. They grow in an incredibly wide range of climates, from the cold mountain plateaus of Peru (where lima beans originated) to the hot, humid tropics (where pigeon peas were first cultivated). With more than seventy varieties of beans currently enjoyed worldwide, it is no surprise that there are so many classic bean dishes. They include Boston Baked Beans and South Carolina's Hoppin' John, Spanish black bean soup, Italian *pasta e fagioli*, Indian *dahl*, Mexican refried beans, Middle Eastern hummus, French lentil salad, and so much more.

The broad category of "beans" includes peas and lentils, though botanically these are legumes, as are beans. When we say "beans," we are including all legumes. The Europeans call this category of food "pulses," from the ancient Roman word *puls,* which means pottage. Whatever you call legumes, when you eat them you are consuming high-protein vegetables that are cholesterol-free and high in vitamin B, minerals (iron, calcium, phosphorus, and potassium), and soluble fiber. A cup of cooked kidney beans, for example, supplies 219 calories, 16 grams of protein, and less than a gram of fat.

Beans are often enjoyed green, when the pods are still tender enough to eat and the seed, or bean, within the pod is undeveloped. These are called snap beans because the pods crack crisply in two when broken. They haven't had strings since 1894, when stringless varieties were introduced and universally adopted. A green bean has more vitamins A and C but much less protein than a dried bean. A bean that is left to grow for about nine to eleven weeks becomes a shell bean, at which stage the pods are tough and inedible, but the beans in the pod can be enjoyed after a brief cooking period. At the dry bean stage (twelve to fourteen weeks after planting), the beans are dry and ready to be stored.

Beans may have been the inspiration for the development of the art of cooking, since all beans and lentils, whether fresh or dried, will cause abdominal pain, nausea, and diarrhea if eaten raw. (With green beans, the beans are not developed; you are eating the pod not the bean, which is why it also has a different nutritional profile.) Boiling beans for 2 to 3 minutes destroys the toxic lectins that cause all of these problems.

Glossary of Beans

The legume family has five main branches. Lentils are the oldest cultivated legume; they were domesticated around the same time as wheat and barley, some eight thousand years ago. They originated in Southwest Asia, probably Syria, and spread throughout the Middle East. The pea is also a legume and includes sweet peas and split peas, but not chickpeas, which belong to a family of their own, or black-eyed peas, which are related to mung beans. Fava beans, or broad beans, originated in Europe. Mung beans and soy beans originated in Asia. The lima bean and the common bean (*Phaseolus vulgaris*) are both New World beans. The so-called "common bean" is a huge family of beans that includes kidney beans, black beans, navy beans, pinto beans, and dozens more.

Beans are a great study in how foods move around the world. Today China produces about seventy percent of the international fava bean crop, while the U.S. is the leading producer of soybeans, most of which are fed to livestock. Africa is the major producer of lima beans. Here is a glossary of the most commonly found beans, with descriptions, cooking times, and name variations.

Adzuki Beans (also known as Azuki, Aduki, Asuki)

Adzuki beans are popular in Asia, where they are called "the king of beans." They are small, oval, red beans with a thin white ridge line (which distinguishes them from small red beans). Adzuki beans are served in both sweet and savory dishes. In Japan, the cooking water from red beans is used to color rice in a festive wedding dish. But, more commonly, the beans are made into a sweetened paste and used as a filling for pastries and confections.

Adzuki beans have a tough skin and should always be presoaked before cooking. Then boil gently for 30 to 45 minutes. Adzuki beans can be found canned.

Black Beans (also known as Turtle, Frijoles Negros, Mexican Black, Spanish Black)

Black beans are central to the cooking of Central and South America as well as the Caribbean. Cuban black bean soup and Moors and Christians (black beans and white rice) are just two of the favorite ways these rich-tasting beans are served. Black beans have a sweet but nutty flavor and a soft creamy texture. The beans have an affinity for chiles, cilantro, and goat cheese. They make an interesting change of pace when substituted for pinto beans in such Mexican or Tex-Mex favorites as refried beans, burritos, and chili.

Gently boil presoaked black beans for about 1 hour. The color of the beans will fade a little. Black beans are readily found canned.

Black-eyed Peas (also known as Brown-eyed Peas, Cow Peas, Southern Peas, Crowder Peas, Black-eyed Suzies)

Black-eyed pea is the most apt name for this cream-colored, kidney-shaped bean with a dark purple circle on its ridge. This native of China (and relative of the mung bean) probably traveled the Silk Route to the Middle East and then to Africa. From there, black-eyed peas were carried by slaves to the New World and established as part of the plantation diet. Black-eyed peas have a buttery texture and mild pea-like flavor. They cook relatively quickly, in 30 to 45 minutes if presoaked. Check frequently when cooking these beans as overcooking causes them to disintegrate. Black-eyed peas are available canned and frozen as well as dried.

Cannellini Beans (also known as White Kidney, Haricot Blancs, Fasiolia, Fagioli)

Popular in the cooking of Italy, France, and Greece, these white, plump, medium-size, oval beans have a slightly nutty, sweet flavor. Their smooth, creamy texture makes them an excellent choice for soups and purees. Cannellini beans are available canned, but the texture is considerably softer than most other canned beans.

Gently boil presoaked cannellini beans for about 45 minutes or until tender and slightly creamy.

Chickpeas (also known as Garbanzos, Ceci)

Chickpeas look like little hazelnuts, though the ancient Romans who gave the beans their name thought they looked like rams' heads. They are one of the most distinctively flavored beans—nutty and chestnutty are two adjectives commonly used to describe their flavor. Chickpeas have a firm texture and hold their shape well with cooking. Even overcooking does little damage to this bean. Of all the canned beans, canned chickpeas hold their shape best.

Gently boil presoaked chickpeas for about 2 hours. If the beans are old, they will take considerably longer to cook. Chickpeas will foam up at the start of the cooking and the foam should be skimmed off. Chickpeas are used extensively in the cooking of the Mediterranean, Middle East, North Africa, and India.

Cranberry Beans (also known as Romans, Barlotti, Shellouts, Shelly)

When cranberry beans are available fresh, connoisseurs eagerly seek them out. The fresh beans are identified by beautiful cream-colored pods with wine-colored marbling. The flavor of these beans is quite delicate, even sweet. This is the traditional bean used for succotash in New England; in the Midwest it is traditionally cooked with sweet spices, such as nutmeg and cinnamon.

Dried cranberry beans, which look like a slightly plumper version of the pinto bean, have a rich, sweet flavor and a creamy texture that makes them a great bean for soups and pasta dishes.

Cook fresh shelled cranberry beans for about 20 minutes. Cook the presoaked dried beans for about 1 hour.

Fava Beans (also known as Broad, Horse, Windsor)

Broad beans were commonplace in colonial American gardens, but they disappeared from American tables until recently, when Mediterranean cooking became popular and they were reintroduced as fava beans. Look for the very large, bright green, fuzzy pods in late spring. Inside each pod is a $3/4$-inch bean that resembles a large lima. You will need 2 pounds in the shell to get $1^1/_2$ cups cooked shelled beans. Unless the pods are harvested when the beans are very young, you will have to remove a tough outer skin from each cooked bean. This is easily done by slicing into the skin with a sharp knife and popping out the bean. The job goes quickly, but you do have to handle each bean. Is it worth the work? If you like the taste of fresh shell beans, you will probably consider fava beans to be the best-tasting of all. Some people say fresh favas taste more like fresh peas than like other shell beans.

Dried fava beans range in color from beige to tan. The skins are often wrinkled and tough and so the beans are best enjoyed pureed. Gently boil the presoaked dried beans for 35 to 40 minutes. The smaller Egyptian favas will cook in 40 to 60 minutes.

Lentils

The oldest known cultivated legume, lentils were mentioned in the Old Testament, when Esau sold his birthright for a bowl of pottage. Lentils play an important role in the diet in India, the Middle East, and Africa. In France, lentils are a common bistro offering.

Lentils vary widely in color, taste, and texture. French green lentils, or *lentilles du Puy*, have a light fresh flavor and a nice firm texture that makes them the only lentil suited for salads. They tend to cost more than other lentils, but are well worth it. Brown lentils, which are actually greenish in color, have a rich flavor but disintegrate readily, making them a good soup candidate. Red lentils, which are really orange, pair beautifully with yellow-hued curry spices and make a nice smooth puree. Cook lentils for about 20 minutes for salads, and 30 to 40 minutes for most other dishes, depending on whether you want the lentils to hold their shape at all.

Lima Beans (also known as Butter, Burma, Christmas, Madagascar, Rangoon, Curry, Pole)

Said to have originated in the high plains near Lima, the capital of Peru, these New World beans have a light buttery flavor and creamy, starchy texture. Two different beans share the same name: the large lima is about $1\frac{1}{2}$ inches long, while the smaller (baby) lima is only about $\frac{1}{2}$ inch long and originated in Mexico. Today limas are grown extensively in Africa.

Fresh limas are available in the pod in late summer. Boil them for 10 to 12 minutes. Presoaked dried limas take about 60 minutes to cook and are quite foamy. Limas are also available canned and frozen.

Mung Beans (also known as Green Grams, Black Grams)

These beans are most familiar to Americans in their sprouted form and are enjoyed in many Asian dishes. They are small, round green beans with a yellow interior. Sometimes the beans are sold hulled and split as *moong dahl* peas. Sprouted mung beans offer about 5 times the nutritive value of the dried beans.

To sprout, place 2 tablespoons mung beans in a quart jar and fill three-quarters full with lukewarm tap water. Cover the jar with cheesecloth or fine mesh and secure the fabric with a rubber band. Shake the jar a few times, then drain. Fill with fresh water and leave to soak overnight. The next day, drain the beans, rinse well, and drain again. Place the jar on its side and store in a warm, dark place. Repeat the rinsing process for 3 to 5 days, until the sprouts are about 2 inches long.

Pink Beans

Small pink versions of the red kidney bean can sometime be found dried or canned. Pink beans can be used interchangeably with pinto beans or small red beans. Cook the presoaked dried beans for about 50 minutes.

Pinto Beans (also known as Mexican Strawberries)

The favorite bean for many Mexican dishes, pinto beans have a meaty flavor and mealy texture. They are closely related to red kidney beans and can be used interchangeably with them when all that matters is taste and texture. With their speckled pink/tan appearance (the name derives from the Spanish word meaning "painted"), they look very similar to cranberry beans. When cooked, the mottled appearance disappears and the beans turn a uniform pink. Two recently developed hybrid versions of pinto beans, rattlesnake and appaloosa beans, are sometimes available.

Cook presoaked dried pinto beans for about 1 hour. Pintos are readily available canned.

Red Kidney Beans

This familiar bean lives up to its name: It is about ¹/₂ inch long, kidney-shaped, and ranges in color from deep reddish brown (almost purple) to light red. When cooked, these beans have a fairly mealy texture and meaty taste. Gently boil presoaked dried red kidney beans for about 1 hour, skimming off any foam that rises to the top of the cooking pot.

Soybeans

In the sixties and seventies, when many Americans started to embrace vegetarianism, it seemed that we would all have to get used to soybeans. These dried beans, which come in a multitude of colors, are easiest to find in the pea-size yellow form. They take 3 to 4 hours to cook. Although rich in protein, plain cooked soybeans have a strong—even unpleasant—earthy flavor. Fortunately, the good nutritional value of soybeans can be enjoyed in tofu and tempeh, ingredients that are outside the scope of this book. I have included one recipe for roasted soybeans (see Chapter 2), which makes an outstanding snack.

White Beans (also known as Haricots)

Many different varieties of white beans are used interchangeably in recipes. Great Northern beans are about ¹/₂ inch long, slightly flattened, and bright white in color. Yellow-eyed peas are white with an amber eye; they are frequently used in baked bean recipes, as are soldier beans, which have a reddish eye shaped like a soldier. Navy beans are small, plump white beans. Pea beans look like navy beans but are half as big. These beans are all available dried and some are also available canned. Presoaked soldier beans will cook in about 25 minutes; most other dried white beans take 60 to 90 minutes.

Buying and Storing Beans

Although beans will keep indefinitely, very old beans will become brittle and take forever to cook. So don't go out and buy a 25-pound sack of beans at a great price, unless you *really* eat a lot of beans. Stored at room temperature, dried beans will remain at good quality for up to 1 year.

Your best bet is to buy beans from a natural food store that has good turnover. If you aren't sure of your source, check for tiny holes in the beans, which are a sign of insect infestation. Look for plump dried beans and discard any that are discolored or shriveled. When you get the beans home, store them in airtight containers. Glass jars are ideal.

One pound raw beans (about $2^1/_2$ cups) will yield about $5^1/_2$ to $6^1/_2$ cups cooked beans.

You can also buy canned beans, which are often softer in texture than home-cooked beans but can't be beat for convenience. When using canned beans, always rinse off and drain the canning liquid, which tends to be salty and gummy. A 15-ounce can of beans yields about $1^1/_2$ cups. I have standardized many of my recipes so that you can use canned or freshly cooked beans interchangeably. Some companies pack their beans in 19-ounce cans, which yield just under 2 cups. Don't discard the extra beans. Use the whole can in the recipe; it won't hurt at all.

Cooked beans can be refrigerated for up to 5 days, or stored in the freezer for up to 6 months.

Presoaking Is Necessary Before Cooking

Most dried beans should be soaked in water for several hours (or overnight) before they are cooked. Yes, you can skip this step, but your cooking time will lengthen by at least an hour and you will have to nearly double the amount of cooking liquid required in the recipes. However, there is a quick-soak method that takes only an hour or two and is described below. Lentils and split peas do not require presoaking.

Before soaking the beans, first pick over and rinse them, discarding any foreign debris and shriveled beans. Then place the beans in a large pot or bowl. Cover with cold tap water. Make sure the beans are covered by at least 3 inches of water. Leave for at least 8 hours.

Quick-Soak Method. Put the rinsed and sorted beans in a pot. Cover with cold tap water by at least 3 inches. Cover and bring to a boil. Remove from the heat, cover, and let stand for 1 to 2 hours.

Cooking Dried Beans

To cook beans, drain off the presoaking liquid and start with fresh tap water. You can enhance the flavor of your beans by cooking them with aromatic vegetables, such as onions, garlic, celery, and herbs and spices. Do not cook the beans with acidic foods, such as tomatoes or wine; these will lengthen the cooking time and toughen the skin of the beans. It is a myth that adding salt will also significantly add to the cooking time. However, when salt is added to a large volume of liquid, the salt flavor concentrates as the liquid cooks down. It, therefore, makes more sense to me to salt to taste at the end of the cooking process.

Bring the beans to a boil. With some beans, the liquid will get quite foamy, and this foam should be skimmed off or it will leave a residue on the beans. Then reduce the heat and simmer. Boiling tends to cause the beans to break apart. Unless I am cooking the beans for soup or a puree, I partially cover the pot. This eliminates the risk of running out of cooking liquid but doesn't turn the beans to mush.

The beans should always be covered by the cooking liquid or they will not soften properly. If too much liquid is lost to evaporation (the beans boiled too vigorously, the lid was left off, the age of the beans required additional cooking time), add *boiling hot* water to cover the beans. Cold water will toughen the skin of the beans.

The cooking times in the recipes should be regarded as guidelines only; times will vary depending on age of the beans, size of the pot, and heat levels. So taste or squeeze a bean for doneness. The bean should be firm but tender throughout. Beans cook from the outside in, so be sure the core of the bean is not hard.

When the beans are done, immediately drain off the cooking liquid if the beans are to be used in a salad or another dish where a firm texture is desired. Otherwise, the beans will continue to cook slightly in the warm cooking liquid.

Pressure Cookers and Crockpots

Most cooks have an appliance or gadget that perfectly suits them and that they wouldn't dream of living without, while the rest of us get by quite well without it. That's how I feel about pressure cookers and crockpots—each does a fine job on beans, if you happen to already own one and have it in a handy spot.

In a pressure cooker, cook lentils and split peas at 15 pounds pressure for 7 minutes; cook medium-size beans, such as navy beans and black beans, for 15 minutes; and cook larger beans, such as chickpeas and kidney beans, for 25 to 35 minutes. If you are cooking a bean that gives up a lot of foam, such as chickpeas, add a tablespoon of vegetable oil to the cooking water to prevent the foam from clogging the steam release valve.

I used to use a pressure cooker for cooking beans, but I've switched to cooking in a regular saucepan on top of the stove. Between the time it takes to build the pressure up to 15 pounds, and the time it takes to cool off the pot before it can be opened, I didn't feel as though I was saving a significant amount of time. Plus it is easy to undercook or overcook the beans without knowing it until the pot is opened.

A slow cooker works well with beans. Follow the manufacturer's directions for timing. Over the long cooking time, certain flavors are lost, so add herbs, spices, and aromatic vegetables during the last 30 to 40 minutes of cooking.

BEANS	COOKING TIMES*
Fresh beans	
Fresh shell beans	5 minutes for small
	10 minutes for medium
	18 minutes for large
Fresh cranberry beans	30 minutes
Dried beans	
Adzuki	30 to 45 minutes
Black beans	About 1 hour
Black-eyed peas	30 to 45 minutes
Chickpeas	2 to $2^1/_2$ hours
Cranberry beans	40 to 45 minutes
Kidney beans	About 1 hour
Lentils, green	25 to 30 minutes
brown	35 minutes
red	30 minutes
Limas, large	1 hour
Christmas	$1^1/_4$ hours
small	1 to $1^1/_4$ hours
Dixie speckled butter beans	1 to $1^1/_4$ hours
Pink beans	50 minutes

BEANS	COOKING TIMES*
Pinto beans	1 to 1^1/$_2$ hours
Split peas	30 minutes
Soy beans	3 to 4 hours
White beans	
Great Northern	1 to 1^1/$_2$ hours
Cannellini	1 to 1^1/$_2$ hours
Navy beans	1 hour
Pea beans	1 hour
Soldier beans	25 minutes
Yellow-eyed beans	30 minutes

* Assumes the beans have been presoaked and are gently boiled with the lid partially on. Times are approximate.

All About Grains

The very first crops cultivated by early farmers were probably grains. These grass plants had many virtues that attracted our ancestors (and continue to attract us). Grasses are extremely easy to grow, which made them rewarding for early farmers and keeps them reasonably inexpensive today. When grasses mature, their seeds contain significant amounts of protein, vitamins, minerals, and fiber. The harvested seeds are quite dry, which means they store well. Grains are pretty simple to cook and offer variety in the diet, depending on whether they are left whole or ground into grits or flour.

Although our forebears were limited to the grains that grew well in their particular climate, we tend to look for more variety in our diets. Today we have a choice of at least eight different grains in many different forms. Here's a look at those that are readily available to us.

Glossary of Grains

Whole grains are sometimes called groats (as in oat or buckwheat) or berries (as in wheat berries). These are the seeds of the plant, with the outer hull removed. The grain may then be polished (if it is rice) or pearled (if it is barley). Whatever the name, this milling step removes most or all of the bran layer and the germ, leaving the endosperm, or kernel, whole. This results in a grain with a shortened cooking time. To speed cooking further, the grain may also be pressed flat to form flakes (as with wheat and barley) or rolled (as with oats). Or the grains may be cracked (as with wheat) or ground into grits (as with corn). They may even be popped (as with corn, millet, and amaranth). Corn has such a tough bran layer that to remove it the kernels are sometimes soaked in a lye or a limestone solution; this is how hominy is made.

Amaranth

Amaranth is an ancient grain that was cultivated by the Aztecs, Mayans, and Incas. According to food historians, the Spanish conquistadors banned the growing of the grain because of its association with human sacrifice (a favorite preparation mixed it with human blood). Cortés ordered the burning of all of the amaranth fields between the Gulf of California and the Bay of Campeche, in effect destroying both a culture and an important food source.

Amaranth is currently enjoying new popularity, in part because it is unusually nutritious. Of all the grains, amaranth provides the most complete protein. It also contains significant levels of calcium, iron, magnesium, phosphorus, and potassium. Amaranth is also unusual in that it is perhaps the only grain that is grown in vegetable gardens for its delicate green leaves, which can be compared to spinach. Home gardeners, however, take note: Amaranth is closely related to an annoying weed called pigweed; once planted, amaranth has the potential for becoming a "volunteer" plant for many more years to come.

Amaranth grains are tiny, like mustard seeds. You can buy amaranth as a flour or in whole grain or popped form. When baked into a bread or cake (my favorite way to utilize this high-powered grain), the flour or popped grains add a toasted seed flavor. Popped amaranth can also be added to cereals, used as a topping for casseroles, or sprinkled on breads and rolls instead of poppy seeds. Although I have experimented with popping the grain in a dry skillet, I have never been satisfied with the results and prefer to buy commercially popped amaranth.

Boiled like rice on top of the stove, amaranth has a rather grassy flavor, not unlike spinach. To cook amaranth like rice, use 1 cup amaranth to 3 cups water. As amaranth cooks, the grains soften and swell. The resulting dish is gelatinous in texture—perhaps an acquired taste.

Barley

Barley is one of the most ancient of cultivated grains, tracing back at least to the Stone Age. It grows in a wide range of climates, from the Arctic to the equator. Until the sixteenth century, it was the staple grain of most of Europe. It is eaten as a whole grain, ground into flour, and brewed into beer. The cooked grain has a chewy texture and a nutty flavor. It makes a delicious alternative to rice in pilafs and salads. Pearled barley can even be cooked as rice to make a creamy barley risotto.

Barley can be bought hulled, pearled, flaked, or unhulled. Hulled barley, which may also be called pot or Scotch barley, takes slightly longer to cook than pearled barley, but it is somewhat higher in fiber and vitamin B. Still, pearled barley is a nutritional bargain, rich in protein, vitamins, and potassium. Boil 1 part pearled or hulled barley to 3 parts salted water in a covered pot for 35 to 45 minutes. Both hulled barley and pearled barley can be simmered to tenderness in a long-cooking soup, which is my favorite way to enjoy this grain. Barley absorbs a lot of the liquid in a soup and acts as a thickener.

Unhulled barley should be presoaked overnight. Then cook 1 part grain in 4 parts water in a covered pot for about 60 minutes.

Rolled barley can be cooked like oatmeal (1 part rolled barley to 2 parts water), which is another one of my favorite barley preparations. Its sweet, toasty flavor is unlike oatmeal but just as satisfying. Rolled barley flakes can also be added to granola mixes.

Buckwheat

Buckwheat is not truly a grain because the buckwheat plant is not a grass. The part of the plant we eat is actually a fruit, not a seed. However, in the kitchen, we treat buckwheat as a grain, enjoying the whole or ground groats as kasha and the flour in pancakes.

Buckwheat does not enjoy much of an ancient history. It originated in Central Asia and was spread throughout Europe in the Middle Ages by invaders—either the Moors or the Tartars. Barley flour became very popular in Japan in soba noodles and in the U.S. for very hearty pancakes. In Eastern Europe, roasted buckwheat grits are enjoyed as kasha.

In this country, buckwheat is most often found as whole roasted groats (they may not be labeled as roasted but the heady aroma will confirm it) or ground roasted groats in fine, medium, or coarse grinds. Either way it may be labeled as "buckwheat," "buckwheat groats," or "kasha." The roasting gives this grain a rich toasted aroma and flavor. When you open a container of buckwheat, the kitchen fills with this appealing aroma.

Because buckwheat groats have a tendency to become mushy when cooked, it is a good idea to mix the groats with a beaten egg or egg white prior to cooking; the egg coating helps the grains separate. Gently boil

1 part buckwheat in 2 parts water or broth in a covered saucepan for about 15 minutes.

Corn

Corn began in the Americas as a wild grass, but it was intensely culti-vated by Native Americans. At the time of the European exploration of the Americas, many different varieties of corn—or maize as it was called—existed. Maize comes from the Native American name for the grain. Corn was so closely associated with Native Americans that it came to be known as Indian corn, "corn" being an English word meaning the grain of any cereal crop. Eventually, the grain became known as corn in the U.S., although Europeans still refer to it as maize.

When Columbus returned from his exploration of Cuba he brought with him four bags of corn. This seed corn yielded very well when planted in European soil, and eventually spread throughout the continent. Italian cooks were the most intrigued with corn, which they made into a thick mush known as polenta. Meanwhile, American settlers came to depend on corn for their own sustenance and for the sustenance of their livestock. At that time, most of the corn was field corn, good for drying and grinding. Sweet corn was grown by Native Americans in New York State as early as 1779, but it wasn't commonly grown by the settlers until the mid-1800s. Popcorn is much older, by about eight thousand years. Native Americans believed that each kernel of popcorn contained a demon who exploded when exposed to heat.

Field corn is dried right in the fields, usually for animal fodder. As it dries, the kernels become dented at the top, hence its other name, dent corn. Besides feeding animals, field corn is processed into breakfast cereals, cornstarch, corn oils, and corn syrup. Flint (or Indian) corn comes in many different colors and may be ground into meal.

Today we enjoy corn in many forms. We eat sweet corn fresh or frozen (or even canned), on or off the cob. Popcorn is a special variety that is dried. Any type of corn may be dried and ground into meal. If it is ground very fine it will be called corn flour in the U.S. (cornflour in Great Britain refers to cornstarch). Any type of corn may also be treated with lime, which sweetens the kernels and causes them to swell and burst, to make hominy, or *posole*. Hominy is sold canned or dried. Hominy may be ground into grits or into a fine meal that is called *masa harina* and is used to make corn tortillas.

Cornmeal. Yellow, white, and even blue corn is ground into cornmeal. When the cornmeal is stone-ground, it retains some of the germ and hull, which boosts its nutritional content but makes it vulnerable to spoilage. When the cornmeal is steel-ground, the husk and germ are removed, lowering its nutritional content but increasing its shelf life; to compensate for the nutritional loss most steel-ground cornmeal is enriched with vitamins and minerals. I prefer the fresh flavor of the stone-ground cornmeal I get from my local co-op to any I have ever bought in a supermarket.

The grind can be fine (in which case it is probably called corn flour), medium, or coarse.

Polenta is the Italian name for cornmeal and also for the Italian dish made with it, which is basically cornmeal mush. You can buy polenta at specialty food stores, but this is no more and no less than stone-ground cornmeal. For polenta, my preference is a medium-grind cornmeal. I have found boxes of "corn grits" at my natural food store that declare its contents perfect for polenta. This is simply a coarse grind of cornmeal and it makes a very gritty polenta.

Hominy. If you've ever bought whole dried kernels of corn to grind your own cornmeal, then you know how tough the outer bran layer is. Native Americans used to boil whole kernel corn in a wood ash or lime solution to remove the hull. The boiling process causes the kernels to swell and become slightly sweet, with a distinctive, almost smoky flavor. The resulting product is called hominy.

Whole yellow or white hominy can be found dried or canned. Canned hominy is a perfectly acceptable and convenient product. Dried hominy, which must be soaked in water overnight and then simmered in water for about 3 hours, has more "corn" flavor. Either way, hominy is truly delicious and underutilized in many parts of the country.

In the Southwest, hominy may be called *posole*, which is also the name of a stew that is made with hominy.

Grits. Ground hominy is called grits. Very finely ground hominy is called *masa harina* and is used to make corn chips and corn tortillas.

In many ways grits are similar to polenta, sharing many common cooking methods. Grits, however, are "cornier" in flavor and grittier in texture. Grits can be served sweetened or with a little salt and butter. Like polenta, grits can be chilled, cut into slices or other shapes, then grilled or fried.

Grits are available in instant, quick-cooking, and regular forms. The instant version lacks flavor and texture, while the quick-cooking variety cooks only slightly faster than the regular kind. To cook regular grits, slowly add 1 part white or yellow grits to 3 parts boiling, salted water. Reduce the heat and simmer for 10 to 15 minutes, stirring almost constantly as the mixture thickens.

Millet

Most Americans encounter millet as bird seed, and while that is a fine use for the grain, millet also belongs on the table. Indeed, millet is a staple grain for about a third of the world's population. In many parts of Asia, millet is a commonly grown alternative to rice.

Millet was probably first cultivated in the Neolithic era. Some scientists propose that the grain is even older than that, perhaps one of the grasses that sustained vegetarian dinosaurs. We know it was grown in China and India at least as far back as 2800 B.C. Like most grains, millet is rich in phosphorus, iron, calcium, B vitamins, and protein.

Hulled millet looks like small mustard seeds and is sold in most natural food stores. As the grains cook, they swell and burst. Millet has a bland, slightly sweet and nutty flavor that adapts to many different flavorings. Millet is sometimes sold puffed.

I like to grind millet in my blender and use it in baked goods, where it adds a crunchy texture and a toasty flavor. You can get the same effect from puffed millet, if you can find it.

Millet can be cooked like rice. Combine 1 part millet to $2\frac{1}{2}$ parts water and gently boil in a covered saucepan for 25 to 30 minutes. Toasting the millet in a lightly oiled skillet before adding the liquid will enhance the flavor and reduce the stickiness of the grain. I have tried to make popped millet in a dry skillet, toasting the grains until they puff, but I have found (as with amaranth) that this method is not well suited to a home kitchen.

Oats

We make our acquaintance with oats early. It is cooked into the porridge we are served as children (oatmeal), baked into chewy cookies, and toasted to make granola. Interestingly, oats are one of the few grains that are rarely seen on the dinner table, except in the form of bread.

Oats thrive in cool, wet climates where wheat and barley do not. It is likely that the plant started as an unwanted weed. Although oats were probably gathered and eaten in Neolithic times, they were spread throughout Europe as animal feed. Only the poorest of the poor ate oats. In Scotland, where the damp climate was unsuited to wheat, oats became the staple grain, and today many oat recipes have Scottish origins.

Oats are promoted for being rich in soluble fiber, which can have a positive effect on blood cholesterol levels. They are also good sources of B vitamins, vitamin E, protein, and calcium.

Rolled oats, both "old-fashioned" and "quick," are readily available in most supermarkets and natural food stores. Rolled oats are oats that have been steamed and then flattened into flakes. Quick oats are rolled thinner over a heat source, which precooks the grain; this enables quick oats to cook fast, but some flavor and nutrition is lost in the process. Steel-cut oats, also called Irish oatmeal or Scotch oatmeal, are cut to speed cooking but are not rolled. They make a distinctively textured oatmeal that takes close to an hour to cook. You can both enhance the flavor and reduce the cooking time of steel-cut oats to about 20 minutes by first toasting the oats in a 350 degree oven for about 20 minutes. The pretoasted oats can be stored for a few months in an airtight container and used as needed.

Oat bran can be added to baked goods. Its positive effect on lowering blood cholesterol levels is well documented. The bitter-tasting bran is best added with a light hand.

Quinoa

One cup of cooked quinoa (pronounced keen-wah) is equivalent in calcium to 1 quart of milk. It is a complete protein and is high in iron. Now there are some good reasons to try this ancient grain!

Quinoa was the staple grain of the Incas. It grew well on the high mountain plains of Peru, sustaining life where little else would grow. Francisco Pizarro, the Spanish conquistador, envisioned a more European-style beef-based agricultural—and cultural—lifestyle in Peru. He banned the growing of this "mother grain" and imported Spanish livestock, vegetables, and barley to replace it. The vegetables could not grow in the harsh mountain climates, and the vegetarian Incas would not eat meat. Pizarro conducted regular raids on the mountainside to destroy any quinoa, but eventually ill-health caused him to remove himself and his army from Peru. Although quinoa agriculture was restored, yet another native culture was left seriously weakened by its contact with Europeans.

Technically quinoa is not a grain at all but the seeds of an herb. The tiny beads look like millet, except each seed seems to have a little eye. When cooked, this "eye," which is the seed's external germ, forms a tiny white squiggle, like a tail, at one end. Cooked quinoa expands to about 4 times its volume and has a delicate, slightly grassy flavor. Some cooks compare it to couscous.

Quinoa has a natural protective coating called saponin that protects it from insects and the radiation of the high-altitude sun. The saponin will give the grain a bitter flavor if it is not washed off before cooking. Although most processors take care of the washing, if you buy the grain in bulk, you can't be sure of how it has been handled.

To remove the saponin, place 1 cup quinoa in a blender with 2 cups water. Pulse the motor on and off a few times, until the water becomes cloudy. Strain off the water. Repeat with fresh water in the blender, until the water remains clear. Strain the quinoa through a fine-mesh strainer.

To cook quinoa, add 1 part quinoa to 2 parts hot liquid. Cover and bring to a boil, then reduce the heat and simmer until the quinoa is tender and looks translucent, about 12 minutes. Fluff with a fork.

Wheat

It is rare that a day goes by when a Westerner doesn't consume wheat in one form or another. It is our staple crop, that which contributes the most bulk to our diet, our staff of life.

Wheat is an ancient grain, perhaps as old as barley. Some food historians believe that wheat was consumed in Iraq at least eighty-five hundred years ago. The Egyptians made the first yeasted wheat breads about six thousand years ago. As wheat cultivation spread across the world, some thirty thousand different varieties were developed. Some wheat is called "spring wheat" because it is planted in the spring; some is called "winter wheat" because it is planted in winter. A more important distinction is based on the gluten content of the grain. Hard wheat has the highest, and it is ground into bread flour; soft wheat flour is used for pastries. Hard durum wheat is used for pasta; it is ground into semolina flour or made into couscous.

Wheat flours sold in supermarkets are usually defined by their uses: cake, bread, or all-purpose (a mixture of hard and soft wheats). In natural food stores, we are also given the choice of wheat in its many forms: whole berries, cracked wheat, flakes, germ, bran, flour, bulgur, and couscous. Wheat germ, wheat bran, and flour are all used in baking but are almost never served on their own.

Wheat Berries. The whole grain form of wheat, wheat berries can be cooked and served in many of the same ways as barley, such as in salads, soups, and pilafs. It takes about $1^{1}/_{4}$ to $1^{1}/_{2}$ hours of simmering to render the berries chewy but tender, using 1 part berries to 4 parts water. That time can be reduced to 50 to 60 minutes by presoaking the berries overnight.

Some people like to eat sprouted wheat berries in salads and sandwiches. You can sprout wheat berries just as you would mung beans. See page 18.

Cracked Wheat. Wheat berries that have been cracked and ground to form coarse grits are called cracked wheat. Cracked wheat looks similar to bulgur in both its cooked and uncooked state but is more uniform in color.

It also tastes similar to bulgur. Whereas bulgur can be steamed, cracked wheat must be boiled. Gently boil 1 part cracked wheat in 2$\frac{1}{3}$ cups liquid in a covered saucepan for about 15 minutes. If your cooked cracked wheat is mushy in texture, you may be inadvertently cooking with bulgur.

The cracked wheat you find in most natural food stores will be a medium or coarse grind. A fine grind becomes a breakfast cereal. Wheatina cereal is an example of finely ground cracked wheat.

Bulgur. Most of us were introduced to bulgur in tabouli, the Middle Eastern salad of bulgur, parsley, cucumbers, and tomatoes in a lemon-mint dressing. Bulgur has a very distinctive nutty flavor that ensures it will not be lost in a crowd of ingredients.

Bulgur was created in the Middle East, which helps explain the variant spellings of this grain—bulgur, bulghur, bulgar, burgul. However it is spelled, it is always made from wheat berries that have been washed, steamed, hulled, and dried. You can often find it crushed to different grinds—fine, medium, and coarse. Because it is precooked, bulgur requires very little additional handling. Soaking it in boiling water for about 15 minutes should do the trick. Always drain off any excess water once the grains are tender.

Bulgur is easy to confuse with cracked wheat because the two look nearly identical—so be sure to label your jars if you buy your grains in bulk. Cracked wheat is more uniform in color. On occasion you will even find bulgur mislabeled as cracked wheat—or vice versa—in a bin at a natural food store. If soaking the bulgur in boiling water for 15 minutes doesn't result in a tender grain, you may have inadvertently bought cracked wheat.

Rolled Wheat Flakes. Like rolled oats, rolled wheat flakes make a delicious breakfast cereal. The homemade flavor is quite like Ralston and other packaged wheat cereals. Cook 1 part rolled wheat in 3 parts liquid, just as you would oatmeal. Rolled wheat flakes can also be used in granola mixes.

Couscous. Traditionally made from hand-rolled semolina wheat, couscous is more like a pasta than a grain. Nonetheless, it is cooked and served like a grain, so it is treated as such in this book. Couscous has a very mild flavor, which makes it an excellent foil for spicy stews. Use it in place of rice for variety.

Virtually all of the couscous sold in this country is precooked. All that is required to cook it is to steep it in boiling water, as with bulgur. Use 1 part couscous to 1$\frac{1}{2}$ cups boiling water or broth. Combine in a bowl, cover, and let steep for about 5 minutes. Fluff with a fork and let stand for another 5 minutes before serving.

366 Delicious Ways to Cook Rice, Beans, and Grains

Because whole grains are rich in natural oils, they will go rancid over a period of 1 to 12 months, depending on the grain and the temperature at which they are stored. Even before the grains smell rancid, the vitamins will oxidize, which means the grains won't have the same nutritional value. It is, therefore, a good idea to buy grains from a natural food store with rapid turnover.

When you buy grains in bulk, it is very important to label the storage containers in which you keep them in order to avoid confusion later on.

Dating the containers is also a good idea so you can keep track of the freshness of the grains. To keep whole grains at their nutritious best, store in tightly sealed containers for up to 1 month at room temperature or for up to 5 months in the refrigerator. Oats, pearled barley, and hominy will keep for up to 1 year on a cool, dry shelf.

Cooked grains can be stored in the refrigerator for 2 to 3 days in an airtight container. They do not freeze particularly well.

2
Dips, Spreads, Starters, and Snacks

Grilled Tomato Salsa with Black Beans

Chunky Avocado Black Bean Dip

Piquant Black Bean Dip

Cheesy Black Bean Dip

Hummus

Roasted Red Pepper Hummus

Curried Hummus

Caramelized Onion and Kidney Bean Spread

Egyptian-style Lima Bean Dip

Herbed White Bean Spread

Roasted Garlic, Red Pepper, and White Bean Spread

Eggplant Caviar

Black Bean Roll-Ups

Black Bean and Goat Cheese Quesadillas

Black Bean Turnovers

Polenta-Fontina Bites

Stuffed Grape Leaves (Dolmades)

Vegetarian Nori Rolls

Pizza-flavored Popcorn

Crunchy Chickpea Snacks

Garlic-roasted Soy Nuts

Barley Water

I can't remember the last party I attended where I didn't find the ubiquitous bowl of chips and salsa. I'm happy for the offering—it sure beats the potato chips and onion dip of my youth—and I often make it myself, but I also like to prepare many of the other wonderful appetizers that can be thrown together quickly, from bean dips to quesadillas to flavored popcorn.

For potluck gatherings, I particularly enjoy making special appetizers, such as Stuffed Grape Leaves, Vegetarian Nori Rolls, or Polenta-Fontina Bites. These pretty little bites inevitably disappear in a matter of minutes.

Crunchy Chickpea Snacks—mildly spiced roasted chickpeas—and Garlic-roasted Soy Nuts have become staples in my house. They are a favorite at parties and a necessity (with a beer) while watching football games on television on Sunday afternoons.

Grilled Tomato Salsa with Black Beans

YIELD: 10 TO 12 SERVINGS

When this salsa is first made, all you can taste is the heat of the peppers, with a floral note from the lime. Wait a while and the smoky-floral flavor of cilantro begins to assert itself. Finally, the charred tomatoes and black beans begin to contribute their sweet, earthy flavors, while the onion and garlic add an herbal essence in the background. This is a wonderfully complex, beautifully balanced salsa, great as a dip with chips or as a condiment with grilled foods. It is at its best on the day it is made.

2 pounds vine-ripened tomatoes
   (about 6 medium)
2 garlic cloves
3 jalapeño peppers
$1/_2$ red bell pepper
$1/_4$ sweet red onion

$1^1/_2$ cups cooked black beans
$1/_4$ cup chopped fresh cilantro
3 tablespoons freshly squeezed
   lime juice
Salt

Preheat the grill. Slice the tomatoes in half. Peel and skewer the garlic. Lightly mist the vegetables with nonstick cooking spray. Place the tomatoes (cut side down), garlic, jalapeño and bell peppers, and onion on the grill, and grill until the vegetables are slightly charred, 6 to 10 minutes, removing each vegetable as it becomes ready. The timing will vary depending on the vegetable (the bell pepper will be done last) and the heat of the grill.

Seed the jalapeños. Peel the tomatoes, jalapeños, and bell pepper if you wish. Combine the jalapeños, bell pepper, onion, and garlic and process in a food processor fitted with a steel blade until finely chopped. Add the tomatoes and pulse until you have a chunky sauce. Stir black beans, in the cilantro, lime juice, and salt to taste. Transfer to a serving bowl and let stand for at least 1 hour at room temperature to allow the flavors to blend before serving.

Calories 60 • Protein 3 gm • Fat 1 gm • Percent of calories from fat 7% • Cholesterol 0 mg • Dietary fiber 4 gm • Sodium 10 mg • Calcium 17 mg

Chunky Avocado Black Bean Dip

YIELD: 10 TO 12 SERVINGS

By using all salsa or half salsa and half chopped tomatoes and by adding or not adding additional chile peppers, you can make this dip mild or mouth-searing. Either way it is a great party dip. Serve with tortilla chips. This dip is best served the day it is made.

1½ cups cooked black beans
2 cups homemade or store-bought
  salsa or 1 cup salsa and 1 cup
  diced tomatoes with juice
½ green bell pepper, finely
  chopped
2 hot green chiles, finely chopped
  (optional)

¼ cup chopped fresh cilantro
2 scallions, finely chopped
1 ripe avocado, finely chopped
Salt and freshly ground black
  pepper

In a large bowl, coarsely mash half the beans. Stir in the remaining beans, salsa, bell pepper, chiles, cilantro, scallions, and avocado. (If you prefer, you can use a food processor to chop the peppers, chiles, cilantro, and scallions. Add the beans and briefly puree. The avocado should be chopped by hand and stirred in.) Taste and add salt and pepper if needed. Cover and let stand for at least 30 minutes to allow the flavors to blend.

Calories 74 • Protein 3 gm • Fat 4 gm • Percent of calories from fat 40% •
Cholesterol 0 mg • Dietary fiber 5 gm • Sodium 6 mg • Calcium 15 mg

Piquant Black Bean Dip

❧❧❧

YIELD: 6 TO 8 SERVINGS

Capers are the unexpected ingredient in this boldly seasoned dip. Serve with tortilla chips. The dip may be made up to 3 days in advance and stored in an airtight container in the refrigerator.

1½ cups cooked black beans
½ green bell pepper,
   finely chopped
4 scallions, finely chopped
2 garlic cloves, finely minced

1 to 2 green chiles, finely chopped
½ cup homemade or store-bought
   salsa
2 tablespoons capers, drained

In a medium bowl, coarsely mash the beans. Stir in the bell pepper, scallions, garlic, chiles, salsa, and capers. Taste and adjust seasonings. Let stand for at least 30 minutes to allow the flavors to blend.

Calories 67 • Protein 4 gm • Fat 0 gm • Percent of calories from fat 4% • Cholesterol 0 mg • Dietary fiber 4 gm • Sodium 109 mg • Calcium 19 mg

Cheesy Black Bean Dip

YIELD: ABOUT 6 SERVINGS

Chipotle en adobo adds a hot, smoky flavor to this bean dip. It is a paste made of smoke-dried jalapeños, oil, vinegar, and spices. Look for it wherever Mexican foods are sold.

1¹/₂ cups cooked black beans
¹/₂ cup homemade
   or store-bought salsa
1 to 3 teaspoons chipotle
   en adobo
   (optional but recommended)

1¹/₂ cups diced fresh or canned
   tomatoes
8 ounces reduced-fat cheddar
   cheese, shredded
Tortilla chips

Preheat the oven to 350 degrees. In a food processor fitted with a steel blade, combine the beans and salsa and process until smooth. Taste and add chipotle en adobo (if using). Stir in the tomatoes. Spoon the mixture into a 1-quart baking dish. Stir in the cheese. Heat for about 15 minutes in the oven, until the cheese is melted. Serve hot, with tortilla chips for scooping up the dip.

Calories 164 • Protein 18 gm • Fat 4.4 gm • Percent of calories from fat 23% • Cholesterol 13 mg • Dietary fiber 4 gm • Sodium 113 mg • Calcium 415 mg

Hummus

YIELD: 6 TO 10 SERVINGS

Hummus is a Middle Eastern dip made with mashed cooked chickpeas seasoned with lemon juice, garlic, and sesame paste or sesame oil. It makes a great dip for raw vegetables or can be stuffed into a pita pocket, along with lettuce, sliced cucumbers, tomatoes, and sprouts, as a delicious and hearty vegetarian sandwich. Here it is presented quite simply, with wedges of pita pockets.

1 cup chopped fresh parsley

4 garlic cloves

3 cups cooked chickpeas

$1/2$ cup tahini (sesame paste)

4 to 6 tablespoons freshly squeezed lemon juice

1 to 4 tablespoons water (optional)

Salt and freshly ground black pepper

$1/4$ cup chopped scallions

4 pita pockets, cut into wedges

To make the hummus, combine the parsley and garlic in a food processor fitted with a steel blade. Process until finely chopped. Add the chickpeas, tahini, and lemon juice, and process until smooth, adding the water, 1 tablespoon at a time, if needed to make a smooth paste. Taste and adjust seasoning, adding salt, pepper, garlic, and/or additional lemon juice. Allow to sit for at least 30 minutes to allow the flavors to blend.

To serve, mound the hummus in a bowl. Garnish with the chopped scallions. Serve the pita wedges on the side. The hummus can be made in advance and stored in a tightly closed container in the refrigerator for up to 3 days.

Calories 403 • Protein 18 gm • Fat 16 gm • Percent of calories from fat 35% • Cholesterol 0 mg • Dietary fiber 6 gm • Sodium 228 mg • Calcium 139 mg

Roasted Red Pepper Hummus

YIELD: 6 TO 10 SERVINGS

This hummus boasts a touch of sweetness from the roasted peppers and a whisper of heat from the hot pepper sauce. It makes a delightful change of pace from the classic hummus.

4 garlic cloves
2 homemade or store-bought
   roasted red bell peppers
   (see Note)
3 cups cooked chickpeas, drained
1/3 cup tahini (sesame paste)
4 tablespoons freshly squeezed
   lemon juice

1 teaspoon Louisiana-style hot
   pepper sauce, or more to taste
Salt and freshly ground black
   pepper
4 pita pockets, cut into wedges

In a food processor fitted with a steel blade, process the garlic until finely chopped. Add the roasted peppers, chickpeas, tahini, and lemon juice, and process until smooth. Add the hot pepper sauce and salt and pepper to taste. Set aside for at least 30 minutes to allow the flavors to blend.

To serve, mound the hummus in a bowl. Serve the pita wedges on the side. Hummus can be made in advance and stored in a tightly closed container in the refrigerator for up to 3 days.

Note: To roast the peppers, hold over a gas burner or place under a broiler until well charred all over, turning frequently. Place in a paper bag, seal, and set aside in the freezer for about 10 minutes. Then peel and seed.

Calories 354 • Protein 15 gm • Fat 12 gm • Percent of calories from fat 28% • Cholesterol 0 mg • Dietary fiber 6 gm • Sodium 225 mg • Calcium 108 mg

Curried Hummus

❧❧❧

YIELD: 6 TO 10 SERVINGS

Yet another way to vary the flavor of hummus, this time with Indian spices. I like to serve this dip with pappadams—crisp wafers made from lentils and spices. If you can't find pappadams in a specialty store near you, pita pockets, cut into wedges and baked in the oven until crisp, can be substituted. The hummus can be made in advance and stored in a tightly closed container in the refrigerator for up to 3 days.

¼ cup chopped fresh cilantro
¼ cup chopped fresh parsley
4 garlic cloves
3 cups cooked chickpeas, drained
¼ cup tahini (sesame paste)
3 tablespoons freshly squeezed
    lemon juice
1 teaspoon Louisiana-style hot
    pepper sauce

1 to 4 tablespoons water (optional)
1½ teaspoons curry powder
Salt and freshly ground black
    pepper
¼ cup chopped scallions or chives
Pappadams

In a food processor fitted with a steel blade, combine the cilantro, parsley, and garlic and process until very finely chopped. Add the chickpeas, tahini, lemon juice, and hot sauce, and process until smooth and creamy, adding the water, 1 tablespoon at a time, if needed to make a light, smooth consistency. Stir in the curry powder, salt, and pepper to taste, and chopped scallions. Transfer to a serving bowl and set aside for at least 30 minutes to allow the flavors to blend.

Calories 218 • Protein 11 gm • Fat 9 gm • Percent of calories from fat 35% •
Cholesterol 0 mg • Dietary fiber 5 gm • Sodium 13 mg • Calcium 79 mg

Caramelized Onion and Kidney Bean Spread

YIELD: 6 TO 8 SERVINGS

Those of us who were raised on our mother's chopped liver experience regular cravings for that traditional food—even when the rest of the time we can't conceive of ever eating the stuff again. This vegetarian dip conveys the flavor of chopped liver—without the gamy overtones or chewy texture. It is delicious on flatbreads, crackers, and matzoh. The spread may be made in advance and stored in a tightly closed container in the refrigerator for up to 3 days.

1 tablespoon extra-virgin olive oil
2 large onions, thinly sliced
1½ cups cooked kidney beans

1 hard-cooked egg, crumbled
Salt and freshly ground black
   pepper

In a medium skillet, heat the olive oil over medium heat. Add the onions and sauté until golden, about 10 minutes. In a food processor fitted with a steel blade, combine the onions and beans and process until smooth. Stir in the egg and salt and pepper to taste. Transfer to a serving bowl and set aside for at least 30 minutes to allow the flavor to develop. Serve at room temperature.

Calories 109 • Protein 5 gm • Fat 3 gm • Percent of calories from fat 27% •
Cholesterol 35 mg • Dietary fiber 4 gm • Sodium 13 mg • Calcium 27 mg

Egyptian-style Lima Bean Dip

YIELD: 4 TO 6 SERVINGS

*F*ul mesdames, *a dip made with fava beans, is a staple all over the Middle East. Since fava beans are difficult to find in the U.S., I make this deliciously simple dish—pureed beans flavored with olive oil, garlic, and lemon—with fresh or frozen lima beans.*

2 cups fresh or frozen shelled
   lima beans (about 1³/₄ pounds
   before shelling)
2 garlic cloves
1 cup fresh parsley leaves

2 tablespoons extra-virgin olive oil
Juice of 1 lemon, or to taste
Salt and freshly ground black
   pepper
2 pita pockets, cut into wedges

Steam the beans for 15 to 18 minutes, until quite soft. Reserve the steaming liquid

In a food processor fitted with a steel blade, finely mince the garlic and parsley. Add the beans plus ¹/₂ cup of the cooking liquid and puree. Stir in the olive oil and lemon juice. Season generously with salt and pepper.

Transfer to a serving bowl and serve at room temperature, offering the pita pockets as scoops.

Calories 261 • Protein 11 gm • Fat 8 gm • Percent of calories from fat 26% •
Cholesterol 0 mg • Dietary fiber 8 gm • Sodium 172 mg • Calcium 66 mg

Herbed White Bean Spread

YIELD: 6 TO 8 SERVINGS

A great dish to add to your party repertoire, this garlicky and lemony bean spread serves equally well as a dip for vegetables as it does a spread for crackers and slices of French bread. The spread can also be used sparingly on sandwiches as a mayonnaise substitute or stuffed into a pita as a change from hummus. The dip may be made in advance and stored in a tightly closed container in the refrigerator for up to 3 days.

5 garlic cloves
1/2 cup chopped fresh parsley
1 1/2 cups cooked cannellini beans
   (white kidney beans)
Juice of 1 lemon, or more to taste

1 teaspoon extra-virgin olive oil
1 tablespoon chopped fresh sage
   or thyme, or 1 teaspoon dried
Salt and freshly ground black
   pepper

In a food processor fitted with a steel blade, finely chop the garlic and parsley. Add the beans and puree. Stir in the lemon juice, olive oil, and sage. Season with salt and pepper to taste. Taste and adjust seasoning. Transfer to a serving bowl and set aside for at least 30 minutes before serving.

Calories 72 • Protein 4 gm • Fat 1 gm • Percent of calories from fat 13% •
Cholesterol 0 mg • Dietary fiber 3 gm • Sodium 4 mg • Calcium 30 mg

Roasted Garlic, Red Pepper, and White Bean Spread

YIELD: 6 TO 8 SERVINGS

Serve as a spread for crackers or French bread or as a dip for vegetables. The spread may be made in advance and stored in a tightly closed container in the refrigerator for up to 3 days.

2 whole garlic bulbs
1 tablespoon extra-virgin olive oil
1 homemade or store-bought
   roasted red bell pepper
   (see Note on page 40)
1¹/₂ cups cooked cannellini beans
   (white kidney beans)

1 tablespoon balsamic vinegar
¹/₄ cup finely chopped fresh basil
Salt and freshly ground black
   pepper

Preheat the oven to 400 degrees. Remove as much of the outer papery skin from the garlic as possible. Place the garlic in an ovenproof dish, drizzle with the olive oil, cover with aluminum foil, and roast until soft, about 30 minutes. When cool enough to handle, squeeze the pulp out of the skin.

In a food processor fitted with a steel blade, combine the garlic, roasted pepper, and beans. Puree until smooth. Stir in the balsamic vinegar, basil, and salt and pepper to taste. Taste and adjust seasoning. Transfer to a serving bowl and set aside for at least 30 minutes before serving.

Calories 113 • Protein 5 gm • Fat 3 gm • Percent of calories from fat 20% • Cholesterol 0 mg • Dietary fiber 3 gm • Sodium 5 mg • Calcium 53 mg

Eggplant Caviar

YIELD: 4 TO 6 SERVINGS

Dips made from eggplant are often called "vegetarian caviar" because of the texture derived from the seeds. I think this dip is even more deserving of this name thanks to the addition of chewy wheat berries. Serve with flatbreads or crisp sesame crackers.

1 large eggplant
1 cup cooked wheat berries
  (¹/₃ cup uncooked; see page 30
  for cooking instructions)
¹/₄ cup minced onion
¹/₄ cup chopped fresh parsley

2 garlic cloves, minced
Salt and freshly ground black
  pepper
2 tablespoons extra-virgin olive oil
3 tablespoons freshly squeezed
  lemon juice

Preheat the oven to 450 degrees. Prick the eggplant in several places with a fork. Place on a baking sheet and roast until soft and collapsed, about 30 minutes. Set aside to cool.

Scrape the eggplant flesh onto a wooden chopping board and chop. Combine in a bowl with the cooked wheat berries, onion, parsley, garlic, and salt and pepper to taste. Beat in the oil and lemon juice. Taste and adjust seasonings. Cover and set aside at room temperature for several hours before serving to allow the flavors to blend

Calories 149 • Protein 4 gm • Fat 7 gm • Percent of calories from fat 41% • Cholesterol 0 mg • Dietary fiber 5 gm • Sodium 6 mg • Calcium 20 mg

Black Bean Roll-Ups

꧁꧂

YIELD: 36 PIECES

You won't find many recipes for finger foods that are as easy as this one to execute, or as tasty to eat. Starting with canned beans, I can make up a garnished plate of these roll-ups in less than 15 minutes. You can experiment with other fillings, such as refried beans.

1½ cups cooked black beans	¼ cup homemade
1 tablespoon chipotle en adobo	or store-bought salsa
(optional but highly	6 large flour tortillas
recommended)	¼ cup chopped fresh cilantro

In a food processor fitted with a steel blade, combine the beans, chipotle en adobo, and salsa. Process briefly to make a smooth paste. Warm one tortilla in a dry skillet or over an open flame until soft and pliable, about 30 seconds. Use a spatula to spread about ¼ cup of the mixture in a thin layer on the tortilla. Sprinkle with about 2 teaspoons of the cilantro. Roll up to form a tight tube. Repeat with the remaining ingredients.

Just before serving, slice the tortilla tubes into 1-inch pieces. To get uniform pieces, trim off the ragged ends first, then slice. Arrange, cut-side up, on a serving tray. Cover tightly with plastic wrap if you can't serve at once.

Calories 29 • Protein 1 gm • Fat 1 gm • Percent of calories from fat 14% •
Cholesterol 0 mg • Dietary fiber 1 gm • Sodium 28 mg • Calcium 10 mg

Black Bean and Goat Cheese Quesadillas

YIELD: 4 SERVINGS

The combination of goat cheese and black beans is a culinary marriage made in heaven. Even those who don't care for goat cheese find the flavor combination irresistible. I often make these as an accompaniment to soup.

2 large green chiles, such as
   Anaheims or poblanos
1½ cups cooked black beans
1 tomato, diced
1 tablespoon homemade
   or store-bought salsa, or more
   to taste

Salt
8 large flour tortillas
4 to 6 ounces soft, fresh
   goat cheese (chèvre)
4 scallions, chopped
2 tablespoons chopped fresh
   cilantro

Roast the chiles directly over a gas burner or under a broiler, turning often until charred all over. Place the chiles in a bag, close tightly, and set aside to steam for 10 minutes. Using a sharp knife, scrape off the blackened skins. Remove and discard the stems, seeds, and ribs. Place in a food processor fitted with a steel blade. Add the beans, tomato, and salsa, and process until well mixed but not completely smooth. Taste and add salt and additional salsa, as needed.

Preheat the oven to 200 degrees.

In a large ungreased skillet, warm 1 tortilla over moderate heat until softened. Flip and warm the other side. Remove from the skillet and set aside. Repeat with the remaining tortillas.

Return 1 of the warm tortillas to the skillet. Spread a quarter of the bean mixture evenly on the tortilla. Top with a quarter of the cheese, scallions, and cilantro. Place another tortilla on top, pressing firmly to make a sandwich. Flip and cook on the other side. Remove from the skillet and place in the oven while you make 3 more quesadillas, using the remaining ingredients. Cut into wedges and serve at once or cover with a dampened towel and hold in the oven for up to 30 minutes.

Calories 406 • Protein 18 gm • Fat 12 gm • Percent of calories from fat 25% •
Cholesterol 13 mg • Dietary fiber 9 gm • Sodium 444 mg • Calcium 156 mg

Black Bean Turnovers

❧

YIELD: **24** TURNOVERS

Here's another variation on the sublime black bean and goat cheese combination. Phyllo dough is surprisingly easy to work with and yields impressive results—as long as you avoid the temptation to overstuff the turnovers; the filling expands as it heats and will burst out of the seams if you're not careful.

Although the traditional way to handle phyllo dough is to brush it freely with butter, fat-conscious cooks have discovered that they can get excellent results with far less fat when they spray the dough with nonstick cooking spray. Having tried both ways, I think the low-fat technique yields superior results because the pastries are never greasy.

1^1/$_2$ cups cooked black beans
^{1}/$_2$ cup homemade
or store-bought salsa
4 ounces soft goat cheese (chèvre)

5 sheets phyllo, thawed according to package directions
Nonstick cooking spray

In a medium mixing bowl, combine the beans, salsa, and cheese. Mash with a potato masher to create a roughly textured paste.

Cut the stack of phyllo sheets lengthwise into 5 strips, each about 2^1/$_2$ inches wide. Keep the phyllo covered with plastic wrap or damp paper toweling to prevent drying out. Place 1 strip of phyllo on your work surface. Spray with nonstick cooking spray. Place a *scant* tablespoon of filling at the end of the strip. Fold 1 corner of the strip diagonally over the filling so the short end meets the long end, forming a right angle. Continue folding at right angles, like a flag, until the strip ends. Place the turnover, seam side down, on a baking sheet. Spray with nonstick cooking spray. Repeat with the remaining phyllo strips and filling. You can make these up to 1 day in advance and store them, tightly covered, in the refrigerator.

Just before serving, preheat the oven to 375 degrees. Bake the turnovers for 12 to 15 minutes, until golden brown. Let cool for a few minutes, then serve warm.

Calories 40 • Protein 2 gm • Fat 1 gm • Percent of calories from fat 30% •
Cholesterol 2 mg • Dietary fiber 1 gm • Sodium 37 mg • Calcium 10 mg

Stuffed Grape Leaves (Dolmades)

YIELD: 36 PIECES

Stuffed and wrapped appetizers are probably everyone's favorite. The great thing about stuffed grape leaves is they can be made up to a day in advance and served chilled—unlike dumplings, empanadas, eggrolls, and other classic stuffed appetizers, which must be made pretty much on the spot. Brown rice can be substituted for the white as long as the cooking liquid and times are increased accordingly.

2 tablespoons extra-virgin
   olive oil
1 large onion, finely chopped
3 garlic cloves, minced
1 cup uncooked long-grain
   white rice
2 cups plus 3 tablespoons water
4 strips lemon zest

2 tablespoons finely chopped
   fresh dill
$1/2$ teaspoon salt
$1/4$ cup dried currants
Freshly ground black pepper
1 (8-ounce) jar grape leaves
Juice of 1 lemon

In a medium saucepan, heat 1 tablespoon of the oil. Add the onion, garlic, and rice, and sauté until the rice appears toasted and the vegetables are limp, about 5 minutes. Add 2 cups of the water, the lemon zest, dill, and salt, and cover. Bring to a boil, then reduce the heat and boil gently until the rice is tender and all the liquid is absorbed, about 12 minutes. Remove from the heat. Discard the lemon zest. Stir in the currants. Season to taste with pepper.

Rinse the grape leaves in cool water, drain, then blot dry. Cut off any stems. Set aside any torn or very small leaves.

Preheat the oven to 350 degrees. Line a lidded 2-quart casserole dish with the torn and small grape leaves.

Place a grape leaf, vein side up, on your work surface. Place a heaping teaspoon of filling in the center of the leaf near the stem end. Fold the stem end up over the filling. Fold in both sides of the leaf toward the middle and roll up the leaf tightly (like a cigar). Place the stuffed leaves in the lined casserole dish, seam side down. Repeat until all the grape leaves and filling are used.

In a small bowl, combine the remaining 1 tablespoon oil and 3 tablespoons water with the lemon juice. Pour over the grape leaves. Cover and bake for 30 minutes. Remove from the oven and let cool to room temperature or chill well before serving.

Calories 37 • Protein 0 gm • Fat 1 gm • Percent of calories from fat 23% • Cholesterol 0 mg • Dietary fiber 0 gm • Sodium 134 mg • Calcium 4 mg

Vegetarian Nori Rolls

YIELD: 6 SERVINGS (48 PIECES SUSHI)

It takes almost as long to describe how to make nori rolls as it does to actually assemble them, so don't be put off by the length of the instructions. Nori rolls can be served as a light lunch, but they also make a beautiful and tasty hors d'oeuvre platter.

3 cups uncooked short-grain
    white rice
3³/₄ cups water
2¹/₃ tablespoons mirin
    (sweet rice wine)
¹/₂ cup rice vinegar
1 tablespoon plus 1¹/₂ teaspoons
    sugar
2¹/₄ teaspoons salt

6 dried nori seaweed sheets
    (about 8 inches square)
1 tablespoon wasabi powder
    mixed with 1 tablespoon water
¹/₂ avocado, thinly sliced
¹/₂ red bell pepper, thinly sliced
¹/₂ cup pickled ginger slices
4 scallions, thinly sliced

Dipping Sauce
¹/₂ cup soy sauce
1 tablespoon rice vinegar
1 teaspoon sesame oil

1 teaspoon sugar
1 scallion, finely chopped

To make the rice, combine the rice, water, and mirin in a medium saucepan and bring to a boil. Cover and simmer until the rice is tender and the water is absorbed, 12 to 15 minutes.

In a small saucepan, combine the vinegar, sugar, and salt, and bring to a boil.

Transfer the cooked rice to a shallow bowl or baking pan. Gradually pour the hot vinegar mixture over the rice and toss with a spoon or rice paddle held in one hand while fanning the rice with the other hand. (Alternatively, set the rice in front of a fan and let the fan cool the rice while you toss.) Continue until the rice is cooled to the touch and appears glossy.

To assemble, pass each seaweed sheet over an open flame or electric burner to lightly toast it. Place on a bamboo rolling mat. (Or substitute a bamboo table mat or clean dish towel.) Set a small bowl of rice vinegar nearby to use to moisten your fingertips. With moistened fingertips, spread 1 cup of rice in an even layer over the seaweed sheet, leaving about 1 inch at the top edge of the sheet. Spread about 1 teaspoon wasabi paste in a line over the bottom of the rice. Arrange the avocado slices on the wasabi. Top with a band of pepper strips, then ginger slices, then scallions. Brush the top edge of the seaweed with warm water. Using the bamboo rolling mat as a guide, roll the seaweed into a tight cylinder, starting with the bottom edge closest to you. Press on the moistened seaweed flap to seal the roll, then set aside, seam side down, while you repeat with the remaining ingredients, making 6 rolls in all.

To make the dipping sauce, combine the soy sauce, rice vinegar, sesame oil, sugar, and scallion in a nonreactive bowl.

To serve, cut each roll into 1-inch slices. Serve with the dipping sauce.

Nori Rolls: Calories 443 • Protein 8 gm • Fat 3 gm • Percent of calories from fat 7% • Cholesterol 0 mg • Dietary fiber 6 gm • Sodium 898 mg • Calcium 13 mg

Dipping Sauce: Calories 24 • Protein 1 gm • Fat 1 gm • Percent of calories from fat 30% • Cholesterol 0 mg • Dietary fiber 0 gm • Sodium 1372 mg • Calcium 5 mg

VARIATION

Smoked Salmon Nori Rolls. Replace the avocado with 3 ounces very thinly sliced smoked salmon, cut in thin strips.

Calories 436 • Protein 11 gm • Fat 1 gm • Percent of calories from fat 3% • Cholesterol 3 mg • Dietary fiber 4 gm • Sodium 1007 mg • Calcium 13 mg

Pizza-flavored Popcorn

YIELD: 6 CUPS (1-CUP SERVING)

Air-popped popcorn can be pretty spartan. Here's a tasty way to add a powerful punch of flavor without much fat.

6 cups air-popped popcorn
  (made from ³/₄ cup kernels)
1¹/₂ teaspoons butter
1¹/₂ teaspoons tomato paste

1 teaspoon salt
¹/₂ teaspoon garlic powder
¹/₂ teaspoon Italian seasoning

While the popcorn pops, heat the butter and tomato paste in a microwave set on high until the butter is melted, about 30 seconds. Stir in the salt, garlic powder, and Italian seasoning. Toss with the hot popcorn. Serve at once.

Calories 102 • Protein 3 gm • Fat 2 gm • Percent of calories from fat 17% • Cholesterol 3 mg • Dietary fiber 5 gm • Sodium 401 mg • Calcium 3 mg

Polenta-Fontina Bites

❦

YIELD: 24 PIECES

1 recipe Basic Double-boiler
  (Foolproof) Polenta (page 278)
1 teaspoon crushed dried rosemary
1 tablespoon chopped sun-dried
  tomatoes, packed in oil or
  reconstituted from dried

3 ounces Fontina cheese, thinly
  sliced
1 tablespoon extra-virgin olive oil
  or oil from sun-dried tomatoes

Prepare the polenta according to the recipe directions, stirring in the rosemary and sun-dried tomatoes at the end of the cooking time. While the polenta cooks, spray a 15-inch cooking sheet or jelly roll pan with non-stick cooking spray. Spread the cooked polenta in the pan and smooth the top with a spatula. Let cool for at least 1 hour, until firm.

Spray a griddle with nonstick cooking spray and heat over medium heat. Cut the polenta into uniform-size squares, triangles, or other shapes. Make sandwiches by placing a slice of Fontina between 2 pieces of polenta. Lightly brush the top of each piece with the oil and place, oiled side down, on the griddle. Fry until lightly browned, about 4 minutes. Brush with oil and flip. Cook until browned on the second side. Serve hot.

Calories 38 • Protein 1 gm • Fat 2 gm • Percent of calories from fat 44% •
Cholesterol 4 mg • Dietary fiber 0 gm • Sodium 129 mg • Calcium 21 mg

Crunchy Chickpea Snacks

YIELD: 1 1/2 CUPS

For the gotta-munch bunch, these crunchy alternatives to roasted nuts are similar to the roasted chickpeas sold by street vendors throughout the Middle East.

1 cup uncooked chickpeas
6 cups water
2 tablespoons Louisiana-style
   hot sauce

1 teaspoon ground cumin
Garlic powder
Salt

In a medium saucepan, combine the beans with the water and bring to a boil. Boil for 5 minutes. Remove from the heat and let stand for 1 hour. Drain well. Toss the beans with the hot sauce and cumin.

Preheat the oven to 400 degrees. Lightly spray a baking sheet with non-stick cooking spray. Spread the beans on the baking sheet. Mist the beans with the nonstick spray. Bake for about 25 minutes, until the beans start popping, shaking the baking sheet a few times while they bake. Reduce the heat to 325 degrees and continue to bake for another 30 minutes, until the beans are well-browned and crunchy. Sprinkle the chickpeas with garlic powder and salt to taste and let cool completely before storing in an airtight container for up to 1 month.

Calories 123 • Protein 7 gm • Fat 2 gm • Percent of calories from fat 15% •
Cholesterol 0 mg • Dietary fiber 6 gm • Sodium 38 mg • Calcium 43 mg

Garlic-roasted Soy Nuts

YIELD: ABOUT 1¼ CUPS (¼-CUP SERVING)

Warning! These terrific high-protein, high-fiber, low-fat alternatives to peanuts are highly addictive. Don't even think about making soy nuts unless you want to make a weekly commitment to making more. And you thought you didn't like soybeans!

1 cup soybeans	**2 cloves garlic, minced**
4 cups water	**Garlic powder**
2 tablespoons soy sauce	**Salt**

In a medium saucepan, combine the beans, water, soy sauce, and garlic and bring to a boil. Boil for 5 minutes. Remove from the heat and let sit for 1 hour.

Preheat the oven to 400 degrees. Lightly spray a baking sheet with non-stick cooking spray. Spread the beans on the baking sheet. Mist the beans with the nonstick spray and bake for 30 minutes, until the beans are browned, shaking the baking sheet a few times as they bake. Reduce the heat to 325 degrees and continue baking until crisp, about 30 minutes. Sprinkle with garlic powder and salt to taste and let cool completely before storing in an airtight container for up to 1 month.

Calories 117 • Protein 11 gm • Fat 6 gm • Percent of calories from fat 42% • Cholesterol 0 mg • Dietary fiber 3 gm • Sodium 212 mg • Calcium 73 mg

Barley Water

YIELD: 2 SERVINGS

I had read enough British novels to be curious about barley water when I finally came across a recipe for it. The drink is quite similar to lemonade in taste, but the barley gives it an almost silken feeling in the mouth. I assume that in the days of uncertain sanitary conditions, barley water was a way of making boiled water more palatable. I find it delicious and refreshing.

3 tablespoons pearled barley
4 cups water
Approximately 3 tablespoons
freshly squeezed lemon juice

Approximately 2 tablespoons
honey
Thinly sliced lemon

Combine the barley and water in a saucepan. Bring to a boil, uncovered, and boil until the liquid is reduced by half, about 30 minutes. Strain and discard the solids. Add the lemon juice and honey to taste. Chill well. Serve over ice, if desired, and garnish each glass with a lemon slice.

Calories 70 • Protein 0 gm • Fat 0 gm • Percent of calories from fat 0% • Cholesterol 0 mg • Dietary fiber 0 gm • Sodium 15 mg • Calcium 12 mg

3

Splendid Soups

❦

Mediterranean Vegetable Soup with Barley

Hearty Barley-Vegetable Soup

Barley-Mushroom Soup

Barley-Leek Soup

Barley-Kale Soup

Quick Hominy–Pinto Bean Soup

Tomato-Hominy Soup

Spanish Tomato-Rice Soup

Fresh Tomato-Rice Soup

Risi e Bisi

Japanese Thick Rice Soup

Wild Rice and Mushroom Soup

Black Bean Soup with Red Peppers and Corn

Smoky Black Bean and Tomato Soup

Black Bean Soup with Indian Spices

Butternut Squash Soup with Black Beans and Cilantro

Moroccan Chickpea and Rice Soup

Ton-o'-Garlic Cranberry Bean Soup

Spinach-Bean Soup

Lentil-Vegetable Soup

Curried Red Lentil Soup

Gingered Red Lentil Soup with Sweet Potatoes

Tomato-Cabbage Soup with Lima Beans

Moong Dahl Soup

Split Pea Soup

Split Pea–Barley Soup

Split Pea–Vegetable Soup

Quick Garlicky White Bean Soup

Quick Roasted Red Pepper and White Bean Soup

Mediterranean White Bean and Vegetable Soup with Fennel

Tomato Soup with White Beans and Fennel

Minestrone alla Genovese

Minestrone with Greens

Vegetable Stock

Mushroom Stock

Chicken Stock

I love to make soup. No culinary adventure is as open to improvisation, as forgiving to neglect or substitution as soup. And no culinary endeavor is as ultimately hospitable as a pot of soup.

A pot of soup brought to cheer a sick friend or relieve a family under stress is always welcome—and easy to accomplish. Bean soups, in particular, freeze well, so I keep large quantities on hand, ready to be called into service as a meal for my family or someone else's.

Many of the recipes in this chapter were tested on a group of potters who gathered once a week at the Frog Hollow Studio in Middlebury, Vermont. I made them early in the morning before class, or sometimes a day ahead (fortunately, most soups only get better with time). At these weekly potlucks, others were sure to bring some bread and salad, and no matter how many sat down to share, there was always enough.

The basis for many soups is broth. At the end of this chapter you will find recipes for chicken, vegetable, and mushroom broths. All three can be made ahead and stored in the freezer for four to six months. I have tasted many different canned and dried vegetable broths, but I have found only one vegetarian broth that I like (Westbrae Natural UnChicken Broth). Most taste too strongly of either tomatoes or sweet root vegetables, especially carrots. In recipes that require broth, I prefer to use homemade vegetable broth or Campbell's Healthy Request canned chicken broth. I recommend tasting a few brands of broth until you find a favorite—and then stock it regularly so you can make any of these soups whenever the spirit strikes.

This chapter begins with some of my favorite soups made with grains, specifically barley, hominy, and rice. Rice soup, in particular, defines comfort food for me. The final half of the chapter includes a wide variety of bean soups, with flavor combinations drawn from all over the world. With the exception of the rice soups, most of these dishes taste even better the second day, but will thicken on standing. If a soup becomes too thick, thin with additional broth or water and add more salt and pepper, if needed.

Mediterranean Vegetable Soup with Barley

YIELD: 4 TO 6 SERVINGS

While many barley soups are very thick and hearty, this one is quite delicate. The sweet flavor of the barley is highlighted by the natural sweetness of the fennel, carrots, and tomatoes. This soup doesn't take much cooking—just long enough to cook the barley, about 50 minutes. Along the way, you can speed up your work by using a food processor to chop the vegetables and relying on canned or frozen broth.

1 tablespoon extra-virgin olive oil
1 leek, finely chopped
1 carrot, finely chopped
1 small fennel bulb, finely chopped
4 garlic cloves, minced
6 cups high-quality chicken or vegetable broth
1/3 cup uncooked pearled or hulled barley

1 (15-ounce) can diced tomatoes, well drained
1/2 teaspoon dried rosemary, crumbled
Salt and freshly ground black pepper
1/2 pound spinach, stems removed and leaves cut into 1 1/2-inch pieces

In a large soup pot, heat the oil over medium heat. Add the leek, carrot, fennel, and garlic. Sauté until the vegetables are soft, about 5 minutes. Add the broth, barley, tomatoes, and rosemary. Bring to a boil. Then reduce the heat and simmer for 40 to 60 minutes, until the barley is tender. Taste and adjust seasonings. Add the spinach and continue to simmer until the spinach is wilted, about 5 minutes. Serve at once.

Calories 190 • Protein 10 gm • Fat 4.2 gm • Percent of calories from fat 19% • Cholesterol 0 mg • Dietary fiber 7 gm • Sodium 919 mg • Calcium 130 mg

Hearty Barley-Vegetable Soup

YIELD: 6 TO 8 SERVINGS

A thick, hearty vegetable soup.

1 tablespoon extra-virgin olive oil
1 leek, finely chopped
1 small carrot, finely chopped
2 garlic cloves, minced
1 cup chopped white mushrooms
4 cups high-quality chicken
    or vegetable broth
2 cups water
1 large ripe tomato, chopped,
    or 1 cup canned diced tomatoes,
    drained

$2/3$ cup uncooked pearled or
    hulled barley
$1/2$ cup frozen lima beans
$1/2$ cup frozen corn
1 teaspoon dried marjoram
Salt and freshly ground black
    pepper

In a large soup pot, heat the oil over medium heat. Add the leek, carrot, garlic, and mushrooms. Sauté until the vegetables are soft, about 5 minutes. Add the broth, water, tomato, barley, lima beans, corn, marjoram and salt and pepper, and bring to a boil. Then reduce the heat and simmer for 40 to 60 minutes, until the barley is tender. Taste and adjust seasonings. Serve hot.

Calories 164 • Protein 6 gm • Fat 2.8 gm • Percent of calories from fat 15% • Cholesterol 0 mg • Dietary fiber 6 gm • Sodium 323 mg • Calcium 35 mg

Barley-Mushroom Soup

YIELD: 6 TO 8 SERVINGS

The porcini mushrooms create a deep, rich flavor background for the nutty-sweet barley. This soup makes a very satisfying meal with whole-grain bread and a salad.

1 cup dried sliced porcini
    mushrooms (1 ounce)
2 cups boiling water
2 onions, quartered
2 carrots, chopped
2 garlic cloves
1½ pounds white mushrooms
1 tablespoon olive or canola oil
8 cups water or high-quality
    chicken, vegetable, or
    mushroom broth

²/₃ cup uncooked pearled or hulled
    barley
1 teaspoon dried thyme
¼ cup dry sherry
¼ cup chopped fresh parsley
Salt and freshly ground black
    pepper

Place the dried porcini mushrooms in a medium bowl. Pour the boiling water over the mushrooms and set aside to soak.

In a food processor fitted with a metal blade, finely chop the onions, carrots, and garlic. Set aside. Finely chop about 1 pound of the white mushrooms and slice the remaining ½ pound.

Heat the oil in a large soup pot over medium heat. Add the chopped vegetables and sauté until the vegetables are well browned and the liquid has mostly evaporated, about 15 minutes. Add the water or broth, barley, thyme, and sliced white mushrooms. Add the soaked porcini mushrooms and their soaking liquid, avoiding any grit that has settled in the bottom of the bowl. Bring to a boil, then reduce the heat and simmer until the barley is tender, about 40 to 60 minutes. Add the sherry, parsley, and plenty of salt and pepper. Taste and adjust the seasonings. Serve hot.

Calories 207 • Protein 10 gm • Fat 3.2 gm • Percent of calories from fat 13% • Cholesterol 0 mg • Dietary fiber 7 gm • Sodium 624 mg • Calcium 60 mg

Barley-Leek Soup

YIELD: 6 TO 8 SERVINGS

The success of this soup really depends on the quality of the broth you use. If you are using canned broth, select one with good—and fairly neutral—flavor.

1 tablespoon extra-virgin olive oil
4 medium leeks, sliced
  (1¹/₄ to 1¹/₂ pounds)
3 cups sliced mushrooms
  (about ¹/₂ pound)
2 garlic cloves, minced
8 cups high-quality chicken or
  vegetable broth

²/₃ cup uncooked pearled
  or hulled barley
2 carrots, diced
1 tablespoon chopped fresh sage
  or 1 teaspoon dried
¹/₄ cup sherry
Salt and freshly ground black
  pepper

Heat the oil in a large soup pot over medium heat. Add the leeks, mushrooms, and garlic, and sauté until the leeks are limp and the mushrooms are beginning to color, about 8 minutes. Add the broth, barley, carrots, and sage. Bring to a boil, then reduce the heat and simmer until the barley is tender, 40 to 60 minutes. Add the sherry and salt and pepper to taste. Serve hot.

Calories 210 • Protein 9 gm • Fat 3 gm • Percent of calories from fat 13% • Cholesterol 0 mg • Dietary fiber 6 gm • Sodium 629 mg • Calcium 71 mg

Barley-Kale Soup

YIELD: 6 TO 8 SERVINGS

Because I don't enjoy overcooked kale, I think this is one barley soup that tastes best on the day it is made.

1 tablespoon extra-virgin olive oil
1 large onion, diced
1 red bell pepper, diced
2 garlic cloves, minced
8 cups high-quality chicken
   or vegetable broth
²/₃ cup uncooked pearled
   or hulled barley

1 medium tomato, diced
1 tablespoon chopped fresh sage
   or 1 teaspoon dried
Salt and freshly ground black
   pepper
4 cups finely chopped kale

Heat the olive oil in a large soup pot over medium heat. Add the onion, bell pepper, and garlic, and sauté until the onion is limp, about 4 minutes. Add the broth, barley, tomato, and sage. Bring to a boil, then reduce the heat and simmer until the barley is tender, 40 to 60 minutes. Season with salt and pepper to taste. Add the kale and simmer until the kale is tender but not overcooked, 5 to 10 minutes. Serve at once.

Calories 163 • Protein 8 gm • Fat 2.9 gm • Percent of calories from fat 16 % •
Cholesterol 0 mg • Dietary fiber 6 gm • Sodium 618 mg • Calcium 61 mg

Quick Hominy—Pinto Bean Soup

YIELD: 6 TO 8 SERVINGS

This soup is quick to make because it requires already cooked—or canned—hominy and pinto beans. However, the flavor much improves if it is made a few hours or a day in advance.

1 tablespoon extra-virgin olive oil
1 onion, finely chopped
1 green bell pepper,
   finely chopped
2 jalapeño peppers, finely
   chopped (seeded, if desired)
4 garlic cloves, minced
1 teaspoon chili powder
1 (28-ounce) can peeled tomatoes

4 cups high-quality chicken
   or vegetable broth
1 teaspoon dried oregano
1 (15-ounce) can hominy,
   rinsed and drained
1½ cups cooked pinto beans
Salt and freshly ground black
   pepper

In a large pot, heat the olive oil over medium heat. Add the onion, green pepper, jalapeños, garlic, and chili powder. Sauté until the onion is limp, about 4 minutes. Add the tomatoes, broth, and oregano. Bring to a boil. Then reduce the heat and simmer for about 30 minutes. Add the hominy, pinto beans, and salt and pepper to taste. Simmer for another 30 minutes. Serve hot.

Calories 189 • Protein 9 gm • Fat 3.6 gm • Percent of calories from fat 16% • Cholesterol 0 mg • Dietary fiber 8 gm • Sodium 701 mg • Calcium 80 mg

Tomato-Hominy Soup

YIELD: 4 TO 6 SERVINGS

Like many foods, hominy tastes best when it is least processed—in this case, dried not canned. If you have the time, dried hominy makes a delicious soup.

1 cup posole (dried hominy),
   soaked overnight
6 cups water
1 tablespoon extra-virgin olive oil
1 onion, finely chopped
1 celery stalk, finely chopped
4 garlic cloves, minced
1 (28-ounce) can tomato puree

6 cups high-quality chicken
   or vegetable broth
1 tablespoon ground cumin
Salt and freshly ground black
   pepper
1/4 cup chopped fresh parsley
   or cilantro (optional)

Drain the posole. Combine with the water in a large pot. Bring to a boil, then reduce the heat and simmer, partially covered, for about 1 1/2 hours, until the hominy is slightly tender.

In a large pot, heat the olive oil over medium heat. Add the onion, celery, and garlic, and sauté until the onion is limp, about 4 minutes. Add the tomato puree, broth, cumin, and hominy plus any cooking water. Bring to a boil. Then reduce the heat and simmer for about 2 more hours. Season with salt and pepper to taste. Add the cilantro and parsley (if using). Serve hot.

Calories 260 • Protein 11 gm • Fat 4.1 gm • Percent of calories from fat 14% •
Cholesterol 0 mg • Dietary fiber 6 gm • Sodium 749 mg • Calcium 40 mg

Spanish Tomato-Rice Soup

YIELD: 6 TO 8 SERVINGS

1 tablespoon extra-virgin olive oil

1 leek, white part only, thinly sliced

2 shallots, minced

4 garlic cloves, minced

2 (35-ounce) cans Italian tomatoes, chopped

4 cups vegetable or chicken broth or water

$1/2$ cup white wine

$1/4$ teaspoon crushed saffron threads

$1/4$ teaspoon hot paprika

Salt and freshly ground pepper

$1/2$ cup uncooked Arborio or medium-grain rice

1 (4-ounce) jar chopped pimiento, drained

Heat the olive oil in a large soup pot over medium heat. Add the leek, shallots, and garlic, and sauté until tender, about 4 minutes. Add the tomatoes, broth, wine, saffron, and paprika. Season to taste with salt and pepper. Bring to a boil. Add the rice and pimiento and simmer, partially covered, until the rice is tender, about 20 minutes. Serve hot.

Calories 205 • Protein 7 gm • Fat 3.1 gm • Percent of calories from fat 13% • Cholesterol 0 mg • Dietary fiber 4 gm • Sodium 898 mg • Calcium 117 mg

Fresh Tomato-Rice Soup

YIELD: 4 TO 6 SERVINGS

When fresh tomatoes and corn are in season, this is a great soup to make. The corn can be added raw, scraped right off the ear, but if you have a couple of leftover ears of grilled corn, so much the better. And, of course, out of season, feel free to substitute canned tomatoes and frozen corn.

2 tablespoons extra-virgin olive oil

4 garlic cloves, minced

1 shallot, minced

1 celery stalk, minced

3 cups fresh or canned chopped tomatoes

3 cups high-quality chicken or vegetable broth

1/2 cup uncooked long-grain or medium-grain white rice

Kernels from 2 ears corn, grilled or raw, or 1 cup frozen corn

2 tablespoons chopped fresh basil

1 teaspoon chopped fresh tarragon, oregano, summer savory, or chervil

1 tablespoon balsamic vinegar

Salt and freshly ground black pepper

In a heavy saucepan over low heat, heat the olive oil. Add the garlic, shallot, and celery, and sauté until soft, about 10 minutes. Add the tomatoes and broth, increase the heat to medium, and simmer for 10 minutes. Add the rice, corn, and herbs, and simmer until the rice is cooked, about 15 minutes. Add the vinegar and salt and pepper to taste. Let simmer for about 5 more minutes. Serve hot.

Calories 241 • Protein 7 gm • Fat 7.9 gm • Percent of calories from fat 28% • Cholesterol 0 mg • Dietary fiber 3 gm • Sodium 367 mg • Calcium 27 mg

Risi e Bisi

YIELD: 4 TO 6 SERVINGS

Rice with peas is considered a soup in Italy, though it can be eaten with a fork and has the consistency of a wet risotto. A specialty of Venice, it was supposedly a banquet dish served to the doges of Venice to celebrate the Feast of St. Mark. I like to make it with fresh homegrown peas as a celebration of summer, but frozen peas can be substituted.

5 cups high-quality chicken
  or vegetable broth
2 tablespoons extra-virgin
  olive oil
1 tablespoon butter
2 scallions, sliced
3/4 cup uncooked medium-grain
  or Arborio rice

Salt (optional)
2 cups fresh shelled peas
  (about 2 pounds in the pod)
1/3 cup freshly grated Parmesan
  cheese
1 tablespoon chopped fresh
  parsley

Heat the broth to a simmer in a saucepan on top of the stove or in a heatproof container in the microwave.

In a large saucepan, heat the olive oil and butter over medium heat. Add the scallions and sauté for 2 minutes. Add the hot broth and rice, stir well, cover, reduce the heat, and simmer until the rice is just tender, 15 minutes. Taste and add salt if needed. Stir in the peas and cook gently until the peas are done enough to suit you, 2 to 5 minutes. Stir in the Parmesan and parsley. If the mixture is too thick, stir in additional broth or water. Serve at once.

Calories 333 • Protein 13 gm • Fat 12.3 gm • Percent of calories from fat 34% • Cholesterol 13 mg • Dietary fiber 4 gm • Sodium 721 mg • Calcium 117 mg

Japanese Thick Rice Soup

YIELD: 4 SERVINGS

A cure for hangovers and overindulgence, this is a bowl of comfort—Japanese style. I eat it for dinner or breakfast when I am feeling digestively challenged.

6 cups high-quality chicken
   or vegetable broth
3 cups cooked white rice
1 tablespoon tamari
   or soy sauce, or more to taste

1 teaspoon grated fresh ginger
2 scallions, thinly sliced
2 large eggs, lightly beaten

In a large saucepan, heat the broth to boiling. Add the rice, tamari, ginger, and scallions. Reduce the heat to low and simmer for 10 minutes, until the rice is quite soft. Vigorously stir in the eggs. Simmer for another 2 minutes, until the eggs are cooked. Serve at once. This will thicken to a porridge-like consistency on standing.

Calories 253 • Protein 11 gm • Fat 2.8 gm • Percent of calories from fat 11% • Cholesterol 106 mg • Dietary fiber 1 gm • Sodium 958 mg • Calcium 20 mg

Wild Rice and Mushroom Soup

YIELD: 6 TO 8 SERVINGS

A variation on the barley-mushroom theme.

1 cup dried sliced porcini
   mushrooms (1 ounce)
2 cups boiling water
2 onions, quartered
2 celery stalks, chopped
2 garlic cloves
1$^1/_2$ pounds white mushrooms
1 tablespoon olive or canola oil
6 cups water or high-quality
   chicken, vegetable, or
   mushroom broth

1$^1/_2$ cups diced canned tomatoes
   with juice
$^2/_3$ cup uncooked wild rice
$^1/_3$ cup uncooked brown rice
2 teaspoons dried thyme
2 bay leaves
$^1/_2$ cup dry sherry
$^1/_2$ cup chopped fresh parsley
Salt and freshly ground black
   pepper

Place the dried porcini mushrooms in a small bowl. Pour in the boiling water and set aside to soak.

In a food processor, finely chop the onions, celery, and garlic. Set aside. Finely chop about 1 pound of the white mushrooms and slice the remaining $^1/_2$ pound.

Heat the oil in a large soup pot over medium heat. Add the chopped vegetables and sauté until the vegetables are well browned and most of the liquid has evaporated, 10 to 15 minutes. Add the water or broth, tomatoes, wild rice, brown rice, sliced white mushrooms, thyme, and bay leaves. Add the soaked porcini mushrooms and their soaking liquid, avoiding any grit that has settled in the bottom of the bowl. Bring to a boil, then reduce the heat and simmer, partially covered, until the rice is tender, about 1 hour. Remove the bay leaves and discard. Add the sherry, parsley, and plenty of salt and pepper. Taste and adjust seasonings. Serve hot.

Calories 238 • Protein 11 gm • Fat 3.3 gm • Percent of calories from fat 12% •
Cholesterol 0 mg • Dietary fiber 4 gm • Sodium 716 mg • Calcium 66 mg

Black Bean Soup with Red Peppers and Corn

YIELD: 6 TO 8 SERVINGS

The sherry echoes the sweetness of the carrots, peppers, and corn and smoothes all the rough edges from this lovely soup.

2 cups dried black beans,
　soaked overnight or
　using quick-soak
　method on page 20
8 cups water
2 onions, chopped
2 carrots, chopped
3 garlic cloves, halved

2 bay leaves
1 red bell pepper, diced
2 cups fresh or frozen corn kernels
1/4 cup dry sherry
Salt and freshly ground black
　pepper
Sour cream or mashed
　hard-cooked egg (optional)

Drain the beans. Combine the beans in a large soup pot with the 8 cups fresh water, onions, carrots, garlic, and bay leaves. Bring to a boil, then skim off any foam that rises to the top. Reduce the heat, cover, and simmer until the beans are very tender, about 2 hours. Remove the bay leaves and discard; puree the soup in a blender.

Return the soup to the pot and bring to a boil. Again, skim off any foam that rises to the top. Add the red pepper, corn, and sherry. Season generously with salt and pepper and heat through.

If desired, serve with a dollop of sour cream or a spoonful of hard-cooked egg on top.

Calories 315 • Protein 17 gm • Fat 1 gm • Percent of calories from fat 3% • Cholesterol 0 mg • Dietary fiber 13 gm • Sodium 26 mg • Calcium 109 mg

Smoky Black Bean and Tomato Soup

YIELD: 6 TO 8 SERVINGS

The smoky flavor comes from the chipotle chile, a smoked-dried jalapeño. Its flavor is particularly well suited to black beans.

2 cups dried black beans, soaked
   overnight or using quick-soak
   method on page 20
8 cups water
4 garlic cloves, minced
1 onion, finely chopped
1 dried chipotle chile or
   1 tablespoon chipotle en
   adobo

2 bay leaves
1 (28-ounce) can Italian tomatoes
1/4 cup chopped fresh cilantro
1 tablespoon freshly squeezed
   lime juice
Salt and freshly ground black
   pepper
Cilantro or sour cream,
   for garnish (optional)

Drain the beans. Combine the beans in a large soup pot with the 8 cups fresh water, garlic, onion, chipotle, and bay leaves. Bring to a boil, then skim off any foam that rises to the top. Reduce the heat, cover, and simmer until the beans are very tender, about 2 hours.

Remove the bay leaves and discard. Remove the chile from the pot. Discard the seeds and finely chop the flesh; return to the pot. Remove about 3 cups of the soup from the pot and let cool slightly. Puree in the blender and return to the pot. Chop the tomatoes and add to the soup along with the juice from the can. Add the cilantro, lime juice, and salt and pepper to taste. Simmer for about 15 minutes to blend the flavors. Serve hot, garnishing with additional chopped cilantro or a dollop of sour cream, if desired.

Calories 262 • Protein 16 gm • Fat 1 gm • Percent of calories from fat 4% •
Cholesterol 0 mg • Dietary fiber 12 gm • Sodium 251 mg • Calcium 134 mg

Black Bean Soup with Indian Spices

YIELD: 6 TO 8 SERVINGS

Black beans, which are usually associated with New World seasonings, pair well with Indian spices. Coconut milk is the secret ingredient in this soup.

2 cups dried black beans,
   soaked overnight or using quick-
   soak method on page 20
8 cups water
2 medium onions, chopped
2 garlic cloves
1-inch piece fresh ginger, peeled
   and sliced

1 tablespoon ground cumin
2 teaspoons salt
1 tablespoon ground cardamom
1 teaspoon ground coriander
1 (14-ounce) can light coconut
   milk
1/3 cup chopped fresh cilantro

Drain the beans. Combine the beans, 8 cups fresh water, onions, garlic, and ginger in a soup pot and bring to a boil over medium heat. Skim off any foam that rises to the top. Cover, reduce the heat, and simmer until the beans are very tender, about 2 hours.

Let the beans cool slightly, then puree in a blender or food processor or strain through a food mill. Return to the pot and add the cumin, salt, cardamom, and coriander. Simmer for at least 30 minutes. Taste and adjust the seasoning.

Just before serving, stir in the coconut milk and cilantro. Serve hot. Do not allow the soup to boil once the coconut milk has been added.

Calories 291 • Protein 15 gm • Fat 4.6 gm • Percent of calories from fat 14% •
Cholesterol 0 mg • Dietary fiber 12 gm • Sodium 810 mg • Calcium 117 mg

Butternut Squash Soup with Black Beans and Cilantro

❧❧❧

YIELD: 4 TO 6 SERVINGS

1 medium-size butternut squash
  (about 2¹/₂ pounds)
4 cups high-quality chicken
  or vegetable broth
1¹/₂ cups cooked black beans
¹/₄ cup chopped fresh cilantro

¹/₄ cup chopped fresh chives
  or scallions
Salt and black and white pepper
4 to 6 tablespoons light coconut
  milk

Peel the squash, remove any seeds and fibers, and cut into chunks. Combine with the broth in a large saucepan and simmer until the squash is tender, about 1 hour. Let cool slightly, then puree in a food processor or blender. Return to the pot and add the black beans, cilantro, chives, and salt and pepper. Heat through over low heat.

To serve, ladle the soup into individual bowls. Drizzle a tablespoon of coconut milk over each bowl and swirl gently with a spoon. Do not mix in completely.

Calories 229 • Protein 11 gm • Fat 1.4 gm • Percent of calories from fat 5% • Cholesterol 0 mg • Dietary fiber 10 gm • Sodium 467 mg • Calcium 141 mg

Moroccan Chickpea and Rice Soup

YIELD: 6 TO 8 SERVINGS

1¹/₂ cups chickpeas, soaked
 overnight or using quick-soak
 method on page 20
8 cups water
2 onions, finely diced
2 garlic cloves, minced
1 teaspoon freshly ground black
 pepper
¹/₂ teaspoon crushed saffron
 threads

³/₄ cup long-grain white rice
1¹/₂ cups chopped tomatoes
 with juice
¹/₄ cup tomato paste
Salt and freshly ground black
 pepper
¹/₃ cup chopped fresh parsley
¹/₄ cup chopped fresh cilantro

Drain the chickpeas. In a large pot, combine the chickpeas with the 8 cups fresh water, onions, garlic, pepper, and saffron. Bring to a boil, then reduce the heat and simmer, partially covered, until the beans are tender but not mushy, 1¹/₂ to 2 hours.

Add the rice, tomatoes, tomato paste, and salt and pepper to taste. Bring the soup to a boil, then reduce the heat and simmer, covered, until the rice and chickpeas are both completely cooked, about 30 minutes. Add the parsley and cilantro, then taste and adjust the seasoning with more salt and pepper, if needed. Let simmer for at least 15 minutes to blend the flavors. Serve hot.

Calories 292 • Protein 13 gm • Fat 3 gm • Percent of calories from fat 9% •
Cholesterol 3 mg • Dietary fiber 4 gm • Sodium 30 mg • Calcium 106 mg

Ton-o'-Garlic Cranberry Bean Soup

YIELD: 4 TO 6 SERVINGS

Good for what ails you, this extraordinarily simple and flavorful soup contains a lot of garlic, which is said to have immune-system boosting properties. The garlic mellows as it cooks, resulting in a rich background flavor that matches the meaty, sweet flavor of the cranberry beans quite well. My favorite way to serve this soup is with toasted whole-wheat bread or croutons.

A simple way to peel a garlic bulb is to first break it into individual cloves. Then smash each clove with the side of your chef's knife or cleaver, pressing down hard with the heel of your hand. At this point the paper will separate easily from the squashed cloves.

2 cups dried cranberry beans
   (or substitute white beans,
   such as Great Northerns),
   soaked overnight or using
   quick-soak method on
   page 20
10 cups water

1 large garlic bulb
10 stems parsley
6 sprigs fresh thyme
2 bay leaves
1^1/$_2$ tablespoons red wine vinegar
Salt and freshly ground black
   pepper

Drain the beans. Combine the beans in a large soup pot with the 10 cups fresh water and bring to a boil. Skim off any foam that rises to the surface. Reduce the heat to a simmer. Peel the garlic cloves and add to the soup. Tie together the parsley and thyme stems with cotton thread and add to the soup, along with the bay leaves. Partially cover and simmer until the beans are quite tender—even mushy—about 2 hours. Discard the tied bunch of herbs.

Let the soup cool slightly, then puree in the blender. Return to the pot and add the vinegar and salt and pepper to taste. Simmer for another 5 minutes, then serve.

Calories 365 • Protein 25 gm • Fat 1 gm • Percent of calories from fat 3% •
Cholesterol 0 mg • Dietary fiber 16 gm • Sodium 39 mg • Calcium 310 mg

Spinach-Bean Soup

YIELD: 6 TO 8 SERVINGS

This is a comforting soup for whatever ails you. The spinach in the rich bean broth gives me the feeling that I am imbibing a spring tonic.

1 cup dried cranberry beans
   (or substitute white beans,
   such as Great Northerns),
   soaked overnight or using
   the quick-soak method on
   page 20
8 cups water
1 onion, diced
2 carrots, sliced

8 garlic cloves, minced
2 teaspoons dried sage
1 teaspoon dried thyme
1 pound spinach, stemmed and
   chopped
1 tablespoon balsamic vinegar,
   or more to taste
Salt and freshly ground black
   pepper

Drain the beans. In a large soup pot, combine the beans, 8 cups fresh water, onion, carrots, garlic, sage, and thyme. Bring to a boil, then reduce the heat, partially cover, and simmer until the beans are tender, about 2 hours. Add the spinach and simmer for 15 minutes, partially covered. Add the balsamic vinegar and salt and pepper to taste. Serve hot.

Calories 157 • Protein 11 gm • Fat 1 gm • Percent of calories from fat 4% •
Cholesterol 0 mg • Dietary fiber 11 gm • Sodium 82 mg • Calcium 150 mg

Lentil-Vegetable Soup

YIELD: 6 TO 8 SERVINGS

1 tablespoon olive or canola oil

1 onion, coarsely chopped

2 celery stalks, coarsely chopped

4 garlic cloves, halved

2 cups dried green or brown
   lentils, rinsed

6 cups water or broth,
   or more as needed

1 tablespoon plus 1¹/₂ teaspoons
   dried thyme

2 cups chopped fresh or canned
   tomatoes

4 cups diced mixed vegetables
   (green beans, carrots, corn,
   zucchini, turnips, etc.)

Salt and freshly ground black
   pepper

In a large soup pot, heat the oil over medium-low heat. Add the onion, celery, and garlic, and sauté until the onions are golden, about 7 minutes. Add the lentils, water or broth, and 1 tablespoon of the dried thyme. Bring to a boil, then skim off any foam that rises to the top. Reduce the heat, cover, and simmer until the lentils are mushy, about 45 to 60 minutes, depending on the variety and age of the lentils.

Let cool slightly, then puree in a blender. Return to the pot and thin with additional water, if desired. Add the tomatoes and mixed vegetables. Simmer for about 15 minutes, until the vegetables are tender but still slightly crunchy. Add the remaining 1¹/₂ teaspoons thyme and the salt and pepper with a liberal hand. Serve hot.

Calories 251 • Protein 12 gm • Fat 3 gm • Percent of calories from fat 9% • Cholesterol 0 mg • Dietary fiber 14 gm • Sodium 48 mg • Calcium 114 mg

Curried Red Lentil Soup

YIELD: 6 TO 8 SERVINGS

2½ cups dried red lentils, rinsed
8 cups water
4 garlic cloves, minced
2 teaspoons ground coriander
½ teaspoon ground turmeric
½ teaspoon ground red pepper,
 or more to taste
3 bay leaves
2 tablespoons olive or canola oil

2 large onions, finely chopped
1 tablespoon minced fresh ginger
1 teaspoon ground cumin
3 tablespoons freshly squeezed
 lemon juice
1 cup light coconut milk
¼ cup minced fresh cilantro
Salt and freshly ground pepper

Combine the lentils, water, garlic, coriander, turmeric, ground red pepper, and bay leaves in a large soup pot. Bring to a boil, then skim off any foam that rises to the top. Reduce the heat, cover, and simmer until the lentils are very tender, 45 to 60 minutes. Let cool slightly. Discard the bay leaves. Then process the soup in a blender until smooth.

In a large skillet over medium-low heat, heat the oil. Add the onions, ginger, and cumin, and sauté until the onions are golden, about 10 minutes. Stir into the lentil puree. Add the lemon juice. Simmer for about 30 minutes. Just before serving, add the coconut milk, cilantro, and salt and pepper to taste. Serve hot. Do not allow the soup to boil once the coconut milk has been added.

Calories 366 • Protein 24 gm • Fat 7.6 gm • Percent of calories from fat 18% • Cholesterol 0 mg • Dietary fiber 26 gm • Sodium 32 mg • Calcium 74 mg

Gingered Red Lentil Soup with Sweet Potatoes

YIELD: 8 TO 10 SERVINGS

A rich, smooth soup packed with a hefty dose of everything that's good for you—beta carotene, fiber, protein, flavor.

2 tablespoons olive or canola oil
1 large onion, diced
6 garlic cloves, minced
**4 tablespoons finely chopped
   fresh, peeled ginger**
2$^1/_2$ cups red lentils, rinsed
8 cups water

2 large carrots, cubed
2 sweet potatoes, peeled and cubed
$^1/_4$ cup dry sherry
**2 tablespoons freshly squeezed
   lemon juice**
Salt and white pepper

In a large soup pot, heat the oil over medium heat. Add the onion, garlic, and ginger, and sauté until the onion is transparent, about 4 minutes. Add the lentils, water, carrots, and sweet potatoes. Bring to a boil, then reduce the heat and simmer, partially covered, until the lentils are very tender, 45 to 60 minutes. Let cool slightly. Then process in a blender until smooth. Return to the pot and add the sherry, lemon juice, and salt and pepper to taste. Simmer over very low heat for about 30 minutes. Serve hot.

Calories 294 • Protein 18 gm • Fat 4 gm • Percent of calories from fat 12% •
Cholesterol 0 mg • Dietary fiber 20 gm • Sodium 24 mg • Calcium 58 mg

Tomato-Cabbage Soup with Lima Beans

YIELD: 6 TO 8 SERVINGS

2 tablespoons olive or canola oil
3 cups shredded green cabbage
1 onion, thinly sliced
1 (28-ounce) can crushed tomatoes
   or tomato puree

6 cups chicken or vegetable broth
1 teaspoon ground cumin
$1/_8$ teaspoon ground allspice
1 cup fresh or frozen lima beans
Salt and black and white pepper

In a large soup pot, heat the oil over medium heat. Add the cabbage and onion and sauté until golden, about 10 minutes. Add the tomatoes, broth, cumin, and allspice. Bring to a boil, then reduce the heat and simmer for 30 minutes. Add the lima beans and simmer until tender and heated through, about 20 minutes. Taste and adjust seasonings; be generous with the pepper. Serve hot.

Calories 141 • Protein 8 gm • Fat 5.1 gm • Percent of calories from fat 32% • Cholesterol 0 mg • Dietary fiber 5 gm • Sodium 813 mg • Calcium 65 mg

Moong Dahl Soup

❧❦❧

YIELD: 4 TO 5 SERVINGS

*Y*ellow split mung beans, or *moong dahl*, are somewhat reminiscent of red lentils in flavor and make for a very creamy soup. They can be found where Indian foods are sold, likewise all curry seasonings, including fenugreek. I find all of these ingredients in my local natural food store.

2 tablespoons olive or canola oil

1 large onion, diced

4 garlic cloves, minced

2 tablespoons finely chopped fresh, peeled ginger

1 teaspoon fenugreek seeds

1/2 teaspoon ground cumin

1/2 teaspoon ground coriander

1/8 teaspoon ground turmeric

2 1/2 cups dried yellow split mung beans, rinsed

8 cups water

2 large carrots, cubed

1/4 cup dry sherry

2 tablespoons freshly squeezed lemon juice

Salt and white pepper

1/4 cup chopped fresh scallions

2 tablespoons chopped fresh cilantro

In a large soup pot, heat the oil over medium heat. Add the onion, garlic, ginger, fenugreek, cumin, coriander, and turmeric, and sauté until the onion is transparent, about 4 minutes. Add the beans, water, and carrots. Bring to a boil, then reduce the heat and simmer, partially covered, until the beans are tender, about 45 minutes. Let cool slightly. Then process in a blender until smooth. Return to the pot and add the sherry, lemon juice, and salt and pepper to taste. Stir in the scallions and cilantro. Simmer over very low heat for about 30 minutes. Serve hot.

Calories 577 • Protein 33 gm • Fat 9 gm • Percent of calories from fat 13% • Cholesterol 0 mg • Dietary fiber 23 gm • Sodium 53 mg • Calcium 222 mg

Split Pea Soup

YIELD: 4 TO 5 SERVINGS

It's hard to conceive of a rich pea soup without some smoked flavor. This one can get that requisite flavor boost from either smoked turkey or a chipotle chile (a smoke-dried jalapeño). If you want smoke flavor but none of the heat, cook the soup with the chile, but do not return the chile to the pot after the soup is pureed. If you want only some of the flavor and heat, remove the seeds from the chile but return the flesh to the soup.

2 cups dried split peas, rinsed
8 cups water
1 chipotle chile
2 onions, quartered
2 celery stalks, quartered
1 carrot, quartered
1 bay leaf
Salt and freshly ground black pepper

In a large soup pot, combine the peas, water, and chipotle. Bring to a boil, then reduce the heat. Skim off any foam that rises to the top of the pot. Add the onions, celery, carrots, and bay leaf. Simmer for 1 hour.

Remove the soup from the heat to cool slightly. Remove the chile and bay leaf. Process the soup in the blender until smooth. Return the soup to the pot. Finely dice the chile (remove the seeds first, if desired) and return to the soup. Add salt and pepper to taste. Thin the soup with water, if desired. Heat through before serving. The soup improves in flavor and thickens on standing. Thin with water as needed.

Calories 378 • Protein 25 gm • Fat 1 gm • Percent of calories from fat 3 % • Cholesterol 0 mg • Dietary fiber 28 gm • Sodium 126 mg • Calcium 99 mg

VARIATION

Split Pea Soup with Smoked Turkey. Lean smoked turkey contributes the flavor—but none of the fat—of the traditional ham bone. Omit the chipotle chile and add $1/2$ pound smoked turkey—all in one piece—along with the onions, celery, and carrot. Remove the turkey before processing the soup in the blender and finely dice. Return the diced turkey to the processed soup and add salt and pepper to taste.

Calories 439 • Protein 36 gm • Fat 2 gm • Percent of calories from fat 5% • Cholesterol 20 mg • Dietary fiber 28 gm • Sodium 653 mg • Calcium 99 mg

Split Pea–Barley Soup

YIELD: 5 TO 6 SERVINGS

1¹/₂ cups dried split peas, rinsed
¹/₂ cup pearled barley
8 cups water
1 dried chipotle chile (optional)
1 onion, diced

2 celery stalks, diced
2 carrots, diced
1 bay leaf
Salt and freshly ground black
   pepper

In a large soup pot, combine the split peas, barley, water, and chipotle (if using). Bring to a boil, then reduce the heat. Skim off any foam that rises to the top of the pot. Add the onion, celery, carrots, and bay leaf. Simmer for 1 hour. Remove the chipotle and bay leaf and discard. Add salt and pepper to taste. Thin the soup with water, if desired. Heat through before serving. The soup improves in flavor and thickens on standing. Thin with water as needed.

Calories 299 • Protein 17 gm • Fat 1 gm • Percent of calories from fat 3% •
Cholesterol 0 mg • Dietary fiber 20 gm • Sodium 47 mg • Calcium 67 mg

Split Pea—Vegetable Soup

YIELD: 4 TO 5 SERVINGS

Buttery dill has a special affinity for split peas.

1¹/₂ cups dried split peas, rinsed
6 cups water
2 onions, quartered
6 garlic cloves
1 tablespoon chopped fresh dill
    or 1 teaspoon dried, or more
    to taste

1 pound potatoes (3 medium),
    peeled and diced
1 large carrot, diced
1 yellow summer squash, diced
1 cup fresh or frozen corn kernels
Salt and freshly ground black
    pepper

In a large soup pot, combine the split peas and water. Bring to a boil, then reduce the heat. Skim off any foam that rises to the top of the pot. Add the onions, garlic, and dill. Simmer for 1 hour.

Remove the soup from the heat to cool slightly. Process the soup in a blender until smooth. Return to the pot. Add the potatoes, carrot, squash, and corn. Simmer until the potatoes are tender, about 1 hour. Taste and adjust the seasoning, adding salt, pepper, and additional dill to taste. The soup improves in flavor and thickens on standing. Thin with water as needed. Serve hot.

Calories 437 • Protein 23 gm • Fat 1 gm • Percent of calories from fat 3% •
Cholesterol 0 mg • Dietary fiber 24 gm • Sodium 40 mg • Calcium 99 mg

Quick Garlicky White Bean Soup

YIELD: 4 SERVINGS

In this soup, cannellini beans are blended with a rich broth, then combined with garlic and thyme. Barely cooked carrots and fennel add a sweet and crunchy touch. In the variation at the end of the recipe, turkey sausage adds considerable interest and heartiness. This is the kind of soup that can be made with little or no planning if the kitchen is well stocked.

6 cups cooked or canned cannellini (white kidney) beans
4 cups high-quality chicken or vegetable broth
6 garlic cloves, minced
2 teaspoons fresh thyme or 1 teaspoon dried

1 tablespoon extra-virgin olive oil
2 medium carrots, diced
1/2 medium fennel bulb, diced
Salt and freshly ground black pepper

In a large soup pot, combine the beans, broth, garlic, and thyme. Cover and bring to a boil. Simmer for 10 minutes.

Meanwhile, in a separate skillet, heat the olive oil. Add the carrots and fennel and sauté until limp, about 4 minutes.

Process the soup until smooth in the blender. Return the soup to the pot. Add the sautéed carrots and fennel. Simmer for 10 minutes. Skim off any foam that rises to the top. Taste and adjust seasoning, adding salt, pepper, and additional thyme if necessary. Serve hot.

Calories 415 • Protein 27 gm • Fat 4.9 gm • Percent of calories from fat 10% • Cholesterol 0 mg • Dietary fiber 18 gm • Sodium 475 mg • Calcium 113 mg

VARIATION

Quick Garlicky White Bean Soup with Sausage. Replace the olive oil and fennel with 1/2 pound Italian turkey sausage, casings removed. In a nonstick skillet, crumble the sausage and brown with the carrots over medium-high heat until the sausage is cooked through, about 5 minutes. Remove from the skillet with a slotted spoon and place on paper towels to drain off any excess fat. Add to the blended soup and simmer as indicated in the recipe.

Calories 463 • Protein 36 gm • Fat 6.5 gm • Percent of calories from fat 12% • Cholesterol 35 mg • Dietary fiber 18 gm • Sodium 975 mg • Calcium 108 mg

Quick Roasted Red Pepper and White Bean Soup

YIELD: 4 TO 6 SERVINGS

This is a simple soup, completely dependent on the quality of the broth.

6 cups high-quality chicken or vegetable broth

2 store-bought or homemade roasted red bell peppers (see Note on page 40), julienned

1½ cups cooked or canned cannellini or other white beans

Salt and freshly ground black pepper

8 basil leaves, cut in shreds

Heat the broth to simmering. Add the bell pepper strips and cooked white beans. Heat through. Taste and add salt and pepper, if needed. Pour into soup bowls. Sprinkle the basil leaves on top. Serve hot.

Calories 134 • Protein 11 gm • Fat .3 gm • Percent of calories from fat 2% • Cholesterol 0 mg • Dietary fiber 5 gm • Sodium 680 mg • Calcium 65 mg

Mediterranean White Bean and Vegetable Soup with Fennel

YIELD: 6 TO 8 SERVINGS

1 cup dried white beans
(small white, Great Northern,
or cannellini), soaked overnight
or using quick-soak method
on page 20
1 tablespoon extra-virgin olive oil
1 leek, finely chopped
2 carrots, finely chopped
2 celery stalks, finely chopped
6 garlic cloves, finely chopped
8 cups water

2 bay leaves
1 teaspoon dried oregano
1 teaspoon dried sage
1 teaspoon dried thyme
2 cups fresh or canned diced
tomatoes
1 fennel bulb, diced
Salt and freshly ground black
pepper
1/2 cup chopped fresh parsley
1/4 cup chopped fennel ferns

Drain the beans. In a large soup pot, heat the olive oil over medium-high heat. Add the leek, carrots, celery, and garlic, and sauté until limp, about 5 minutes. Add the beans, 8 cups fresh water, bay leaves, oregano, sage, and thyme. Bring to a boil, then reduce the heat, partially cover, and simmer until the beans are tender, about 1 hour. Add the tomatoes, fennel bulb, and salt and pepper to taste. Simmer for 30 minutes, partially covered. Discard the bay leaves. Then add the parsley and fennel ferns. Taste again and adjust the seasoning. Serve hot.

Calories 181 • Protein 10 gm • Fat 3 gm • Percent of calories from fat 14% •
Cholesterol 0 mg • Dietary fiber 8 gm • Sodium 52 mg • Calcium 144 mg

Tomato Soup with White Beans and Fennel

YIELD: 4 TO 6 SERVINGS

A simpler, faster version of Mediterranean White Bean and Vegetable Soup with Fennel, but full of flavor and very satisfying. I use a food processor to chop the vegetables. Canned broth and canned beans can be used in this soup, with no loss of flavor.

1 tablespoon extra-virgin olive oil
1 onion, finely chopped
1 carrot, finely chopped
1 small fennel bulb, finely chopped
4 garlic cloves, minced
1 teaspoon dried rosemary, crumbled
1 (28-ounce) can crushed tomatoes
4 cups high-quality chicken or vegetable broth

1 bay leaf
Salt and freshly ground black pepper
1½ cups cooked or canned cannellini beans (white kidney) beans
2 tablespoons chopped fennel ferns
Freshly grated Parmesan cheese

In a large pot, heat the olive oil over medium heat. Add the onion, carrot, fennel, garlic, and rosemary, and sauté until the vegetables are quite soft, about 10 minutes. Add the tomatoes, broth, bay leaf, and salt and pepper to taste. Bring to a boil. Then reduce the heat and simmer for 25 minutes. Taste and adjust seasonings. Discard the bay leaf. Add the beans and fennel ferns. Cover and simmer until the beans are heated through, about 5 minutes. Serve hot, passing the Parmesan cheese at the table.

Calories 236 • Protein 13 gm • Fat 3.9 gm • Percent of calories from fat 15% • Cholesterol 0 mg • Dietary fiber 10 gm • Sodium 780 mg • Calcium 121 mg

Minestrone alla Genovese

YIELD: 6 TO 8 SERVINGS

There are as many versions of minestrone as there are cooks in Italy. What distinguishes minestrone from Genoa is the last-minute addition of pesto. This hearty soup is rich with beans, pasta, and vegetables, and scented with tomatoes, rosemary, and basil.

1 tablespoon extra-virgin olive oil
1 leek, sliced
4 garlic cloves, minced
6 cups vegetable or chicken broth
1 (28-ounce) can crushed tomatoes
1 carrot, diced
1 celery stalk, diced
2 teaspoons dried rosemary
1 teaspoon dried thyme
1 cup small soup pasta (such as
   rings, ditalini, alphabets, or
   bowties)

4 cups chopped Swiss chard,
   cabbage, or kale
2 cups cooked cannellini (white
   kidney) beans
4 tablespoons store-bought or
   homemade pesto (page 263)
Salt and freshly ground pepper

Heat the olive oil in a large soup pot over medium heat. Add the leek and garlic and sauté for 2 minutes. Add the broth, tomatoes, carrot, celery, rosemary, and thyme. Bring to a boil, then reduce the heat and simmer for about 20 minutes. Return the soup to boiling. Add the pasta and boil gently until the pasta is cooked through, about 5 minutes. Add the greens and cannellini. Simmer for 5 minutes more. Add the pesto and salt and pepper to taste. Serve. The soup will thicken on standing. Thin with additional broth or water if needed.

Calories 315 • Protein 15 gm • Fat 9.6 gm • Percent of calories from fat 26% • Cholesterol 1 mg • Dietary fiber 8 gm • Sodium 791 mg • Calcium 131 mg

Minestrone with Greens

YIELD: 6 TO 8 SERVINGS

1/2 cup chopped dried porcini
mushrooms
2 cups boiling water
1 tablespoon extra-virgin olive oil
1 onion, sliced
4 garlic cloves, minced
1 carrot, diced
1 small zucchini, diced
1/2 cup chopped fresh parsley
1/4 cup chopped fresh basil
6 cups water
1 cup small soup pasta (such as
rings, ditalini, alphabets, or
bowties)

4 cups chopped Swiss chard or
spinach, packed
1 cup chopped fresh arugula
(optional)
11/2 cups cooked cannellini
(white kidney) beans
Salt and freshly ground black
pepper
Freshly grated Parmesan cheese

Soak the mushrooms in the boiling water until soft, about 10 minutes.

Meanwhile, heat the olive oil in a large soup pot over medium heat. Add the onion and garlic and sauté for 1 minute. Add the carrot and zucchini and sauté for another minute. Then add the parsley, basil, remaining 6 cups water, and the mushrooms with their soaking liquid, taking care to avoid any grit that may have sunk to the bottom of the liquid. Bring to a boil, then reduce the heat and simmer for at least 20 minutes. Return the soup to boiling. Add the pasta and boil gently until the pasta is cooked through, about 5 minutes. Add the greens and cannellini. Simmer for 5 minutes more. Season with salt and pepper to taste.

Serve with a sprinkling of Parmesan on top of each soup bowl and pass additional cheese at the table. The soup will thicken on standing. Thin with additional broth or water if needed.

Calories 172 • Protein 8 gm • Fat 3 gm • Percent of calories from fat 15% •
Cholesterol 0 mg • Dietary fiber 5 gm • Sodium 73 mg • Calcium 69 mg

Vegetable Stock

YIELD: 3½ TO 4 QUARTS

2 carrots
2 leeks
1 large onion
¼ small head cabbage
1 fennel bulb
4 garlic cloves
1 bunch parsley

4 sprigs fresh thyme
1 cup dried porcini mushrooms
4 quarts water
1 cup dry white wine
1 tablespoon black peppercorns
Salt (optional)

Quarter all the vegetables. Combine all of the vegetables, herbs, and mushrooms in a large soup pot. Add the water. Cover, bring to a boil, then reduce the heat and simmer for 30 minutes. Add the wine and black peppercorns and continue to simmer, covered, for 10 minutes. Strain, avoiding any grit that has settled to the bottom, and discard solids. To make broth, season to taste with salt. Or leave unsalted and use as a base for soups and grain dishes. Use immediately or cool, then refrigerate. It will keep for about 5 days in the refrigerator or 4 to 6 months in the freezer.

Calories 31 • Protein 3 gm • Fat 0 gm • Percent of calories from fat 0% •
Cholesterol 0 mg • Dietary fiber 0 gm • Sodium 141 mg • Calcium 2 mg

Mushroom Stock

YIELD: 3½ TO 4 QUARTS

3 cups stems and pieces of
   mixed fresh mushrooms
   (such as white, shiitake,
   oyster, and portobello)
1 cup dried porcini mushrooms
1 carrot, quartered
3 celery stalks, quartered

1 small bunch parsley
4 quarts water
1 cup dry white wine
1 tablespoon black peppercorns
1 tablespoon soy sauce
Salt (optional)

Combine the mushrooms, carrot, celery, and parsley in a large soup pot. Add the water. Cover, bring to a boil, then reduce the heat and simmer for 1 hour. Add the wine, peppercorns, and soy sauce, and continue to simmer, uncovered, for 30 minutes. Strain and discard the solids. To make broth, season to taste with salt. Or leave unsalted and use as a base for soups and grain dishes. Use immediately or cool, then refrigerate. It will keep for about 5 days in the refrigerator or 4 to 6 months in the freezer.

Calories 32 • Protein 3 gm • Fat 0 gm • Percent of calories from fat 0% • Cholesterol 0 mg • Dietary fiber 0 gm • Sodium 214 mg • Calcium 2 mg

Chicken Stock

YIELD: 2 TO 3 QUARTS

3 to 4 pounds chicken parts
1 large onion, quartered
4 stalks celery
4 garlic cloves

1 bunch parsley
4 quarts water
Salt (optional)

Combine the chicken, onion, celery, and garlic in a large soup pot. Add the water. Cover and bring just to a boil. Immediately reduce the heat and simmer gently, partially covered, for 2 hours. Do not allow the soup to boil.

Strain. Save the meat for another use, such as chicken salad. Chill for several hours. Skim off the fat that rises to the top and hardens.

To make broth, season to taste with salt. Or leave unsalted and use as a base for soups and grain dishes. Use immediately or cool, then refrigerate. It will keep for about 3 days in the refrigerator or 4 to 6 months in the freezer.

Calories 20 • Protein 3 gm • Fat 0 gm • Percent of calories from fat 0% •
Cholesterol 0 mg • Dietary fiber 0 gm • Sodium 140 mg • Calcium 0 mg

4

Sensational Salads

Barley-Vegetable Salad with Orange-Buttermilk Dressing

Tabouli

Couscous and Black Bean Salad

Lemony Couscous Salad with Chickpeas and Feta

Sugar Snap–Millet Salad

New World Quinoa Salad

Quinoa Tabouli

Wheat Berry and Parsley Salad

Wild Rice Salad with Walnuts and Dried Cranberries

Mediterranean Tomato-Rice Salad with Feta and Dill

Lemony Broccoli Slaw Rice Salad

Japanese-style Rice Salad

Curried Rice and Fruit Salad with Mango Chutney Dressing

Kimchee Rice Salad with Tofu

Southwestern Rice and Bean Salad

Yellow Rice and Black Bean Salad

Southwestern Bean and Corn Salad

Hominy and Pinto Bean Salad

Black Bean Salad with Chipotle-Honey Vinaigrette

Tomato-Corn Salad with Black Beans

Black Bean Salad with Goat Cheese

Tropical Black Bean Salad

Summertime Black-eyed Pea Salad

Chickpea Salad with Tomatoes and Feta

Marinated Fava Bean Salad with Roasted Garlic and Onion

Marinated Vegetable Salad with Kidney Beans

Smoky Corn and Kidney Bean Salad

Three-Bean Salad

French Lentil Salad with Lemon-Garlic Vinaigrette

Tomato, Green Bean, and White Bean Salad with Basil and Mint

French Lentil Salad with Goat Cheese

Tomato, White Bean, and Arugula Salad with Roasted Garlic Vinaigrette

White Bean Salad with Sun-dried Tomatoes

Dilled White Bean Salad with Tomatoes

Artichoke Pasta Salad with Basil Vinaigrette

Wagon Train Pasta Salad

I never tire of salads. I love the endless variety of tastes and textures that are possible. With rice, beans, or grains as the key ingredient, salads can make a hearty main course, especially during the summer when hot foods are not particularly appealing.

Just about any salad in this chapter can be made into a main course by serving it on a generous bed of greens, and I do mean generous. Twelve cups of greens is about right for four servings. The greens mix with the rest of the salad and usually no extra dressing is needed, though extra can be passed at the table.

I grow my own salad greens when I can, and buy the best when I can't. The best are usually found at farmer's markets and natural food stores that buy directly from farmers. At the farmer's market, inquire about varieties and ask for samples. You will be amazed at the difference you can taste. I will definitely pay extra for certain varieties of lettuce I have tasted, like Lolla Rossa, a deeply ruffled red lettuce that has a very distinctive green flavor. In recent years, mesclun mixes have become increasingly available. Mesclun is a mixture of baby greens—lettuces, mustards, cabbages, herbs, even flowers. The concept of this type of mix was developed in the French-Italian border region. I grow my own mesclun from seeds sold by the Cook's Garden of Londonderry, Vermont (P.O. Box 535, Londonderry, VT 05148; 802-824-3400). When buying mesclun, look for greens that are crisp and bright. Be wary of supermarket mesclun mixes—you may be paying a premium price for tasteless, old greens.

Arugula is one of my favorite greens. Its smoky mustard flavor is positively addictive. When arugula isn't in season, watercress contributes a nice peppery note instead.

Bread is a necessary accompaniment when you are creating a menu around a salad. A good loaf of French bread, a rustic wheat bread, or a fresh hot corn bread will round out a memorable meal.

Barley-Vegetable Salad
with Orange-Buttermilk Dressing

YIELD: 4 TO 6 SERVINGS

The sweet nutty flavor and chewy texture of barley lends itself to wonderful grain salads. I like to highlight barley's natural sweetness with complementary sweet vegetables—red bell peppers, carrots, and peas—and a light citrusy dressing. This attractive salad can be made into a light supper by serving it on a bed of greens. Sliced tomatoes and whole wheat bread are great accompaniments.

3¹/₂ cups cooked pearled
  or hulled barley
  (1 cup uncooked)
1 red bell pepper, diced
4 scallions, diced
1 carrot, diced
1 celery stalk, diced
1 cup fresh or frozen peas
¹/₂ cup chopped fresh parsley

2 tablespoons chopped fresh basil
1 tablespoon chopped fresh mint
¹/₂ cup nonfat buttermilk
2 tablespoons extra-virgin
  olive oil
2 tablespoons fresh lemon juice
2 tablespoons fresh orange juice
Salt and freshly ground black
  pepper

In a large salad bowl, combine the barley with the bell pepper, scallions, carrot, celery, peas, parsley, basil, and mint. Toss well. In a separate bowl, combine the buttermilk, olive oil, lemon juice, and orange juice, and blend well. Pour over the salad. Taste and adjust seasonings. Serve at once.

Calories 295 • Protein 7 gm • Fat 8 gm • Percent of calories from fat 23% • Cholesterol 1 mg • Dietary fiber 9 gm • Sodium 59 mg • Calcium 91 mg

Tabouli

❦

YIELD: 4 TO 8 SERVINGS

Tabouli originated in the Middle East as a parsley salad dressed with olive oil, lemon, and mint, with bulgur or cracked wheat added for bulk. Americans generally make tabouli as a grain salad with a generous grace note of parsley. This tabouli is a hearty grain salad, filling enough to satisfy a hungry appetite as a main course.

2 cups uncooked bulgur	$\frac{1}{4}$ cup chopped fresh mint
5 cups boiling water	or 1 tablespoon dried
2 cups chopped fresh parsley	Juice of 1 lemon, or more to taste
1 cucumber, seeded and chopped	3 tablespoons extra-virgin olive oil
2 large ripe tomatoes, seeded and	Salt and freshly ground black
chopped	pepper
6 scallions, chopped	Romaine lettuce leaves

Combine the bulgur and boiling water in a large bowl. Cover and let stand for 15 minutes, until the grains are tender and most of the water is absorbed. Drain off any excess water.

Add the parsley, cucumber, tomatoes, scallions, and mint to the bulgur. Toss to mix. Add the lemon juice, olive oil, and salt and pepper to taste. Toss again. Chill for 30 to 60 minutes to allow the flavors to blend.

To serve, arrange the romaine lettuce leaves like spokes around individual plates or a serving platter. Mound the tabouli on top. If desired, diners can use the lettuce leaves to scoop up portions of the tabouli.

Calories 375 • Protein 11 gm • Fat 12 gm • Percent of calories from fat 26% •
Cholesterol 0 mg • Dietary fiber 15 gm • Sodium 47 mg • Calcium 105 mg

Couscous and Black Bean Salad

YIELD: 4 TO 6 SERVINGS

Because couscous tastes so mild, it can provide a background for any number of flavor combinations. In this salad, the flavors of the American Southwest meet the grain of the Middle East.

1 cup uncooked couscous
1/2 teaspoon salt
1 1/2 cups boiling water
1 1/2 cups cooked black beans
1 cup julienned red bell pepper
1 cup julienned jicama
1/4 cup chopped red onion

1/4 cup chopped fresh cilantro
2 tablespoons extra-virgin
 olive oil
3 tablespoons lime juice
Salt and freshly ground black
 pepper

Combine the couscous, salt, and boiling water in a large bowl. Cover and set aside to steam for about 10 minutes, until all of the liquid is absorbed. Fluff with a fork. Let cool to room temperature.

Add the black beans, bell pepper, jicama, onion, cilantro, olive oil, lime juice, and salt and pepper to taste, and toss to mix. Let stand for at least 30 minutes to allow the flavors to blend before serving.

Calories 350 • Protein 12 gm • Fat 8 gm • Percent of calories from fat 19% •
Cholesterol 0 mg • Dietary fiber 11 gm • Sodium 302 mg • Calcium 46 mg

Lemony Couscous Salad
with Chickpeas and Feta

YIELD: 6 TO 8 SERVINGS

Couscous combined with sharp lemons, tingly mint, salty feta cheese, and grassy parsley makes for a bold salad that, served with assorted warmed flatbreads, makes a great, light summer meal. This salad holds up well, which makes it a good choice for summer potlucks, when it may sit around for a while.

2 cups uncooked couscous
1 teaspoon salt
3 cups boiling water
6 scallions, chopped
1 cucumber, peeled and diced
2 large ripe tomatoes, peeled
   and diced
1 1/2 cups cooked chickpeas
1/2 cup crumbled feta cheese

1 cup chopped fresh parsley
1/4 cup chopped fresh mint
   or 1 tablespoon dried
3 tablespoons extra-virgin
   olive oil
Juice of 2 lemons
Salt and freshly ground black
   pepper

Combine the couscous, salt, and boiling water in a large mixing bowl. Cover and set aside for 10 minutes. Fluff with a fork. All the liquid should be absorbed. Let cool to room temperature.

Add the scallions, cucumber, tomatoes, chickpeas, feta cheese, parsley, mint, olive oil, lemon juice, and salt and pepper to taste. Toss gently. If you are making this salad ahead of time, add the olive oil and lemon juice just before serving.

Calories 440 • Protein 16 gm • Fat 13 gm • Percent of calories from fat 26% •
Cholesterol 19 mg • Dietary fiber 7 gm • Sodium 648 mg • Calcium 175 mg

Sugar Snap-Millet Salad

YIELD: 4 TO 6 SERVINGS

A great way to enjoy fresh sugar snap peas. If you don't grow your own or have a ready source, substitute snow peas.

3½ cups cooked millet
   (1 cup uncooked)
½ red bell pepper, diced
2 scallions, diced
1½ cups fresh sugar snap peas
1 medium tomato, chopped
2 tablespoons capers
2 tablespoons chopped fresh basil

½ cup nonfat buttermilk
2 tablespoons extra-virgin
   olive oil
2 tablespoons freshly squeezed
   lemon juice
Salt and freshly ground black
   pepper

In a large salad bowl, combine the millet with the bell pepper, scallions, peas, tomato, capers, and basil. Toss well.

In a separate bowl, combine the buttermilk, olive oil, and lemon juice and blend well. Pour over the salad. Add salt and pepper to taste. Taste and adjust seasonings. Serve at once.

Calories 362 • Protein 11 gm • Fat 9 gm • Percent of calories from fat 22% • Cholesterol 1 mg • Dietary fiber 5 gm • Sodium 251 mg • Calcium 83 mg

New World Quinoa Salad

YIELD: 6 SERVINGS

I took my inspiration for this salad from vegetables that originated in the New World. The Incas might not have combined them with their quinoa, but you never know . . .

1 cup quinoa
2 cups water
1¹/₂ cups cooked black beans
1 cup diced jicama
1 cup halved cherry tomatoes
¹/₂ red bell pepper, diced
¹/₄ cup finely chopped fresh
  cilantro

2 tablespoons extra-virgin
  olive oil
2 tablespoons freshly squeezed
  lime juice
1 tablespoon red wine vinegar
Salt and freshly ground black
  pepper

To remove the sticky, bitter-tasting saponin that may still cling to the surface of the quinoa, place in a blender with a couple of cups of water. Pulse the motor on and off a few times, until the water becomes cloudy. Strain off the water. Repeat with fresh water in the blender, until the water remains clear. Strain the quinoa through a fine-mesh strainer and discard the water.

Place the quinoa in a medium saucepan over medium heat. Toast until the grains are fragrant and lightly colored, about 5 minutes. Add the 2 cups water, cover, and bring to a boil. Reduce the heat and simmer slowly for about 12 minutes, until the water is all absorbed.

Fluff the quinoa with a fork. Turn out into a bowl and let cool, stirring occasionally with a fork. When the quinoa is cool, add the black beans, jicama, tomatoes, bell pepper, and cilantro. Toss to mix. Add the olive oil and toss again. Then add the lime juice and vinegar and toss again. Season with salt and pepper to taste. Serve at once.

Calories 228 • Protein 8 gm • Fat 7 gm • Percent of calories from fat 25% •
Cholesterol 0 mg • Dietary fiber 8 gm • Sodium 16 mg • Calcium 40 mg

Quinoa Tabouli

YIELD: 6 TO 8 SERVINGS

Versatile quinoa combines well with the traditional Middle Eastern flavors of tabouli.

1 cup uncooked quinoa
2 cups water
2 cups parsley leaves, snipped
   or pulled from the stems
1¹/₂ cups halved or
   quartered cherry tomatoes
1 cucumber, peeled, seeded,
   and diced
¹/₂ Vidalia or other sweet onion,
   diced (about ¹/₂ cup)

¹/₄ cup chopped fresh mint leaves
   or 1 tablespoon dried
2 tablespoons extra-virgin
   olive oil
3 tablespoons freshly squeezed
   lemon juice
Salt and freshly ground black
   pepper

To remove the sticky, bitter-tasting saponin that may still cling to the surface of the quinoa, place in a blender with a couple of cups of water. Pulse the motor on and off a few times, until the water becomes cloudy. Strain off the water. Repeat with fresh water in the blender, until the water remains clear. Strain the quinoa through a fine-mesh strainer and discard the water.

Place the quinoa in a medium saucepan over medium heat. Toast until the grains are fragrant and lightly colored, about 5 minutes. Add the 2 cups fresh water, cover, and bring to a boil. Reduce the heat and simmer slowly for about 12 minutes, until the water is all absorbed.

Fluff the quinoa with a fork. Turn out into a bowl and let cool, stirring occasionally with a fork. When the quinoa is cooled, add the parsley, tomatoes, cucumber, onion, mint, olive oil, lemon juice, and salt and pepper to taste. Toss to mix. Taste and adjust the seasoning before serving.

Calories 182 • Protein 5 gm • Fat 7 gm • Percent of calories from fat 31% • Cholesterol 0 mg • Dietary fiber 4 gm • Sodium 28 mg • Calcium 65 mg

Wheat Berry and Parsley Salad

YIELD: 4 TO 6 SERVINGS

This salad is yet another variation on tabouli, which is traditionally made with bulgur or cracked wheat. Here wheat berries provide a chewy texture and a somewhat sweeter flavor.

1 cup uncooked wheat berries
4 cups water
3 cups Italian parsley leaves,
   snipped or pulled from
   the stems
3/4 cup thinly sliced red radishes
1/4 cup chopped fresh mint leaves
   or 1 tablespoon dried

1/4 cup chopped scallions or chives
1/2 teaspoon dried marjoram
2 tablespoons extra-virgin olive oil
3 tablespoons fresh lemon juice
Salt and freshly ground black
   pepper

Combine the wheat berries and water in a medium saucepan. Bring to a boil, reduce the heat, cover, and cook until tender, about 1 1/2 hours. (You can reduce the cooking time to 50 to 60 minutes by soaking the berries overnight before cooking.) When the berries are tender, drain off any excess water. Allow to cool.

In a large salad bowl, combine the cooked wheat berries, parsley, radishes, mint, scallions, and marjoram. Toss to mix. Add the olive oil and toss again. Add the lemon juice and salt and pepper and toss again.

Calories 243 • Protein 8 gm • Fat 8 gm • Percent of calories from fat 27% • Cholesterol 0 mg • Dietary fiber 8 gm • Sodium 38 mg • Calcium 104 mg

Wild Rice Salad with Walnuts and Dried Cranberries

YIELD: 6 TO 8 SERVINGS

A Thanksgiving feast is incomplete without this jewel of a salad! Besides combining native American ingredients (wild rice and cranberries), it has a bejeweled appearance thanks to the ruby-colored cranberries.

Salad

About 4^1/$_2$ cups cooked wild rice
  (1^1/$_2$ cups uncooked)
1^1/$_4$ cups dried sweetened
  cranberries
2 heads Belgian endive, cut
  crosswise into ^{1}/$_2$-inch slices

^{3}/$_4$ cup toasted walnut pieces
1 red bell pepper, diced
4 scallions, chopped
Salt and freshly ground black
  pepper

Citrus Vinaigrette

^{1}/$_4$ cup freshly squeezed
  orange juice
^{1}/$_2$ teaspoon grated orange zest
2 tablespoons freshly squeezed
  lemon juice

1 teaspoon Dijon mustard
2 tablespoons extra-virgin
  olive oil

In a large bowl, combine the wild rice, cranberries, endive, walnuts, bell pepper, and scallions. Toss to mix.

In a small bowl, combine the orange juice, orange zest, lemon juice, and mustard. Slowly whisk in the olive oil. Pour over the salad and toss to mix. Season to taste with salt and pepper. Allow to stand for at least 30 minutes to allow the flavors to blend.

Calories 366 • Protein 9 gm • Fat 14 gm • Percent of calories from fat 34% •
Cholesterol 0 mg • Dietary fiber 6 gm • Sodium 11 mg • Calcium 24 mg

Wild Rice Turkey Salad. Add 3 cups diced roasted turkey to this salad for a truly interesting flavor combination.

Calories 476 • Protein 30 gm • Fat 16 gm • Percent of calories from fat 31% • Cholesterol 48 mg • Dietary fiber 6 gm • Sodium 56 mg • Calcium 37 mg

Mediterranean Tomato-Rice Salad with Feta and Dill

❧

YIELD: 4 TO 6 SERVINGS

Because feta cheese adds so much flavor, it is possible to make a very tasty salad with a very light dressing. This quick, summery salad contains rice, tomatoes, feta cheese, and dill. Serve it on a bed of greens to transform it into a delicious main course.

3 cups cooked white rice	1/4 cup diced red onion
3 ripe tomatoes, diced	3 tablespoons freshly squeezed
1 zucchini, diced	lemon juice
1 red bell pepper, diced	2 tablespoons extra-virgin olive oil
1 cup fresh or frozen peas	1/2 cup crumbled feta cheese
1/4 cup chopped fresh dill	Salt and freshly ground pepper

Combine all of the ingredients and toss lightly. Serve at once.

Calories 390 • Protein 11 gm • Fat 14 gm • Percent of calories from fat 33% • Cholesterol 28 mg • Dietary fiber 4 gm • Sodium 367 mg • Calcium 185 mg

Lemony Broccoli Slaw Rice Salad

YIELD: 4 TO 8 SERVINGS

Broccoli slaw is a convenience food—prepackaged matchsticks of broccoli, carrot, and red cabbage. I like to have a package on hand for quick salads like this one.

**4 cups cooked white or
   brown rice or a combination**
4 cups broccoli slaw
6 scallions, chopped
¼ cup extra-virgin olive oil
**¼ cup freshly squeezed
   lemon juice**

**1 tablespoon mirin
   (sweet Japanese rice wine)**
1 teaspoon grated lemon zest
**Salt and freshly ground black
   pepper**

In a large salad bowl, combine the rice, broccoli slaw, and scallions and toss to mix. In a separate bowl, whisk together the olive oil, lemon juice, mirin, and lemon zest. Pour over the rice mixture and toss well. Season with salt and pepper to taste and set aside for about 15 minutes before serving to allow the flavors to blend.

Calories 403 • Protein 7 gm • Fat 14 gm • Percent of calories from fat 31% •
Cholesterol 0 mg • Dietary fiber 4 gm • Sodium 29 mg • Calcium 56 mg

Japanese-style Rice Salad

YIELD: 4 TO 6 SERVINGS

Salad

4 cups cooked white or brown rice, cooled

1¹/₂ cups bean sprouts

1 cup snow peas or sugar snap peas

1 cup grated daikon (giant white radish)

1 carrot, grated

4 scallions, chopped

¹/₄ cup chopped fresh cilantro

Dressing

1-inch piece fresh ginger, peeled and minced

1 garlic clove, minced

3 tablespoons tamari

3 tablespoons rice wine vinegar

1 tablespoon mirin (sweet Japanese rice wine)

1 tablespoon sugar

1 tablespoon sesame oil

Combine the cooled rice with the bean sprouts, peas, daikon, carrot, scallions, and cilantro. Combine the dressing ingredients in the order given, beating in the sesame oil last. Just before serving, pour the dressing over the salad and toss lightly. Serve at once.

Calories 325 • Protein 8 gm • Fat 5 gm • Percent of calories from fat 15% • Cholesterol 0 mg • Dietary fiber 3 gm • Sodium 778 mg • Calcium 59 mg

Curried Rice and Fruit Salad
with Mango Chutney Dressing

YIELD: 6 TO 8 SERVINGS

Mango chutney forms a light and flavorful base for the salad dressing. This beautiful salad makes an exotic and flavorful contribution to any party spread.

Salad

2 cups uncooked basmati
   or long-grain white rice
1 tablespoon peanut or canola oil
1/4 cup minced shallots
2 garlic cloves, minced
1 tablespoon curry powder
1 tablespoon minced fresh ginger
1 teaspoon salt, or more to taste
3 1/2 cups water
2 apples, diced (Cortland
   is recommended)

1 1/2 cups well-drained crushed
   pineapple
1/2 cup diced dried apricots
1/4 cup unsweetened flaked
   coconut
1/4 cup chopped fresh mint
1/4 cup chopped fresh cilantro
Salt and freshly ground black
   pepper

Dressing

1/2 cup mango chutney
2 tablespoons freshly
   squeezed lemon juice

1 tablespoon canola oil
1 teaspoon honey

Wash the rice in several changes of water until the water runs clear. Drain well.

In a medium saucepan, heat the oil over medium heat. Add the shallots, garlic, curry powder, ginger, and rice, and sauté until the rice appears dry, about 4 minutes. Add the 1 teaspoon salt and the water, cover, reduce the heat to low, and cook at a gentle boil until the rice is tender and the water is absorbed, about 15 minutes. Fluff with a fork and allow the rice to cool.

In a large salad bowl, combine the cooled rice, apples, pineapple, apricots, coconut, mint, and cilantro.

To make the dressing, combine the chutney, lemon juice, oil, and honey in a blender or food processor and process until smooth. Pour the dressing over the salad and toss well. Season with salt and pepper and serve at once.

Calories 392 • Protein 5 gm • Fat 7 gm • Percent of calories from fat 16% •
Cholesterol 0 mg • Dietary fiber 6 gm • Sodium 401 mg • Calcium 68 mg

Kimchee Rice Salad with Tofu

YIELD: 4 TO 6 SERVINGS

Kimchee is a hot and sour pickle that adds pep to all manner of foods. It is eaten daily in most Korean homes. Many Westerners also find it addictive. There are those who claim that kimchee is the solution to all problems related to digestion. I don't know about that, but I do know that this salad is rich in good-for-you fiber and vitamins. Look for kimchee in natural food stores and wherever Asian foods are sold. If you have a choice, the kimchee that is kept in refrigerator cases is usually fresher and crisper than canned kimchee.

1 pound firm tofu
1 tablespoon sesame oil
2 tablespoons soy sauce
2 tablespoons mirin (sweet Japanese rice wine)
2 cups cooked brown or white rice

1 carrot diced
2 scallions, chopped
1 cup fresh or frozen peas
1½ cups cabbage kimchee
Soy sauce or salt (optional)
2 tablespoons toasted sesame seeds (optional), see Note

Wrap the tofu in a clean kitchen towel or paper towel. Place on a plate or cutting board and weight down with another board or heavy plate topped with a weight (such as a filled juice can). This will force out excess moisture from the tofu. Leave to drain for 30 minutes.

Dice the drained tofu. In a large salad bowl, combine the sesame oil, soy sauce, and mirin. Add the tofu and let marinate for about 30 minutes. Add the rice, carrot, scallions, and peas. Toss well. Add the kimchee and toss again. Taste and add soy sauce or salt, if desired. Garnish with toasted sesame seeds, if desired.

Note: To toast sesame seeds, place the seeds in a dry skillet over medium heat for about 5 minutes, stirring often. Remove from the heat as soon as they begin to turn golden. Do not allow the seeds to scorch; burnt seeds taste bitter.

Calories 281 • Protein 14 gm • Fat 8 gm • Percent of calories from fat 24% • Cholesterol 0 mg • Dietary fiber 3 gm • Sodium 945 mg • Calcium 109 mg

Southwestern Rice and Bean Salad

❧

YIELD: 4 TO 8 SERVINGS

The perfume of lime juice and cilantro is well matched by the earthy flavors of the black beans and green olives in this colorful salad. A guaranteed crowd-pleaser, it is easy to transport and holds up well on a buffet table. Add even more color with a garnish of tomato wedges.

2 cups cooked white or brown rice
2 cups fresh or frozen corn kernels
1½ cups cooked black beans
1 red bell pepper, finely diced
1 green bell pepper, finely diced
½ cup chopped scallions
½ cup chopped fresh cilantro
2 tablespoons chopped green
 pimiento-stuffed olives

2 tablespoons extra-virgin
 olive oil
3 tablespoons freshly squeezed
 lime juice
Salt and freshly ground black
 pepper
Tomato wedges, for garnish
 (optional)

Combine the rice, corn, beans, peppers, scallions, cilantro, and olives in a large salad bowl. Toss to mix. Add the olive oil and lime juice and toss to mix. Season to taste with salt and pepper. Serve at once or refrigerate for a few hours, then bring to room temperature before serving. Garnish with tomato wedges (if using).

Calories 360 • Protein 11 gm • Fat 9 gm • Percent of calories from fat 20% •
Cholesterol 0 mg • Dietary fiber 9 gm • Sodium 119 mg • Calcium 40 mg

Yellow Rice and Black Bean Salad

YIELD: 6 TO 8 SERVINGS

This salad is based on a classic Caribbean rice and bean combination that features rice flavored with annatto and combined with black beans. Brick red annatto seeds, which have a floral, mildly earthy flavor, are widely used to color foods yellow. Look for them in markets that specialize in Mexican or Caribbean cooking. The whole or ground seeds may be labeled as either annatto or achiote. No substitutes are possible.

1½ cups uncooked long-grain white rice

2 tablespoons annatto oil (see Note)

2 shallots, finely diced

2 garlic cloves, finely minced

2¾ cups water

1 teaspoon salt

1½ cups cooked black beans

1 red or green bell pepper, diced

1 ripe tomato, diced

¼ cup chopped scallions

2 tablespoons chopped fresh cilantro

2 tablespoons extra-virgin olive oil

3 tablespoons freshly squeezed lime juice

1 tablespoon red wine vinegar

Salt and freshly ground black pepper

Rinse the rice in several changes of water. Drain.

In a large skillet, heat the oil over medium heat. Add the rice, shallots, and garlic, and sauté until the rice appears toasted and dry, about 5 minutes. Add the water and salt, cover, and bring to a boil, then reduce the heat and boil gently until all the liquid is absorbed, about 15 minutes. Remove from the heat. Fluff the rice with a fork. Set aside to cool.

When the rice has cooled, combine in a large salad bowl with the black beans, bell pepper, tomato, scallions, and cilantro. Toss to mix. In a small bowl, combine the olive oil, lime juice, and vinegar. Pour over the salad. Toss to mix. Taste and add salt, pepper, and additional lime juice as needed. Serve at once.

Note: To make annatto oil, heat ½ cup canola oil in a small saucepan over low heat. Add $1/4$ cup annatto seeds and cook over low heat, stirring occasionally, for about 5 minutes, until the oil takes on a rich orange color. Cool, then strain. You can store the oil in an airtight jar in the refrigerator for several months.

Calories 320 • Protein 8 gm • Fat 10 gm • Percent of calories from fat 27% • Cholesterol 0 mg • Dietary fiber 5 gm • Sodium 398 mg • Calcium 39 mg

Southwestern Bean and Corn Salad

YIELD: 4 TO 8 SERVINGS

In the summer, I like to eat my beans cold, in a salad. In this recipe the beans and corn combine well with a spicy tomato-based dressing. This is a great dish to take to a barbecue.

Salad

1¹/₂ cups cooked black beans
1¹/₂ cups cooked pinto beans
1¹/₂ cups fresh or frozen corn
   kernels, thawed
1 cup diced fresh tomato
1 green bell pepper, diced
¹/₄ cup diced red onion

1 small hot pepper, diced
   (optional)
2 tablespoons chopped fresh
   cilantro
¹/₄ cup chopped fresh parsley
Shredded lettuce
Baked tortilla chips, for garnish

Dressing

2 tablespoons olive or canola oil
2 tablespoons freshly squeezed
   lime juice
1 tablespoon white wine vinegar
2 tablespoons ketchup
2 teaspoons sugar

1 teaspoon chili powder
¹/₂ teaspoon ground cumin
2 garlic cloves, minced
Salt and freshly ground black
   pepper

In a large salad bowl, combine the black and pinto beans, corn, tomato, bell pepper, onion, hot pepper (if using), cilantro, and parsley.

To make the dressing, in a separate bowl whisk together the oil, lime juice, vinegar, ketchup, sugar, chili powder, cumin, garlic, and salt and pepper to taste. Pour the dressing over the salad and set aside for at least 30 minutes to allow the flavors to blend.

To serve, make a bed of lettuce on a large platter or individual salad plates. Mound the bean salad on top. Garnish with the tortilla chips.

Calories 321 • Protein 14 gm • Fat 8 gm • Percent of calories from fat 21% •
Cholesterol 0 mg • Dietary fiber 14 gm • Sodium 103 mg • Calcium 70 mg

Hominy and Pinto Bean Salad

YIELD: **4** SERVINGS

V8 Juice adds lots of flavor but no fat to this delicious combination of hominy and pinto beans.

1 (15-ounce) can hominy,
  rinsed and drained
1¹/₂ cups cooked pinto beans
¹/₂ green bell pepper, chopped
¹/₄ cup chopped sweet red onion
¹/₂ cup chopped celery
1 (5.5-ounce) can V8 juice
¹/₂ teaspoon chili powder

¹/₂ teaspoon ground cumin
¹/₄ teaspoon dried oregano
2 tablespoons red wine vinegar
2 tablespoons extra-virgin
  olive oil
Salt and freshly ground black
  pepper

Combine all the ingredients in a bowl and toss to mix. Let stand for at least 30 minutes to allow the flavors to blend. Serve at room temperature.

Calories 229 • Protein 8 gm • Fat 7 gm • Percent of calories from fat 26% •
Cholesterol 0 mg • Dietary fiber 9 gm • Sodium 509 mg • Calcium 51 mg

Black Bean Salad with Chipotle-Honey Vinaigrette

YIELD: 4 SERVINGS

English cucumbers are long and narrow with small seeds. They are sold unwaxed and keep because they are tightly wrapped in plastic. Because they don't require peeling, and because the flesh is firmer than regular salad cucumbers, they add extra crunch to a salad.

Salad

1¹/₂ cups cooked black beans
1 English cucumber, diced
1 red bell pepper, diced
4 scallions, chopped

1 large tomato, diced
Salt and freshly ground black
    pepper

Vinaigrette

1 teaspoon chipotle en adobo,
    or more to taste
2 teaspoons honey
1 garlic clove, minced
2 tablespoons chopped fresh
    cilantro

2 tablespoons white wine vinegar
    or champagne vinegar
1¹/₂ tablespoons extra-virgin
    olive oil

In a salad bowl, combine the beans, cucumber, bell pepper, scallions, and tomato. Toss to mix.

To make the dressing, in a small bowl whisk together the chipotle en adobo, honey, garlic, cilantro, and vinegar. Whisk in the olive oil. Pour over the beans and toss well. Season to taste with salt and pepper. Serve at room temperature.

Calories 340 • Protein 14 gm • Fat 11 gm • Percent of calories from fat 29% • Cholesterol 0 mg • Dietary fiber 15 gm • Sodium 100 mg • Calcium 80 mg

Tomato-Corn Salad with Black Beans

❧

YIELD: 4 TO 8 SERVINGS

This summer feast—luscious tomatoes, sweet corn, crunchy peppers, and crisp cucumbers tied together with the smoky earth flavors of cilantro and black beans—can only be enjoyed during the local fresh tomato season. Bread is essential with this salad—and anything goes. Corn bread is lovely, but a good French bread or even a hearty whole wheat loaf will also make a pleasing accompaniment.

1 yellow bell pepper, diced
1 green bell pepper, diced
1 English cucumber, diced
$1/2$ red onion, diced
3 cups corn, scraped off the cob
(about 6 ears)
3 large vine-ripened tomatoes, cubed

$1/4$ cup chopped fresh parsley
$1/4$ cup chopped fresh cilantro
4 tablespoons red wine vinegar
2 tablespoons extra-virgin olive oil
Salt and freshly ground black pepper
3 cups cooked black beans

At least 1 hour before serving, combine the yellow and green bell peppers, cucumber, onion, corn, tomatoes, parsley, and cilantro in a large bowl. Add the vinegar, olive oil, and salt and pepper to taste and toss well. Taste and add more salt if needed. Set aside for at least 1 hour. Just before serving, mix in the black beans.

Calories 403 • Protein 17 gm • Fat 10 gm • Percent of calories from fat 19% • Cholesterol 0 mg • Dietary fiber 17 gm • Sodium 35 mg • Calcium 67 mg

Black Bean Salad with Goat Cheese

YIELD: 6 TO 8 SERVINGS

Cilantro might be expected in this salad, so mint makes a surprising and delicious alternative. Of course, cilantro could be substituted if you have no mint on hand.

1 cup dried black beans, soaked overnight or using the quick-soak method on page 20
1 onion, halved
1 bay leaf
1 dried ancho chile
8 cups water
5 tablespoons freshly squeezed lime juice, or more to taste
1/2 teaspoon salt
2 tablespoons white wine
2 garlic cloves, minced
2 tablespoons extra-virgin olive oil

3 bell peppers (green, yellow, red, or a combination), diced
2 tablespoons chopped fresh parsley
2 tablespoons chopped fresh mint or 2 teaspoons dried
2 scallions, chopped
Salt and freshly ground black pepper
4 ounces mild goat cheese (chèvre), such as Montrachet, crumbled

Drain the beans. Combine the beans in a large saucepan with the onion, bay leaf, chile, and 8 cups fresh water. Bring to a boil. Then reduce the heat and simmer, partially covered, until the beans are tender, about 1 1/2 hours. Drain the beans and discard the bay leaf and onion.

Remove the skin and seeds from the ancho and finely chop. Set aside.

Toss the still-warm beans with 3 tablespoons of the lime juice and the 1/2 teaspoon salt.

To make the dressing, combine the remaining 2 tablespoons lime juice, wine, garlic, and chopped ancho. Add the olive oil in a slow drizzle until fully incorporated.

Combine the beans, bell peppers, parsley, mint, and scallions in a large bowl. Pour in the dressing and toss. Taste and adjust seasonings, adding salt and pepper to taste. Let stand for at least 30 minutes to blend the flavors. At this point the salad may be held in the refrigerator for several hours. Serve at room temperature with the goat cheese sprinkled on top of the beans.

Calories 234 • Protein 11 gm • Fat 9 gm • Percent of calories from fat 34% • Cholesterol 9 mg • Dietary fiber 6 gm • Sodium 278 mg • Calcium 93 mg

Tropical Black Bean Salad

YIELD: 4 TO 6 SERVINGS

Here's a flavorful salad made sweet with pineapple, spicy with allspice, and fragrant with lime.

1/4 cup freshly squeezed lime juice
2 tablespoons freshly squeezed
  orange juice
2 tablespoons extra-virgin
  olive oil
2 garlic cloves, minced
3 cups cooked black beans
1 red or green bell pepper, diced

1 cup crushed pineapple, drained
1 small green chile pepper, diced
2 scallions, diced
1/2 teaspoon ground allspice
1 tablespoon chopped fresh mint
Salt and freshly ground black
  pepper

Combine the lime juice, orange juice, oil, and garlic in a medium bowl. Add the beans and toss to coat well. Add the bell pepper, pineapple, chile pepper, scallions, allspice, mint, and salt and pepper to taste. Set aside for at least 30 minutes at room temperature to allow the flavors to blend. This salad can be held for several hours in the refrigerator, if desired, but bring to room temperature before serving.

Calories 267 • Protein 12 gm • Fat 8 gm • Percent of calories from fat 25% •
Cholesterol 0 mg • Dietary fiber 12 gm • Sodium 29 mg • Calcium 57 mg

Summertime Black-eyed Pea Salad

YIELD: 6 SERVINGS

Black-eyed peas are best fresh, second best frozen, though cooked dried peas or canned peas are perfectly acceptable. I keep a supply of canned black-eyed peas in the pantry so that I can assemble dishes like this one on the spur of the moment.

1¹/₂ cups cooked black-eyed peas

1¹/₂ cups fresh or frozen
   corn kernels, thawed

1 large celery stalk, diced

¹/₄ cup diced Vidalia
   or other sweet onion

2 homemade or store-bought
   roasted red bell peppers, diced
   (see Note on page 40)

2 tablespoons chopped fresh mint

2 tablespoons chopped fresh
   parsley

2 tablespoons red wine vinegar

1 teaspoon Dijon mustard

¹/₄ teaspoon sugar

3 tablespoons extra-virgin
   olive oil

Salt and freshly ground black
   pepper

2 medium tomatoes, diced

Lettuce

In a large mixing bowl, combine the black-eyed peas, corn, celery, onion, bell peppers, mint, and parsley. In a small bowl, combine the vinegar, mustard, and sugar. Whisk in the olive oil. Pour over the vegetables, season to taste with salt and pepper, and toss well. Set aside for at least 1 hour before serving.

Before serving, mix in the tomatoes. Serve on a bed of lettuce.

Calories 164 • Protein 5 gm • Fat 7 gm • Percent of calories from fat 37% •
Cholesterol 0 mg • Dietary fiber 5 gm • Sodium 20 mg • Calcium 26 mg

Chickpea Salad with Tomatoes and Feta

YIELD: 6 SERVINGS

This versatile salad can be served as an accompaniment to a main course, or it can be the main course, served on a bed of greens. Include some sharp-tasting greens, such as arugula or watercress, in your mix.

4 cups cooked chickpeas
3 medium to large ripe tomatoes, diced
1/2 onion, finely chopped
1/4 cup chopped fresh mint
2 tablespoons freshly squeezed lemon juice
2 tablespoons dry white wine

1 teaspoon Dijon mustard
2 garlic cloves, minced
2 tablespoons extra-virgin olive oil
3 ounces feta cheese
Salt and freshly ground black pepper
12 cups salad greens (optional)

In a large salad bowl, combine the chickpeas, tomatoes, onion, and mint. Toss to mix.

In a small bowl, combine the lemon juice, wine, mustard, and garlic. Slowly whisk in the olive oil. Pour over the chickpeas and toss to mix. Add the feta cheese and toss again. Season to taste with salt and pepper. Let stand for at least 30 minutes to allow the flavors to blend. Serve plain or on a bed of greens.

Calories 284 • Protein 13 gm • Fat 11 gm • Percent of calories from fat 33% • Cholesterol 13 mg • Dietary fiber 7 gm • Sodium 183 mg • Calcium 142 mg

Smoky Corn and Kidney Bean Salad

YIELD: 4 TO 6 SERVINGS

This summery combination of grilled corn, bell peppers, vine-ripened tomatoes, and kidney beans gets its kick from a light dressing made with lime juice and chipotle en adobo, that character-building mixture of smoke-dried jalapeños in a vinegar sauce.

Salad

6 ears corn

1 red or yellow bell pepper, halved and seeded

1 green bell pepper, halved and seeded

2 cups cooked red kidney beans

1/4 cup chopped scallion

2 vine-ripened tomatoes, diced

1/4 cup chopped fresh cilantro

1/4 cup chopped fresh parsley

1 tablespoon sugar (optional, not needed if corn is sweet and fresh)

Salt and freshly ground black pepper

Dressing

1 tablespoon extra-virgin olive oil

2 tablespoons freshly squeezed lime juice

1 teaspoon honey

3 teaspoons chipotle en adobo, or more to taste

Salt

Place the ears of corn in water to soak for 30 minutes; do not husk first. Prepare a medium-hot fire on the grill. Grill the corn until the kernels are lightly toasted, about 20 minutes. Spray the bell peppers with nonstick cooking spray. Grill until lightly charred, about 5 minutes. Shuck and remove the corn from the cobs with a sharp knife (you should have about 2 cups kernels). Dice the peppers.

To make the dressing, combine the olive oil, lime juice, honey, chipotle en adobo, and salt to taste in a small bowl and blend well.

In a large bowl, combine the corn and peppers with the beans, scallion, tomatoes, cilantro, and parsley. Add the sugar (if using). Add the dressing and toss to mix. Season with salt and pepper to taste.

Calories 252 • Protein 11 gm • Fat 4 gm • Percent of calories from fat 14% • Cholesterol 0 mg • Dietary fiber 11 gm • Sodium 145 mg • Calcium 52 mg

Marinated Fava Bean Salad with Roasted Garlic and Onion

YIELD: 4 TO 6 SERVINGS

The season for fresh fava beans is brief—late spring to early summer. They taste like a cross between limas and fresh peas and are considered a superior bean by shell-bean fanciers.

1 garlic bulb

1 Vidalia or other sweet onion, sliced $1/4$ inch thick

$1/4$ cup high-quality chicken or vegetable broth

$2^{1}/_{2}$ pounds fresh fava beans in pods, shelled (about $3^{1}/_{2}$ cups)

1 red bell pepper, diced

2 celery stalks, diced

$1/4$ cup minced fresh Italian parsley

2 teaspoons fresh thyme leaves

$1/4$ cup dry white wine

2 tablespoons white wine vinegar

2 tablespoons extra-virgin olive oil

Salt and freshly ground black pepper

1 tomato, diced

1 cup finely slivered radicchio

2 ounces Parmesan cheese, thinly shaved

Preheat the oven to 450 degrees. Peel the garlic and separate the cloves. Spray an 8-inch baking dish or small roasting pan with nonstick cooking spray. Add the onion and garlic and spray again. Drizzle the broth over the vegetables. Roast until golden, about 30 minutes. Set aside.

Boil the shelled fava beans in lightly salted water for 5 minutes. Drain into a colander and run under cold water. Use a sharp knife to slice open the outer skin of the beans and pop or squeeze out the beans. You will now have a little less than 3 cups beans. Place in a large salad bowl, along with the bell pepper, celery, parsley, and thyme. Add the white wine, vinegar, and olive oil. Season with salt and pepper and toss to coat. Set aside to marinate for at least 1 hour.

Just before serving, toss in the roasted onion and garlic, tomato, and slivered radicchio. Arrange on individual plates or a large serving platter. Top with the Parmesan. Serve at once.

Calories 344 • Protein 19 gm • Fat 12 gm • Percent of calories from fat 31% • Cholesterol 11 mg • Dietary fiber 10 gm • Sodium 357 mg • Calcium 313 mg

Marinated Vegetable Salad
with Kidney Beans

YIELD: 4 SERVINGS

This crunchy vegetable salad is lightly dressed and requires hours of marination to allow the full flavor to develop.

Salad

2 cups small cauliflower florets
  (1/2 pound)
1 cup green beans cut into 1-inch
  pieces
1 carrot, cubed
1 (14-ounce) can artichoke hearts,
  drained and rinsed

1/4 cup diced red onion
1 green bell pepper, diced
2 celery stalks, sliced
2 cups cooked red kidney beans
20 Greek olives (optional)
Salt and freshly ground black
  pepper

Dressing

3 tablespoons extra-virgin
  olive oil
2 tablespoons dry white wine
2 tablespoons red wine vinegar
4 garlic cloves, minced

1 tablespoon chopped fresh
  oregano or 1 1/2 teaspoons dried

Blanch the cauliflower, green beans, and carrot in boiling water to cover for 45 seconds. Plunge into cold water and drain.

Combine the blanched vegetables plus the artichoke hearts, onion, bell pepper, celery, kidney beans, olives (if using), and salt and pepper to taste in a large salad bowl.

To make the dressing, in a small bowl, whisk together the olive oil, wine, vinegar, garlic, and oregano. Pour over the vegetables. Cover and refrigerate for at least 4 hours and up to 8 hours, tossing occasionally. Taste and adjust seasonings before serving.

Calories 288 • Protein 13 gm • Fat 11 gm • Percent of calories from fat 32% • Cholesterol 0 mg • Dietary fiber 9 gm • Sodium 287 mg • Calcium 112 mg

Three-Bean Salad

YIELD: 4 TO 6 SERVINGS

The addition of seasoned bread cubes (found in stuffing mixes) gives this classic salad extra flavor and crunch. If wax beans are unavailable, use green beans only.

2 cups green beans cut into 1-inch
    pieces
2 cups wax beans cut into 1-inch
    pieces
1$^1/_2$ cups cooked red kidney beans
$^3/_4$ cup seasoned bread cubes
$^1/_2$ cup diced celery
$^1/_4$ cup diced red onion

2 garlic cloves
1 teaspoon dried oregano
2 tablespoon extra-virgin olive oil
2 tablespoons red wine vinegar
1 teaspoon sugar
Salt and freshly ground black
    pepper
1 head butter lettuce (optional)

Blanch the green and wax beans in boiling water for 1 minute. Plunge into cold water to stop the cooking, then drain.

In a large bowl, combine the beans, bread cubes, celery, onion, garlic, oregano, oil, vinegar, sugar, and salt and pepper. Let sit for at least 30 minutes to allow the flavor to develop. Taste and adjust the seasonings.

Line a salad bowl or individual salad plates with the lettuce leaves (if using). Spoon the salad onto the leaves and serve.

Calories 279 • Protein 11 gm • Fat 8 gm • Percent of calories from fat 25% •
Cholesterol 0 mg • Dietary fiber 8 gm • Sodium 616 mg • Calcium 107 mg

French Lentil Salad
with Lemon-Garlic Vinaigrette

YIELD: 6 TO 8 SERVINGS

French lentils hold their shape well, so they are the best choice for a salad.

1½ cups dried French lentils, rinsed

2 strips fresh lemon peel

2 garlic cloves

3 tablespoons freshly squeezed lemon juice, or more to taste

2 tablespoons dry white wine

½ teaspoon Dijon mustard

3 tablespoons extra-virgin olive oil

½ cup chopped fresh parsley

2 scallions, chopped

Salt and freshly ground black pepper

1 head butter lettuce

Cook the lentils in plenty of water until tender but not mushy, about 25 minutes. Drain the lentils and set aside.

To make the dressing, finely chop the lemon peel and garlic using a knife or food processor. In a small bowl or in the food processor, combine the lemon peel and garlic with the lemon juice, white wine, and mustard. Beat well. Mix in the olive oil in a slow drizzle and beat until fully incorporated.

Combine the lentils and dressing in a mixing bowl. Toss in the parsley, scallions, and salt and pepper to taste. Taste and adjust seasonings, adding more lemon juice if needed.

To serve, line individual salad bowls with the lettuce leaves. Spoon the lentils on top and serve at once.

Calories 193 • Protein 8 gm • Fat 7 gm • Percent of calories from fat 32% • Cholesterol 0 mg • Dietary fiber 9 gm • Sodium 17 mg • Calcium 61 mg

Tomato, Green Bean, and White Bean Salad with Basil and Mint

YIELD: 4 TO 6 SERVINGS

Don't let the summer go by without making this delicious salad at least once. The crunchy green beans provide just the right snap, while the combination of vine-ripened tomatoes, white beans, and herbs in vinaigrette is a marriage made in culinary heaven. This salad makes a delicious accompaniment for a simple cheese and pasta dish (in which case, it would stretch to feed six), but it is also delicious on its own with a loaf of bread and a summer breeze.

1/2 **pound green beans cut into**
 11/2**-inch lengths**
1**1/2 pounds vine-ripened**
 tomatoes, diced
2 **cups cooked white beans**
2 **tablespoons extra-virgin olive oil**

1 **tablespoon balsamic vinegar**
2 **garlic cloves, minced**
1/2 **cup chopped fresh basil**
1/4 **cup chopped fresh mint**
Salt and freshly ground pepper

About 1 hour before serving, blanch the green beans in boiling water to cover for 1 minute. Drain, plunge into ice water to stop the cooking, and drain again.

In a large bowl, combine the green beans, tomatoes, white beans, oil, vinegar, garlic, basil, and mint and toss gently. Set aside at room temperature for 1 hour to allow the flavors to blend. Add salt and pepper to taste before serving.

Calories 248 • Protein 11 gm • Fat 8 gm • Percent of calories from fat 26% • Cholesterol 0 mg • Dietary fiber 9 gm • Sodium 26 mg • Calcium 132 mg

French Lentil Salad with Goat Cheese

YIELD: 6 TO 8 SERVINGS

Tangy goat cheese proves to be a wonderful foil for the nutty, earthy flavor of lentils. Again, French green lentils are the best choice because they hold their shape well.

1½ cups dried French lentils, rinsed
1 onion, finely chopped
1 bay leaf
1 tablespoon chopped fresh thyme or 1 teaspoon dried
1 teaspoon salt
6 tablespoons freshly squeezed lemon juice, or more to taste
1 teaspoon Dijon mustard
2 tablespoons dry white wine
2 garlic cloves, minced
4 tablespoons extra-virgin olive oil

Salt and freshly ground black pepper
3 bell peppers (green, yellow, red, or a combination), diced
½ cup chopped fresh parsley
2 tablespoons chopped fresh mint
5 ounces mild goat cheese (chèvre), such as Montrachet, crumbled
12 cups mixed salad greens (about ½ pound)

Cook the lentils with the onion, bay leaf, thyme, and 1 teaspoon salt in plenty of water until tender but not mushy, about 25 minutes. Drain the lentils and discard the bay leaf. Toss the lentils with 3 tablespoons of the lemon juice.

To make the dressing, combine the remaining 3 tablespoons lemon juice, the mustard, wine, and garlic. Whisk in the olive oil in a slow drizzle until fully incorporated.

Combine the lentils, bell peppers, parsley, and mint in a large bowl. Pour in half to two-thirds of the dressing. Taste and adjust seasonings. Gently toss in about 3 ounces of the goat cheese.

To serve, line individual salad bowls or a large serving platter with the greens. Spoon the lentils on top. Crumble the remaining 2 ounces goat cheese over the top and serve at once. Pass the remaining dressing at the table.

Calories 304 • Protein 13 gm • Fat 14 gm • Percent of calories from fat 41% • Cholesterol 11 mg • Dietary fiber 10 gm • Sodium 500 mg • Calcium 132 mg

Tomato, White Bean, and Arugula Salad with Roasted Garlic Vinaigrette

YIELD: 3 TO 6 SERVINGS

Sweet tomatoes, peppery arugula, and nutty roasted garlic combine in this delicious salad. Serve it as a starter for a pasta meal or as a main course accompanied by a crusty loaf of bread.

Vinaigrette
1 bulb garlic
3 tablespoons extra-virgin olive oil
3 tablespoons dry white wine
1 tablespoon red wine vinegar
Salt

Salad
3 cups cooked cannellini (white kidney) beans
4 medium to large ripe tomatoes, cut in wedges
12 cups torn arugula (8 ounces)
1/2 cup thinly sliced Vidalia or similar sweet onion
2 teaspoons capers

To make the vinaigrette, preheat the oven to 450 degrees. Remove the papery outer skin of the garlic and slice the top off the bulb to expose the tips of the cloves. Place in a small bowl and pour in enough water to cover the bottom of the bowl by about 1/4 inch. Roast for about 30 minutes, until the garlic is soft and browned, but not charred. Remove the garlic from the water and set aside until cool enough to handle. (You can speed the cooling process by separating the cloves.) Remove the cloves from the papery skins. Combine in a blender with the olive oil, wine, vinegar, and salt to taste, and process until smooth.

In a large salad bowl, combine the beans and tomatoes. Add the dressing and toss to mix well. (You can hold the salad at this point for about an hour.)

To serve, make a bed of arugula on individual plates. Spoon the beans and tomatoes over the greens. Scatter the onions and capers on top. Serve at once.

Calories 447 • Protein 20 gm • Fat 16 gm • Percent of calories from fat 30% •
Cholesterol 0 mg • Dietary fiber 14 gm • Sodium 114 mg • Calcium 222 mg

White Bean Salad with Sun-dried Tomatoes

❧❧❧

YIELD: 4 TO 6 SERVINGS

Since the beans in this recipe are seasoned while they are cooking, they do not need much dressing. Make sure the beans are completely tender before removing them from the heat—undercooked beans in a salad can be quite unpleasant.

1 cup dried Great Northern or navy beans, soaked overnight or using the quick-soak method on page 20

1 onion, quartered

1 celery stalk, quartered

2 bay leaves

6 cups water

1 tablespoon chopped sun-dried tomato (refresh in hot water if not packed in oil)

2 tablespoons red wine vinegar

2 tablespoons chopped fresh parsley

1 tablespoon capers

1 large shallot, finely chopped

2 garlic cloves, minced

1/4 teaspoon Dijon mustard

1/4 teaspoon salt

1/4 teaspoon freshly ground black pepper

3 tablespoons extra-virgin olive oil or sun-dried tomato oil

2 carrots, thinly sliced

Drain the beans. Combine the beans in a large pot with the quartered onion and celery stalk, bay leaves, and 8 cups fresh water. Bring to a boil, then reduce the heat and simmer, partially covered, until the beans are completely tender but still whole, 1 1/2 to 2 hours. Drain and discard the onion, celery, and bay leaves.

Place the beans in a large salad bowl. Toss with the sun-dried tomatoes. In a small bowl, combine the vinegar, parsley, capers, shallot, garlic, mustard, salt, and pepper. Whisk in the oil. Pour over the still-warm beans, toss gently, and set aside to allow the beans to cool to room temperature. Just before serving, add the carrots. Toss to mix, adding additional salt and pepper if needed.

Calories 284 • Protein 11 gm • Fat 11 gm • Percent of calories from fat 34% • Cholesterol 0 mg • Dietary fiber 15 gm • Sodium 271 mg • Calcium 116 mg

Dilled White Bean Salad with Tomatoes

YIELD: 4 TO 6 SERVINGS

1 cup dried Great Northern or
navy beans, soaked overnight
or using the quick-soak
method on page 20
1 onion, halved
1 celery stalk, halved
2 bay leaves
8 cups water
1/2 small red onion, thinly sliced

2 tablespoons freshly squeezed
lemon juice
2 tablespoons dry white wine
3 tablespoons chopped fresh dill
1 teaspoon salt
1/4 teaspoon freshly ground black
pepper
3 tablespoons extra-virgin olive oil
1 large ripe tomato, chopped

Drain the beans. Combine the beans in a large pot with the halved onion and celery stalk, bay leaves, and 8 cups fresh water. Bring to a boil, then reduce the heat and simmer, partially covered, until the beans are tender, 1 1/2 to 2 hours. Drain and discard the onion, celery, and bay leaves.

Place the beans in a large salad bowl and toss with the red onion. In a small bowl, combine the lemon juice, white wine, dill, salt, and pepper. Whisk in the olive oil. Pour over the still-warm beans, toss gently, and set aside to allow the beans to cool to room temperature. Just before serving, add the tomato. Toss to mix.

Calories 283 • Protein 11 gm • Fat 11 gm • Percent of calories from fat 33% • Cholesterol 0 mg • Dietary fiber 14 gm • Sodium 616 mg • Calcium 110 mg

Artichoke Pasta Salad with Basil Vinaigrette

❦

YIELD: 6 SERVINGS

³/₄ pound shells, rotelle, or farfalle

2 tablespoons extra-virgin
   olive oil

(6-ounce) jar marinated artichoke
   hearts

2 cups cooked cannellini (white
   kidney) beans

1 red bell pepper, diced

1 carrot, diced

1 cup fresh or frozen peas

¹/₄ cup diced red onion

2 tablespoons capers

4 garlic cloves

12 large basil leaves

3 tablespoons freshly squeezed
   lemon juice

Salt and freshly ground black
   pepper

Cook the pasta in plenty of boiling salted water until al dente. Drain and rinse thoroughly to cool. Add the olive oil to the pasta and toss.

Drain the marinated artichoke hearts, reserving the liquid. Combine the artichokes with the pasta, cannellini, bell pepper, carrot, peas, onion, and capers. Toss to mix.

To make the dressing, finely chop the garlic and basil in a food processor. Mix in the lemon juice. With the motor running, drizzle in the liquid from the marinated artichokes. Pour over the salad. Toss to mix. Season with salt and pepper to taste and toss again. Serve at once. If the salad is to be held for a few hours, taste before serving. You may want to brighten the flavors with additional lemon juice or salt.

Calories 381 • Protein 14 gm • Fat 8 gm • Percent of calories from fat 18% •
Cholesterol 0 mg • Dietary fiber 8 gm • Sodium 198 mg • Calcium 44 mg

Wagon Train Pasta Salad

YIELD: 4 TO 8 SERVINGS

Sweet, crunchy jicama adds immeasurably to this delicious salad. It serves 8 as a side dish, but I enjoy eating it as a main course. It is equally delicious made with pinto, black, or red kidney beans.

1 pound wagon-wheel pasta
1 tablespoon extra-virgin olive oil
1½ cups cooked pinto, black, or red kidney beans
2 cups julienned jicama
1 cup julienned green or red bell pepper
½ cup diced Vidalia or other sweet onion

1 cup plain nonfat yogurt
¼ cup reduced-fat mayonnaise
½ cup homemade or store-bought salsa
¼ cup chopped fresh cilantro
Salt and freshly ground black pepper
1 avocado, diced

Boil the pasta in plenty of boiling salted water until just al dente. Drain. Toss with the olive oil. Add the beans, jicama, bell pepper, and onion and toss again.

In a separate bowl, combine the yogurt, mayonnaise, salsa, and cilantro.

Just before serving, pour the dressing on the salad and toss lightly. Taste and season with salt and pepper. Add the avocado, toss, and serve.

Leftovers can be be refreshed with a little more yogurt, salsa, and salt and pepper.

Calories 740 • Protein 25 gm • Fat 18 gm • Percent of calories from fat 22% • Cholesterol 1 mg • Dietary fiber 14 gm • Sodium 174 mg • Calcium 189 mg

5
Risottos, Rice Pilafs, and More

Steamed White Rice

Steamed Brown Rice

Steamed Sticky Rice

Steamed Black Rice

Baked White Rice

Baked Brown Rice

Basic Cooked Wild Rice

Pesto Risotto

Risotto alla Milanese

Risotto with Butternut Squash

Risotto with Caramelized Onions and Cabbage

Lemon-Thyme Risotto with Asparagus

Cheddar-Broccoli Risotto

Corn Harvest Risotto

Pistachio-Lemon Pilaf

Vegetarian Paella

Vegetable Pilau

Curried Rice and Broccoli Pilaf

Caribbean Rice Pilaf

Vermicelli-Rice Pilaf

Tex-Mex Vermicelli-Rice Pilaf

Wild Rice–Orzo Pilaf

Brown and Wild Rice Pilaf

Mixed Grain Pilaf

Garlic Rice Timbales

Chirashi Sushi

Festive Yellow Rice

Hazelnut–Wild Rice Dressing

Spanakorizzo

Baked Rice Mediterranean

Chinese Vegetable Fried Rice

Nasi Goreng (Indonesian Fried Rice)

Sesame Stir-fried Broccoli and Brown Rice

Zucchini–Brown Rice Squares

Rice-stuffed Cabbage in Sweet and Sour Sauce

If I had to choose only one grain to exist on for the rest of my life, I would probably choose rice over wheat, despite my Western upbringing. Rice as a main course can take inspiration from the great cuisines of the world (and rice pudding *is* my favorite dessert, but that's for another chapter).

The recipes collected here range from Italian risottos to Indian pilafs to Japanese vinegared rice dishes. The flavors are as American as corn and as exotic as annatto, a spice popular in the Caribbean and Central America. Clearly rice is adaptable to many different flavorings.

A certain delicacy is called for when cooking with rice. Flavoring broths should be neutral, not dominated by mushrooms or sweet root vegetables. It is also important to respect the texture of the rice. Certain pilafs should be almost dry in texture, which is why those recipes call for rinsing the rice of the surface starch. Other dishes, such as risottos, should be almost soupy. For those dishes, the liquid is added in stages, allowing each grain of rice to absorb as much liquid as possible.

Steamed White Rice

YIELD: ABOUT 3 CUPS

This basic recipe will work for any domestic or aromatic long-grain white rice. The goal is fluffy rice, each grain separate rather than in a gummy clump. In India it is said that rice should be like two brothers: close, but not stuck together.

1 cup uncooked long-grain white rice

1³/₄ cups cold water
¹/₂ teaspoon salt (optional)

Rinse the rice in several changes of water until the rinse water runs clear. This step is optional, but it will result in a fluffier, drier rice.

In a saucepan, combine the rice, water, and salt (if using). Cover and bring to a boil over high heat. Reduce the heat to a gentle boil and cook until the liquid has been absorbed and the rice is tender, 12 to 15 minutes. Fluff the rice with a fork. Dry the pot lid. Crumple a clean kitchen cotton or paper towel and place over the rice. Return the dried lid to the pot and let stand for 5 minutes before serving.

Calories 225 • Protein 4 gm • Fat .4 gm • Percent of calories from fat 2% •
Cholesterol 0 mg • Dietary fiber 1 gm • Sodium 7 mg • Calcium 20 mg

Steamed Brown Rice

YIELD: 3 CUPS

This basic recipe will work for any long-grain or medium-grain brown rice, including the specialty brown rices, such as Wehani. Again, the goal is to have fluffy grains of cooked rice, not a gummy clump.

**1 cup uncooked long-grain
  or medium-grain brown rice**
2¹/₄ cups cold water

**¹/₂ teaspoon salt (optional;
  do not use with Wehani)**

In a saucepan, combine the rice, water, and salt (if using). Cover and bring to a boil over high heat. Reduce the heat to a gentle boil and cook until the liquid has been absorbed and the rice is tender, about 40 minutes. Fluff the rice with a fork. Dry the pot lid. Crumple a clean kitchen cotton or paper towel and place over the rice. Return the dried lid to the pot and let stand for 5 minutes before serving.

Calories 228 • Protein 5 gm • Fat 1.8 gm • Percent of calories from fat 7% • Cholesterol 0 mg • Dietary fiber 2 gm • Sodium 10 mg • Calcium 18 mg

Steamed Black Rice

YIELD: ABOUT 3 CUPS

Black rice has a sticky texture and a flavor that is a cross between basmati and wild rice. It will become purple-black in color when cooked.

1 cup black rice
2¹/₂ cups cold water

¹/₂ teaspoon salt (optional)

In a saucepan, combine the rice, water, and salt (if using). Cover and bring to a boil over high heat. Reduce the heat to a gentle boil and cook until the liquid has been absorbed and the rice is tender, about 25 minutes. Fluff the rice with a fork. Dry the pot lid. Crumple a clean kitchen cotton or paper towel and place over the rice. Return the dried lid to the pot and let stand for 5 minutes before serving.

Calories 223 • Protein 6 gm • Fat 1.5 gm • Percent of calories from fat 6% • Cholesterol 0 mg • Dietary fiber 3 gm • Sodium 7 mg • Calcium 17 mg

Steamed Sticky Rice

❦

YIELD: 2 CUPS

Unlike the previous two recipes, this rice is truly steamed. Sticky rice is rarely served plain.

**1 cup uncooked sticky rice,
   soaked overnight**

Drain the rice. Rinse well and drain again. Place the rice in a steamer over boiling water and steam for 20 minutes, or until the rice is tender. As the rice steams, sprinkle a little water on it from time to time.

Calories 342 • Protein 6 gm • Fat 1 gm • Percent of calories from fat 1% •
Cholesterol 0 mg • Dietary fiber 3 gm • Sodium 6 mg • Calcium 10 mg

Baked White Rice

YIELD: ABOUT 3 CUPS

Usually I cook rice on top of the stove or in a rice cooker. However, baking rice has the same advantages as preparing it in a rice cooker—it is a foolproof method that allows me to hold the rice at a good serving temperature, without running the risk of scorching the bottom of the pan.

1 cup uncooked long-grain or medium-grain white rice

2 cups water or broth
¹/₂ teaspoon salt (optional)

Rinse the rice in several changes of water until the rinse water runs clear. This step is optional, but it will result in a fluffier, drier rice. Preheat the oven to 400 degrees.

In a flameproof Dutch oven or casserole, combine the rice, liquid, and salt (if using), cover, and bring to a boil. Transfer the pan, still covered, to the oven and bake until the liquid is absorbed and the rice is tender, about 15 minutes. Remove from the oven and let stand for 3 to 4 minutes. You can hold the rice for up to 30 minutes in the covered Dutch oven without any noticeable loss in heat or texture. Fluff with a fork before serving.

Calories 225 • Protein 4 gm • Fat .5 gm • Percent of calories from fat 2% • Cholesterol 0 mg • Dietary fiber 1 gm • Sodium 8 mg • Calcium 20 mg

Baked Brown Rice

YIELD: ABOUT $3^1/_4$ CUPS

**1 cup uncooked long-grain
or medium-grain brown rice**

**$2^1/_4$ cups water or broth
$^1/_2$ teaspoon salt (optional)**

Preheat the oven to 400 degrees.

In a flameproof Dutch oven or casserole, combine the rice, liquid, and salt (if using), cover, and bring to a boil. Transfer the pan, still covered, to the oven and bake until the liquid has been absorbed and the rice is tender, about 40 minutes. Remove from the oven and let stand for 3 to 4 minutes. You can hold the rice for up to 30 minutes in the covered Dutch oven without any noticeable loss in heat or texture. Fluff with a fork before serving.

Calories 208 • Protein 4 gm • Fat .4 gm • Percent of calories from fat 2% •
Cholesterol 0 mg • Dietary fiber 1 gm • Sodium 8 mg • Calcium 19 mg

Basic Cooked Wild Rice

YIELD: ABOUT 3 CUPS

There is tremendous variety among wild rice in terms of size, age, and degree of processing, which means you'll need to use this recipe as a guide, and adjust as needed. It is especially important to begin checking the grain for doneness (take a taste) after 30 minutes to avoid overcooking.

1 cup uncooked wild rice   **1 teaspoon salt**
3 cups water

Rinse the rice in a sieve under cold running water. Drain. In a saucepan, combine the wild rice, water, and salt. Cover, bring to a boil, then reduce the heat and simmer until the rice is tender and most of the grains have burst open, 40 to 60 minutes. Drain off any excess water. Let stand for about 10 minutes before serving.

Calories 190 • Protein 8 gm • Fat 1 gm • Percent of calories from fat 3% • Cholesterol 0 mg • Dietary fiber 3 gm • Sodium 786 mg • Calcium 16 mg

Pesto Risotto

YIELD: 4 TO 6 SERVINGS

This is a great dish to make in the summer, when tomatoes, basil, and summer squash are near at hand. Add arugula if you like its peppery flavor.

5¹/₂ cups high-quality vegetable or chicken broth

1/₂ cup dry white wine

2 tablespoons extra-virgin olive oil

3 garlic cloves, minced

1 small yellow summer squash, diced

1¹/₂ cups uncooked Arborio rice

1/₂ cup homemade or store-bought pesto (page 263)

1 cup halved cherry tomatoes

2 cups chopped arugula (optional)

Salt and freshly ground black pepper

In a medium saucepan, heat the broth and wine to simmering.

In a large nonstick skillet, heat the olive oil over medium heat. Add the garlic, yellow squash, and rice and toss to coat with the oil. Sauté for 3 to 5 minutes, until the rice appears toasted.

Add 1 cup of the simmering broth to the rice mixture and reduce the heat to medium. Stir until most of the liquid has been absorbed. Continue adding more broth, 1 cup at a time, cooking and stirring as the liquid is absorbed. It will take a total of 18 to 35 minutes for the liquid to be absorbed and the rice to become tender and creamy. Stir in the pesto, tomatoes, and arugula (if using). Season to taste with salt and pepper, if needed. Serve hot.

Calories 650 • Protein 12 gm • Fat 26 gm • Percent of calories from fat 37% •
Cholesterol 2 mg • Dietary fiber 3 gm • Sodium 315 mg • Calcium 70 mg

Risotto alla Milanese

YIELD: 4 TO 6 SERVINGS

In her book, Gastronomy of Italy, *Anna Del Conte relates the mythical origin of Risotto alla Milanese (risotto with saffron). It seems that a fifteenth-century craftsman who used saffron to tint stained glass was inspired to have saffron added to the risotto served at his daughter's wedding. Since serving food with gold in it was considered healthful, this golden risotto became the height of fashion. It lives on today because it is also a very delicious combination. The carrot is a nontraditional addition, but a welcome touch if you are going to serve this dish as a vegetarian main course.*

5¹/₂ cups high-quality vegetable or chicken broth

¹/₂ cup dry white wine

¹/₄ teaspoon crushed saffron

1 tablespoon extra-virgin olive oil

2 shallots, minced

3 garlic cloves, minced

1¹/₂ cups uncooked Arborio rice

1 large carrot, diced (optional)

Salt and freshly ground black pepper

In a medium saucepan, heat the broth, wine, and saffron to simmering.

In a large nonstick skillet, heat the olive oil over medium heat. Add the shallots, garlic, and rice and toss to coat with the oil. Sauté for 3 to 5 minutes, until the rice appears toasted. Add the carrot (if using).

Add 1 cup of the simmering broth to the rice and reduce the heat to medium. Stir until most of the liquid has been absorbed. Continue adding more broth, 1 cup at a time, cooking and stirring as the liquid is absorbed. It will take a total of about 18 to 35 minutes for the liquid to be absorbed and the rice to become tender and creamy. Season to taste with salt and pepper, if needed. Serve hot.

Calories 416 • Protein 7 gm • Fat 3 gm • Percent of calories from fat 8% • Cholesterol 0 mg • Dietary fiber 2 gm • Sodium 115 mg • Calcium 7 mg

Golden Risotto with Shrimp. Add 1 pound unpeeled medium shrimp to the simmering broth. Poach until firm and pink throughout, about 5 minutes. Remove from the broth with a slotted spoon and set aside to cool enough to handle. Peel. Proceed with the recipe as written, but do not add the carrot. Stir in the shrimp when the risotto has absorbed all the liquid and is tender and creamy. Taste and add salt and pepper. Serve at once.

Calories 528 • Protein 31 gm • Fat 5 gm • Percent of calories from fat 8% • Cholesterol 222 mg • Dietary fiber 2 gm • Sodium 369 mg • Calcium 51 mg

Golden Risotto with Chicken. Add 1 pound boneless, skinless chicken breast to the simmering broth. Poach for 5 minutes. Remove the pan from the heat and let the chicken sit in the broth for another 5 minutes to finish cooking. Remove the chicken from the broth with a slotted spoon and set aside until cool enough to handle. Dice. Return the broth to simmering and proceed with the recipe as written, but do not add the carrot. Stir in the chicken when the risotto has absorbed all the liquid and is tender and creamy. Taste and add salt and pepper. Serve at once.

Calories 541 • Protein 34 gm • Fat 5 gm • Percent of calories from fat 8% • Cholesterol 66 mg • Dietary fiber 2 gm • Sodium 189 mg • Calcium 19 mg

Risottos, Rice Pilafs, and More

Risotto with Butternut Squash

YIELD: 2 TO 4 SERVINGS

This is one of my favorite ways to enjoy winter squash, and possibly my favorite risotto—an outstanding combination!

1/2 cup white wine

31/2 cups water

2 tablespoons extra-virgin olive oil

1 onion, finely diced

2 garlic cloves, minced

1 teaspoon fresh, or 1/4 teaspoon dried rosemary

1 cup uncooked Arborio rice

1 teaspoon salt

1/2 small butternut squash (about 1 pound), peeled and diced

1/3 cup freshly grated Parmesan cheese

Freshly ground black pepper

In a medium saucepan, heat the wine and water to simmering.

Heat the olive oil in a large nonstick skillet over medium heat. Add the onion, garlic, and rosemary, and sauté until the onion appears transparent. Add the rice and salt and toss to coat with the oil. Sauté for 3 to 5 minutes, until the rice appears toasted. Stir in the squash.

Add 1/2 cup of the simmering water mixture to the rice mixture and reduce the heat to medium. Stir until most of the liquid has been absorbed. Continue adding more water, 1/2 cup at a time, cooking and stirring occasionally as the liquid is absorbed. It will take a total of 18 to 35 minutes for the liquid to be absorbed and the rice and squash to become tender. Vigorously stir in the Parmesan. Season to taste with pepper and additional salt, if needed. Serve hot.

Calories 710 • Protein 12 gm • Fat 14 gm • Percent of calories from fat 18% • Cholesterol 1 mg • Dietary fiber 7 gm • Sodium 1205 mg • Calcium 144 mg

Risotto with Caramelized Onions and Cabbage

YIELD: 4 TO 6 SERVINGS

A warming bowl of comfort for a wintry night, this rustic risotto is rather soupy. A green salad and a crusty loaf of bread finishes the meal nicely.

2 tablespoon extra-virgin olive oil
2 onions, thinly sliced
6 cups shredded green or Savoy cabbage
2 teaspoons dried thyme
5$^1/_2$ cups high-quality vegetable or chicken broth
$^1/_2$ cup dry white wine
1$^1/_2$ cups uncooked Arborio rice
$^1/_2$ cup freshly grated Parmesan cheese
Salt and freshly ground black pepper

In a large nonstick skillet, heat the olive oil over medium heat. Add the onions, cabbage, and thyme, and sauté until the onions are golden, 10 to 12 minutes, stirring frequently.

Meanwhile, in a medium saucepan, combine the broth and wine and heat to simmering.

When the onions are golden, add the rice and toss to coat with the oil. Add 1 cup of the simmering broth to the rice and stir until most of the liquid has been absorbed. Continue adding more broth, 1 cup at a time, cooking and stirring as the liquid is absorbed. It will take a total of 18 to 35 minutes for most of the liquid to be absorbed and the rice to become tender and creamy. Stir in the Parmesan. Season to taste with salt and pepper, if needed. Serve hot.

Calories 549 • Protein 14 gm • Fat 10 gm • Percent of calories from fat 17% •
Cholesterol 8 mg • Dietary fiber 6 gm • Sodium 333 mg • Calcium 206 mg

Lemon-Thyme Risotto with Asparagus

YIELD: 4 TO 6 SERVINGS

This is a fine way to salute asparagus season. Lemon-thyme adds a delicate lemony aroma to this risotto. If you don't have access to it, use regular thyme leaves and increase the lemon zest in the recipe to 3/4 teaspoon.

1 pound asparagus, cut into
  1-inch pieces
5 1/2 cups high-quality vegetable
  or chicken broth
1/2 cup dry white wine
1/2 teaspoon grated lemon zest
1 teaspoon fresh lemon-thyme
  or regular thyme leaves

1 tablespoon extra-virgin olive oil
2 shallots, minced
3 garlic cloves, minced
1 1/2 cups uncooked Arborio rice
1/4 cup freshly grated Parmesan
  cheese
Salt and freshly ground black
  pepper

Blanch the asparagus in boiling water to cover until just tender, about 4 minutes. Plunge into cold water to stop the cooking. Drain and set aside.

In a medium saucepan, combine the broth, wine, lemon zest, and thyme. Heat to simmering.

In a large nonstick skillet, heat the olive oil over medium heat. Add the shallots, garlic, and rice, and toss to coat with the oil. Sauté for 3 to 5 minutes, until the rice appears toasted.

Add 1 cup of the simmering broth to the rice and reduce the heat to medium. Stir until the liquid is mostly absorbed. Continue adding more broth, 1 cup at a time, cooking and stirring as the liquid is absorbed. It will take a total of 18 to 35 minutes for the liquid to be absorbed and the rice to become tender and creamy. Stir in the cheese, then the asparagus. Season to taste with salt and pepper, if needed. Serve hot.

Calories 467 • Protein 12 gm • Fat 5 gm • Percent of calories from fat 10% • Cholesterol 4 mg • Dietary fiber 4 gm • Sodium 221 mg • Calcium 102 mg

Cheddar-Broccoli Risotto

YIELD: 4 TO 6 SERVINGS

4 cups chopped broccoli
5 cups high-quality vegetable
  or chicken broth
1 cup dry white wine
1 tablespoon extra-virgin olive oil
2 shallots, minced
3 garlic cloves, minced

1¹/₂ cups uncooked Arborio rice
1¹/₂ cups coarsely grated
  reduced-fat cheddar cheese
¹/₂ cup freshly grated Parmesan
  cheese
Salt and freshly ground black
  pepper

Steam the broccoli until just tender, about 3 minutes. Plunge into cold water to stop the cooking. Drain and set aside.

In a medium saucepan, heat the broth and wine to simmering.

In a large nonstick skillet, heat the olive oil over medium heat. Add the shallots, garlic, and rice, and toss to coat with the oil. Sauté for 3 to 5 minutes, until the rice appears toasted.

Add 1 cup of the simmering broth to the rice and reduce the heat to medium. Stir until most of the liquid has been absorbed. Continue adding more broth, 1 cup at a time, cooking and stirring as the liquid is absorbed. It will take a total of 18 to 35 minutes for the liquid to be absorbed and the rice to become tender and creamy. Stir in the broccoli. Stir in the cheeses and continue to stir until the cheese is well melted. Season to taste with salt and pepper, if needed. Serve hot.

Calories 626 • Protein 31 gm • Fat 11.4 gm • Percent of calories from fat 17% • Cholesterol 23 mg • Dietary fiber 6 gm • Sodium 453 mg • Calcium 698 mg

Corn Harvest Risotto

YIELD: 6 TO 8 SERVINGS

This risotto is infused with the sweet flavor of corn. Red peppers, tomato, and basil add to the summery flavors.

5 cups water
3 cups fresh or frozen
    corn kernels
1 cup dry white wine
1 tablespoon sugar (optional;
    needed only if corn is frozen
    or not recently harvested)
1 teaspoon salt
1/2 teaspoon turmeric
1 tablespoon extra-virgin olive oil

1³/₄ cups uncooked Arborio rice
2 shallots, minced
3 garlic cloves, minced
1 red bell pepper, diced
2 tablespoons chopped fresh basil,
    plus extra for garnish
1 ripe tomato, diced
Salt and freshly ground black
    pepper

In a medium saucepan, bring 1 cup of the water to a boil. Add the corn, cover, and cook for 4 minutes. Pour into a blender and puree. Return the pureed corn to the saucepan. Add the remaining 4 cups water, the wine, sugar (if using), salt, and turmeric. Heat to simmering.

In a large nonstick skillet, heat the olive oil over medium heat. Add the rice, shallots, garlic, and bell pepper and toss to coat with the oil. Sauté for 3 to 5 minutes, until the rice appears toasted.

Add 1 cup of the simmering corn broth to the rice and reduce the heat to medium. Stir until most of the liquid has been absorbed. Continue adding more corn broth, 1 cup at a time, cooking and stirring as the liquid is absorbed. When half the corn broth has been absorbed, stir in the basil. It will take between 18 and 35 minutes for the liquid to be absorbed and the rice to become tender and creamy. Stir in the tomato. Season to taste with salt and pepper, if needed. Serve immediately, garnished with fresh basil leaves, if desired.

Calories 369 • Protein 8 gm • Fat 2 gm • Percent of calories from fat 6% •
Cholesterol 0 mg • Dietary fiber 3 gm • Sodium 402 mg • Calcium 16 mg

Pistachio-Lemon Pilaf

YIELD: 4 TO 6 SERVINGS

For this delicately flavored pilaf, only the most neutral-tasting broth will do. If you don't want to use chicken broth, then use water—most vegetable broths are just too assertive in flavor.

1¹/₂ cups uncooked basmati
   or other long-grain white rice
1 tablespoon extra-virgin olive oil
2 shallots, minced
2 garlic cloves, minced
2³/₄ cups high-quality chicken
   broth or water
1 teaspoon grated lemon zest

¹/₈ teaspoon ground turmeric
¹/₂ cup shelled roasted pistachio
   nuts (salted or unsalted), finely
   chopped
2 tablespoons chopped fresh
   parsley or cilantro
Salt and freshly ground black
   pepper

Wash the rice in cold running water until the rinse water runs clear. Drain.

Heat the oil in a saucepan over medium-high heat. Add the shallots and garlic and sauté until softened, about 2 minutes. Add the rice and sauté until the rice appears toasted and dry, 3 to 5 minutes. Stir in the chicken broth or water, lemon zest, and turmeric. Cover and bring to a boil, then reduce the heat and boil gently until the liquid has been absorbed and the rice is tender, 12 to 15 minutes.

Fluff the rice with a fork. Stir in the pistachio nuts and parsley, and season to taste with salt and pepper. Dry the pot lid. Crumple a clean kitchen cotton or paper towel and place on top of the rice. Cover with the dried lid and let rest for 5 minutes before serving.

Calories 376 • Protein 9 gm • Fat 14 gm • Percent of calories from fat 33% •
Cholesterol 3 mg • Dietary fiber 5 gm • Sodium 72 mg • Calcium 57 mg

Vegetarian Paella

YIELD: 4 TO 6 SERVINGS

4 cups high-quality chicken or
   vegetable broth
1/4 teaspoon crushed saffron
   threads
1 tablespoon extra-virgin olive oil
1 onion, minced
3 garlic cloves, minced
1 1/2 cups chopped fresh or
   canned tomatoes
2 cups green beans cut into 1-inch
   lengths

2 teaspoons dried rosemary
2 cups uncooked medium-grain
   or Arborio rice
1/4 cup diced pimientos
1 cup fresh or frozen peas
1 (14-ounce) can artichoke hearts
   quartered, rinsed, and drained
Salt

In a saucepan, combine the broth and saffron. Heat to simmering, then reduce the heat to low and continue simmering.

In a large nonstick skillet, heat the olive oil over medium-low heat. Add the onion and garlic and sauté until golden, about 6 minutes. Add the tomatoes, green beans, and rosemary, and sauté until the mixture is quite thick, about 4 minutes. Add the rice and simmering stock. Stir well. Cover and let simmer for about 30 minutes, until the rice is tender and has absorbed all of the liquid. Remove from the heat and fluff with a fork. Stir in the pimientos, peas, and artichokes. Add salt to taste. Cover and let stand for 5 minutes before serving.

Calories 596 • Protein 18 gm • Fat 4.1 gm • Percent of calories from fat 6% • Cholesterol 0 mg • Dietary fiber 8 gm • Sodium 711 mg • Calcium 102 mg

VARIATIONS

Paella with Chicken and Sausage. Dice 1/2 pound boneless skinless chicken breast. Remove 1/2 pound turkey or smoked chicken sausage from its casing. Add to the skillet along with the onion and garlic and sauté until the chicken is firm and white throughout, about 6 minutes. Proceed with the recipe as written. Serves 6.

Calories 513 • Protein 30 gm • Fat 7.5 gm • Percent of calories from fat 13% • Cholesterol 59 mg • Dietary fiber 5 gm • Sodium 839 mg • Calcium 74 mg

Seafood Paella. Add 1 pound unpeeled medium shrimp to the simmering broth. Poach until firm and pink throughout, about 5 minutes. Remove from the broth with a slotted spoon and set aside until cool enough to handle. Peel. Proceed with the recipe as written, until the rice has cooked for 25 minutes and has absorbed most of its liquid. Remove the cover and quickly cover the top of the rice with 2 pounds of clams or mussels (or a combination). Replace the lid and continue to cook until the rice is tender and has absorbed all its liquid and the shells have opened, about 5 minutes more. Fluff the rice with a fork. Stir in the peas and shrimp, but omit the pimientos and artichoke hearts. Serves 6.

Calories 473 • Protein 31 gm • Fat 3.9 gm • Percent of calories from fat 8% • Cholesterol 161 mg • Dietary fiber 5 gm • Sodium 498 mg • Calcium 114 mg

Vegetable Pilau

YIELD: 4 TO 6 SERVINGS

A pilau is to Indian cuisine what a pilaf is to Middle Eastern. Pilau are fragrant with aromatic spices, including fenugreek, a spice that can be hard to locate but is worth seeking out for authentic flavor. Try a natural food store or an Asian grocery.

2 cups uncooked basmati rice
2 tablespoons canola or olive oil
1 medium onion, diced
1 tablespoon minced fresh ginger
1 green chile (jalapeño or serrano), minced
4 garlic cloves, minced
1 teaspoon cumin seeds

1 teaspoon fenugreek seeds
1/4 teaspoon ground turmeric
1 teaspoon salt, or more to taste
3 3/4 cups water
1 large carrot, peeled and diced
1 cup frozen peas
1/4 cup chopped fresh cilantro

Wash the rice in several changes of water until the rinse water runs clear. Drain.

In a large saucepan, heat the oil over medium heat. Add the onion, ginger, chile, garlic, cumin, fenugreek, and turmeric, and sauté until the onion is golden and the spices are fragrant, about 8 minutes. Add the rice and continue to sauté until the rice appears dry and toasted, 3 to 5 minutes more. Stir in the salt, water, and carrot. Cover and bring rapidly to a boil, then reduce the heat to low and boil very gently until all of the liquid has been absorbed, 12 to 15 minutes.

Fluff the rice with a fork. Stir in the peas and cilantro. Dry the pot lid. Crumple a clean kitchen cotton or paper towel and place over the rice. Replace the dried lid. Set the rice aside for 5 minutes, then fluff again with a fork and serve hot.

Calories 429 • Protein 9 gm • Fat 9 gm • Percent of calories from fat 19% •
Cholesterol 0 mg • Dietary fiber 8 gm • Sodium 634 mg • Calcium 86 mg

Curried Rice and Broccoli Pilaf

YIELD: 4 TO 6 SERVINGS

Garam masala is an aromatic Indian spice blend used to add warm flavors to a dish. In this dish it blends with fresh ginger, cumin, and coriander to add a sweet fragrance to the rice.

1½ cups uncooked basmati
  or long-grain white rice
2 tablespoons canola or olive oil
1 onion, chopped
2 garlic cloves, minced
2 tablespoons minced fresh ginger
1 teaspoon garam masala

½ teaspoon ground cumin
½ teaspoon ground coriander
Pinch ground turmeric
2¾ cups water
1 large stalk broccoli (about
  ½ pound), florets and peeled,
  chopped stem

Wash the rice in several changes of water until the water runs clear. Drain and set aside.

In a large nonstick skillet, heat the oil over medium heat. Add the onion, garlic, ginger, garam masala, cumin, coriander, and turmeric. Sauté for about 8 minutes, until the onion is golden and the mixture is fragrant. Add the rice and continue to sauté for another 3 to 5 minutes, until the rice appears toasted. Add the water. Cover and bring to a boil. Then reduce the heat to maintain a gentle boil and cook for 12 to 15 minutes, or until the liquid has been absorbed and the rice is tender.

While the rice cooks, steam the broccoli until just tender, about 3 minutes. Plunge into cold water to stop the cooking. Drain well.

When the rice is cooked, fluff with a fork. Stir in the broccoli. Dry the lid. Crumple a clean kitchen cotton or paper towel and place over the rice. Replace the dried lid and let the heat of the rice warm the broccoli for about 5 minutes. Serve warm.

Calories 328 • Protein 7 gm • Fat 9 gm • Percent of calories from fat 24% •
Cholesterol 0 mg • Dietary fiber 6 gm • Sodium 24 mg • Calcium 85 mg

Caribbean Rice Pilaf

YIELD: 4 TO 6 SERVINGS

This orange-yellow pilaf derives its color and floral, musky flavor from the annatto seed (also known as achiote), a spice found in Hispanic and Indian food stores. If you can't find annatto, you can substitute saffron, which is more expensive. It will lend the same yellow coloring and its aroma and flavor is also floral, but annatto has a musky undertone that is quite unique.

2 cups uncooked long-grain
  white rice
2 tablespoons annatto oil
  (see Note)
1 red bell pepper, diced
1 green bell pepper, diced
1 shallot, minced
2 garlic cloves, minced
1 teaspoon salt

3³/₄ cups boiling water
1 cup frozen peas
2 scallions, chopped
2 tablespoons chopped fresh
  cilantro
1 tablespoon capers
Salt, freshly ground black pepper,
  and Tabasco sauce (optional)

Wash the rice in several changes of water until the rinse water runs clear. Drain.

In a large skillet, heat the oil over medium heat. Add the rice, red and green bell peppers, shallot, and garlic. Sauté until the rice appears toasted and dry, 3 to 5 minutes. Add the salt and water, cover, and bring to a boil. Then reduce the heat and boil gently until all of the liquid has been absorbed, 12 to 15 minutes.

Remove from the heat. Fluff the rice with a fork. Stir in the peas, scallions, cilantro, and capers. Dry the pot lid. Crumple a clean kitchen cotton or paper towel and place over the rice. Cover with the dried lid and allow the heat of the rice to cook the peas, about 5 minutes. Taste and add additional salt, pepper, and Tabasco sauce as desired. Serve hot.

Note: To make annatto oil, heat ¹/₂ cup canola oil in a small saucepan over low heat. Add ¹/₄ cup annatto seeds and cook over low heat for about 5 minutes, stirring occasionally, until the oil takes on a rich orange color.

Cool, then strain. You can store the oil in an airtight jar in the refrigerator for several months.

Calories 443 • Protein 9 gm • Fat 8 gm • Percent of calories from fat 16% • Cholesterol 0 mg • Dietary fiber 4 gm • Sodium 708 mg • Calcium 51 mg

VARIATIONS

Caribbean Rice Pilaf with Chicken. Dice 1 pound boneless, skinless chicken breast. Add to the oil and sauté until white and firm throughout, about 5 minutes. Then add the rice, bell peppers, shallot, and garlic and proceed with the recipe as written.

Calories 628 • Protein 44 gm • Fat 12 gm • Percent of calories from fat 17% • Cholesterol 107 mg • Dietary fiber 4 gm • Sodium 791 mg • Calcium 68 mg

Caribbean Rice Pilaf with Sausage. Remove 1 pound turkey or chicken sausage from its casing. Add to the oil and sauté until cooked through, about 5 minutes. Then add the rice, bell peppers, shallot, and garlic and proceed with the recipe as written.

Calories 622 • Protein 31 gm • Fat 20 gm • Percent of calories from fat 28% • Cholesterol 90 mg • Dietary fiber 4 gm • Sodium 1643 mg • Calcium 51 mg

Vermicelli-Rice Pilaf

YIELD: 6 TO 8 SERVINGS

Rice A Roni by any name is still a favorite with children. This famed convenience food began as a classic Middle Eastern pilaf. It can be made into a hearty main dish by stirring in cooked chickpeas after the rice is done. In order to get little bits of pasta, you will have to break up dry vermicelli—a somewhat messy proposition. I advise breaking it up with your hands over a very large bowl.

1½ cups uncooked long-grain
    white rice
2 tablespoons extra-virgin olive oil
1 small onion, finely chopped
2 garlic cloves, minced
8 ounces uncooked vermicelli,
    broken into small
    (1-inch) pieces

4 cups high-quality chicken
    or vegetable broth or water
    (or a combination)
½ teaspoon ground cumin
¼ teaspoon freshly ground black
    pepper
Salt

Wash the rice in several changes of water until the rinse water runs clear. Drain well.

Heat the olive oil in a large skillet or saucepan. Add the onion, garlic, vermicelli, and rice, and sauté until the rice and vermicelli are well toasted, about 5 minutes. Add the broth or water, cumin, pepper, and salt to taste. Cover and bring to a boil. Then reduce the heat and boil gently for 12 to 15 minutes, until the liquid has been absorbed.

Fluff the pilaf with a fork. Dry the pot lid. Crumple a clean kitchen cotton or paper towel and place over the pilaf. Cover with the dried lid and let stand for 5 minutes. Serve hot.

Calories 374 • Protein 11 gm • Fat 5.5 gm • Percent of calories from fat 13% •
Cholesterol 0 mg • Dietary fiber 2 gm • Sodium 306 mg • Calcium 29 mg

Tex-Mex Vermicelli-Rice Pilaf

YIELD: 6 TO 8 SERVINGS

This is close to the Rice A Roni of my childhood. A true comfort food.

2 cups uncooked medium-grain or long-grain rice	4 ounces vermicelli, broken into small pieces (about 1 cup)
2 tablespoons canola or olive oil	1 (15-ounce) can diced tomatoes
1 tablespoon chili powder	About 3^1/$_2$ cups water
1 small onion, finely diced	1 teaspoon salt
1 green bell pepper, finely diced	^{1}/$_2$ teaspoon freshly ground black pepper
2 garlic cloves, minced	

Wash the rice in several changes of water until the rinse water runs clear. Drain.

Heat the oil in a large cast-iron or nonstick skillet. Add the rice, chili powder, onion, green pepper, garlic, and vermicelli, and sauté until the rice appears toasted, about 5 minutes.

Drain the tomatoes, reserving the juice. Combine the juice with enough water to make 4 cups. Add the tomatoes, water, salt, and pepper to the skillet. Stir. Cover, bring to a boil, then reduce the heat and gently boil until all of the liquid has been absorbed, about 15 minutes.

Fluff with a fork. Dry the pot lid. Crumple a clean kitchen cotton or paper towel and place over the rice. Cover with the dried lid and let stand for 5 minutes. Serve hot.

Calories 377 • Protein 8 gm • Fat 6 gm • Percent of calories from fat 14% • Cholesterol 0 mg • Dietary fiber 3 gm • Sodium 557 mg • Calcium 31 mg

Wild Rice—Orzo Pilaf

YIELD: 4 TO 6 SERVINGS

Wild rice alone can have a bitter flavor. But combined with orzo, a rice-shaped pasta, its nutty flavor shines through.

3/4 cup uncooked wild rice, rinsed
2 1/4 cups water
1/2 teaspoon salt
8 ounces uncooked orzo (1 1/4 cups)
1 tablespoon extra-virgin olive oil
1 shallot, diced
2 garlic cloves, minced

1 red bell pepper, diced
2 tablespoons soy sauce
2 tablespoons finely chopped
  fresh parsley
1 teaspoon dried marjoram
Salt and freshly ground black
  pepper

In a small saucepan, combine the wild rice, water, and salt. Cover, bring to a boil, then reduce the heat and simmer until the rice is tender and most of the grains have burst open, 40 to 60 minutes. Drain off any excess water.

Meanwhile, cook the orzo in plenty of boiling salted water until al dente. Drain well.

In a large skillet, heat the oil over medium heat. Add the shallot, garlic, and bell pepper and sauté until the pepper is tender, about 3 minutes. Add the drained wild rice and drained orzo and toss well. Stir in the soy sauce, parsley, marjoram, and salt and pepper to taste. Serve hot.

Calories 353 • Protein 12 gm • Fat 5 gm • Percent of calories from fat 12% •
Cholesterol 0 mg • Dietary fiber 4 gm • Sodium 813 mg • Calcium 21 mg

Brown and Wild Rice Pilaf

YIELD: 4 TO 6 SERVINGS

1 tablespoon olive or canola oil
3 garlic cloves, minced
1 celery stalk, minced
1 carrot, minced
1 large shallot, minced
1/3 cup uncooked wild rice, rinsed
4 cups high-quality chicken
   or vegetable broth

Salt and freshly ground black
   pepper
1½ cups uncooked brown rice
2 tablespoons chopped fresh
   parsley
2 cups fresh or frozen peas

Heat the oil in a small saucepan over medium-high heat. Add the garlic, celery, carrot, shallot, and wild rice, and sauté until the shallot is transparent, about 2 minutes. Stir in 1 cup of the broth and season to taste with salt and pepper. Increase the heat to high and bring to a boil. Reduce the heat to low, cover, and cook until the rice has burst open and is tender, about 40 to 60 minutes.

Meanwhile, combine the brown rice and the remaining 3 cups broth in a large saucepan. Season to taste with salt and pepper, cover, and bring to a boil over high heat. Reduce the heat to low and boil gently for 35 to 40 minutes, until the rice is tender. Remove from the heat and let sit, covered, for 10 minutes. Then fluff with a fork. Fold in the wild rice, parsley, and peas. Season to taste. Let sit for 5 more minutes to heat the peas. Serve hot.

Calories 427 • Protein 15 gm • Fat 5.8 gm • Percent of calories from fat 12% • Cholesterol 0 mg • Dietary fiber 8 gm • Sodium 474 mg • Calcium 60 mg

Mixed Grain Pilaf

YIELD: 6 SIDE-DISH SERVINGS

The trick to cooking long-cooking grains with short-cooking grains is to soak the long-cooking grains overnight.

1/2 cup uncooked brown rice
1/2 cup uncooked Wehani rice
2 tablespoons extra-virgin
  olive oil
2 garlic cloves, minced
1 shallot, minced

3/4 cup long-grain white rice
1/4 cup cracked wheat
33/4 cups water
1 teaspoon salt
1 tablespoon chopped fresh
  parsley

Soak the brown and Wehani rice in plenty of water overnight. Drain well.

In a large saucepan, heat the olive oil over medium heat. Add the garlic and shallot and sauté for 1 minute. Add the drained rices, the white rice, and cracked wheat. Sauté until the white rice appears toasted and dry, about 4 minutes. Add the water and salt. Cover and bring to a boil. Reduce the heat and boil gently until the water has been absorbed and the rice is tender, about 30 minutes. Fluff with a fork. Stir in the parsley. Serve hot.

Calories 263 • Protein 5 gm • Fat 6 gm • Percent of calories from fat 19% • Cholesterol 0 mg • Dietary fiber 3 gm • Sodium 394 mg • Calcium 18 mg

Garlic Rice Timbales

YIELD: 6 SIDE-DISH SERVINGS

You can take any freshly cooked white rice, add flavoring, and mold it in ramekins for a presentation worthy of a special occasion. Spoon some cooked beans around the base and you have a most elegant rice and bean supper. The flavorings for the timbale presented here are simple, but they can be endlessly varied. Add mushrooms to the garlic while sautéing, or finely chop some sun-dried tomatoes or olives and add to the rice. Fresh herbs also make a nice addition.

**2 cups uncooked long-grain
or medium-grain white rice**
3¹/₂ cups water
1 teaspoon salt
**2 tablespoons extra-virgin
olive oil**

1 tablespoon butter
4 garlic cloves, minced
2 scallions, minced

Combine the rice, water, and salt in a saucepan. Cover and bring to a boil. Reduce the heat and boil gently until the rice is tender and the water has been absorbed, 12 to 15 minutes.

Meanwhile, heat the olive oil and butter in a small skillet over medium-low heat. Add the garlic and scallions and simmer gently until the garlic is lightly colored, 5 to 7 minutes.

When the rice is cooked, mix in the garlic and scallions. Spray 6 small custard cups with nonstick cooking spray. Pack with the rice. Cover with aluminum foil and keep warm until you are ready to serve. Then unmold onto serving plates. Or pack 1 custard cup with the hot rice and unmold onto a serving plate. Cover with a kitchen towel to keep warm. Working quickly so the rice won't get cold, repeat this procedure for the remaining servings.

Calories 286 • Protein 5 gm • Fat 7 gm • Percent of calories from fat 22% •
Cholesterol 5 mg • Dietary fiber 1 gm • Sodium 416 mg • Calcium 26 mg

Chirashi Sushi

YIELD: 6 SERVINGS

The flavors of sushi—vegetarian-style—without the fuss of rolling it all up inside a nori wrapper. This is a traditional Japanese dish—vinegared rice mounded in a bowl and topped with vegetables. Chirashi sushi makes a wonderful supper on a hot summer night. It takes far less time to make than the length of the recipe might suggest.

Seasoned Rice

3 cups uncooked short-grain
   white rice
3³/₄ cups water
2 tablespoons mirin
   (sweet rice wine)

¹/₂ cup rice wine vinegar
2 tablespoons sugar
2 teaspoons salt

Vegetables

10 dried shiitake mushrooms
2 tablespoons tamari
2 tablespoons mirin
1 carrot, julienned

1 cup julienned snow peas
1 sheet nori
¹/₄ cup pickled ginger
2 scallions, thinly sliced

Thin Egg Omelets

2 large eggs
1 teaspoon sugar

To make the seasoned rice, combine the rice, water, and mirin in medium saucepan and bring to a boil. Cover and boil gently until the rice is tender and the water has been absorbed, 12 to 15 minutes.

In a small saucepan, combine the vinegar, sugar, and salt, and bring to a boil.

Transfer the rice to a shallow bowl or pan. Gradually pour the hot vinegar mixture over the rice and toss with a spoon or rice paddle held in one hand while fanning the rice with the other hand. (Alternatively, set the rice in front of an electric fan and let the fan cool the rice while you toss.) Continue until the rice is cooled to the touch and appears glossy.

To make the vegetables, soak the dried shiitakes in water to cover until soft, about 30 minutes. Drain. Remove the stems and any hard pieces. Cut into shreds. Combine in a small saucepan or microwave-safe container with the tamari and mirin. Simmer over low heat until the mushrooms absorb most of the liquid, about 1 minute, or heat on high in the microwave for 1 minute. Set aside.

Blanch the carrot and snow peas in boiling water to cover until just tender-crisp, about 1 minute. Drain, plunge into cold water to stop the cooking, and drain again. Set aside.

Pass the nori over an open flame or electric burner to lightly toast it. Crumble it into small pieces. Set aside.

To make the thin egg omelets, beat 1 of the eggs with $1/2$ teaspoon sugar. Heat a nonstick skillet over medium heat. Spray with nonstick cooking spray. Pour the beaten egg into the skillet, tilting the skillet to coat the bottom evenly. Cook for about 30 seconds, or until the egg is set and the edges are dry. Flip the egg over and cook for another 12 seconds, or until the bottom is dry. Transfer to a plate to cool while you make the second omelet. Roll each cooled egg sheet into a tube and cut into $1/4$-inch-wide slices. Set aside.

To serve, spoon the rice into individual serving bowls. Top with the mushrooms, blanched vegetables, pickled ginger, scallions, and omelet slices. Sprinkle the crumbled nori on top. Serve at once.

Calories 482 • Protein 11 gm • Fat 2 gm • Percent of calories from fat 4% •
Cholesterol 71 mg • Dietary fiber 5 gm • Sodium 1163 mg • Calcium 32 mg

Risottos, Rice Pilafs, and More

Festive Yellow Rice

YIELD: 4 SIDE-DISH SERVINGS

Throughout Southeast Asia, the color yellow is sacred, associated with gods, royalty, and festivities. This aromatic rice dish is served on special occasions, mounded in a great yellow cone on large platters. The rice is flavored with lemongrass, ginger, and shallots and tinted yellow with turmeric.

Lemongrass is found wherever Asian foods are sold. It can be stored in the freezer, wrapped tightly in plastic, for up to 4 months. Use only the bottom 4 to 6 inches of the stem and peel away the woody outer leaves before mincing. To save time, you can mince the shallots, ginger, and lemongrass together in a food processor.

1 cup uncooked jasmine
   or basmati rice
1 tablespoon canola oil
2 shallots, minced
2-inch piece fresh ginger,
   peeled and minced
1 stem lemongrass (bottom
   4 inches only), minced

$^1/_2$ teaspoon ground coriander
$^1/_2$ teaspoon ground turmeric
$1^3/_4$ cups plus 2 tablespoons
   water
$^1/_2$ teaspoon salt

Wash the rice in several changes of water until the rinse water runs clear. Drain.

In a medium saucepan, heat the oil over medium-high heat. Add the shallots, ginger, and lemongrass, and sauté until the shallots are limp, about 2 minutes. Stir in the rice, coriander, and turmeric, and sauté until the rice appears dry and toasted, 3 to 5 minutes. Add the water and salt and bring to a boil. Cover, reduce the heat, and boil gently until all of the liquid has been absorbed, 12 to 15 minutes.

Remove from the heat and fluff with a fork. Dry the pot lid. Crumple a clean kitchen cotton or paper towel and place over the rice. Cover with the dried pot lid and let stand for 5 minutes before serving.

Calories 207 • Protein 3 gm • Fat 4 gm • Percent of calories from fat 16% •
Cholesterol 0 mg • Dietary fiber 1 gm • Sodium 294 mg • Calcium 6 mg

Hazelnut–Wild Rice Dressing

❦❦❦

YIELD: 6 TO 12 SERVINGS

This nutty–flavored wild rice dressing makes a delicious alternative to the bread dressing traditionally served with the Thanksgiving feast. It can also be served as a main course.

1½ cups uncooked long-grain
  brown rice
½ cup uncooked wild rice
1 tablespoon extra-virgin olive oil
1 onion, finely chopped
2 celery stalks with leaves,
  finely chopped
1 red bell pepper, finely chopped
4 cups water

1½ teaspoons salt
1 tablespoon fresh thyme
¾ teaspoon poultry seasoning
  or dried sage
1 cup hazelnuts (or substitute
  walnuts, or pecans)
2 tart apples, chopped
1 cup dried currants
Salt and freshly ground black pepper

Rinse the wild rice and brown rice. Drain.

Heat the oil in a large skillet or saucepan. Add the onion, celery, and bell pepper, and sauté for 2 minutes, until limp. Add the rices and sauté for another 4 minutes, until lightly toasted. Add the water, salt, thyme, and poultry seasoning. Cover and bring to a boil. Then reduce the heat and boil gently for about 40 minutes, until all of the liquid has been absorbed.

Preheat the oven to 325 degrees.

Meanwhile, toast the hazelnuts in a dry skillet over medium heat until they darken slightly and smell fragrant, about 5 minutes. Place the nuts in a clean kitchen towel and rub off the skins.

Add the apples, currants, and toasted nuts to the skillet with the rice and mix well. Season to taste with salt and pepper, adding additional thyme if desired.

Spoon into a greased 9×13-inch baking dish, cover, and bake for 30 minutes, uncovering for the last 15 minutes.

Calories 510 • Protein 11 gm • Fat 17 gm • Percent of calories from fat 29% • Cholesterol 0 mg • Dietary fiber 10 gm • Sodium 610 mg • Calcium 87 mg

Spanakorizzo

YIELD: 4 TO 6 SERVINGS

Spinach, rice, feta cheese, and pine nuts make a wonderful combination in this Greek classic.

2 cups uncooked long-grain
   white rice
3³/₄ cups water
1 pound spinach
2 tablespoons extra-virgin
   olive oil
1 small onion, finely chopped
2 garlic cloves, minced

4 ounces feta cheese, crumbled
4 tablespoons pine nuts
2 tablespoons chopped fresh mint
   or 2 teaspoons dried
1 tablespoon chopped fresh
   oregano or 1 teaspoon dried
Salt and freshly ground black
   pepper

Wash the rice in several changes of water until the rinse water runs clear. Drain. Combine the rice with the 3³/₄ cups fresh water in a medium saucepan. Cover and bring to a boil. Reduce the heat to maintain a gentle boil and boil until the rice is tender and all of the water has been absorbed, 12 to 15 minutes.

Wash and stem the spinach. Place in a large pot, with the water still clinging to the leaves, and steam until limp, about 7 minutes. Immediately plunge into ice water to stop the cooking. Drain well. Remove the excess water from the spinach by taking the spinach up in handfuls and squeezing hard. Chop the spinach and set aside.

Preheat the oven to 350 degrees. In a large saucepan, heat the olive oil over medium-high heat. Add the onion and garlic and sauté until the onion is limp, about 3 minutes. Add the spinach and toss well. Remove from the heat, add the feta cheese, pine nuts, mint, oregano, and salt and pepper to taste and mix well. Turn out into a 2-quart casserole dish and cover with foil or the casserole lid. Bake until heated through, 15 to 20 minutes. Serve hot.

Calories 568 • Protein 17 gm • Fat 19 gm • Percent of calories from fat 29% • Cholesterol 25 mg • Dietary fiber 5 gm • Sodium 420 mg • Calcium 309 mg

Baked Rice Mediterranean

YIELD: 4 TO 6 SERVINGS

1¹/₂ cups uncooked long-grain white rice

2³/₄ cups water

1 homemade or store-bought roasted red bell pepper, chopped (page 40)

1 tablespoon chopped sun-dried tomatoes (reconstituted in water if not packed in oil)

2 scallions, chopped

2 garlic cloves, minced

3 ounces feta cheese, crumbled

3 tablespoons chopped black olives

3 tablespoons chopped fresh parsley

Salt and freshly ground black pepper

Preheat the oven to 400 degrees.

In a flameproof casserole, combine the rice and water. Cover and bring to a boil over high heat. Stir in the bell pepper, sun-dried tomatoes, scallions, and garlic. Cover tightly and place in the oven. Bake for about 15 minutes, until the rice is tender and the liquid has been absorbed.

Fluff the rice with a fork. Stir in the feta cheese, olives, parsley, and salt and pepper to taste. Dry the pot lid. Crumple a clean kitchen cotton or paper towel and place over the rice. Cover with the dried lid and let stand for 5 minutes before serving.

Calories 335 • Protein 8 gm • Fat 6 gm • Percent of calories from fat 17% • Cholesterol 19 mg • Dietary fiber 1 gm • Sodium 321 mg • Calcium 139 mg

Chinese Vegetable Fried Rice

YIELD: 4 TO 6 SERVINGS

The secret to making restaurant-style fried rice is to begin with properly cooked rice. The rice should be dry, not mushy. To achieve this, be sure to wash the rice until the rinse water runs clear before cooking.

2 large eggs	1 large carrot, diced
1 tablespoon water	2 garlic cloves, minced
6 teaspoons soy sauce	6 cups cooked white rice
1 tablespoon peanut oil	5 tablespoons oyster sauce
1/4 cup diced onion	2 cups bean sprouts
4 cups very thinly sliced green or Chinese cabbage	1 cup fresh or frozen peas
	3 to 4 scallions, chopped

Beat the eggs with the water and 1 teaspoon of the soy sauce. Heat 1 teaspoon of the peanut oil in a large skillet or wok over high heat. Pour in the eggs, swirling the pan to make a large omelet. When the bottom has set, flip over and cook on the other side. Remove from the wok. Dice into 1/2-inch pieces and set aside.

Add the remaining 2 teaspoons oil to the wok. Add the onion and stir-fry for 1 minute. Then add the cabbage, carrot, garlic, and 1 teaspoon of the soy sauce to the skillet. Stir-fry until the cabbage is limp, about 2 minutes.

Add the rice, oyster sauce, and the remaining 4 teaspoons soy sauce to the wok. Cook over high heat, continuously stirring and tossing, until rice is heated through. Taste and add more oyster sauce or soy sauce if needed. Carefully mix in the bean sprouts, peas, scallions, and egg pieces. Cook, carefully tossing and stirring, until heated through, about 2 minutes. Serve hot.

Calories 527 • Protein 15 gm • Fat 7 gm • Percent of calories from fat 12% • Cholesterol 106 mg • Dietary fiber 6 gm • Sodium 978 mg • Calcium 86 mg

Shrimp Fried Rice. Peel and devein 1 pound medium shrimp. Cook the eggs as directed. Heat the 2 teaspoons oil in the wok or skillet. Add the shrimp and stir-fry until pink and firm throughout, about 3 minutes. Remove from the wok with a slotted spoon and set aside. Proceed with the recipe as written, returning the shrimp to the wok along with the bean sprouts, peas, scallions, and egg pieces.

Calories 639 • Protein 39 gm • Fat 8 gm • Percent of calories from fat 12% •
Cholesterol 328 mg • Dietary fiber 6 gm • Sodium 1231 mg • Calcium 131 mg

Pork Fried Rice. Dice $1/2$ pound pork tenderloin. Cook the egg as directed. Heat the 2 teaspoons oil in the wok or skillet. Add the pork and stir-fry until firm and cooked throughout, about 3 minutes. Add the cabbage, carrot, garlic, and soy sauce, and proceed with the recipe as written.

Calories 620 • Protein 31 gm • Fat 10 gm • Percent of calories from fat 14% •
Cholesterol 151 mg • Dietary fiber 6 gm • Sodium 1009 mg • Calcium 90 mg

Nasi Goreng (Indonesian Fried Rice)

YIELD: 4 TO 6 SERVINGS

What makes nasi goreng *different from Chinese fried rice is the dark sweet soy sauce,* ketjap manis, *with which it is traditionally made. Our own tomato ketchup takes its name, but not its ingredients, from this rich, mellow sauce. Since* ketjap *is so hard to find, I substitute soy sauce sweetened with molasses. If you eat seafood, you might enjoy adding boiled or grilled shrimp to the garnishes. Asian fish sauce is available wherever Thai and Vietnamese foods are sold.*

2 large eggs
1 tablespoon water
1 tablespoon peanut oil
1/4 cup soy sauce
3 tablespoons molasses
5 teaspoons Asian fish sauce
   (*nam bla* or *nuoc cham*)
2 garlic cloves, minced
1 hot pepper, minced
1 onion, finely chopped

4 cups finely chopped Chinese
   cabbage
6 cups cooked white rice
2 cups bean sprouts
4 scallions, chopped
1 tomato, cut in wedges
1/2 cup dry-roasted peanuts
2 tablespoons chopped fresh
   cilantro

Beat the eggs with the water. Heat 1 teaspoon of the oil in a wok or large nonstick skillet over high heat. Pour in the eggs, swirling the pan to make a large omelet. When the bottom has set, flip and cook on the other side. Remove from the wok, roll into a tube, and cut into strips. Set aside.

Combine the soy sauce, molasses, and fish sauce. Set aside.

In the same wok or skillet, heat the remaining 2 teaspoons oil. Add the garlic, hot pepper, and onion. Stir-fry for about 1 minute. Add the cabbage and stir-fry for 2 to 3 minutes, until limp. Add the rice, bean sprouts, and scallions. Pour in the sweetenend soy sauce mixture and carefully toss until well mixed and heated through. Spoon out onto a large serving platter or individual serving plates.

Garnish with the egg strips, tomato wedges, peanuts, and cilantro. Serve hot.

Calories 597 • Protein 19 gm • Fat 16 gm • Percent of calories from fat 24% • Cholesterol 108 mg • Dietary fiber 6 gm • Sodium 1516 mg • Calcium 140 mg

VARIATION

Nasi Goreng with Shrimp. Peel and devein 1 pound medium shrimp. Add to the wok along with the garlic, hot pepper, and onion. Stir-fry until pink and firm throughout, about 3 minutes. Remove from the wok with a slotted spoon. Proceed with the recipe as written. Use the cooked shrimp as a garnish, along with the egg strips, tomato wedges, peanuts, and cilantro.

Calories 709 • Protein 42 gm • Fat 17 gm • Percent of calories from fat 22% • Cholesterol 330 mg • Dietary fiber 6 gm • Sodium 1770 mg • Calcium 184 mg

Sesame Stir-fried Broccoli and Brown Rice

YIELD: 4 TO 6 SERVINGS

This was satisfying when it was a house standard in my first apartment and it is satisfying today. Along the way there has been a little refinement—draining the tofu and steaming the broccoli to improve texture, and adding a little chili paste with garlic for those who insist on a little spice with every meal.

1 pound firm tofu
1½ cups uncooked brown rice
3⅓ cups water
3 large stalks broccoli, florets and
    peeled, chopped stems
2 tablespoons sesame oil
4 garlic cloves, minced

1 small onion, cut in slivers
3 tablespoon soy sauce or tamari
2 teaspoons chili paste with garlic
    (optional)
2 tablespoons toasted sesame
    seeds

Wrap the tofu in a clean kitchen towel or paper towels. Place on a plate or cutting board and weight down with another board or heavy plate topped with a weight (such as a filled juice can). This will force out excess moisture from the tofu. Leave to drain for 30 minutes. Cut into ½-inch cubes.

Meanwhile, combine the rice with the water in a medium saucepan. Cover and bring to a boil. Then reduce the heat and cook at a gentle boil until the rice is tender, 35 to 40 minutes. Drain off any excess water, if necessary.

Steam the broccoli until just barely tender, about 3 minutes. Plunge into cold water to stop the cooking. Drain.

In a large wok or skillet, heat the oil. Add the garlic and onion and sauté until the onion is limp, about 3 minutes. Add the broccoli and stir-fry for 2 minutes. Add the cooked rice, tofu, soy sauce, and chili paste (if using) and stir-fry until the tofu is heated through and the mixture is well combined, about 3 minutes. Serve at once, topping each serving with a sprinkling of sesame seeds.

Calories 450 • Protein 17 gm • Fat 14 gm • Percent of calories from fat 28% •
Cholesterol 0 mg • Dietary fiber 2 gm • Sodium 834 mg • Calcium 125 mg

Zucchini–Brown Rice Squares

YIELD: 9 SQUARES

Leftover brown rice and zucchini from the garden find a wonderful marriage in this baked dish. Serve the squares as an appetizer or as a side dish. This recipe can be doubled and baked in a 9×13-inch baking dish.

3 cups grated zucchini
   (about $3/4$ pound)
1 teaspoon salt
1 tablespoon extra-virgin
   olive oil
1 shallot, minced
2 garlic cloves, minced
$1^1/2$ cups cooked brown rice

$1/2$ red bell pepper, diced
2 large eggs, slightly beaten
$1/2$ cup skim milk
1 teaspoon dried oregano
Freshly ground black pepper
1 tablespoon dried bread crumbs
1 tablespoon freshly grated
   Parmesan cheese

Toss the zucchini with the salt. Place in a colander and weight down (I use a plate on which I place a heavy juice can). Set aside to drain for about 20 minutes.

Preheat the oven to 350 degrees. Spray an 8-inch baking dish with non-stick spray.

In a large skillet, heat the olive oil over medium heat. Add the shallot, garlic, and drained zucchini. Sauté for about 5 minutes, until the zucchini is limp.

Meanwhile, combine the rice, bell pepper, eggs, and milk in a mixing bowl. Remove the zucchini from the skillet with a slotted spoon and add to the mixing bowl. Stir in the oregano and pepper to taste. Spoon into the baking dish. Sprinkle the bread crumbs, then the Parmesan cheese on top. Bake until golden and firm, about 35 minutes. Let stand for 10 minutes before serving.

Calories 84 • Protein 3 gm • Fat 3 gm • Percent of calories from fat 33% •
Cholesterol 48 mg • Dietary fiber 1 gm • Sodium 314 mg • Calcium 44 mg

Rice-stuffed Cabbage in Sweet and Sour Sauce

YIELD: 4 TO 8 SERVINGS

You'll want to serve this with plenty of bread for sopping up the extra tomato sauce. A good rye bread is delicious with this rustic dish.

Sweet and Sour Sauce

1 tablespoon extra-virgin
   olive oil
1 small onion, diced
4 garlic cloves, minced
1 teaspoon grated fresh ginger
1 (28-ounce) can tomato sauce

1 tablespoon honey
1 tablespoon freshly squeezed
   lemon juice
Salt and freshly ground black
   pepper

Cabbage Rolls

8 large Savoy or green cabbage
   leaves
1 tablespoon extra-virgin olive oil
4 garlic cloves, minced
1 green bell pepper, finely diced

¹/₂ cup chopped scallions
2 cups cooked white or brown rice
1 teaspoon caraway seeds, or to taste
Salt and freshly ground black
   pepper

To make the sauce, heat the oil in a medium saucepan. Add the onion and garlic and sauté until the onion is limp, about 3 minutes. Add the ginger, tomato sauce, honey, lemon juice, and salt and pepper to taste, and simmer while you prepare the cabbage and filling.

Blanch the cabbage leaves in boiling water for 3 minutes, then plunge into cold water to stop the cooking. Drain well.

To prepare the filling, heat the oil in a large skillet. Add the garlic, bell pepper, and scallions, and sauté until limp, about 3 minutes. Add the rice and sauté for another minute. Season to taste with the caraway seeds and salt and pepper.

Preheat the oven to 350 degrees. Spray a large baking dish with non-stick cooking spray. Spoon about 1 cup of sauce into the baking dish.

To stuff the cabbage, place about 3 tablespoons of the filling near the base of each cabbage leaf. Fold in the sides, then roll up to enclose the filling. Do not roll too tightly or the cabbage roll will burst while cooking. Place the rolls, seam side down, in the baking dish. Pour the remaining sauce over the rolls. Cover and bake until heated through, about 30 minutes. Serve hot.

Calories 304 • Protein 7 gm • Fat 8 gm • Percent of calories from fat 21% •
Cholesterol 0 mg • Dietary fiber 6 gm • Sodium 728 mg • Calcium 88 mg

6
Beans, Beans, Beans

❧

Braised Fresh Shell Beans

Fresh Fava Bean and New Potato Sauté

Fresh Lima Beans with Lemon and Dill

Sautéed Fresh Lima Beans with Thyme

Mediterranean Fresh Lima Beans with Tomatoes and Dill

Braised Fresh Lima Beans with Summer Vegetables

Succotash

10-minute Black Beans

Mexican Black Beans

Cuban Black Beans

Refried Black Beans

Huevos Rancheros

Smoky Black Bean Burritos

Breakfast Black Bean and Egg Burritos

Black Bean–Potato Cakes

Black Bean–Sweet Potato Cakes

Quick Middle Eastern Chickpeas

Sautéed Broccoli and Cauliflower with Chickpeas

Curried Cauliflower and Chickpeas with Tomato

Curried Spinach with Chickpeas

Falafel

Old Bay Cranberry Beans

Almost Mom's Quick Chili

Honey-Mustard Quick Baked Beans

Kidney Bean and Sweet Potato Stew

Vegetarian Chili for a Crowd

French Green Lentils with Roasted Onions

Syrian Lentils in a Spicy Tomato Sauce

Red Lentil Vegetable Stew

Dried Lima Bean Gratin

Tomato-baked Lima Beans

French Country White Beans

Lebanese Navy Beans with Tomatoes and Onions

Old-fashioned Baked Beans

Honey-Mustard Baked Beans

Maple Baked Beans

Mexican Vegetable Sauté with Pink Beans

Cowboy Frijoles

Spicy Slow-baked Barbecued Beans

15-minute Barbecued Beans

Barbecued Bean Sandwiches with Slaw

Refried Pinto Beans

Pinto Chili–Cheese Burritos

Grilled Veggie Burritos

Quick Cannellini and Broccoli Ragout

Kale with White Beans and Garlic

White Bean Chili Verde

Roasted Garlic–White Bean Chili

Recently an unfamiliar bean appeared in local food stores. The pods were huge, 10 to 12 inches long, and light green in color. The sign at the supermarket simply read "fresh shell beans," but the sign at the co-op was more specific: fresh fava beans.

Finally! The bean I had been reading about had reached Vermont. Greedily, I took home a few pounds—and good thing I did, as a few pounds in the shell yielded only about 2 cups cooked beans. Many recipe tests later, I concluded that fava beans are superior lima beans—more work to prepare, more costly to buy, more flavorful—but, still, not too much different than a good fresh lima.

Fresh shell beans are all too uncommon in American markets—perhaps because of the time it takes to shell them (a good job for the kids) or because we have all had unpleasant experiences with overcooked limas. Look for them at farm stands, farmer's markets, and specialty produce stores. Eating fresh shell beans is a flavor revelation!

I like to steam fresh shell beans and then combine them with summer vegetables in a quickly cooked sauté. (They are also great in combination with pasta; see Chapter 7.) This chapter begins with the fresh shell bean recipes.

Fall and winter are the seasons for dried beans, which require slow cooking, unless you are using canned beans. In some of the recipes in this chapter, dried beans are cooked with seasonings, which adds lots of extra flavor to the finished dish. However, many recipes start with 1½ cups cooked beans, the amount found in a 15-ounce can, so you have a choice between starting from scratch or using a convenient can. Remember, if you do use canned beans, rinse and drain them before incorporating into the recipe.

Braised Fresh Shell Beans

YIELD: 4 SIDE-DISH SERVINGS

With fresh-picked vegetables you can't go wrong with simple preparations. This basic recipe will work with any fresh shell bean—lima, cranberry, fava, whatever. Remember that large fava beans may need to be skinned after blanching.

2 pounds fresh shell beans in
   pod, shelled (about 2½ cups)
2 tablespoons extra-virgin
   olive oil
2 shallots, minced
¼ cup water or broth

Salt and freshly ground black
   pepper
2 tablespoons chopped fresh herbs
   (thyme, oregano, basil, rosemary,
   marjoram, parsley, etc. or any
   combination) (optional)

In a saucepan, cover the beans with lightly salted water. Cover the pan and bring to a boil. Then reduce the heat and boil gently until the beans are barely tender, 5 minutes for tiny beans, 10 minutes for medium-size beans, and up to 18 minutes for large beans. Cranberry beans will take close to 30 minutes. Drain.

Heat the oil in a saucepan over medium heat. Add the shallots and sauté until limp, about 2 minutes. Add the beans and water or broth and simmer, covered, until the beans are completely tender, about 5 minutes. Season with salt and pepper and sprinkle with herbs (if using). Serve hot.

Calories 352 • Protein 16 gm • Fat 14 gm • Percent of calories from fat 36% • Cholesterol 0 mg • Dietary fiber 11 gm • Sodium 52 mg • Calcium 78 mg

Fresh Fava Bean and New Potato Sauté

❧

YIELD: 4 SERVINGS

"What a nice bed for the beans!" my son exclaimed when he felt the fuzzy insides of the fava bean pods. They are nice beds—but they represent a lot of waste: 2 pounds fresh beans in pod yield about 1½ cups cooked, peeled beans. If you can't find fresh fava beans, substitute 1½ cups of another cooked fresh shell bean.

2 pounds fresh fava beans in
    pods, shelled (about 2½ cups)
1 pound new potatoes
2 tablespoons extra-virgin
    olive oil
1 small onion, finely chopped

4 garlic cloves
3 tablespoons chopped fresh
    parsley
1 tablespoon capers
2 tablespoons freshly squeezed
    lemon juice

In a saucepan, cover the shelled beans with lightly salted water. Cover the pan and boil for 5 minutes. Drain into a colander and run under cold water. Use a sharp knife to slice open the outer skin of the beans and pop or squeeze the beans out of their skins. You will have about 1½ cups cooked beans. Set aside.

Cut the potatoes into quarters or eighths or leave whole, depending on their size; do not peel. Combine with water to cover in a medium saucepan. Bring to a boil and boil for 5 to 8 minutes, until tender when pierced with a fork. Drain and set aside.

Heat the oil in a medium saucepan over medium-high heat. Add the onion and garlic and sauté until the onion is limp, about 3 minutes. Add the beans, potatoes, parsley, capers, and lemon juice. Toss until the beans and potatoes are hot and cooked through, about 3 minutes. Season with salt and pepper to taste. Serve at once.

Calories 322 • Protein 11 gm • Fat 7 gm • Percent of calories from fat 20% •
Cholesterol 0 mg • Dietary fiber 9 gm • Sodium 117 mg • Calcium 68 mg

Fresh Lima Beans with Lemon and Dill

YIELD: 4 SIDE-DISH SERVINGS

The simple Greek-inspired flavoring of lemon, dill, and mint works with a variety of fresh shell beans; so feel free to substitute another type of bean. You can even substitute frozen lima beans, if you must.

2 pounds fresh lima beans in
   pods, shelled (about 2½ cups)
1 tablespoon extra-virgin
   olive oil
1 medium onion, diced
2 tablespoons chopped fresh dill

1 tablespoon minced fresh mint
   leaves
3 to 4 tablespoons freshly squeezed
   lemon juice
Salt and freshly ground black
   pepper

In a saucepan, cover the beans with lightly salted water. Cover the pan and bring to a boil. Boil until completely tender, 5 to 18 minutes, depending on the size of the beans. Drain and set aside.

In a large skillet, heat the oil. Add the onion and sauté until limp, about 3 minutes. Add the beans, dill, mint, 3 tablespoons of the lemon juice, and salt and pepper to taste. Remove from the heat and let stand for about 15 minutes, until the flavors have a chance to blend. Taste and adjust seasonings, adding more lemon juice, salt, and pepper as needed.

Calories 192 • Protein 10 gm • Fat 4 gm • Percent of calories from fat 17% •
Cholesterol 0 mg • Dietary fiber 10 gm • Sodium 5 mg • Calcium 48 mg

Sautéed Fresh Lima Beans with Thyme

❧❧❧

YIELD: 4 SIDE-DISH SERVINGS

This is the dish that changed my whole attitude toward lima beans—fresh, nutty-tasting beans sautéed in aromatic olive oil and flavored with thyme, with a touch of balsamic vinegar to bring out their natural sweetness. The result is utterly simple and absolutely heavenly. With a complement of rice, this dish could serve as a main course for two bean lovers.

2 pounds fresh lima beans in
    pods, shelled (about 2½ cups)
2 teaspoons extra-virgin olive oil
1 shallot, minced

2 teaspoons chopped fresh thyme
1 teaspoon balsamic vinegar
Salt and freshly ground black
    pepper

In a saucepan, cover the beans with lightly salted water. Cover the pan and bring to a boil. Boil until the beans are completely tender, 5 to 18 minutes, depending on the size of the beans. Drain, reserving the cooking liquid.

Heat the olive oil in a large skillet. Add the shallot and sauté until limp, about 2 minutes. Add the drained beans and thyme and toss to coat with the oil. Then add ½ cup of the reserved cooking liquid and the balsamic vinegar. Bring to a boil. Remove from the heat and season to taste with salt and pepper. Serve hot.

Calories 155 • Protein 9 gm • Fat 2 gm • Percent of calories from fat 9% •
Cholesterol 0 mg • Dietary fiber 9 gm • Sodium 4 mg • Calcium 36 mg

Mediterranean Fresh Lima Beans with Tomatoes and Dill

YIELD: 4 TO 6 SERVINGS

Fresh lima beans baked in a tomato-dill sauce and topped with feta cheese makes a delicious feast. Serve it with crusty French bread for mopping up the extra sauce. You can substitute frozen limas if you must.

2 pounds fresh lima beans in
   pods, shelled (about 2¹/₂ cups)
1¹/₂ tablespoons extra-virgin
   olive oil
1 onion, finely chopped
3 garlic cloves, minced
3 cups chopped fresh tomatoes
   or drained canned tomatoes

2 tablespoons chopped fresh dill
Salt and freshly ground black
   pepper
¹/₄ cup fine bread crumbs
¹/₄ cup crumbled feta cheese

In a saucepan, cover the shelled beans with lightly salted water. Cover the pan and bring to a boil. Boil until tender, 5 to 18 minutes, depending on the size of the beans. Drain and set aside. Preheat the oven to 350 degrees.

In a medium saucepan, heat the oil over medium-low heat. Add the onion and garlic and sauté until the onion is golden, about 10 minutes. Add the tomatoes, dill, and salt and pepper, and simmer for 5 minutes. Taste and adjust the seasonings, adding salt and pepper as needed.

Combine the beans and sauce in a 1¹/₂-quart baking dish. Sprinkle the bread crumbs, then the cheese, on top. Bake for about 30 minutes, until the topping is golden and the beans are tender. Serve hot.

Calories 295 • Protein 14 gm • Fat 10 gm • Percent of calories from fat 28% • Cholesterol 14 mg • Dietary fiber 11 gm • Sodium 326 mg • Calcium 142 mg

Braised Fresh Lima Beans
with Summer Vegetables

❧❧❧

YIELD: 4 SERVINGS

This delicious feast of summer vegetables makes a wonderful topping for rice, pasta, or couscous. You can substitute frozen lima beans if you can't find fresh.

1³/₄ pounds fresh lima beans
   in pods, shelled (about
   2 cups)
2 tablespoons extra-virgin
   olive oil
4 garlic cloves, minced
1 shallot, minced
1 red or orange bell pepper,
   cut into 1-inch squares
1 cup green beans cut into 1-inch
   pieces

2 tablespoons chopped fresh basil
³/₄ cup high-quality chicken
   or vegetable broth
Salt and freshly ground black
   pepper
1 small yellow summer squash,
   quartered and sliced ¹/₂ inch thick
1 small zucchini, quartered
   and sliced ¹/₂ inch thick
2 tablespoons capers
Juice of 1 lemon

If using fresh lima beans, blanch in lightly salted boiling water to cover in a covered saucepan until just tender, 5 to 18 minutes, depending on the size of the bean. Drain well.

Heat the olive oil in a large skillet over medium-high heat. Add the garlic, shallot, and red pepper and sauté for 2 minutes. Add the lima beans and green beans and sauté for 3 minutes. Add the basil, broth, and salt and pepper; cover and simmer until the green beans are tender, about 8 minutes. Add the summer squash, zucchini, capers, and lemon juice, and cook until the squash pieces are tender, about 5 minutes more. Taste and adjust seasonings. Serve at once.

Calories 211 • Protein 9 gm • Fat 7.3 gm • Percent of calories from fat 30% •
Cholesterol 0 mg • Dietary fiber 9 gm • Sodium 248 mg • Calcium 60 mg

Succotash

YIELD: 4 TO 6 SERVINGS

This classic combination of summer vegetables is best made with fresh, not frozen, corn and limas, and fresh, not canned, tomatoes.

4 large ears corn
1 tablespoon extra-virgin olive oil
1 onion, diced
1 fresh hot green pepper, diced
   (optional)
1 red bell pepper, diced
1 green bell pepper, diced
1 large vine-ripened tomato, diced
2 cups fresh lima beans, shelled
   (1³/₄ pounds limas in shell)
2 tablespoons chopped fresh basil
   (or 1 teaspoon dried)

2 teaspoons fresh thyme
   (or ¹/₂ teaspoon dried)
¹/₄ teaspoon freshly ground black
   pepper
¹/₈ teaspoon white pepper
Salt
2 tablespoons water
2 tablespoons chopped fresh
   parsley
2 scallions, including some green
   tops, chopped

Cu the corn kernels from the cobs. Using a dull knife, scrape the cob to extract as much "milk" as possible. You should have about 3 cups corn plus milk. Set aside.

In a large nonstick or cast-iron skillet, heat the olive oil over medium-high heat. Add the onion and hot pepper (if using) and bell peppers, and sauté until limp, about 3 minutes.

Add the corn, tomato, lima beans, basil, and thyme. Add the black and white pepper and salt to taste. Add the water, cover, and cook gently until the beans are tender, 15 to 20 minutes.

Stir in the parsley and scallions and serve hot.

Calories 262 • Protein 11 gm • Fat 5 gm • Percent of calories from fat 16% •
Cholesterol 0 mg • Dietary fiber 11 gm • Sodium 23 mg • Calcium 53 mg

Succotash with Smoked Turkey. The smoky flavor of the turkey greatly enhances this summertime classic. Just add ³/₄ pound smoked turkey, diced, along with the corn, tomato, and lima beans.

Calories 337 • Protein 26 gm • Fat 5 gm • Percent of calories from fat 13% • Cholesterol 0 mg • Dietary fiber 11 gm • Sodium 1085 mg • Calcium 59 mg

10-minute Black Beans

YIELD: 4 TO 6 SERVINGS

I make these beans in about 10 minutes, starting with canned beans or dried beans that I cooked earlier in the week. They make a delicious topping for rice and can also be used as a filling for tacos or burritos.

1 tablespoon extra-virgin olive oil
1 onion, finely chopped
1 green bell pepper,
   finely chopped
2 garlic cloves, finely chopped

2 tablespoons ground cumin
3 cups cooked black beans
1 cup homemade or
   store-bought salsa
Salt

In a medium saucepan, heat the olive oil. Add the onion, bell pepper, garlic, and cumin, and sauté until the onion is tender, 3 to 5 minutes. Add the beans and salsa and heat through. Season with salt to taste. Serve hot.

Calories 253 • Protein 13 gm • Fat 5 gm • Percent of calories from fat 17% • Cholesterol 0 mg • Dietary fiber 14 gm • Sodium 16 mg • Calcium 81 mg

Mexican Black Beans

❧

YIELD: 6 SERVINGS

Whenever I meet people who say they'd like to eat more vegetarian foods but don't like beans that much, I want to give them this recipe. These beans are rich, smoky, delicious, and versatile. They make a delicious filling for tacos or burritos and are wonderful as a topping for rice.

2 cups dried black beans,
  soaked overnight or using the
  quick-soak method on page 20
6 cups water
1 large onion, diced
2 chipotle chiles
1 dried ancho chile
1 green bell pepper, diced
1 to 2 green chiles, diced (optional)

2 garlic cloves, minced
1 teaspoon ground cumin
1 cup tomato puree
Salt and freshly ground black
  pepper
¼ cup chopped fresh cilantro
  (optional)

Drain the beans. Combine in a large pot with the water, onion, and chipotle and ancho chiles. Bring to a boil, then reduce the heat and simmer, partially covered, until just tender, about 1 hour. Add the bell pepper, green chiles, garlic, cumin, tomato puree, and salt and pepper to taste. Simmer over low heat for about 30 minutes. Discard the dried chiles for a milder flavor, or chop the chiles and return to the pot for a hotter flavor. Taste and adjust the seasonings. Stir in the cilantro (if using).

Calories 256 • Protein 16 gm • Fat 1 gm • Percent of calories from fat 4% •
Cholesterol 0 mg • Dietary fiber 12 gm • Sodium 45 mg • Calcium 103 mg

Cuban Black Beans

YIELD: 4 TO 6 SERVINGS

These are the great-tasting beans that are served as a side dish in Hispanic restaurants. Serve them with good French bread or rice to sop up the cooking liquid.

2 cups dried black beans, soaked overnight or using the quick-soak method on page 20

6 cups water

2 bay leaves

2 tablespoons extra-virgin olive oil

1 onion, diced

2 red bell peppers, diced

1/4 cup dry sherry or red wine

1 teaspoon sugar

1 teaspoon dried oregano

Salt and freshly ground black pepper

Drain the beans. In a large saucepan, combine the beans, 6 cups fresh water, and the bay leaves. Cover and bring to a boil, then reduce the heat and simmer, partially covered, until the beans are tender but not mushy, about 1 hour. Discard the bay leaves.

In another saucepan, heat the olive oil over medium-high heat. Add the onion and red bell peppers and sauté until the onion is limp, about 3 minutes. Add the beans and their cooking liquid, the sherry, sugar, oregano, and salt and pepper to taste. Simmer until the liquid is reduced to a creamy consistency and the beans are completely tender, about 30 minutes. Serve hot.

Calories 441 • Protein 22 gm • Fat 8 gm • Percent of calories from fat 17% • Cholesterol 0 mg • Dietary fiber 16 gm • Sodium 18 mg • Calcium 146 mg

Refried Black Beans

❧

YIELD: 4 TO 6 SERVINGS (ABOUT 2²/₃ CUPS)

Refried beans can be served alone as a side dish or in burritos, enchiladas, or chilaquiles. They can also be used as a filling for chiles rellenos.

1 teaspoon canola or olive oil	1¹/₂ cups diced fresh or canned
1 teaspoon ground cumin	tomatoes
2 garlic cloves, minced	Salt and freshly ground black
3 cups cooked black beans	pepper

Heat the oil in a medium skillet or saucepan. Add the cumin and garlic and sauté for about 2 minutes, until the oil smells fragrant. Add the beans and tomatoes and cook until heated through. Using a potato masher, mash the beans. Then stir with a wooden spoon to make a fairly smooth mixture. Season to taste with salt and pepper and serve hot.

Calories 199 • Protein 12 gm • Fat 2 gm • Percent of calories from fat 9% • Cholesterol 0 mg • Dietary fiber 12 gm • Sodium 9 mg • Calcium 46 mg

Huevos Rancheros

YIELD: 4 SERVINGS

When I lived in Colorado, most Sunday mornings began with huevos rancheros, accompanied by steaming platters of home fries and constantly refilled mugs of dark brewed coffee. It wasn't the bagels and lox I had been raised on, but it sure was a great way to get ready for a day outdoors.

6 large potatoes, peeled and
    sliced 1/4 inch thick
1 onion, thinly sliced
2 garlic cloves, minced
2 tablespoons extra-virgin
    olive oil
Salt and freshly ground black
    pepper
2 cups Refried Black Beans
    (page 203) or Refried Pinto
    Beans (page 237) or canned
    refried beans

8 large eggs
2 tablespoons water
2 roasted jalapeños, finely chopped
4 large flour tortillas
1 1/3 cups grated low-fat Cheddar
    cheese
1/2 cup homemade or
    store-bought salsa
Chopped scallions, for garnish
    (optional)

Preheat the oven to 450 degrees. Spray a large baking dish with nonstick cooking spray. Combine the potatoes, onion, and garlic in the baking dish. Drizzle with the oil and sprinkle with salt and pepper. Toss to coat. Roast in the oven until the potatoes are golden, tossing occasionally, about 30 minutes. During the last 15 minutes of roasting, place the beans in a covered dish in the oven and heat through. Turn off the heat, let the oven cool slightly, and place 4 large dinner plates in the oven to preheat.

Meanwhile, beat the eggs with the water. Stir in the jalapeños and salt to taste. Spray a large skillet with nonstick cooking spray. Heat over medium heat. Add the eggs and cook, stirring constantly, until the eggs are set, about 2 minutes.

To assemble the tortillas, briefly heat both sides of a tortilla over a gas burner or in a dry skillet over medium-high heat until softened. Place on a preheated plate. Sprinkle $1/3$ cup of the cheese on the tortilla, spread $1/4$ of the beans on top. Cover with $1/4$ of the eggs, then top with a saddle of salsa. Arrange a ring of potatoes around the outer edges of the tortilla. Garnish with a sprinkling of scallions, if desired. Return the plate to the oven and repeat with the remaining plates and ingredients. Serve when all the plates have been assembled.

Calories 756 • Protein 43 gm • Fat 25 gm • Percent of calories from fat 29% • Cholesterol 437 mg • Dietary fiber 15 gm • Sodium 757 mg • Calcium 524 mg

Smoky Black Bean Burritos

YIELD: 4 TO 8 SERVINGS

A spoonful of chipotle en adobo gives the black beans a special smoky flavor.

2²/₃ cups Refried Black Beans
    (page 203)
1 tablespoon chipotle en adobo,
    or more to taste

8 (10-inch) flour tortillas
6 ounces reduced-fat Monterey
    Jack cheese, shredded
¹/₄ cup chopped fresh cilantro

Preheat the oven to 350 degrees. Combine the refried beans with the chipotle en adobo. Taste and adjust seasonings.

Heat 1 flour tortilla directly over a gas burner or in a dry skillet over medium-high heat, turning to warm both sides. Sprinkle about ¹/₄ cup of the cheese in a line across the center of the tortilla. Spread about ¹/₃ cup of the beans on the cheese. Sprinkle with 1 to 2 teaspoons of the cilantro. Fold in the sides and roll up the tortilla to enclose the filling. Place on a baking sheet. Repeat with the remaining tortillas.

Cover with aluminum foil and heat in the oven for about 20 minutes. The burritos can be made up to a day in advance and held in the refrigerator until you are ready to heat them. Add a few extra minutes of heating time if the burritos are cold when placed in the oven.

Calories 554 • Protein 32 gm • Fat 15 gm • Percent of calories from fat 24% • Cholesterol 30 mg • Dietary fiber 15 gm • Sodium 763 mg • Calcium 518 mg

VARIATION

Smoky Pinto Bean Burritos. Replace the Refried Black Beans with Refried Pinto Beans (page 237). Proceed with recipe as written.

Calories 537 • Protein 33 gm • Fat 11.6 gm • Percent of calories from fat 19% • Cholesterol 15 mg • Dietary fiber 15 gm • Sodium 549 mg • Calcium 588 mg

Breakfast Black Bean and Egg Burritos

❧❧❧

YIELD: 4 SERVINGS

These hearty burritos are quick to prepare and make a delicious start—or end—to a day dedicated to heavy work or strenuous exercise. Home fries and sliced fresh vegetables make excellent accompaniments.

1¹/₂ cups cooked black beans
¹/₂ cup homemade or store-bought salsa
¹/₄ cup chopped scallions
¹/₄ cup chopped fresh cilantro
5 whole large eggs
2 egg whites
1 tablespoon skim milk

¹/₄ cup chopped green chile peppers, fresh or canned (optional)
Salt and freshly ground black pepper
1 tablespoon butter
4 (10-inch) flour tortillas
¹/₂ cup shredded reduced-fat Cheddar cheese

Preheat the oven to 250 degrees. Place 4 dinner plates in the oven to keep warm.

In a saucepan, combine the beans, salsa, scallions, and cilantro and heat gently. Alternatively, heat them in a microwave.

In a bowl, beat together the eggs, egg whites, milk, chiles (if using), and salt and pepper to taste. Melt the butter in a frying pan over medium heat. Add the eggs and cook, stirring continuously, until the eggs are set.

Heat the tortillas on both sides, one a time, in a dry skillet over medium-high heat or directly over a gas flame. As each tortilla becomes warm and pliable, spoon ¹/₄ of the eggs in a strip down the center. Ladle ¹/₄ of the bean mixture over the eggs, then about 2 tablespoons of the cheese. Fold in the sides of the tortilla over the filling, then fold up the bottom and roll up. Place on a plate and return the plate to the oven to keep warm while you repeat with the remaining ingredients. Serve when all the plates have been assembled.

Calories 370 • Protein 25 gm • Fat 14 gm • Percent of calories from fat 33% •
Cholesterol 278 mg • Dietary fiber 8 gm • Sodium 590 mg • Calcium 263 mg

Black Bean—Potato Cakes

YIELD: 4 TO 8 SERVINGS

A great way to use up leftover mashed potatoes.

2 cups mashed potatoes
1¹/₂ cups cooked black beans
¹/₂ red bell pepper, finely chopped
¹/₄ cup chopped chives
1 tablespoon chopped fresh
   cilantro
2 large eggs, lightly beaten

Salt and freshly ground black
   pepper
1 cup fresh bread crumbs
1 to 2 tablespoons olive or
   canola oil
Homemade or store-bought salsa
   (optional)

Preheat the oven to 250 degrees.

Combine the potatoes, beans, bell pepper, chives, and cilantro in a mixing bowl. Mix well to combine. Add the eggs and salt and pepper to taste and mix well. Form into about eight 4-inch pancakes. Place the bread crumbs in a shallow bowl and dip the pancakes into the crumbs, patting to make the crumbs adhere to the cakes.

Heat 1 tablespoon of the oil in a large nonstick or cast-iron griddle or skillet over medium heat. Add just enough cakes to fit in a single layer. Brown the cakes on one side, then flip and brown the second side. Keep warm in the oven while cooking the rest of the pancakes. Serve hot, passing salsa on the side, if desired.

Calories 270 • Protein 12 gm • Fat 7 gm • Percent of calories from fat 24% •
Cholesterol 108 mg • Dietary fiber 8 gm • Sodium 416 mg • Calcium 79 mg

Black Bean–Sweet Potato Cakes

YIELD: 4 TO 8 SERVINGS

3 medium sweet potatoes,
   peeled and grated
1¹/₂ cups cooked black beans
¹/₄ cup snipped chives or
   chopped scallions
1 tablespoon chopped fresh
   cilantro

2 large eggs, lightly beaten
Salt and freshly ground black
   pepper
1 to 2 tablespoons canola oil

Preheat the oven to 250 degrees.

Combine the potatoes, beans, chives, and cilantro in a large mixing bowl. Mix well to combine. Add the eggs and salt and pepper to taste, and mix well.

Heat 1 tablespoon of the canola oil in a large nonstick or cast-iron griddle or skillet over medium heat. Drop the batter on the griddle by the spoonful to make pancakes about 3 inches in diameter. Brown the pancakes on one side, then flip and brown the second side. Keep warm in the oven while cooking the rest of the pancakes. You should have between 16 and 20 pancakes. Serve hot.

Calories 242 • Protein 10 gm • Fat 7 gm • Percent of calories from fat 24% •
Cholesterol 106 mg • Dietary fiber 8 gm • Sodium 41 mg • Calcium 59 mg

Quick Middle Eastern Chickpeas

YIELD: 4 SIDE-DISH SERVINGS

1 tablespoon extra-virgin olive oil
1 onion, diced
1 fresh jalapeño pepper, diced
4 garlic cloves, minced
2 teaspoons ground cumin
$1/_2$ teaspoon ground coriander

$1^1/_2$ cups diced canned tomatoes
$1^1/_2$ cups cooked chickpeas
$1/_4$ cup chopped fresh cilantro
Salt and freshly ground black
    pepper

In a saucepan, heat the olive oil over medium-high heat. Add the onion, jalapeño, garlic, cumin, and coriander, and sauté until the onion is limp, about 3 minutes. Add the tomatoes, chickpeas, cilantro, and salt and pepper to taste, and simmer for at least 10 minutes. Serve hot.

Calories 177 • Protein 8 gm • Fat 6 gm • Percent of calories from fat 28% •
Cholesterol 0 mg • Dietary fiber 5 gm • Sodium 217 mg • Calcium 71 mg

Sautéed Broccoli and Cauliflower with Chickpeas

YIELD: **4** SERVINGS

This aromatic vegetable combination can be served as a side dish or as a topping for rice as a main course. The anchovies are optional but add a great deal of flavor.

1 stalk broccoli (about 8 ounces), florets and peeled, chopped stem

½ head cauliflower (about 16 ounces), chopped

2 tablespoons extra-virgin olive oil

4 garlic cloves, minced

6 anchovy fillets, minced (optional)

¼ cup chopped fresh Italian parsley

¾ cup cooked chickpeas

Salt and freshly ground black pepper

Steam the broccoli and cauliflower over boiling water until tender, about 6 minutes.

Heat the oil in a large skillet. Add the garlic, anchovies (if using), and parsley, and sauté until fragrant, about 2 minutes. Add the chickpeas and sauté for another minute. Add the broccoli and cauliflower and sauté for 2 minutes. Taste and add salt and pepper if needed (if you include anchovies, the salt may not be needed). Serve hot.

Calories 158 • Protein 7 gm • Fat 8 gm • Percent of calories from fat 44% • Cholesterol 0 mg • Dietary fiber 6 gm • Sodium 37 mg • Calcium 70 mg

Curried Cauliflower and Chickpeas with Tomato

YIELD: 4 TO 6 SERVINGS

Cauliflower and chickpeas swim in a rich tomato-based curry sauce, brightened by a handful of fresh cilantro added at the last minute. This delicious curry can be served on rice to make a hearty soul-warming supper. Or, bring this dish to a potluck—it holds up well on a buffet table.

1 tablespoon canola oil
1 large onion, halved and sliced
1 garlic clove, minced
1 tablespoon curry powder
1 teaspoon garam masala
4 cups chopped canned
  or fresh tomatoes

1 head cauliflower, broken into
  1-inch florets
2 cups cooked chickpeas
Salt and freshly ground
  black pepper
¼ cup chopped fresh cilantro

Heat the oil over medium heat in a large nonstick saucepan or Dutch oven. Add the onion, garlic, curry powder, and garam masala. Sauté until the onion is golden, about 8 minutes.

Add the tomatoes and cauliflower, cover, and simmer until the cauliflower is tender, about 10 minutes. Stir in the chickpeas and salt and pepper to taste. Simmer for an additional 10 minutes to allow the flavors to blend.

Just before serving, stir in the cilantro. Taste and adjust the seasonings. Serve hot.

Calories 268 • Protein 13 gm • Fat 7 gm • Percent of calories from fat 22% •
Cholesterol 0 mg • Dietary fiber 11 gm • Sodium 420 mg • Calcium 153 mg

Curried Spinach with Chickpeas

YIELD: 4 TO 6 SERVINGS

Buttermilk creates a creamy, nonfat sauce to bind together the spinach and chickpeas in this rich-tasting curry. Serve over hot cooked rice.

1½ pounds spinach,
  washed and trimmed
1 tablespoon canola oil
2 onions, thinly sliced
4 garlic cloves, minced
1 to 2 fresh hot green chiles,
  finely chopped

1-inch piece fresh ginger,
  peeled and finely chopped
½ teaspoon garam masala
¼ teaspoon ground coriander
1½ cups nonfat buttermilk
2 cups cooked chickpeas
Salt

Immerse the spinach in a large pan filled with rapidly boiling water and blanch until limp and bright green, about 1 minute. Drain, then immerse into cold water to stop the cooking. Drain again. Taking a handful at a time, squeeze out the excess water from the spinach and chop. Set aside.

In a very large saucepan, heat the oil over medium-low heat. Add the onions, garlic, chiles, ginger, garam masala, and coriander, and sauté until the onions are golden, about 10 minutes. Stir in the buttermilk and chickpeas. Cook over low heat until the chickpeas are heated through, about 5 minutes. Do not let the sauce boil. Stir in the spinach and heat gently until the spinach is heated through.

Calories 283 • Protein 17 gm • Fat 7 gm • Percent of calories from fat 22% • Cholesterol 3 mg • Dietary fiber 11 gm • Sodium 241 mg • Calcium 345 mg

Falafel

YIELD: 4 TO 6 SERVINGS

There are many different recipes for this classic Middle Eastern street food. In this version, the bean patties are made from cooked chickpeas and are baked, not deep-fried, for a significant savings in fat.

Sauce
1/2 cup tahini (sesame paste)
1/3 cup plain nonfat yogurt
1 tablespoon honey
1 tablespoon freshly squeezed
    lemon juice

1 tablespoon water, or more as
    needed

Relish
1 large ripe tomato, diced
1/2 English cucumber, diced
1/2 green bell pepper, diced
1/4 cup diced Vidalia
    or similar sweet onion

1 tablespoon freshly squeezed
    lemon juice
Salt and freshly ground black
    pepper

Falafel
4 cups cooked chickpeas
4 slices bread
4 garlic cloves, chopped
8 scallions, chopped
1/4 cup chopped fresh cilantro
1/4 cup chopped fresh parsley

2 teaspoons baking powder
2 teaspoons ground cumin
1 teaspoon ground coriander
1/2 teaspoon ground red pepper
Pita pockets

Preheat the oven to 350 degrees.

To make the sauce, combine the tahini, honey yogurt, lemon juice, and water in a small bowl and mix well. Add additional water if needed to achieve a consistency of heavy cream. Set aside.

To make the relish, combine the tomato, cucumber, bell pepper, onion, lemon juice, and salt and pepper to taste in a small bowl and mix well. Set aside.

To make the falafel, combine the chickpeas, bread, garlic, scallions, cilantro, parsley, baking powder, cumin, coriander, and ground red pepper in a food processor. Process until well mixed and finely chopped. Knead with your hands to combine.

Spray a baking sheet with nonstick cooking spray. Form the chickpea mixture into balls the size of small limes. Flatten between your hands and place on the baking sheet. Lightly mist the patties with nonstick cooking spray. Bake for 10 minutes, turn over, and bake for another 5 minutes, until golden on both sides.

While the falafel bakes, warm the pita pockets. They can be wrapped in aluminum foil and heated along with the falafel.

To serve, present the falafel, relish, sauce, and warmed pita pockets on a table and invite diners to assemble their own sandwiches.

Calories 624 • Protein 29 gm • Fat 22 gm • Percent of calories from fat 32% •
Cholesterol 0 mg • Dietary fiber 12 gm • Sodium 371 mg • Calcium 337 mg

Old Bay Cranberry Beans

YIELD: 4 SIDE-DISH SERVINGS

This is a quick recipe for a tasty bean that is underutilized in this country. The beans are simply cooked along with aromatic vegetables and Old Bay Seasoning (usually used in crab boils).

1 cup dried cranberry beans,
    soaked overnight or using the
    quick-soak method on
    page 20
6 cups water
1 onion, halved

1 small celery stalk
1 small carrot
3 stems parsley
1 tablespoon Old Bay Seasoning
Salt

    Drain the beans. Combine the beans in a saucepan with the 6 cups fresh water, onion, celery, carrot, parsley, and Old Bay Seasoning. Cover and bring to a boil, then reduce the heat and simmer gently, partially covered, for about 45 minutes. Discard the vegetables and parsley. Add salt to taste. Lift the beans out of the cooking water with a slotted spoon and serve.

Calories 189 • Protein 12 gm • Fat 1 gm • Percent of calories from fat 3% • Cholesterol 0 mg • Dietary fiber 13 gm • Sodium 526 mg • Calcium 89 mg

Almost Mom's Quick Chili

YIELD: 4 TO 6 SERVINGS

I didn't exactly set out to trick people with this recipe. When I made it for the first time with the textured vegetable protein (TVP) I purchased on a whim, I was merely expecting a certain change in the texture of my chili. I never expected that my kids would think the chili had ground meat in it. To me this chili tastes like the Americanized dish my Mom once made—tasty and comforting, great in a taco shell, but not terribly authentic. TVP is available in most natural food stores.

1 tablespoon canola or olive oil
1 onion, diced
1 green bell pepper, diced
4 garlic cloves, minced
2 tablespoons chili powder
1 teaspoon ground cumin
3 cups cooked red kidney beans

1 (28-ounce) can crushed tomatoes
1 teaspoon dried oregano
Salt and freshly ground black pepper
1 cup water
1/2 cup dry textured vegetable protein (TVP)

Heat the oil in a large, heavy-bottomed saucepan or Dutch oven. Add the onion, bell pepper, garlic, chili powder, and cumin, and sauté until the onion is limp, about 5 minutes. Add the beans, tomatoes, oregano, and salt and pepper to taste. Simmer for about 30 minutes.

Meanwhile, bring the water to a boil. Combine the TVP with the boiling water and let stand for 5 minutes. Add to the chili. Simmer for another 15 minutes. Serve hot over rice or in a taco shell or tortilla.

Calories 326 • Protein 25 gm • Fat 4 gm • Percent of calories from fat 11% • Cholesterol 0 mg • Dietary fiber 17 gm • Sodium 323 mg • Calcium 196 mg

Honey-Mustard Quick Baked Beans

YIELD: 4 SIDE-DISH SERVINGS

These distinctively flavored beans have the rich flavor of baked beans, but are quickly made with cooked beans—or canned beans if you have those on hand. These beans make a great side dish for a grain casserole. This recipe is easily doubled.

3 cups cooked red kidney beans
1 small onion, diced
1/2 cup tomato ketchup
1/3 cup honey
3 tablespoons Dijon mustard

1 tablespoon cider vinegar
1/4 teaspoon freshly ground black
    pepper
Salt

Preheat the oven to 350 degrees. Combine the beans, onion, ketchup, honey, mustard, vinegar, pepper, and salt in a 2-quart casserole. Mix well. Cover and bake for about 45 minutes. Serve hot.

Calories 298 • Protein 14 gm • Fat 1 gm • Percent of calories from fat 3% •
Cholesterol 0 mg • Dietary fiber 11 gm • Sodium 273 mg • Calcium 104 mg

Kidney Bean and Sweet Potato Stew

❧❧❧

YIELD: 4 TO 6 SERVINGS

Corn bread and a green salad make the perfect accompaniments for this vitamin- and fiber-rich stew.

1 tablespoon extra-virgin olive oil
1 leek, thinly sliced
4 garlic cloves, minced
2 tablespoons unbleached
   all-purpose flour
1/2 cup dry white wine
1 1/2 pounds sweet potatoes, peeled
   and cut into 1 1/2-inch chunks

1 (28-ounce) can peeled tomatoes
2 cups high-quality chicken
   or vegetable broth
1 teaspoon dried thyme
2 bay leaves
1/4 teaspoon freshly ground black
   pepper
1 1/2 cups cooked red kidney beans

In a large saucepan or Dutch oven, heat the oil over medium heat. Add the leeks, cover, and cook, stirring occasionally until softened, about 5 minutes. Stir in the garlic and sauté for 1 minute longer. Stir in the flour and cook, stirring constantly, for 1 minute.

Add the wine and bring to a boil, scraping up the brown bits that cling to the bottom of the pan. Add the potatoes, tomatoes, broth, thyme, bay leaves, and pepper. Bring to a boil, reduce the heat, cover, and simmer until the potatoes are tender, about 20 minutes. Discard the bay leaves.

Add the beans, cover, and simmer until the beans are heated through, about 10 minutes. Serve hot.

Calories 394 • Protein 14 gm • Fat 4 gm • Percent of calories from fat 10% •
Cholesterol 0 mg • Dietary fiber 13 gm • Sodium 577 mg • Calcium 163 mg

Vegetarian Chili for a Crowd

YIELD: ABOUT 20 SERVINGS

1 tablespoon oil
3 onions, diced
2 green bell peppers, diced
4 garlic cloves, minced
3 tablespoons chili powder
1 tablespoon cumin seeds
8 cups cooked red kidney beans

1 (28-ounce) can tomato puree
4 cups fresh or canned
   diced tomatoes
Salt and freshly ground black
   pepper
1/4 cup chopped fresh cilantro

Heat the oil in a large, heavy-bottomed saucepan or Dutch oven. Add the onions, bell peppers, garlic, chili powder, and cumin, and sauté until the onions are limp, about 5 minutes. Add the beans, tomato puree, and the diced tomatoes. Simmer for about 30 minutes. Add the salt and pepper to taste. Just before serving, stir in the cilantro. Serve hot.

Calories 137 • Protein 8 gm • Fat 2 gm • Percent of calories from fat 9% •
Cholesterol 0 mg • Dietary fiber 7 gm • Sodium 26 mg • Calcium 42 mg

French Green Lentils with Roasted Onions

YIELD: 4 TO 6 SERVINGS

French green lentils are the lentil of choice for this simple combination because they hold their shape so well. Likewise, pearl onions are the onions of choice because of their shape. But, for some reason, pearl onions are not readily available—except during the holiday season, when you are expected to serve them creamed. This dish looks pretty with the whole pearl onions, but you can easily substitute white boiling onions (quartered or cut into eighths if large). But don't use different lentils—they just won't work with this dish.

1 pound white pearl onions
2 tablespoons extra-virgin
   olive oil
1/2 teaspoon dried thyme
1 1/2 cups dried French green
   lentils, rinsed

2 tablespoon balsamic vinegar
Salt and freshly ground black
   pepper

Preheat the oven to 400 degrees. Combine the onions, olive oil, and thyme in a roasting pan. Roast until the onions are lightly browned, 35 to 40 minutes.

Meanwhile, boil the lentils in plenty of salted water until tender but not mushy, about 30 minutes. Drain.

Gently mix the roasted onions into the lentils. Add the balsamic vinegar and salt and pepper to taste. Serve warm.

Calories 293 • Protein 12 gm • Fat 7 gm • Percent of calories from fat 21% • Cholesterol 0 mg • Dietary fiber 14 gm • Sodium 20 mg • Calcium 87 mg

Syrian Lentils in a Spicy Tomato Sauce

YIELD: 6 TO 8 SERVINGS

1 cup dried French green lentils, rinsed

4 cups water

1 tablespoon extra-virgin olive oil

3 onions, sliced

4 garlic cloves, minced

1 (28-ounce) can peeled tomatoes

2 tablespoons tomato paste

1 tablespoon ground cumin, or more to taste

³/₄ teaspoon ground allspice

¹/₂ teaspoon ground coriander

¹/₂ teaspoon hot red pepper flakes

Salt and freshly ground black pepper

Hot cooked rice or couscous (optional)

In a medium saucepan, combine the lentils and water. Cover and bring to a boil. Reduce the heat and simmer until the lentils are tender but still retain their shape, about 30 minutes. Set aside but do not drain.

In another saucepan, heat the oil over medium heat. Add the onions and garlic and sauté until the onions are golden, about 10 minutes. Add the lentils and cooking liquid. Run a knife through the can of tomatoes to chop and add, without draining, to the lentils along with the tomato paste. Add the cumin, allspice, coriander, and red pepper flakes, and simmer for 15 minutes. Add salt and pepper generously. Taste and adjust seasonings.

Serve hot over rice or couscous, if desired.

Calories 172 • Protein 7 gm • Fat 3 gm • Percent of calories from fat 15% • Cholesterol 0 mg • Dietary fiber 9 gm • Sodium 236 mg • Calcium 99 mg

Red Lentil Vegetable Stew

YIELD: 4 SERVINGS

The lentils form the sauce for this Indian-spiced vegetable mélange. It is especially delicious made with garden-fresh summer vegetables.

3/4 cup dried red lentils, rinsed
2 1/2 cups water
2 tablespoons canola oil
1 large onion, halved
    and thinly sliced
2 garlic cloves, minced
1 teaspoon ground cumin
1 teaspoon garam masala
1/2 teaspoon curry powder
Salt

1 small head cauliflower, broken
    into florets (about 4 cups)
2 vine-ripened tomatoes, diced,
    or 1 cup canned tomatoes, well
    drained
Kernels from 2 ears corn or
    1 1/2 cups frozen corn
1 cup fresh or frozen peas
1/4 cup chopped fresh cilantro
Hot cooked rice (optional)

Combine the lentils and water in a saucepan, cover, and bring to a boil. Reduce the heat and simmer for 15 minutes.

Heat the canola oil in a large saucepan or Dutch oven over medium-low heat. Add the onion and cook until slightly limp, about 3 minutes. Stir in the garlic, cumin, garam masala, and curry powder, and cook until fragrant, about 3 minutes. Stir in the lentils and cooking liquid. Add salt to taste. Add the cauliflower and stir to coat well. Bring to a simmer, cover, and cook for 10 minutes. Stir in the tomatoes, corn, and peas, and continue to simmer for another 5 minutes.

Stir in the cilantro. Taste and adjust the seasonings. Serve hot, over rice, if desired.

Calories 314 • Protein 17 gm • Fat 9 gm • Percent of calories from fat 24% • Cholesterol 0 mg • Dietary fiber 19 gm • Sodium 119 mg • Calcium 76 mg

Dried Lima Bean Gratin

YIELD: 6 SIDE-DISH SERVINGS

Layers of flavor envelop the beans to make this delicious side dish. Another type of lima or white bean can be substituted for the large limas, but adjust the cooking time accordingly.

2 cups dried large lima beans, soaked overnight or using the quick-soak method on page 20
8 cups water
2 onions, 1 quartered and 1 diced
2 carrots, 1 quartered and 1 diced
4 sprigs fresh thyme
1 tablespoon fresh or dried rosemary

2 tablespoons extra-virgin olive oil
1 celery stalk, diced
4 garlic cloves, minced
1 (12-ounce) can evaporated skim milk
2 tablespoons dry sherry
Salt and freshly ground black pepper
$1/2$ cup freshly grated Parmesan cheese

Topping
$1/4$ cup dry bread crumbs
$1/4$ cup chopped fresh parsley
$1/2$ teaspoon fresh thyme

2 teaspoons grated lemon zest
2 teaspoons extra-virgin olive oil

Drain the beans. In a large saucepan, combine the beans, 8 cups fresh water, the quartered onion, the quartered carrot, thyme, and rosemary. Cover and bring to a boil. Reduce the heat and simmer, partially covered, until the beans are tender, about 1 hour. Drain and discard the onion, carrot, and thyme.

Preheat the oven to 350 degrees.

Heat the olive oil over medium-high heat in a saucepan. Add the diced onion and carrot, celery, and garlic, and sauté until limp, about 2 minutes. Reduce the heat to medium and stir in the beans, milk, and sherry. Add salt and pepper to taste. Stir in the cheese; do not allow the sauce to boil. Spoon into a lightly buttered $1^1/2$-quart baking dish.

To make the topping, mix together the bread crumbs, parsley, thyme, and lemon zest. Sprinkle over the beans. Drizzle with the olive oil. Bake for 25 minutes or until the topping is golden. Serve hot.

Calories 355 • Protein 21 gm • Fat 7 gm • Percent of calories from fat 16% • Cholesterol 7 mg • Dietary fiber 12 gm • Sodium 355 mg • Calcium 340 mg

Tomato-baked Lima Beans

YIELD: 6 TO 8 SIDE-DISH SERVINGS

2 cups dried large lima beans,
 soaked overnight or using the
 quick-soak method on page 20
6 cups water
1 onion, diced
1 tablespoon fresh (or ¼ teaspoon
 dried rosemary)

1 cup seasoned tomato sauce
4 garlic cloves, minced
Salt and freshly ground black
 pepper
½ cup freshly grated Parmesan
 cheese

Drain the beans. Combine in a large saucepan with the 6 cups fresh water, onion, and rosemary. Bring to a boil, reduce the heat, and simmer, partially covered, until the beans are tender, 1 to 1½ hours. The beans will not soften further, so make sure the texture is pleasing. Drain, reserving 1 cup of the cooking liquid.

Preheat the oven to 350 degrees.

In a lightly buttered 1½-quart baking dish, combine the beans with the reserved cooking liquid and tomato sauce. Stir in the garlic and salt and pepper to taste. Sprinkle the cheese on top. Bake for 25 minutes or until the beans are heated through and the cheese is melted. Serve hot.

Calories 257 • Protein 17 gm • Fat 3 gm • Percent of calories from fat 9% •
Cholesterol 5 mg • Dietary fiber 12 gm • Sodium 290 mg • Calcium 162 mg

French Country White Beans

YIELD: 6 TO 8 SERVINGS

Slow-cooked beans have a marvelous ability to absorb flavors, and these beans are cooked with an abundance of aromatic ingredients. The result is a rich-tasting stew that acts as a wonderful foil for simply cooked vegetables or meat. For convenience, the vegetables can be chopped together in a food processor.

2 cups dried small white navy beans, soaked overnight or using the quick-soak method on page 20

2 tablespoons olive oil

1 large carrot, finely chopped

1 onion, finely chopped

1 celery stalk, finely chopped

1/2 cup finely chopped parsley

4 cloves garlic, finely chopped

4 sprigs fresh thyme

6 fresh sage leaves

3 strips lemon zest

8 cups water

2 cups chopped fresh or canned tomatoes (optional)

Salt and freshly ground black pepper

Drain the beans. In a large saucepan, heat the oil over medium-high heat. Add the carrot, onion, celery, parsley, and garlic, and sauté until limp, about 4 minutes. Add the drained beans, thyme, sage, lemon zest, and the 8 cups fresh water. Cover and bring to a boil. Reduce the heat, partially cover, and simmer until the beans are completely tender, 1 to 1 1/2 hours. Begin checking after 1 hour. Skim off any foam that rises to the top of the pot. Remove the herbs and lemon zest. Add the tomatoes (if using). Season generously with salt and pepper.

Calories 293 • Protein 16 gm • Fat 6 gm • Percent of calories from fat 16% • Cholesterol 0 mg • Dietary fiber 18 gm • Sodium 33 mg • Calcium 135 mg

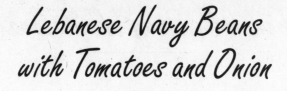

Lebanese Navy Beans with Tomatoes and Onion

YIELD: 4 SERVINGS

In this simple peasant dish, navy beans and onions are simmered in a rich, cumin-scented tomato sauce. This dish is wonderful served hot, over rice or couscous. Or serve it at room temperature and scoop it up with pita pockets.

1 cup dried navy beans or other small white beans, soaked overnight or using the quick-soak method on page 20

6 cups water

1 tablespoon extra-virgin olive oil

2 onions, sliced

4 garlic cloves, minced

2 cups chopped fresh or canned tomatoes with juice

3 tablespoons tomato paste

2 teaspoons cumin

Salt and freshly ground black pepper

Drain the beans. Combine the beans in a saucepan with the 6 cups fresh water, cover, and bring to a boil. Reduce the heat and simmer, partially covered, until just tender, 1 to 1½ hours. Begin checking after 1 hour. Skim off any foam that rises to the top of the pot. Drain and reserve the cooking liquid.

In a heavy-bottomed saucepan, heat the oil over medium heat. Add the onions and garlic and sauté until golden, about 10 minutes. Add the tomatoes, tomato paste, cumin, beans, and enough of the cooking liquid to cover the beans; add salt and pepper to taste. Simmer for 20 minutes, until the beans are quite tender and the sauce has thickened. Serve hot or at room temperature.

Calories 274 • Protein 14 gm • Fat 5 gm • Percent of calories from fat 15% • Cholesterol 0 mg • Dietary fiber 16 gm • Sodium 39 mg • Calcium 128 mg

Old-fashioned Baked Beans

YIELD: 6 SIDE-DISH SERVINGS

Dried chipotle chiles add lovely smoky flavor but little heat to these sweet baked beans. If you like heat, chop the chiles and return them to the beans instead of discarding them before serving.

2 cups dried navy or pea beans,
soaked overnight or using the
quick-soak method on page 20
8 cups water
1 large onion, thinly sliced
2 dried chipolte chiles

1 cup tomato puree
1 cup brown sugar, firmly packed
1 tablespoon prepared mustard
Salt and freshly ground black
pepper

Drain the beans. Combine in a large pot with the water. Bring to a boil, then reduce the heat and simmer, partially covered, until just tender, about 1 hour. Skim off any foam that rises to the top of the pot.

Preheat the oven to 300 degrees. Combine the beans, their cooking liquid, and the onion, chiles, tomato puree, brown sugar, and salt and pepper to taste in a bean pot or baking dish and mix well. Cover and bake for about 3 hours or until the beans are completely tender. Check occasionally to make sure the beans remain moist and add more *hot* water if needed. Remove and discard the chiles. Serve hot.

Calories 401 • Protein 17 gm • Fat 1 gm • Percent of calories from fat 3% •
Cholesterol 0 mg • Dietary fiber 19 gm • Sodium 171 mg • Calcium 168 mg

Honey-Mustard Baked Beans

YIELD: 6 SIDE-DISH SERVINGS

Again, chipotle chiles replace the smoky flavor that might have come from a ham bone or piece of smoked pork. These baked beans have a rich, mustardy flavor.

2 cups dried navy or pea beans,
    soaked overnight or using the
    quick-soak method on
    page 20
8 cups water
1 large onion, diced

2 dried chipotle chiles
1 cup tomato ketchup
1/4 cup honey mustard
1/4 cup honey, or to taste
Salt and freshly ground black
    pepper

Drain the beans. Combine the beans in a large pot with the 8 cups fresh water. Bring to a boil, then reduce the heat and simmer, partially covered, until just tender, about 1 hour. Skim off any foam that rises to the top of the pot.

Preheat the oven to 300 degrees. Combine the beans, their cooking liquid, and the onion, chiles, ketchup, mustard, honey, and salt and pepper to taste in a bean pot or baking dish and mix well. Cover and bake for about 3 hours, or until the beans are completely tender. Check occasionally to make sure the beans remain moist and add more *hot* water if needed. Remove and discard the chiles. Serve hot.

Calories 339 • Protein 16 gm • Fat 1 gm • Percent of calories from fat 3% •
Cholesterol 0 mg • Dietary fiber 18 gm • Sodium 445 mg • Calcium 159 mg

Maple Baked Beans

YIELD: 6 SIDE-DISH SERVINGS

For that traditional baked bean flavor, I sometimes put a 4-ounce piece of salt pork in the bottom of the baking dish. I score the meat in a few places, but keep the rind intact. When the beans have finished baking, I discard the salt pork. A piece of lean smoked turkey can provide the same smoky undertone.

2 cups dried navy or pea beans, soaked overnight or using the quick-soak method on page 20
8 cups water
1 large onion, thinly sliced
³/₄ cup pure maple syrup

¹/₂ cup ketchup
¹/₂ cup brewed coffee
1 tablespoon prepared mustard
1 teaspoon powdered ginger
Salt and freshly ground black pepper

Drain the beans. Combine the beans in a large pot with the 8 cups fresh water. Cover and bring to a boil. Reduce the heat and simmer, partially covered, until just tender, about 1 hour. Skim off any foam that rises to the top of the pot.

Preheat the oven to 300 degrees. Combine the beans, their cooking liquid, and the onion, maple syrup, ketchup, coffee, mustard, ginger, and salt and pepper in a bean pot or baking dish and mix well. Cover and bake for about 3 hours or until the beans are completely tender. Check occasionally to make sure the beans remain moist and add more *hot* water if needed. Serve hot.

Calories 356 • Protein 16 gm • Fat 1 gm • Percent of calories from fat 2% • Cholesterol 0 mg • Dietary fiber 17 gm • Sodium 172 mg • Calcium 176 mg

Mexican Vegetable Sauté with Pink Beans

YIELD: 4 SERVINGS

A great topping for rice or filling for burritos.

2 tablespoons extra-virgin
  olive oil
1 tablespoon chili powder
2 garlic cloves, minced
$1/2$ small onion, diced
$1/2$ green bell pepper, diced
$1/2$ red bell pepper, diced

1 zucchini, quartered and sliced
  $1/4$ inch thick
$1^1/2$ cups diced tomatoes
$1^1/2$ cups cooked pink or pinto beans
$1/4$ cup chopped fresh cilantro
$1/4$ cup chopped black olives
  (optional)

In a large nonstick skillet, heat the olive oil over medium-high heat. Add the chili powder, garlic, and onion, and sauté until the onion is slightly limp, about 2 minutes. Add the bell peppers and sauté for 1 minute. Add the zucchini and continue to sauté until the vegetables are tender-crisp, about 3 minutes. If you are using canned tomatoes, drain slightly. Add the tomatoes to the skillet along with the beans and cilantro, and cook briefly to heat through. Stir in the olives (if using) and serve hot.

Calories 191 • Protein 7 gm • Fat 8 gm • Percent of calories from fat 34% • Cholesterol 0 mg • Dietary fiber 5 gm • Sodium 12 mg • Calcium 57 mg

Cowboy Frijoles

꧁꧂

YIELD: 6 TO 8 SERVINGS

Cowboys used to call pinto beans "Mexican strawberries." I like to think that these beans—a little spicy, a little sweet—would have pleased any cowboy on the trail. I know these beans make a great side dish at a barbecue and combine well with cheese as a filling for burritos and enchiladas.

1¹/₂ cups dried pinto beans, soaked overnight or using the quick-soak method on page 20
1 onion, finely chopped
2 garlic cloves, minced
2 dried ancho chiles
8 cups water

1 cup tomato puree
2 tablespoons cider vinegar
2 tablespoons honey
¹/₂ teaspoon dried oregano
Salt
¹/₄ cup chopped fresh cilantro (optional)

Drain the beans. Combine the beans in a large pot with the onion, garlic, chiles, and 8 cups fresh water. Cover and bring to a boil. Then reduce the heat and simmer, partially covered, until the beans are tender, 1 to 1¹/₂ hours. Skim off any foam that rises to the top of the pot. If the chiles are intact, remove the stem and skin and chop the flesh. Return to the pot along with the tomato puree, vinegar, honey, oregano, and salt to taste. Simmer for 15 minutes, then stir in the cilantro (if using). Serve hot.

Calories 211 • Protein 11 gm • Fat 1 gm • Percent of calories from fat 2% • Cholesterol 0 mg • Dietary fiber 13 gm • Sodium 26 mg • Calcium 73 mg

Spicy Slow-baked Barbecued Beans

YIELD: 4 TO 6 SERVINGS

Smoky and hot, these beans make a wonderful alternative to barbecued meats—or can be served as an accompaniment to more traditional grilled fare. My absolute favorite way to serve these beans is on top of a whole-wheat bun with a dollop of coleslaw (see Barbecued Bean Sandwiches with Slaw, page 236).

2 cups dried pinto beans, soaked overnight or using the quick-soak method on page 20
6 cups water
2 onions, thinly sliced
2 garlic cloves, minced
1 (28-ounce) can tomato puree

1/2 cup dark brown sugar, firmly packed
2 tablespoons chipotle en adobo
1 tablespoon chili powder
2 teaspoons dried oregano
Salt and freshly ground black pepper

Drain the beans. Combine the beans with the 6 cups fresh water in a large saucepan. Cover and bring to a boil. Reduce the heat slightly and boil gently, covered, for 45 to 60 minutes, until the beans are just tender. Skim off any foam that rises to the top of the pot.

Preheat the oven to 300 degrees.

Transfer the beans and their cooking liquid to a bean pot or baking dish. Add the onions, garlic, tomato puree, brown sugar, chipotle en adobo, chili powder, oregano, and salt and pepper to taste. Bake, covered, for 2 to 3 hours, until the beans are completely tender and the sauce is a nice thick consistency. If necessary, uncover during the last half hour to reduce the cooking liquid. Serve hot.

Calories 540 • Protein 25 gm • Fat 1 gm • Percent of calories from fat 2% • Cholesterol 0 mg • Dietary fiber 29 gm • Sodium 211 mg • Calcium 181 mg

15-minute Barbecued Beans

YIELD: 4 SIDE-DISH SERVINGS

These sweet-spicy beans, which my kids love, make a great accompaniment to scrambled eggs and whole-wheat toast for a Sunday night supper. Or serve them with veggie burgers. This recipe is easily doubled to serve 4 as a main course.

1 tablespoon olive or canola oil
1 small onion, diced
1 small green bell pepper, diced
2 green chile peppers, diced
2 garlic cloves, minced
1 teaspoon chili powder
1 teaspoon ground cumin

$1^1/_2$ cups cooked pinto beans
$^3/_4$ cup tomato-based barbecue
   sauce
1 teaspoon sugar
   or more to taste (optional)
Salt and freshly ground black
   pepper

Heat the oil in a medium saucepan over medium heat. Add the onion, bell pepper, chile peppers, garlic, chili powder, and cumin, and sauté until the onion is limp, about 4 minutes. Add the beans and barbecue sauce. Taste and add the sugar, if desired, and salt and pepper. Simmer for 10 minutes to allow the flavors to blend and the beans to heat through. Serve hot.

Calories 226 • Protein 6 gm • Fat 4 gm • Percent of calories from fat 16% • Cholesterol 0 mg • Dietary fiber 7 gm • Sodium 666 mg • Calcium 52 mg

Barbecued Bean Sandwiches with Slaw

YIELD: 6 SERVINGS

The proper accompaniment to these vegetarian sloppy joes is oven-fries. These sandwiches make a hearty, casual dinner that is perfect for hungry appetites.

**1 recipe Spicy Slow-baked Barbecued
    Beans (page 234) or double recipe
    15-minute Barbecued Beans
    (page 235)**

6 hard rolls

Slaw

6 cups finely grated green cabbage
2 carrots, finely grated
$1/4$ cup minced onion
**Salt and freshly ground black
    pepper**

$2/3$ cup fat-free mayonnaise
$1/3$ cup regular mayonnaise
3 tablespoons prepared mustard

Prepare the barbecued beans according to the recipe directions. Keep warm.

To make the slaw, combine the cabbage, carrots, and onion in a large mixing bowl. Season to taste with salt and pepper and toss well. In a small bowl, mix together the mayonnaises and mustard. Add to the cabbage mixture and toss until well combined. Taste and adjust the seasoning.

To serve, slice open the rolls and toast under the broiler. Place one roll on each plate. Ladle a generous amount of beans on one half of each roll. Top with a generous dollop of slaw and place the top on the sandwich. Serve at once, with napkins and a fork and knife.

Calories 673 • Protein 24 gm • Fat 14 gm • Percent of calories from fat 18% •
Cholesterol 9 mg • Dietary fiber 22 gm • Sodium 768 mg • Calcium 226 mg

Refried Pinto Beans

❧

YIELD: 6 TO 8 SIDE-DISH SERVINGS

This recipe makes enough refried beans to fill about 8 large burritos, allowing about 1/2 cup refried beans per tortilla. A word of advice: In this recipe it is very important to cook the beans until they are meltingly tender—a state that would be overcooked for most other recipes.

2 cups dried pinto beans, soaked
   overnight or using the quick-
   soak method on page 20
8 cups water
3 tablespoons canola oil
3 garlic cloves, minced
2 fresh jalapeño or serrano chiles,
   minced (seeding is optional)

1 small onion, minced
1 teaspoon chili powder
1 teaspoon ground cumin
Salt and freshly ground black
   pepper

Drain the beans. Combine the beans with the 8 cups fresh water in a large saucepan. Cover and bring to a boil. Then reduce the heat and simmer, partially covered, until the beans are very, very tender, 1 1/2 to 2 hours. Skim off any foam that rises to the top of the pot.

In a large nonstick skillet over low heat, heat the canola oil. Add the garlic, chiles, onion, chili powder, and cumin, and sauté until the onion and chiles are very soft and fragrant, about 10 minutes. Using a slotted spoon, transfer the beans to the skillet, adding about 1/2 cup of the cooking liquid at the same time. Mash the beans with the back of your spoon or a potato masher, adding additional cooking liquid as needed to achieve a creamy consistency. Season to taste with salt and pepper. Serve warm.

Calories 296 • Protein 14 gm • Fat 8 gm • Percent of calories from fat 23% •
Cholesterol 0 mg • Dietary fiber 17 gm • Sodium 161 mg • Calcium 97 mg

Pinto Chili-Cheese Burritos

YIELD: 6 TO 7 BURRITOS

You get an extra layer of flavor when you cook the beans with seasonings—in this case, an onion, ancho chile, and bay leaf. These burritos, a favorite in my house, are mildly spiced but still assertively flavored with just the ancho chile. Those who take their foods very hot should add the additional fresh chiles.

1 cup dried pinto beans, soaked overnight or using the quick-soak method on page 20

1 onion, halved

1 dried ancho chile

1 bay leaf

7 cups water

1 tablespoon extra-virgin olive oil

2 shallots, minced

2 garlic cloves, minced

1/4 cup chopped fresh green chiles (optional)

1 (15-ounce) can diced tomatoes

1/4 cup chopped fresh cilantro

Salt and freshly ground black pepper

2 cups grated reduced-fat Cheddar cheese (8 ounces)

6 to 7 large flour tortillas

Drain the beans. Combine the beans in a large saucepan with the onion, ancho chile, bay leaf, and 7 cups fresh water. Cover and bring to a boil. Then reduce the heat and skim off any foam that has risen to the top. Simmer, partially covered, until tender, about 60 minutes. Drain the beans and discard the onion and bay leaf. Peel the ancho chile; remove the seeds if desired. Chop the flesh and set aside.

Heat the oil in a medium saucepan. Add the shallots, garlic, and fresh chiles (if using), and sauté until fragrant, about 3 minutes. Add the beans, chopped ancho, tomatoes, cilantro, and salt and pepper to taste. Simmer to blend the flavors for 10 minutes. Taste and adjust seasonings. Stir in the cheese until melted. Remove from the heat.

Heat the tortillas, one at a time, by warming briefly in a dry skillet or directly over a gas flame. As each tortilla becomes warm and pliable, place on a work surface and spoon 1/2 cup of the bean mixture in a strip down the center. Fold in the sides of the tortilla over the filling, then fold up the bottom and roll up. Place on a plate in the oven to keep warm while you make the remaining burritos. Serve hot.

If you aren't serving immediately, cover and hold in the refrigerator for several hours. Reheat, covered, at 350 degrees, for about 30 minutes.

Calories 363 • Protein 24 gm • Fat 9.3 gm • Percent of calories from fat 23% • Cholesterol 13 mg • Dietary fiber 10 gm • Sodium 402 mg • Calcium 517 mg

VARIATION

Black Bean–Cheese Burritos. Replace the cooked pinto beans with $1/2$ recipe (about 3 cups) Mexican Black Beans (page 201). Proceed with the recipe as written.

Calories 397 • Protein 24 gm • Fat 12 gm • Percent of calories from fat 27% • Cholesterol 27 mg • Dietary fiber 8 gm • Sodium 612 mg • Calcium 468 mg

Grilled Veggie Burritos

YIELD: 4 TO 8 SERVINGS

There are very acceptable canned vegetarian refried beans on the market, but I prefer homemade. Still, it's worth taste-testing a few and keeping some in your pantry for recipes like this one.

1 small zucchini, sliced
    lengthwise 1/4 inch thick
6 plum tomatoes, cut in half
1 green bell pepper, halved and
    seeded
4 scallions, trimmed
1 to 2 jalapeños, halved and
    seeded
2 garlic cloves, minced
Salt and freshly ground black
    pepper

2 tablespoons chopped fresh
    cilantro
8 (10-inch) flour tortillas
8 ounces reduced-fat Cheddar
    cheese, shredded
2 cups Refried Black Beans
    (page 203) or Refried Pinto
    Beans (page 237) or store-bought
    vegetarian refried beans,
    heated

Prepare a medium fire in a charcoal or gas grill. To determine if a fire built with charcoal is medium-hot, hold your palm 6 inches above the fire. If you can stand it for 5 to 6 seconds, you have a medium-hot fire. Spray the zucchini, tomatoes, bell pepper, scallions, and jalapeños with nonstick cooking spray. Toss with the garlic.

Place the vegetables on the grill and grill until lightly charred on all sides: about 2 minutes for the scallions, 6 to 10 minutes for the tomatoes, and 8 to 12 minutes for the sweet and hot peppers and zucchini. Peel the bell peppers and tomatoes. Coarsely chop all of the vegetables and season to taste with salt and pepper. Mix with the cilantro.

Heat 1 flour tortilla directly over the grill, the flame of a gas burner, or in a dry skillet over medium-high heat, turning to heat both sides. As each tortilla becomes warm and pliable, place on a work surface. Sprinkle about 1/4 cup of the cheese in a line across the center of the tortilla. Spread about 1/3 cup of the beans on the cheese. Top with about 1/4 cup of the chopped vegetables. Fold in the sides and roll up the tortilla to enclose the filling. Place in a baking pan. Repeat with the remaining tortillas.

Cover with aluminum foil and heat in the oven at 350 degrees for about 15 minutes or on the grill over indirect heat. The burritos can be made up to a day in advance and held in the refrigerator until you are ready to heat them. Add a few extra minutes of heating time if the burritos are cold when you place them in the oven or on the grill.

Calories 553 • Protein 37 gm • Fat 13 gm • Percent of calories from fat 21% • Cholesterol 20 mg • Dietary fiber 14 gm • Sodium 619 mg • Calcium 742 mg

Quick Cannellini and Broccoli Ragout

YIELD: 4 SERVINGS

If you have canned cannellini beans and tomatoes on hand, this dish is very quick to make. You can serve it as a side dish or as a main-course topping for pasta or grains.

1 stalk broccoli, florets and peeled, chopped stem (about 2 cups)
1 tablespoon extra-virgin olive oil
4 garlic cloves
1¹/₂ cups diced fresh or canned tomatoes

1¹/₂ cups cooked cannellini (white kidney) beans
¹/₄ cup chopped fresh basil
Salt and freshly ground black pepper

Blanch the broccoli in boiling water to cover until just tender, about 2 minutes. Drain, plunge into cold water to stop the cooking, and drain again.

Heat the olive oil in a medium saucepan over medium heat. Add the garlic and sauté until fragrant, about 2 minutes. Add the broccoli, tomatoes, beans, basil, and salt and pepper to taste. Simmer for about 15 minutes to heat through and blend the flavors. Serve hot.

Calories 146 • Protein 8 gm • Fat 4 gm • Percent of calories from fat 24% •
Cholesterol 0 mg • Dietary fiber 6 gm • Sodium 20 mg • Calcium 53 mg

Kale with White Beans and Garlic

YIELD: 4 SERVINGS

A mess o' greens, Italian style. Be sure to serve with plenty of bread to sop up the delicious pot liquor.

1 cup dried cannellini (white kidney) beans or Great Northern beans, soaked overnight or using the quick-soak method on page 20

6 cups water or broth

1 onion, halved

2 sprigs fresh thyme or 1 tablespoon dried

1¹/₂ pounds kale, stems removed and chopped

Salt and freshly ground black pepper

¹/₄ cup extra-virgin olive oil

8 large garlic cloves, sliced

¹/₄ teaspoon hot red pepper flakes (optional)

Drain the beans. In a large saucepan, combine the beans with the 6 cups fresh water or broth, onion, and thyme. Cover and bring to a boil. Then reduce the heat and simmer, partially covered, until the beans are tender, approximately 1¹/₂ hours. Skim off any foam that rises to the top of the pot. Do not overcook the beans.

Remove and discard the onion and sprigs of thyme. (At this point the beans can be refrigerated for up to 1 day before continuing the recipe.) Bring the beans to a boil and add the kale and salt and pepper to taste. Simmer, stirring down the kale every few minutes, until the kale is tender, about 10 minutes.

Meanwhile, heat the olive oil in a small heavy pan over very low heat. Add the garlic and cook until tender, stirring occasionally and guarding against overbrowning the garlic, about 10 minutes. Mash the garlic with a fork. Add the hot pepper flakes (if using). Pour over the beans and greens and serve immediately.

Calories 368 • Protein 15 gm • Fat 15 gm • Percent of calories from fat 36% • Cholesterol 0 mg • Dietary fiber 15 gm • Sodium 68 mg • Calcium 232 mg

White Bean Chili Verde

YIELD: 6 TO 8 SERVINGS

This is a spicy chili, rich with the flavors of roasted peppers, tomatillos, and cilantro. The heat can be moderated by seeding the anchos before blending them into the sauce. It tastes even better on the second day, so make it a day ahead if you can. Serve over rice.

1½ cups dried Great Northern or
   other white beans, soaked
   overnight or using the quick-
   soak method on page 20
8 cups water
2 dried ancho chiles
2 bay leaves
2 fresh cubanelle chiles or
   Italian frying peppers

2 green bell peppers
12 ounces spinach, washed well,
   stems removed
12 tomatillos, husked, washed,
   and quartered
1 cup fresh cilantro leaves
Salt

Drain the beans. Combine the beans with the 8 cups fresh water, ancho chiles, and bay leaves in a large saucepan. Cover and bring to a boil. Then reduce the heat and simmer, partially covered, until the beans are tender, 1½ to 2 hours.

Roast the cubanelle and green peppers under a broiler or over a gas flame, turning frequently until the peppers are charred all over. Transfer to a paper or plastic bag, close tightly, and let steam for 10 minutes. Peel and remove the seeds.

Drain the beans, reserving the cooking liquid and anchos but discarding the bay leaves. Bring the cooking liquid to a boil. Add the anchos, roasted peppers, spinach, tomatillos, and cilantro. Cook until the spinach is wilted, 4 to 5 minutes. Spoon the spinach mixture into a food processor or blender and puree until smooth. Return to the pot along with the beans. Add salt to taste. Simmer over very low heat for at least 30 minutes to allow the flavors to blend.

Calories 231 • Protein 14 gm • Fat 1 gm • Percent of calories from fat 5% •
Cholesterol 0 mg • Dietary fiber 18 gm • Sodium 82 mg • Calcium 182 mg

Roasted Garlic-White Bean Chili

YIELD: 6 SERVINGS

For lovers of the stinking rose, this white bean chili is a treat. It can be played off the flavor of either ancho or chipotle chiles. The flavor each chile contributes is very different, but blends well with garlic. With 1 chile, the flavor is well defined but mild; add more if you like your chili hot. This chili just begs to be served with corn bread.

1¹/₂ cups Great Northern or other white beans, soaked overnight or using the quick-soak method on page 20

8 cups water

1 dried ancho or chipotle chile, or more to taste

2 large bulbs garlic, cloves peeled and separated

1 onion, slivered

1 red bell pepper, sliced

12 tomatillos, husked, washed, and quartered

2 tablespoons olive or canola oil

2 teaspoons ground cumin

Salt and freshly ground black pepper

Drain the beans. Combine the beans with the 8 cups fresh water and the chile in a large saucepan. Cover and bring to a boil. Then reduce the heat and simmer, partially covered, until the beans are tender, 1¹/₂ to 2 hours. Skim off any foam that rises to the top of the pot. The cooked beans should be *just* covered by the cooking liquid. If there is excess liquid, increase the heat to high and boil off the extra.

Meanwhile, preheat the oven to 400 degrees. Coat a large baking dish with nonstick cooking spray. Combine the garlic cloves, onion, bell pepper, and tomatillos in the baking dish. In a small bowl, combine the oil and cumin. Drizzle over the vegetables and toss to coat. Roast in the oven until well browned, 30 to 45 minutes.

Remove the chile from the beans and peel, seed, and chop the flesh. Return to the pot and add the roasted vegetables. Add salt and pepper to taste. Simmer for at least 30 minutes to blend the flavors before serving.

Calories 276 • Protein 14 gm • Fat 6 gm • Percent of calories from fat 17% • Cholesterol 0 mg • Dietary fiber 15 gm • Sodium 42 mg • Calcium 146 mg

7
Pasta e Fagioli

Penne with Fresh Fava Beans

Fresh Cranberry Beans with Pasta, Tomatoes, and Rosemary

Pasta with Fresh Lima Beans and Summer Vegetables

Pasta and Black Beans in Saffron-Tomato Sauce

Orecchiette with Black Beans, Goat Cheese, and Fresh Tomato Sauce

Tex-Mex Black Bean Pasta

Cilantro Pesto Rotini with Black Beans

Baked Penne with Spinach and Chickpeas

Cavatelli with Broccoli and Chickpeas

Orecchiette with Broccoli Rabe and Chickpeas

Rotini with Chickpeas and Tomato-Vegetable Sauce

Ziti with Chickpeas, Tomatoes, and Feta

Pesto Pasta with Chickpeas and Tomatoes

Pesto Pasta with Cranberry Beans

Syrian Rishtah

Bowties with White Beans and Fresh Tomato Sauce

White Bean and Fennel Linguine

Penne with White Beans and Greens

Chili Mac

This chapter is devoted to felicitous combinations of pasta and beans that can be served as main courses. Most of the recipes rely on already cooked beans—I often use canned beans in these recipes—so most of the preparation can be done in the time it takes to heat the water for the pasta.

Naturally, most of the recipes have Italian accents. Meaty cranberry beans (also known as borlotti beans), which have served as "poor man's meat" in Italy for centuries, appear in several recipes. Cannellini beans, with their particular affinity for tomatoes, basil, and greens, also play a large role in this chapter.

The surprise bean here is the black bean. Try it in the Saffron-Tomato Sauce on page 253 or with goat cheese and tomatoes on page 254 and you will begin to see what a tremendously versatile bean it is.

This chapter also includes recipes with flavorings from India and the Middle East. More recipes for bean and pasta combinations can be found in the soup and salad chapters. As always, the possibilities are infinite.

Penne with Fresh Fava Beans

YIELD: 4 SERVINGS

The fresh fava bean season is brief; look for the oversized pods in your markets in late spring through early summer. Fresh favas are among the best-tasting beans you'll ever find.

2 pounds fresh fava beans in
    pods, shelled (about 2¹/₂ cups)
2 tablespoons extra-virgin olive oil
4 garlic cloves, minced
1 small onion, finely chopped
¹/₂ cup chopped fresh parsley
1 (28-ounce) can Italian plum
    tomatoes with juice

2 homemade or store-bought
    roasted red bell peppers, diced
    (see Note on page 40)
²/₃ cup dry white wine
Salt and freshly ground black
    pepper
1 pound penne or ziti
Freshly grated Parmesan cheese

Boil the shelled beans in lightly salted water for 5 minutes. Drain in a colander and run under cold water. Use a sharp knife to slit open the beans and squeeze to pop the beans out of their skins. You will have about 1¹/₂ cups beans. Set aside.

Heat the olive oil in a medium saucepan. Add the garlic, onion, and parsley, and sauté until the onion is limp, about 3 minutes. Add the tomatoes, roasted peppers, and wine, and simmer for about 30 minutes or until the flavors have blended and mellowed. Add the fava beans and salt and pepper to taste.

Cook the pasta in plenty of boiling salted water until al dente. Drain well.

Spoon the pasta into a large serving dish. Add the fava bean mixture and toss well. Serve at once, passing the cheese at the table.

Calories 674 • Protein 24 gm • Fat 10 gm • Percent of calories from fat 13% •
Cholesterol 0 mg • Dietary fiber 11 gm • Sodium 361 mg • Calcium 134 mg

Fresh Cranberry Beans with Pasta, Tomatoes, and Rosemary

YIELD: 4 TO 6 SERVINGS

You'll rarely find fresh cranberry beans in the supermarket, but you may find them at a farm stand, and they are more than worth the extra trouble it takes to locate them. Look for them in September, when tomatoes (also featured in this recipe) are also at their peak. The meaty, nutty flavor of fresh cranberry beans goes particularly well with this combination, but you can substitute other fresh shell beans, such as limas or favas. If need be, canned tomatoes and dried rosemary can replace the fresh tomatoes and fresh herb.

1½ pounds fresh cranberry beans
   in pod, shelled (about 2 cups)
1 tablespoon extra-virgin olive oil
1 shallot, minced
2 garlic cloves, minced
1 tablespoon chopped fresh
   rosemary
6 cups chopped vine-ripened
   tomatoes

¾ cup dry white wine
2 tablespoons tomato paste
Salt, freshly ground black pepper,
   and hot red pepper flakes
1 pound fusilli, ziti, or shells
½ cup chopped fresh parsley

Place the beans in a pot and cover with warm water. Place a lid on the pot and bring to a boil, then simmer until just tender, about 30 minutes. Drain and set aside.

In a large nonstick saucepan or Dutch oven, heat the olive oil. Add the shallot and garlic and sauté until fragrant, about 1 minute. Add the rosemary, tomatoes, wine, and tomato paste, and bring to a boil. Add the beans and simmer until the sauce has reduced by about a third, about 10 minutes. Season to taste with salt, pepper, and hot red pepper flakes.

Cook the pasta in plenty of boiling salted water until just al dente. Drain well.

Add the pasta to the sauce and toss well. Add the parsley and toss again. Taste and adjust seasonings. Serve at once.

Calories 671 • Protein 26 gm • Fat 7 gm • Percent of calories from fat 9% • Cholesterol 0 mg • Dietary fiber 11 gm • Sodium 45 mg • Calcium 107 mg

Pasta with Fresh Lima Beans and Summer Vegetables

YIELD: 4 TO 6 SERVINGS

*F*resh lima beans enjoy a brief season—fortunately when corn and tomatoes are also in season. This delicious feast of fresh vegetables and pasta will satisfy the hungriest appetites. You could probably substitute frozen limas and corn and canned tomatoes, but that would be beside the point.

1 tablespoon extra-virgin olive oil
1 shallot, minced
2 garlic cloves, minced
6 cups chopped vine-ripened
   tomatoes
1 carrot, diced
1 tablepoon chopped fresh
   rosemary
1½ pounds fresh lima beans
   in pods, shelled (2 cups)

¾ pound fusilli, ziti, or shells
1 yellow summer squash,
   quartered and sliced
Kernels from 2 ears corn
   (about 1 cup)
Salt and freshly ground black
   pepper
½ cup chopped fresh parsley
   or fresh basil
Freshly grated Parmesan cheese

In a large nonstick saucepan or Dutch oven, heat the olive oil. Add the shallot and garlic and sauté until fragrant, about 1 minute. Add the tomatoes, carrot, and rosemary, and bring to a boil, stirring constantly. Add the lima beans, cover, and simmer until the beans are almost completely tender, about 35 minutes.

Meanwhile, cook the pasta in plenty of boiling salted water until al dente. Drain well.

When the beans are almost completely tender, add the summer squash and corn. Simmer for an additional 5 minutes. Season to taste with salt and pepper.

Add the pasta to the vegetables and toss well. Add the parsley or basil and toss again. Garnish with the Parmesan cheese and serve at once, passing extra cheese at the table.

Calories 576 • Protein 23 gm • Fat 7 gm • Percent of calories from fat 10% • Cholesterol 0 mg • Dietary fiber 14 gm • Sodium 56 mg • Calcium 76 mg

Pasta and Black Beans in Saffron–Tomato Sauce

YIELD: 4 TO 6 SERVINGS

Saffron pairs wonderfully with black beans in this elegant sauce. Choose a twisted pasta that will catch and hold the sauce, such as rotini or gemelli.

1 tablespoon extra-virgin olive oil
1 small onion, finely chopped
1 green bell pepper,
    finely chopped
4 garlic cloves, minced
1 (28-ounce) can crushed tomatoes
1/4 cup dry white wine

1/4 teaspoon crushed saffron
1 1/2 cups cooked black beans
Salt and freshly ground black
    pepper
1 pound pasta
1/4 cup chopped fresh parsley,
    for garnish (optional)

Heat the olive oil in a medium saucepan over medium-high heat. Add the onion, bell pepper, and garlic, and sauté until soft, about 3 minutes. Add the tomatoes, wine, and saffron. Bring to a boil. Reduce the heat and simmer for 20 minutes to allow the flavors to blend. Add the black beans and salt and pepper to taste. Keep warm.

Meanwhile, cook the pasta in plenty of boiling salted water until just al dente. Drain well.

To serve, spoon the sauce over the pasta. Garnish with the parsley, if desired.

Calories 634 • Protein 24 gm • Fat 6 gm • Percent of calories from fat 8% •
Cholesterol 0 mg • Dietary fiber 13 gm • Sodium 321 mg • Calcium 119 mg

Orecchiette with Black Beans, Goat Cheese, and Fresh Tomato Sauce

YIELD: 4 TO 6 SERVINGS

Goat cheese and black beans is one of my favorite combinations. Together they create a flavor that is rich and earthy, yet light. In this recipe the goat cheese also combines with the uncooked tomatoes to make a creamy sauce for the pasta.

2 pounds vine-ripened tomatoes
   (3 to 5 tomatoes), chopped
1 large garlic clove
1/4 cup chopped fresh cilantro
1 tablespoon extra-virgin olive oil
1 1/2 teaspoons salt
1/4 teaspoon freshly ground
   black pepper

1 1/2 cups cooked black beans
1/4 cup chopped pimiento
1 pound orecchiette (or shells,
   rotelle, or bowties)
4 ounces soft goat cheese (chèvre),
   such as Montrachet, crumbled

In a food processor, combine the tomatoes, garlic, cilantro, olive oil, salt, and pepper. Puree. Pour into a large pasta serving bowl. Stir in the beans and pimiento. Set aside.

While the bean mixture sits, heat a large pot of salted water to boiling. Cook the pasta until just done. Drain and toss the pasta with the goat cheese. Add to the bean mixture. Let sit for about 1 minute to allow the pasta to absorb some of the bean mixture. Serve at once.

Calories 663 • Protein 28 gm • Fat 12 gm • Percent of calories from fat 16% •
Cholesterol 13 mg • Dietary fiber 11 gm • Sodium 1007 mg • Calcium 97 mg

Tex-Mex Black Bean Pasta

YIELD: 4 TO 6 SERVINGS

Artichoke hearts, baby corn, and black beans star in another quick-to-make sauce. I like to use a small cup-shaped pasta, such as shells or orecchiette, to catch and hold the vegetables. This way each forkful contains both pasta and delicious vegetables.

1 tablespoon extra-virgin olive oil
1 small onion, finely chopped
2 jalapeño peppers, finely chopped
4 garlic cloves, minced
3 cups diced fresh or canned tomatoes with juice
1 (14-ounce) can quartered artichoke hearts, rinsed and drained

1 (15-ounce) can baby corn, cut into bite-size pieces, rinsed and drained
1 1/2 cups cooked black beans
1/4 cup chopped fresh cilantro
Salt and freshly ground black pepper
1 pound medium shells or orecchiette

Heat the olive oil in a large saucepan over medium heat. Add the onion, jalapeños, and garlic, and sauté until soft, about 5 minutes. Add the tomatoes, artichoke hearts, baby corn, and beans. Add the cilantro and salt and pepper to taste. Simmer over medium heat while you cook the pasta.

Meanwhile, cook the pasta in plenty of boiling salted water until al dente. Drain well.

To serve, spoon the sauce over the pasta. Serve at once.

Calories 672 • Protein 25 gm • Fat 6 gm • Percent of calories from fat 8% • Cholesterol 0 mg • Dietary fiber 11 gm • Sodium 627 mg • Calcium 65 mg

Cilantro Pesto Rotini with Black Beans

YIELD: 4 TO 6 SERVINGS

Although traditionally made with basil, a pesto—herb paste—can be made with cilantro as well. Cilantro pesto combines beautifully with pasta and black beans.

Cilantro Pesto
1½ cups fresh cilantro leaves
2 garlic cloves
3 tablespoons slivered almonds
4 tablespoons extra-virgin olive oil

3 tablespoons freshly grated
   Parmesan cheese
Salt and freshly ground black
   pepper

Beans and Pasta
1½ cups cooked black beans
1 cup fresh or frozen corn
½ cup homemade
   or store-bought salsa

Water, as needed
1 pound rotini

To make the pesto, combine the cilantro, garlic, and almonds in a food processor and process until finely chopped. Add the olive oil through the feed tube with the motor running and continue processing until you have a smooth paste. Briefly mix in the Parmesan and salt and pepper to taste. Set aside for at least 20 minutes to allow the flavors to develop.

In a small saucepan, combine the beans, corn, and salsa and heat gently. Add water as needed to keep the mixture moist. Set aside.

Meanwhile, cook the pasta in plenty of boiling salted water until al dente. Drain well, reserving a few tablespoons of the cooking liquid to thin down the pesto. Place the pasta in a large bowl. Thin the pesto with the reserved cooking liquid. Add the pesto sauce to the pasta and toss to coat well.

To serve, spoon the pasta into individual bowls. Top with the bean mixture. Serve at once.

Calories 726 • Protein 27 gm • Fat 21 gm • Percent of calories from fat 25% •
Cholesterol 3 mg • Dietary fiber 10 gm • Sodium 327 mg • Calcium 133 mg

Baked Penne with Spinach and Chickpeas

YIELD: 4 SERVINGS

$3/4$ pound penne
2 tablespoons extra-virgin
   olive oil
1 shallot, minced
4 garlic cloves, minced
$1^1/_2$ pounds spinach, washed well,
   stemmed and chopped

$1^1/_2$ cups cooked chickpeas
$3/4$ cup freshly grated Parmesan
   cheese
Salt and freshly ground black
   pepper

Cook the pasta in plenty of boiling salted water until just al dente. Drain well. Meanwhile, preheat the oven to 425 degrees.

Heat the olive oil in a large saucepan over medium-high heat. Add the shallot and garlic and sauté for about 1 minute, until fragrant. Add the spinach and stir until coated with the oil and slightly limp, about 2 minutes. Cover and let steam for 2 minutes. Stir in the cooked pasta and chickpeas. Stir in $1/2$ cup of the Parmesan. Season to taste with salt and pepper. Remove from the heat and spoon into a large baking dish. Sprinkle the remaining $1/2$ cup Parmesan on top. Cover the baking dish with a lid or aluminum foil. Bake until the cheese on top is melted, about 20 minutes. Serve hot.

Calories 585 • Protein 28 gm • Fat 15 gm • Percent of calories from fat 22% • Cholesterol 12 mg • Dietary fiber 10 gm • Sodium 424 mg • Calcium 426 mg

Cavatelli with Broccoli and Chickpeas

YIELD: 4 TO 6 SERVINGS

Cavatelli are small lip-shaped shells with curly edges. If you can't find them, substitute any other pasta shape that will catch the bits of vegetable and beans in its cup, such as shells, gnocchi, rotini, or orecchiette.

3 cups peeled, chopped broccoli stems and florets (³/₄ pound)

2 tablespoons extra-virgin olive oil

1 onion, finely chopped

4 garlic cloves, minced

¹/₄ teaspoon hot red pepper flakes, or more to taste

1 (28-ounce) can Italian tomatoes

1¹/₂ cups cooked chickpeas

12 brined black olives, pitted and chopped

¹/₂ cup chopped Italian parsley

1 tablespoon capers

1 pound cavatelli

Freshly grated Parmesan or Romano cheese

Blanch the broccoli in plenty of boiling salted water for 1 minute. Drain, plunge into cold water to stop the cooking, and drain again. Set aside.

In a large saucepan, heat the olive oil over medium-high heat. Add the onion, garlic, and red pepper flakes. Sauté until the onion is limp, about 3 minutes. Add the tomatoes, chickpeas, olives, parsley, and capers, and simmer gently for 5 minutes.

Meanwhile, cook the pasta in plenty of boiling salted water until al dente. Drain well.

Place the pasta in a warmed serving bowl. Add the tomato mixture and toss together. Serve with the cheese on the side or lightly sprinkled over the top.

Calories 714 • Protein 25 gm • Fat 15 gm • Percent of calories from fat 19% • Cholesterol 0 mg • Dietary fiber 11 gm • Sodium 779 mg • Calcium 145 mg

Orecchiette with Broccoli Rabe and Chickpeas

❧❧❧

YIELD: 4 TO 6 SERVINGS

Pasta, greens, and beans are a classic combination that is hard to beat for flavor and nutrition. Anchovies, garlic, and Parmesan cheese heighten the flavors of this simple combination. If broccoli rabe isn't available, substitute kale. You can use a food processor or mortar and pestle to mash and mince the garlic and anchovies.

1 pound orecchiette
2 pounds broccoli rabe, chopped
5 tablespoons extra-virgin olive oil
6 anchovy fillets, mashed (optional, but highly recommended)

6 garlic cloves, minced
3 cups cooked chickpeas
Salt and freshly ground black pepper
1 cup freshly grated Parmesan cheese

Cook the pasta in plenty of boiling salted water until al dente. Drain.

Meanwhile, blanch the broccoli rabe in plenty of boiling salted water until bright green and tender, 2 to 3 minutes. Drain and plunge into cold water to stop the cooking. Drain again.

In a large saucepan, heat the olive oil over medium-low heat. Add the anchovies (if using) and garlic and sauté until the garlic is fragrant and golden, about 3 minutes. Add the broccoli rabe and chickpeas and cook until heated through, about 4 minutes. Season to taste with salt (if needed) and pepper. Combine the pasta and vegetables in a large bowl, sprinkle with half the cheese, and toss well. Pass the remaining cheese at the table.

Calories 931 • Protein 41 gm • Fat 29 gm • Percent of calories from fat 27% • Cholesterol 16 mg • Dietary fiber 16 gm • Sodium 451 mg • Calcium 473 mg

Rotini with Chickpeas and Tomato-Vegetable Sauce

YIELD: 4 TO 6 SERVINGS

I like to use a food processor for chopping the shallots, garlic, anchovies, and herbs, but a mortar and pestle are equally effective. These chopped ingredients form a paste that infuses the eggplant with favor.

3 tablespoons extra-virgin olive oil
2 shallots, finely chopped
4 garlic cloves, finely chopped
6 anchovy fillets, finely chopped (optional, but highly recommended)
$1/4$ cup finely chopped fresh Italian parsley
$1/4$ cup finely chopped fresh basil
1 eggplant, diced (peeling is optional)

1 red bell pepper, diced
1 (28-ounce) can Italian tomatoes in puree
$1^1/_2$ cups cooked chickpeas
$1/4$ teaspoon hot red pepper flakes
$1/2$ teaspoon sugar (optional)
Salt and freshly ground black pepper
1 pound rotini, shells, orecchiette, or similarly shaped pasta
Freshly grated Parmesan cheese

In a large saucepan, heat the olive oil over medium heat. Add the shallots, garlic, anchovies (if using), parsley, basil, eggplant, and bell pepper. Sauté until the eggplant is soft and tender, about 10 minutes. Run a knife through the tomatoes in the can to chop them. Add to the saucepan along with the chickpeas and red pepper flakes. Taste and add the sugar (if using) and salt and pepper, as needed. Simmer for 10 to 20 minutes.

Meanwhile, cook the pasta in plenty of boiling salted water until al dente. Drain well.

To serve, spoon the sauce over the pasta. Pass the cheese at the table.

Calories 691 • Protein 23 gm • Fat 14 gm • Percent of calories from fat 18% • Cholesterol 0 mg • Dietary fiber 10 gm • Sodium 442 mg • Calcium 112 mg

Ziti with Chickpeas, Tomatoes, and Feta

YIELD: 4 TO 6 SERVINGS

If you start with canned chickpeas, you can make the sauce for this dish in the time it takes to boil water for the pasta. The feta cheese melts onto the warm pasta, becoming soft and creamy.

1½ cups cooked chickpeas
1 pint cherry tomatoes, halved
   (2 cups)
4 ounces feta cheese, crumbled
   (about ¾ cup)
¼ cup thinly sliced Vidalia
   or other sweet onion
2 tablespoons extra-virgin
   olive oil

1 tablespoon freshly squeezed
   lemon juice
3 tablespoons chopped fresh
   parsley
¼ teaspoon dried oregano
Salt and freshly ground black
   pepper
1 pound ziti

In a large bowl, combine the chickpeas, tomatoes, feta cheese, onion, olive oil, lemon juice, parsley, oregano, and salt and pepper to taste. Set aside.

Cook the pasta in plenty of boiling salted water until al dente. Drain the pasta and toss with the chickpea mixture until the cheese is completely melted. Serve at once.

Calories 685 • Protein 25 gm • Fat 17 gm • Percent of calories from fat 22% •
Cholesterol 26 mg • Dietary fiber 8 gm • Sodium 351 mg • Calcium 208 mg

Pesto Pasta with Chickpeas and Tomatoes

YIELD: 4 TO 6 SERVINGS

2 tablespoons extra-virgin
olive oil
2 shallots, minced
4 garlic cloves, minced
4 cups diced vine-ripened
or canned tomatoes
1 cup dry white wine
1 cup chicken or vegetable broth

$\frac{1}{2}$ teaspoon hot red pepper flakes
Salt and freshly ground black
pepper
2 cups cooked chickpeas, drained
1 pound orecchiette or shells
$\frac{1}{2}$ cup store-bought or homemade
pesto (page 263)

In a large skillet, heat the olive oil over medium-low heat. Add the shallots and garlic and cook, stirring occasionally, until the shallots are translucent, about 3 minutes. Increase the heat to high. Add the tomatoes, wine, and broth, and cook until the sauce thickens, about 10 minutes. Add the hot pepper flakes and season to taste with salt and pepper. Add the chickpeas and cook another 5 minutes.

Meanwhile, cook the pasta until just al dente. Drain well, reserving a few tablespoons of the cooking liquid to thin down the pesto. Place the pasta in a large serving bowl. Thin the pesto with the reserved cooking liquid, add the pesto sauce to the pasta, and toss well.

To serve, spoon the pasta into individual bowls. Top with the tomato-chickpea mixture. Serve at once.

Calories 795 • Protein 26 gm • Fat 18.9 gm • Percent of calories from fat 22% •
Cholesterol 1 mg • Dietary fiber 9 gm • Sodium 243 mg • Calcium 108 mg

Pesto Pasta with Cranberry Beans

YIELD: 4 TO 6 SERVINGS

$^3/_4$ cup dried cranberry beans, soaked overnight or using the quick-soak method on page 20
6 cups water
2 garlic cloves, minced

Pesto
1$^1/_2$ cups fresh basil leaves
2 garlic cloves
3 tablespoons pine nuts
4 tablespoons extra-virgin olive oil

2 bay leaves
1$^1/_2$ cups diced tomatoes with juice
$^1/_4$ cup dry white wine
Salt and freshly ground black pepper
1 pound rotini

3 tablespoons freshly grated Parmesan cheese
Salt and freshly ground black pepper

Drain the beans. Combine the beans in a saucepan with the 6 cups fresh water, garlic, and bay leaves. Cover and bring to a boil. Then reduce the heat and boil gently, partially covered, until tender, about 1 hour. Drain the beans and discard the bay leaves.

To make the pesto, combine the basil, garlic, and pine nuts in a food processor and process until finely chopped. Add the olive oil through the feed tube with the motor running and continue processing until you have a smooth paste. Briefly mix in the Parmesan and salt and pepper to taste. Set aside for at least 20 minutes to allow the flavors to develop.

In small saucepan, combine the cooked beans, tomatoes, wine, and salt and pepper to taste. Heat gently.

Meanwhile, cook the pasta in plenty of boiling salted water until al dente. Drain well, reserving several tablespoons of the cooking liquid to thin down the pesto. Place the pasta in a large bowl. Thin the pesto with the reserved cooking liquid. Add the pesto to the pasta and toss to coat well.

To serve, spoon the pasta into individual bowls. Top with the bean mixture. Serve at once.

Calories 750 • Protein 27 gm • Fat 21 gm • Percent of calories from fat 25% • Cholesterol 3 mg • Dietary fiber 13 gm • Sodium 99 mg • Calcium 163 mg

Syrian Rishtah

YIELD: 4 TO 6 SERVINGS

Lentils cooked in a spicy-sweet tomato sauce, served over noodles, makes an exotic and unusually tasty combination. Rishtah means "threads," as in "threads" of pasta. If at all possible, use French lentils for this dish as they hold their shape better than other kinds of lentils.

1/2 cup dried French green
    lentils, rinsed
2 1/2 cups water
1 tablespoon extra-virgin
    olive oil
2 onions, diced
3 garlic cloves, minced
2 cups chopped fresh or
    canned tomatoes
1 tablespoon tomato paste

1/2 cup water or chicken or
    vegetable broth
1 teaspoon ground cumin
1/4 teaspoon ground allspice
1/4 teaspoon ground coriander
1/4 teaspoon hot red pepper flakes
Salt and freshly ground black
    pepper
1 1/2 pounds fresh fettuccine
    or tagliatelle (or 1 pound dried)

In a medium saucepan, combine the lentils and the 2 1/2 cups water. Bring to a boil. Reduce the heat and simmer, covered, until the lentils are just tender but still retain their shape, 25 to 35 minutes. Set aside but do not drain.

In another saucepan, heat the olive oil over medium heat. Add the onions and garlic and sauté until the onions are golden, about 10 minutes. Add the lentils and cooking liquid, tomatoes, tomato paste, and water or broth. Add the cumin, allspice, coriander, hot pepper flakes, and salt and pepper to taste, and simmer for 15 minutes. Taste and adjust seasonings.

Cook the pasta in plenty of boiling salted water until al dente. Drain and place in a warm serving bowl. Pour the lentil sauce on top and toss lightly. Serve at once.

Calories 662 • Protein 26 gm • Fat 11 gm • Percent of calories from fat 15% •
Cholesterol 174 mg • Dietary fiber 11 gm • Sodium 87 mg • Calcium 97 mg

Bowties with White Beans and Fresh Tomato Sauce

YIELD: 4 TO 6 SERVINGS

This uncooked tomato sauce can only be made with vine-ripened tomatoes and fresh basil. If you use canned beans, the sauce is made in the time it takes to heat the water and cook the pasta. A delicious and light summer offering.

2 pounds vine-ripened tomatoes
   (3 to 5 tomatoes), chopped
1 large garlic clove
1 cup lightly packed fresh basil
   leaves
2 tablespoons extra-virgin
   olive oil
1^1/$_2$ teaspoons salt

^{1}/$_4$ teaspoon freshly ground black
   pepper
1^1/$_2$ cups cooked cannellini
1 pound bowties
   (or shells, rotelle, or orecchiette)
^{1}/$_3$ cup freshly grated Parmesan
   cheese

   In a food processor, combine the tomatoes, garlic, basil, oil, salt, and pepper. Puree. Pour into a large pasta serving bowl. Stir in the beans. Set aside.

   While the bean mixture sits, heat a large pot of salted water. Cook the pasta until just al dente. Drain and toss the pasta with the bean mixture and Parmesan cheese. Let sit for about 1 minute to allow the pasta to absorb some of the sauce. Serve at once.

Calories 671 • Protein 27 gm • Fat 16 gm • Percent of calories from fat 22% •
Cholesterol 137 mg • Dietary fiber 9 gm • Sodium 1037 mg • Calcium 140 mg

White Bean and Fennel Linguine

YIELD: 4 SERVINGS

1 tablespoon extra-virgin
   olive oil
1 fennel bulb, julienned
1 red bell pepper, julienned
3 garlic cloves, minced
$1/_4$ teaspoon hot red pepper
   flakes
$1^1/_2$ cups cooked cannellini
   or Great Northern beans

2 cups high-quality chicken or
   vegetable broth
2 tablespoons half-and-half
$1/_2$ cup chopped fresh parsley
2 tablespoons chopped fresh basil
Salt and freshly ground black
   pepper
1 pound linguine

Heat the olive oil in a large nonstick skillet over medium heat. Add the fennel and bell pepper, and sauté until translucent, about 4 minutes. Add the garlic, red pepper flakes, and beans, and continue to sauté for another 3 minutes. Reduce the heat to low and add the broth, half-and-half, parsley, and basil. Season with salt and pepper to taste.

Meanwhile, cook the linguine in plenty of boiling salted water until al dente. Drain the pasta and toss with the bean mixture. Serve at once.

Calories 572 • Protein 23 gm • Fat 6.5 gm • Percent of calories from fat 10% • Cholesterol 3 mg • Dietary fiber 8 gm • Sodium 254 mg • Calcium 76 mg

Penne with White Beans and Greens

YIELD: 4 SERVINGS

1 cup dried Great Northern or
    other white beans, soaked
    overnight or using the
    quick soak method page 20
6 cups water
1 onion, halved
1 celery stalk, halved
1 carrot, halved
2 sprigs fresh thyme or sage
3/4 pound kale or other green,
    stemmed and chopped

Salt and freshly ground black
    pepper
1 pound penne or other short pasta
1/4 cup extra-virgin olive oil
8 large garlic cloves, sliced
1/4 teaspoon hot red pepper flakes
    (optional)
Freshly grated Parmesan cheese

Drain the beans. In a large pot, combine the beans with the 6 cups fresh water, onion, celery, carrot, and thyme. Cover and bring to a boil. Then reduce the heat and simmer, partially covered, until the beans are tender, approximately $1^1/_2$ to 2 hours. Do not overcook the beans. (The beans can be held for several hours at this point.)

Remove and discard the onion, celery, carrot, and thyme sprigs. Season the beans with salt and pepper to taste. Bring to a boil, then stir in the greens and simmer until the greens are tender, about 8 minutes.

Meanwhile, cook the pasta in plenty of boiling salted water until al dente. Drain. While the pasta cooks, heat the oil in a small heavy pan over very low heat. Add the garlic and simmer until tender and slightly golden, stirring occasionally and guarding against overbrowning, about 10 minutes. Mash the garlic with a fork. Add the hot pepper flakes (if using). Toss with the pasta.

To serve, spoon the beans and greens on top of the pasta. Sprinkle a little grated Parmesan cheese on top and pass additional cheese at the table.

Calories 729 • Protein 26 gm • Fat 16 gm • Percent of calories from fat 20% •
Cholesterol 0 mg • Dietary fiber 17 gm • Sodium 46 mg • Calcium 180 mg

Chili Mac

YIELD: 8 TO 10 SERVINGS

An all-American dish that combines macaroni with chili and corn.

1 tablespoon olive or canola oil

3 tablespoons chili powder

2 teaspoons ground cumin

1 large onion, chopped

1 green bell pepper, diced

3 cloves garlic, finely chopped

1 (28-ounce) can whole tomatoes in juice

1 (28-ounce) can tomato puree

2 cups fresh or frozen corn kernels

1¹/₂ cups cooked red kidney beans

1¹/₂ cups cooked black beans

1¹/₂ cups cooked pinto beans

1 teaspoon dried oregano

12 ounces beer or chicken or vegetable broth

Salt and freshly ground black pepper

¹/₂ pound uncooked macaroni

Grated Monterey Jack or Cheddar cheese (optional)

Heat the oil in a large pot over medium heat. Add the chili powder, cumin, onion, bell pepper, and garlic. Sauté until the onion is limp, about 4 minutes. Add the tomatoes, tomato puree, corn, and the kidney, black, and pinto beans; stir in the oregano, beer or broth, and salt and pepper to taste. Simmer for 20 minutes, until the flavors are blended. Taste and adjust seasonings.

Meanwhile, cook the macaroni in plenty of salted boiling water until al dente. Drain and stir into the chili.

Serve hot, passing grated cheese at the table, if desired.

Calories 377 • Protein 17 gm • Fat 3 gm • Percent of calories from fat 8% • Cholesterol 0 mg • Dietary fiber 14 gm • Sodium 193 mg • Calcium 99 mg

8

Great Grains

Basic Cooked Amaranth

Basic Cooked Pearled Barley

Basic Cooked Hulled Barley

Basic Kasha

Basic Roasted Buckwheat Groats

Basic Cooked Bulgur

Basic Cooked Cracked Wheat

Basic Polenta

Basic Double-boiler (Foolproof) Polenta

Basic Cooked Couscous

Basic Cracked Wheat

Basic Grits

Basic Cooked Millet

Basic Cooked Wheat Berries

Barley with Roasted Fall Vegetables

Toasted Barley-Vermicelli Pilaf

Baked Barley Pilaf

Barley–Wild Rice Pilaf

Barley Risotto with Wild Mushrooms and Peas

Bulgur Pilaf with Creamy Dill Sauce

Red Pepper Corn Cakes

Southern Spoonbread

Cheesy Soft Polenta with Rich Tomato Sauce

Broiled Garlic-Cheese Polenta Squares

Couscous Pilaf

Couscous Timbales

Egyptian Slow-simmered Vegetables on Couscous

Couscous-stuffed Eggplant

Couscous with Roasted Vegetables

Simple Cracked Wheat Pilaf

Tomato-Vegetable Cracked Wheat Pilaf

Spinach-Cheese Grits

Cheese Grits Soufflé

Kasha with Bowties

Kasha with Wild Mushrooms, Leeks, and Dill

Millet Stir-Fry

Millet-stuffed Golden Nugget Squash

Quinoa Pilaf

I was raised in a household where meat and potatoes ruled the table. But at least once a week, kasha was offered as an alternative to the almighty spud. Barley frequently starred in thick, porridge-like soups, and bulgur began to appear, in the form of tabouli, during the sixties, when many people began to broaden their palates and explore different cuisines.

More recently I have made the acquaintance of millet, quinoa, couscous, and polenta, and have enjoyed them most at restaurants where the chefs like to work with cross-cultural or "exotic" ingredients. Grains all have in common a subtle, nutty flavor that combines well with both mild and assertive seasonings and vegetables. They fill you up and provide good nutrition in the form of fiber and B vitamins. Refer to pages 23 to 32 of the Introduction for a more detailed description of grains.

The recipes collected here are mostly simple combinations. Depending on your mood, they can be enjoyed as side dishes or main courses.

Basic Cooked Amaranth

YIELD: ABOUT 2 1/2 CUPS

Amaranth was the sacred grain of the Aztecs. It was considered to have almost mythical strength-giving properties. On holy days, amaranth was combined with honey and human blood to make cakes in the shapes of snakes, birds, and other deities, which were then broken apart and eaten for their strength-giving powers. This practice infuriated the Spanish conquistadors who saw it as a mockery of Christian communion. Hernando Cortés commanded his troops to burn all the fields of amaranth in Mexico and ordered that anyone found in possession of so much as a grain of amaranth be relieved of his hands. Thus, a whole culture was destroyed.

1 cup uncooked amaranth
3 cups water
1/4 teaspoon salt

Butter
Salt and freshly ground black pepper

Combine the amaranth, water, and salt in a saucepan. Cover and bring to a boil. Reduce the heat and boil gently until the liquid has been absorbed and the grains are tender, about 25 minutes. Whether or not the water looks like it has been absorbed, stir gently after 25 minutes; there is probably just a thin film of water on top that will stir in, revealing the cooked grain. Serve hot, seasoned to taste with a little butter and salt and pepper.

Calories 292 • Protein 11 gm • Fat 5 gm • Percent of calories from fat 15% • Cholesterol 0 mg • Dietary fiber 12 gm • Sodium 257 mg • Calcium 125 mg

Basic Cooked Pearled Barley

❧

YIELD: ABOUT 3 1/2 CUPS

1 cup uncooked pearled barley **1/2 teaspoon salt**
3 cups water **Freshly ground black pepper**

Combine the barley, water, and salt in a saucepan. Cover and bring to a boil. Reduce the heat and simmer until the liquid has been absorbed and the grains are tender but still chewy (not mushy), about 40 minutes. Fluff with a fork. Taste and adjust seasoning, adding a little pepper if desired.

Calories 194 • Protein 6 gm • Fat 1 gm • Percent of calories from fat 5% •
Cholesterol 0 mg • Dietary fiber 6 gm • Sodium 338 mg • Calcium 4 mg

Basic Cooked Hulled Barley

❧

YIELD: ABOUT 3 1/2 CUPS

1 cup uncooked hulled barley **1/2 teaspoon salt**
3 cups water **Freshly ground black pepper**

Combine the barley, water, and salt in a saucepan. Cover and bring to a boil. Reduce the heat and simmer until the liquid has been absorbed and the grains are tender but still chewy (not mushy), 40 to 45 minutes. Fluff with a fork. Taste and adjust seasoning, adding a little pepper, if desired.

Calories 189 • Protein 6 gm • Fat 1 gm • Percent of calories from fat 5% •
Cholesterol 0 mg • Dietary fiber 9 gm • Sodium 345 mg • Calcium 21 mg

Basic Kasha

YIELD: 4 CUPS

Kasha—ground roasted buckwheat groats—is sold in fine and medium granulation. Reduce the cooking time for a fine grind.

1 cup uncooked medium-grind kasha
1 egg white, slightly beaten

2 cups boiling water or broth
¹/₂ teaspoon salt (optional)

Combine the kasha and egg white in a saucepan and stir to coat the kernels. Turn the heat to high and cook, stirring constantly, until the egg has dried on the kasha and the grains are separate. Stir in the boiling water or broth and salt (if using). Cover, reduce the heat, and simmer until the kasha grains are tender and the liquid has been absorbed, about 8 minutes. Serve hot.

Calories 146 • Protein 6 gm • Fat 1 gm • Percent of calories from fat 6% • Cholesterol 0 mg • Dietary fiber 4 gm • Sodium 22 mg • Calcium 10 mg

Basic Roasted Buckwheat Groats

❧

YIELD: 4 CUPS

I have never found unroasted buckwheat groats in the store. Roasted whole groats can be used interchangeably with kasha.

1 cup uncooked roasted buckwheat groats
1 egg white, slightly beaten

2 cups boiling water or broth
$1/_2$ teaspoon salt (optional)

   Combine the buckwheat groats and egg white in a saucepan and stir to coat the kernels. Turn the heat to high and cook, stirring constantly, until the egg has dried and the grains are separate. Stir in the boiling water or broth and salt (if using). Cover, reduce the heat, and simmer until the groats are tender and the liquid has been absorbed, about 15 minutes. Serve hot.

Calories 146 • Protein 6 gm • Fat 1 gm • Percent of calories from fat 6% • Cholesterol 0 mg • Dietary fiber 4 gm • Sodium 22 mg • Calcium 10 mg

Basic Cooked Bulgur

YIELD: 3 CUPS

1 cup fine- or medium-grind bulgur　　　　　**2¹/₂ cups boiling water**

In a large bowl, combine the bulgur and boiling water. Cover and let stand for about 15 minutes. When most of the water has been absorbed and the grains are tender, drain off any excess water. Fluff with a fork.

Calories 160 • Protein 6 gm • Fat 1 gm • Percent of calories from fat 3% •
Cholesterol 0 mg • Dietary fiber 9 gm • Sodium 14 mg • Calcium 20 mg

Basic Polenta

❧

YIELD: ABOUT 4 CUPS

Polenta is a porridge made from cornmeal. It is smoother and seems more refined than grits and is also a trifle more trying for the cook, as it is difficult to avoid lumps in the cooking process. Whisking in the cornmeal with a wire whisk and then persistent stirring with a wooden spoon should take care of the pesky lumps. Basic polenta is a comfort dish for some; for others it is the starting point for other more complex recipes, such as the ones that appear later in this chapter.

4 cups water	**Butter (optional)**
1 teaspoon salt	**Extra-virgin olive oil (optional)**
1¹/₂ cups medium-grind cornmeal	

In a heavy-bottomed saucepan, bring the water and salt to a full boil. Whisk in the cornmeal in a slow steady stream. Reduce the heat and simmer for 20 to 25 minutes, stirring almost constantly with a wooden spoon as the mixture thickens.

If desired, stir in a few tablespoons of butter. Serve hot. Or scrape the polenta into a 9×13-inch baking dish that has been sprayed with nonstick cooking spray. Smooth the top and let cool. The polenta will solidify and can be cut into slices. To reheat, brush lightly with olive oil and place on the grill or under the broiler briefly, until golden and heated through.

Calories 166 • Protein 4 gm • Fat 2 gm • Percent of calories from fat 8% • Cholesterol 0 mg • Dietary fiber 3 gm • Sodium 604 mg • Calcium 8 mg

Basic Double-boiler (Foolproof) Polenta

YIELD: ABOUT 4 CUPS

If you have the time—about an hour and a half—this is the method to use for making polenta. It is almost foolproof. I can guarantee that it will taste great and never be gummy. However, you still have to add the cornmeal slowly—it doesn't do away with the lump problem. I first read about this method in Cook's Illustrated, *a fine magazine that takes pride in questioning conventional cooking wisdom. This method is well tested and time-proven.*

4 cups boiling water
1 teaspoon salt
1 cup medium-grind cornmeal

Butter (optional)
Olive oil (optional)

Pour the boiling water into the top of a double boiler set over simmering water. Add the salt. Gradually sprinkle in the cornmeal, whisking constantly to prevent lumps. Cover and cook over the simmering water until the polenta is soft and fluffy, about 1 1/4 to 1 1/2 hours. Stir for about 1 minute every 15 minutes or so.

If desired, stir in a few tablespoons of butter. Serve hot. Or scrape the polenta into a 9×13-inch baking dish that has been sprayed with nonstick cooking spray. Smooth the top and let cool. The polenta will solidify and can be cut into slices. To reheat, brush lightly with olive oil and place on the grill or under the broiler briefly, until golden and heated through.

Calories 111 • Protein 2 gm • Fat 1 gm • Percent of calories from fat 8% •
Cholesterol 0 mg • Dietary fiber 2 gm • Sodium 599 mg • Calcium 7 mg

Basic Cooked Couscous

YIELD: 2 3/4 CUPS

The mildest of grains, couscous is almost like white rice in its adaptability.

1 cup uncooked couscous
1 1/2 cups boiling water or broth

1/4 teaspoon salt (optional)

Combine the couscous and boiling liquid in a bowl. Add salt, if desired. Cover and let stand for 5 minutes, until all of the liquid has been absorbed and the grain is tender. Fluff with a fork and let stand another 5 minutes before serving.

Calories 252 • Protein 9 gm • Fat 1 gm • Percent of calories from fat 2% • Cholesterol 0 mg • Dietary fiber 3 gm • Sodium 11 mg • Calcium 19 mg

Basic Cracked Wheat

❧❧❦

YIELD: ABOUT 3 CUPS

1 cup uncooked cracked wheat   **2 cups water**

In a saucepan, toast the cracked wheat over medium heat until it smells fragrant, about 3 minutes. Carefully stir in the water, cover, and bring to a boil over high heat. Reduce the heat and simmer until the water has been absorbed, about 15 minutes. Fluff with a fork.

Calories 187 • Protein 7 gm • Fat 1 gm • Percent of calories from fat 3% • Cholesterol 0 mg • Dietary fiber 8 gm • Sodium 5 mg • Calcium 10 mg

Basic Grits

YIELDS: ABOUT 3 CUPS

Corn kernels that have been treated with lime, which removes the husks and alters the starch, becomes hominy. Hominy that has been ground becomes grits, which are cooked in milk or water to make a creamy dish that is grittier than Italian polenta (which is made from cornmeal). Both polenta and grits can be served simply, with perhaps a pat of butter on top. Cheese also makes a fine addition to these two similar dishes.

3 cups water
1 teaspoon salt
1 cup uncooked white or yellow
  grits

Butter (optional)

In a heavy-bottomed saucepan, bring the water and salt to a full boil. Stir in the grits, reduce the heat, and simmer for 10 to 15 minutes, stirring almost constantly as the mixture thickens.

If desired, stir in a few tablespoons of butter. Serve hot.

Calories 187 • Protein 4 gm • Fat 1 gm • Percent of calories from fat 3% • Cholesterol 0 mg • Dietary fiber 3 gm • Sodium 782 mg • Calcium 5 mg

Basic Cooked Millet

YIELD: 3 1/2 CUPS

1 tablespoon olive or canola oil	2 1/2 cups boiling water or broth
1 cup uncooked millet	Salt (optional)

Heat the oil in a saucepan over medium heat. Add the millet and sauté, stirring constantly, until the grains are popping and smell toasted. Stir in the boiling water and salt (if using). Cover and bring to a boil, then reduce the heat to low and simmer until the grains are tender and have absorbed all of the liquid, 25 to 30 minutes. Remove from the heat and let stand for 10 minutes. Then fluff with a fork and serve.

Calories 250 • Protein 6 gm • Fat 6 gm • Percent of calories from fat 23% • Cholesterol 0 mg • Dietary fiber 5 gm • Sodium 8 mg • Calcium 8 mg

Basic Cooked Wheat Berries

✦

YIELD: 3 CUPS

If you think of it, you can soak wheat berries overnight and reduce the cooking time to 50 to 60 minutes. If you forget to presoak, the berries will require $1^1/_4$ to $1^1/_2$ hours of cooking to reach a tender state.

1 cup uncooked wheat berries **4 cups water**

In a medium saucepan, combine the wheat berries and water. Cover and bring to a boil. Reduce the heat and simmer until the berries are tender, $1^1/_4$ to $1^1/_2$ hours. Drain well.

Calories 209 • Protein 8 gm • Fat 1 gm • Percent of calories from fat 4% • Cholesterol 0 mg • Dietary fiber 8 gm • Sodium 11 mg • Calcium 25 mg

Barley with Roasted Fall Vegetables

YIELD: 4 TO 6 SERVINGS

This dazzling feast of fall vegetables turns a bright magenta from the beets. A more conservative version would substitute turnips or rutabagas, but I think the color is exciting.

1½ pounds winter squash, such as butternut, peeled and diced
1 pound beets, peeled and diced
1 garlic bulb, cloves separated (halved if large) and peeled
1 tablespoon fresh rosemary leaves
3 tablespoons extra-virgin olive oil

1 leek, white part only, thinly sliced
1 cup uncooked pearled barley
4 cups high-quality chicken or vegetable broth
6 tablespoons freshly grated Parmesan cheese
Salt and freshly ground black pepper

Preheat the oven to 400 degrees. Spray a large shallow roasting pan or 2 baking trays with nonstick cooking spray. In a large bowl, combine the squash, beets, garlic, rosemary, and 2 tablespoons of the oil. Arrange in a single layer in the roasting pan and roast for 30 to 45 minutes, stirring every 15 minutes or so, until the vegetables are browned and tender.

Meanwhile, heat the remaining 1 tablespoon oil in a large saucepan. Add the leek and sauté until limp, about 2 minutes. Add the barley and sauté another minute. Add the broth. Bring to a boil, then cover, reduce the heat, and simmer until the barley is quite tender and most of the liquid has been absorbed, about 40 minutes. Increase the heat to high and stir the barley as the last amount of liquid is absorbed. Remove from the heat and stir in the Parmesan cheese, then the roasted vegetables. Season with salt and pepper to taste. Serve hot.

Calories 474 • Protein 17 gm • Fat 14 gm • Percent of calories from fat 25% • Cholesterol 6 mg • Dietary fiber 14 gm • Sodium 698 mg • Calcium 239 mg

Toasted Barley-Vermicelli Pilaf

YIELD: 4 TO 6 SERVINGS

Barley A Roni? You won't find this in a convenience mix, but it is easy to make. This is a light-hearted dish, filled with little jewels of sweet vegetables.

2 tablespoons extra-virgin
  olive oil
3 ounces vermicelli, broken
  into 1½-inch pieces
2 shallots, minced
4 garlic cloves, minced
1 red bell pepper, diced
1 carrot, diced

1 cup uncooked pearled barley
2½ cups high-quality chicken
  or vegetable broth
1 cup fresh or frozen green peas
2 tablespoons chopped fresh
  parsley
Salt and freshly ground black
  pepper

Heat 1 tablespoon of the olive oil in a large cast-iron or nonstick skillet over medium heat. Add the vermicelli and sauté until lightly browned, about 3 minutes. Remove from the pan with a slotted spoon and set aside.

Add the remaining 1 tablespoon olive oil to the skillet. Heat for 1 minute, then add the shallots, garlic, bell pepper, carrot, and barley, and sauté until the vegetables are barely softened and the barley smells toasted, about 3 minutes. Add 2 cups of the broth. Bring to a boil, then reduce the heat, cover, and simmer for 20 minutes.

Stir in the remaining ½ cup broth and the vermicelli. Cover and simmer, stirring frequently, until the barley and vermicelli are tender and the liquid has been absorbed, about 10 minutes. Remove from the heat. Stir in the peas and parsley. Season to taste with salt and pepper. Dry the lid and cover the pan. Let stand for 5 minutes before serving.

Calories 378 • Protein 12 gm • Fat 8 gm • Percent of calories from fat 18% •
Cholesterol 0 mg • Dietary fiber 12 gm • Sodium 297 mg • Calcium 44 mg

Baked Barley Pilaf

YIELD: 4 TO 6 SERVINGS

Barley and mushrooms have a great affinity for each other. For extra flavor, use several different kinds of mushrooms, such as shiitake, chanterelle, and oyster.

2 tablespoons extra-virgin
  olive oil
2 cups thinly sliced mushrooms
1 onion, diced
1 cup uncooked pearled barley
4 cups high-quality chicken or
  vegetable broth

1 tablespoon chopped fresh sage
  or 1 teaspoon dried
$1/_2$ cup finely chopped scallions
Salt and freshly ground black
  pepper

Preheat the oven to 350 degrees.

In a 2-quart or larger Dutch oven, heat the olive oil over medium-high heat. Add the mushrooms, onion, and barley, and sauté until the barley appears toasted and the mushrooms are well browned, about 8 minutes. Stir in 2 cups of the broth and the sage, mix well, cover, and bake for 30 minutes. Add the remaining 2 cups broth, cover again, and bake for an additional 30 minutes. Carefully stir in the scallions and salt and plenty of pepper, leave the Dutch oven uncovered, and bake for 15 minutes more, until most of the liquid is absorbed and the barley is tender. Fluff with a fork before serving.

Calories 286 • Protein 9 gm • Fat 8 gm • Percent of calories from fat 24% •
Cholesterol 0 mg • Dietary fiber 9 gm • Sodium 459 mg • Calcium 48 mg

Barley—Wild Rice Pilaf

❦

YIELD: 4 TO 6 SERVINGS

A great pairing—the sweetness of the barley perfectly complements the slight bitterness of the wild rice, while the wild rice adds an especially pleasant chewy texture.

2 tablespoons extra-virgin
  olive oil
2 shallots, finely chopped
2 garlic cloves, minced
3 cups chopped mushrooms

$1/2$ cup uncooked wild rice
$1/2$ cup uncooked pearled barley
3 cups water
1 teaspoon salt
Freshly ground black pepper

Heat the olive oil in a large skillet over medium-high heat. Add the shallots, garlic, and mushrooms, and sauté until well coated with the oil, about 2 minutes. Add the wild rice and barley and sauté until the barley appears toasted and the wild rice is fragrant, about 5 minutes. Add the water, salt, and pepper, and bring to a boil. Reduce the heat to a gentle boil, cover, and cook until all of the liquid has been absorbed and the barley and rice grains are tender, about 50 minutes. Fluff with a fork. Serve hot.

Calories 233 • Protein 7 gm • Fat 7 gm • Percent of calories from fat 28% • Cholesterol 0 mg • Dietary fiber 6 gm • Sodium 591 mg • Calcium 17 mg

Barley Risotto with Wild Mushrooms and Peas

YIELD: 2 TO 4 SERVINGS

Cooking barley as you would rice in a risotto results in a creamy, moist dish. The grain creates its own gravy, wonderfully fragrant with the woodsy flavors of wild mushrooms. This is a great dish.

4³/₄ cups high-quality chicken, mushroom, or vegetable broth

¹/₂ cup dry white wine

2 tablespoons extra-virgin olive oil

¹/₄ pound fresh mixed wild mushrooms (such as shiitakes, chanterelles, and oysters), trimmed

2 shallots, minced

2 garlic cloves, minced

³/₄ cup uncooked pearled barley

1 cup fresh or frozen peas

Salt and freshly ground black pepper

Heat the broth and wine to a simmer. Keep over low heat.

In a large skillet, heat 1 tablespoon of the oil. Add the mushrooms and sauté until browned and limp, about 4 minutes. Remove from the skillet with a slotted spoon and set aside.

Add the remaining 1 tablespoon oil to the skillet. Add the shallots and garlic and sauté for 2 minutes, until limp. Add the barley and continue to sauté until the barley appears toasted and is slightly fragrant, about 4 minutes. Stir in 1 cup of the hot broth, reduce the heat to low, and cook, stirring frequently, until the liquid has been absorbed, about 10 minutes. Continue adding the broth, 1 cup at a time, stirring frequently and cooking slowly, until all of the broth has been absorbed. The total cooking time will be about 40 minutes. After the addition of the last cup of broth, stir in the mushrooms. When the barley is tender and creamy, stir in the peas and salt and pepper to taste. Continue cooking and stirring gently until the peas are heated through, about 3 minutes. Serve immediately.

Calories 574 • Protein 20 gm • Fat 15 gm • Percent of calories from fat 23% • Cholesterol 0 mg • Dietary fiber 17 gm • Sodium 1083 mg • Calcium 56 mg

Bulgur Pilaf with Creamy Dill Sauce

YIELD: 4 TO 6 SERVINGS

2 cups medium-grind bulgur

4 cups boiling water

2 tablespoons extra-virgin
    olive oil

2 garlic cloves, minced

1 leek, white portion only,
    thinly sliced

1 carrot, cubed

2 cups fresh or frozen peas

Salt and freshly ground black
    pepper

1/2 cup sour cream

1/2 cup nonfat plain yogurt

1/4 cup chopped fresh dill

Combine the bulgur and boiling water in a large saucepan. Remove from the heat, cover, and set aside for 10 to 15 minutes, until the water has been absorbed and the grains are tender.

Meanwhile, heat the olive oil in a large saucepan or skillet. Add the garlic, leek, and carrot, and sauté until the leek and carrot are tender, about 5 minutes. Set aside.

When the bulgur is tender, stir in the carrot-leek mixture. Stir in the peas. Dry the pot lid. Place a crumpled kitchen towel over the pilaf to absorb excess steam, replace the cover, and let stand for about 10 minutes. Fluff with a fork and season to taste with salt and pepper.

Combine the sour cream, yogurt, and dill in a small bowl. Stir 1/4 cup of the sauce into the pilaf. Pass the remaining sauce at the table.

Calories 464 • Protein 16 gm • Fat 14 gm • Percent of calories from fat 26% •
Cholesterol 13 mg • Dietary fiber 18 gm • Sodium 73 mg • Calcium 164 mg

Red Pepper Corn Cakes

YIELD: 4 TO 6 SERVINGS

Silken cornmeal pancakes studded with fresh sweet corn and sweet red bell peppers are delicious, hot out of the pan, just as they are. But to gild the lily, you can garnish them with a sprinkling of chopped cilantro and pass salsa or sour cream (or both) on the side. During corn and tomato season, I like to serve these as a main course with a chopped tomato salad on the side.

2 tablespoons coarse yellow
   stone-ground cornmeal
$^1/_2$ cup water
1 tablespoon butter
6 tablespoons unbleached
   all-purpose flour
$^1/_4$ teaspoon salt
$^1/_4$ teaspoon freshly ground black
   pepper
$^1/_4$ teaspoon baking powder

$^1/_4$ teaspoon baking soda
2 large eggs
6 tablespoons nonfat buttermilk
2 cups corn kernels (fresh
   or frozen and thawed)
$^1/_2$ cup finely chopped red bell
   pepper
$^1/_4$ cup finely snipped chives
   or chopped scallions

Combine the cornmeal and water in a small saucepan and cook over medium heat, stirring constantly, until thick, about 3 minutes. Add the butter and stir until smooth. Set aside to cool slightly.

Combine the flour, salt, pepper, baking powder, and baking soda in a mixing bowl.

Stir the eggs and buttermilk into the cornmeal mixture. Fold in the flour mixture. Stir in the corn, bell pepper, and chives or scallions.

Preheat the oven to 250 degrees. Spray a well-seasoned cast-iron griddle or large nonstick frying pan with nonstick cooking spray and heat over medium heat. Spoon the batter, about $^1/_4$ cup at a time, onto the heated surface and cook for 2 to 3 minutes per side. Transfer the cooked corn cakes to the oven to keep warm while you cook the remaining batter. Serve warm.

Calories 197 • Protein 8 gm • Fat 6 gm • Percent of calories from fat 26% •
Cholesterol 115 mg • Dietary fiber 3 gm • Sodium 342 mg • Calcium 58 mg

Southern Spoonbread

❧❧❧

YIELD: 4 TO 6 SERVINGS

Spoonbread is a soft, custardy cross between a soufflé and a corn bread. Here it is jazzed up with diced red bell peppers and scallions.

1¹/₂ cups fresh or frozen corn
   kernels
2 cups skim milk
1 cup evaporated skim milk
2 teaspoons salt
1 cup white or yellow
   stone-ground cornmeal

2 tablespoons butter
¹/₂ red bell pepper, diced
¹/₄ cup chopped scallions
1 teaspoon sugar
¹/₄ teaspoon freshly ground black
   pepper
4 large eggs, separated

Preheat the oven to 350 degrees. Butter a 2-quart baking dish.

In a heavy-bottomed saucepan, combine the corn, skim milk, evaporated milk, and salt, and heat almost to a boil over high heat. Add the cornmeal in a thin stream, stirring constantly. Reduce the heat to low and cook, stirring constantly, for about 5 minutes, until the mixture is thick enough for a spoon to stand up in it. Remove from the heat and beat in the butter, bell pepper, scallions, sugar, and pepper.

Beat the egg yolks in a small bowl. Add about ¹/₂ cup of the cornmeal mixture and beat until well mixed. Add to the cornmeal mixture and beat until well incorporated.

In a separate bowl, beat the egg whites until stiff. Fold into the cornmeal mixture.

Pour the batter into the prepared baking dish. Bake for 35 to 45 minutes, until the spoonbread is puffed and browned. Serve at once.

Calories 408 • Protein 20 gm • Fat 12 gm • Percent of calories from fat 26% •
Cholesterol 233 mg • Dietary fiber 5 gm • Sodium 1430 mg • Calcium 376 mg

Cheesy Soft Polenta with Rich Tomato Sauce

YIELD: 4 TO 6 SERVINGS

The creamy polenta forms a wonderful base for the vegetable-rich tomato sauce—a lovely change from pasta.

1 tablespoon extra-virgin olive oil
1/2 pound mushrooms, sliced
   (4 cups)
1 onion, finely chopped
1 carrot, finely chopped
1 celery stalk, finely chopped
4 garlic cloves, minced
1 (28-ounce) can crushed tomatoes
2 tablespoons chopped fresh
   parsley
2 tablespoons chopped fresh basil
1 teaspoon dried thyme
1/2 teaspoon dried rosemary
Salt and freshly ground black
   pepper
8 cups water
1 teaspoon salt
2 cups medium-grind cornmeal
1 tablespoon butter
5 tablespoons freshly grated
   Parmesan cheese,
   plus extra for serving

In a medium saucepan, heat the oil over medium heat. Add the mushrooms, onion, carrot, celery, and garlic, and sauté until soft, about 5 minutes. Add the tomatoes, parsley, basil, thyme, and rosemary. Simmer for 15 minutes. Taste and season with salt and pepper to taste.

Meanwhile, heat the water with 1 teaspoon salt in a large, heavy-bottomed saucepan. Add the cornmeal in a slow stream, whisking constantly. Reduce the heat and simmer, stirring frequently with a wooden spoon, until the polenta is thick and pulls away from the sides of the pan, about 20 minutes. Stir in the butter and Parmesan.

Serve the polenta in bowls, topped with the tomato sauce. Pass extra Parmesan at the table, if desired.

Calories 417 • Protein 13 gm • Fat 11 gm • Percent of calories from fat 23% • Cholesterol 13 mg • Dietary fiber 10 gm • Sodium 1093 mg • Calcium 204 mg

Broiled Garlic-Cheese Polenta Squares

YIELD: 10 SERVINGS

1 recipe Basic Polenta (page 277) or Basic Double-boiler (Fool-proof) Polenta (page 278)
2 garlic cloves, minced
1 tablespoon butter

¼ cup freshly grated Parmesan cheese
2 tomatoes, sliced
2 tablespoons chopped fresh basil
1 cup grated mozzarella cheese

Prepare the polenta according to the recipe, adding the garlic to the cooking water along with the salt. When the polenta is cooked, stir in the butter. Spray a 15-inch cookie sheet or jelly roll pan with nonstick cooking spray. Quickly spread the cooked polenta in the pan, using a spatula to make a level surface. Sprinkle the grated Parmesan over the top. Let cool for an hour or more, until firm. You can make this a day ahead, if desired.

Preheat the broiler. Arrange the tomatoes on the polenta. Sprinkle the basil, then the mozzarella on top. Broil until lightly browned, about 5 minutes. Cut into squares and serve hot.

Calories 125 • Protein 5 gm • Fat 5 gm • Percent of calories from fat 34% • Cholesterol 11 mg • Dietary fiber 2 gm • Sodium 354 mg • Calcium 114 mg

Couscous Pilaf

YIELD: 4 TO 6 SERVINGS

1 tablespoon extra-virgin olive oil
2 shallots, minced
3 garlic cloves, minced
1 carrot, minced
1 celery stalk, with leaves, minced
1 ripe tomato, diced

$1/4$ cup chopped fresh parsley
$1^1/2$ cups couscous
$2^1/4$ cups boiling water
1 teaspoon salt
Freshly ground black pepper
$1/2$ cup chopped black olives

In a large skillet, heat the olive oil over medium-high heat. Add the shallots, garlic, carrot, and celery, and sauté until the vegetables are limp and fragrant, about 4 minutes. Stir in the tomato and parsley and sauté for 1 minute more. Add the couscous and boiling water. Remove from the heat. Stir in the salt and pepper to taste. Cover and set aside until the couscous has absorbed all of the liquid, about 10 minutes. Fluff with a fork, mix in the olives, taste, and adjust seasonings as needed. Serve hot.

Calories 327 • Protein 10 gm • Fat 5 gm • Percent of calories from fat 15% •
Cholesterol 0 mg • Dietary fiber 5 gm • Sodium 703 mg • Calcium 39 mg

Couscous Timbales

❧✦❧

YIELD: 5 SERVINGS

Pressed into molds, these grains become a very elegant dish.

2 cups water
Pinch saffron
$1/4$ teaspoon ground coriander
$1/2$ teaspoon salt
1 tablespoon extra-virgin olive oil
2 scallions, chopped
$1/2$ red bell pepper, finely chopped

$1/4$ cup chopped pistachio nuts
$1/4$ cup currants
1 cup couscous
2 tablespoons chopped fresh cilantro
Salt and freshly ground black pepper

In a small saucepan, combine the water, saffron, coriander, and salt. Bring to a boil.

Meanwhile, in a large skillet, heat the olive oil over medium heat. Add the scallions and bell pepper and sauté for 2 minutes. Remove from the heat and stir in the pistachios, currants, couscous, and boiling water mixture. Cover and set aside for 10 minutes, until the couscous is tender and the water has been completely absorbed.

Mix the cilantro into the couscous. Taste and adjust seasonings. Spray 5 small custard cups or timbale molds with nonstick cooking spray. Press the couscous mixture into the cups. Cover and keep warm until you are ready to serve.

To serve, unmold the warm timbales directly onto the serving plates.

Calories 231 • Protein 6 gm • Fat 6 gm • Percent of calories from fat 24% • Cholesterol 0 mg • Dietary fiber 3 gm • Sodium 243 mg • Calcium 25 mg

Egyptian Slow-simmered Vegetables on Couscous

YIELD: 4 TO 6 SERVINGS

It is the combination of herbs and spices that makes this dish so tasty. The mint brings all the flavors together in a most harmonious manner.

2 tablespoons extra-virgin olive oil

4 garlic cloves, minced

1 large onion, diced

1 green bell pepper, diced

1 small zucchini, diced

1 small yellow summer squash, diced

1 (28-ounce) can peeled tomatoes with juice

1/2 pound green beans, trimmed and cut into 1 1/2-inch lengths (about 2 cups)

2 teaspoons ground cumin

1/4 teaspoon ground cinnamon

3 tablespoons chopped fresh mint

3 tablespoons chopped fresh parsley

Salt and freshly ground black pepper

1 1/2 cups couscous

3 cups boiling water

In a large, nonstick saucepan, heat the olive oil over medium-high heat. Add the garlic, onion, green pepper, zucchini, and summer squash, and sauté until the vegetables are slightly tender, about 3 minutes. Add the tomatoes, green beans, cumin, and cinnamon. Simmer for about 1 hour, until the vegetables are meltingly tender (the green beans will still have some crunch). Stir in the mint and parsley. Season with salt and pepper to taste. Let simmer while you prepare the couscous.

In a large bowl, combine the couscous with the boiling water. Cover and let steam for about 10 minutes. When all of the liquid has been absorbed, fluff with a fork.

To serve, spoon the couscous onto a large platter or into individual serving bowls and shape into a mound. With a spoon, pat a depression in the center of the mound. Spoon the vegetable mixture on top. Serve hot.

Calories 420 • Protein 14 gm • Fat 8 gm • Percent of calories from fat 17% • Cholesterol 0 mg • Dietary fiber 10 gm • Sodium 346 mg • Calcium 144 mg

Egyptian Slow-simmered Chicken Stew on Couscous. Place $^1/_2$ cup all-purpose flour in a shallow bowl. Season with $^1/_4$ teaspoon black pepper, $^1/_4$ teaspoon cumin, and $^1/_2$ teaspoon salt. Slice 1 pound boneless skinless chicken breast into $^1/_2$-inch cubes. Toss with the seasoned flour. Brown the chicken cubes in the hot oil, turning to brown all sides, about 8 minutes. Remove from the saucepan with a slotted spoon and set aside. Proceed with the recipe as written, sautéing the garlic, onion, green pepper, zucchini, and summer squash in the oil remaining in the saucepan. Return the chicken to the saucepan when you add the tomatoes and green beans. Proceed with the recipe as above, skimming off any fat that rises to the surface before serving.

Calories 659 • Protein 50 gm • Fat 12 gm • Percent of calories from fat 17% • Cholesterol 107 mg • Dietary fiber 10 gm • Sodium 720 mg • Calcium 165 mg

Couscous-stuffed Eggplant

YIELD: 6 TO 8 SERVINGS

Eggplants come in all sizes, colors, and shapes. For stuffing, it is worth seeking out small, preferably Japanese ones. Then you can serve a half to each person.

4 small Japanese eggplants
   or 1 large purple eggplant
2 tablespoons extra-virgin olive oil
1 cup uncooked couscous
2 cups boiling water
1 onion, finely chopped
1 fresh green chile pepper, finely
   diced
2 garlic cloves, minced

1 tablespoon ground cumin
1/2 teaspoon ground coriander
1 1/2 cups diced fresh
   or canned tomatoes, drained
2 tablespoons capers
Salt and freshly ground black
   pepper
1/2 cup crumbled feta cheese

Preheat the oven to 425 degrees. Slice the eggplants in half lengthwise. Run a knife along the inside edges of the eggplants, about 1/2 inch from the skin. Brush with 1 tablespoon of the oil. Set the eggplants, cut sides up, in a baking dish. Add about 1/2 inch water to the bottom of the dish. Bake for 25 to 40 minutes, until the eggplants are just tender.

While the eggplant bakes, prepare the couscous. Place the couscous in a medium bowl. Add the boiling water, stir once, cover, and set aside.

When the eggplants are tender, remove from the oven and reduce the oven temperature to 325 degrees. Scoop out the flesh, chop, and set aside. Reserve the skins. Pour out any water that remains and set the baking dish aside.

In a large skillet, heat the remaining 1 tablespoon oil over medium-high heat. Add the chopped eggplant, onion, chile pepper, garlic, cumin, and coriander, and sauté until the onion is tender, about 5 minutes. Stir in the prepared couscous, tomatoes, and capers. Taste and season with salt and pepper.

Stuff the couscous filling into the eggplant skins. Sprinkle the crumbled feta cheese on top. Return the stuffed eggplants to the baking dish. Bake for 20 minutes or until heated through. Serve hot.

Calories 253 • Protein 9 gm • Fat 10 gm • Percent of calories from fat 34% •
Cholesterol 19 mg • Dietary fiber 4 gm • Sodium 356 mg • Calcium 138 mg

Couscous- and Sausage-stuffed Eggplant. Remove 1 pound turkey or smoked chicken sausage from its casings and crumble. Add to the skillet along with the chopped eggplant, onion, chile pepper, garlic, cumin, and coriander, and cook until the sausage is browned. Proceed with the recipe as written.

Calories 373 • Protein 19 gm • Fat 16 gm • Percent of calories from fat 39% • Cholesterol 59 mg • Dietary fiber 4 gm • Sodium 1021 mg • Calcium 202 mg

Couscous with Roasted Vegetables

YIELD: 4 SERVINGS

Roasting vegetables renders their flavor rich, sweet, and mellow. This vegetarian feast, which combines roasted vegetables with couscous and tangy feta cheese, is delicious served with a green salad and flatbread. The vegetables you choose for the recipe can be varied; use whatever is in season and looks good to you.

$^1/_2$ pound beets, peeled
  and julienned
$^1/_4$ pound green beans, trimmed
  and cut into $1^1/_2$-inch lengths
$^1/_4$ pound baby carrots
1 small onion, halved
  and cut into slivers
1 red bell pepper, julienned
1 green bell pepper, julienned
1 garlic bulb, cloves
  separated and peeled
3 tablespoons chopped mixed
  fresh herbs (such as basil,
  thyme, oregano, and rosemary)
  or 1 tablespoon dried

2 tablespoons extra-virgin olive oil
Salt and freshly ground black
  pepper
Approximately $^1/_2$ cup high-quality
  chicken or vegetable broth
$^1/_4$ pound feta cheese, crumbled
$1^1/_2$ cups uncooked couscous
$2^1/_4$ cups boiling water

Preheat the oven to 400 degrees. Spray a large roasting pan with nonstick cooking spray.

In a large bowl, combine the beets, green beans, carrots, onion, red and green bell peppers, garlic, dried herbs (if using), olive oil, and salt and pepper to taste. Place in a single layer in the roasting pan. Pour the broth over the vegetables. Roast in the oven for about 30 minutes. During the last 10 minutes, add the feta cheese and fresh herbs (if using).

While the vegetables roast, combine the couscous with the boiling water and a pinch of salt. Cover and set aside to steam.

When the vegetables are roasted and the couscous is tender, mix together. If the mixture is a little dry, stir in a little more broth. Taste and add more salt and pepper, if needed. Serve hot.

Calories 494 • Protein 17 gm • Fat 13.9 gm • Percent of calories from fat 25% •
Cholesterol 26 mg • Dietary fiber 9 gm • Sodium 450 mg • Calcium 235 mg

Simple Cracked Wheat Pilaf

❧❧❧

YIELD: **4** SERVINGS

1 tablespoon extra-virgin olive oil
1 small onion, finely diced
1 cup uncooked cracked wheat
2 cups high-quality chicken
  or vegetable broth

$1/_4$ teaspoon freshly ground black
  pepper
1 cup fresh or frozen peas
Salt

In a medium saucepan over medium heat, heat the olive oil. Add the onion and sauté until soft, about 3 minutes. Add the cracked wheat and sauté until well coated in the oil. Pour in the broth and add the pepper. Cover and bring to a boil, then reduce the heat and simmer until the liquid has been absorbed and the grains are tender and fluffy, about 15 minutes. Fluff with a fork. Stir in the peas and season with salt, if needed. Dry the pot lid. Place a crumpled clean kitchen cotton or paper towel over the pilaf and replace the lid. Let sit for about 5 minutes before serving.

Calories 225 • Protein 9 gm • Fat 4.1 gm • Percent of calories from fat 16% •
Cholesterol 0 mg • Dietary fiber 9 gm • Sodium 228 mg • Calcium 23 mg

Tomato-Vegetable Cracked Wheat Pilaf

YIELD: 2 TO 4 SERVINGS

Cooking the cracked wheat in V8 juice or tomato juice is a fuss-free way to infuse the grain with flavor. The addition of summer vegetables makes this dish irresistible.

2¼ cups V8 or tomato juice
1 cup uncooked cracked wheat
1 tablespoon olive or canola oil
2 garlic cloves, minced
1 small onion, slivered
1 green bell pepper, diced

1 medium zucchini, diced (about
½ pound)
2 tablespoons chopped fresh basil
Salt and freshly ground black
pepper

In a medium saucepan, combine the V8 Juice and cracked wheat and bring to a boil. Reduce the heat to low, cover, and cook gently until the cracked wheat has absorbed all of the juice, about 15 minutes.

Meanwhile, in a large skillet, heat the oil over medium-high heat. Add the garlic, onion, and bell pepper, and sauté until the onion is limp, about 3 minutes. Add the zucchini and sauté until tender-crisp, about 3 minutes.

Fluff the cracked wheat with a fork. Stir in the sautéed vegetables and basil. Season to taste with salt and pepper. Serve hot.

Calories 457 • Protein 14 gm • Fat 8 gm • Percent of calories from fat 16% •
Cholesterol 0 mg • Dietary fiber 17 gm • Sodium 705 mg • Calcium 101 mg

Spinach-Cheese Grits

YIELD: 4 SERVINGS

12 ounces fresh spinach

1 tablespoon extra-virgin olive oil

4 garlic cloves, minced

1 shallot, minced

2¼ cups skim milk

¾ cup yellow or white
  quick-cooking grits

1 large egg, lightly beaten

1 large egg white, lightly beaten

1 cup reduced-fat cheddar cheese

2 tablespoons freshly grated
  Parmesan cheese

Salt and freshly ground black
  pepper

Preheat the oven to 350 degrees. Spray a 1½-quart casserole dish with nonstick cooking spray.

Steam the spinach until tender, plunge into ice water to stop the cooking, then drain. Squeeze the spinach in your hands to remove as much liquid as possible. Finely chop.

Heat the olive oil in a large saucepan. Add the garlic and shallot and sauté until the shallot is translucent, about 2 minutes. Add the milk and bring to a boil. Stir in the grits, cover, reduce the heat, and simmer until thickened, about 10 minutes, stirring occasionally. Remove from the heat.

Combine the chopped spinach, whole egg, egg white, and cheddar and Parmesan cheeses. Stir about one-fourth of the grits into the egg mixture, then stir the mixture into the grits. Continue stirring until the cheese melts.

Pour the mixture into the prepared baking dish. Bake for 30 to 35 minutes, until set. Serve hot.

Calories 295 • Protein 23 gm • Fat 9.3 gm • Percent of calories from fat 27% • Cholesterol 67 mg • Dietary fiber 4 gm • Sodium 294 mg • Calcium 600 mg

Cheese Grits Soufflé

YIELD: 4 TO 6 SERVINGS

4 cups water
1 cup yellow or white
    quick-cooking grits
1 teaspoon salt
1 cup coarsely grated reduced-fat
    cheddar cheese (4 ounces)
1/2 cup coarsely grated sharp
    cheddar cheese (2 ounces)

1 carrot, grated
2 scallions, chopped
2 teaspoons Louisiana-style hot
    sauce
1/2 teaspoon freshly ground black
    pepper
4 large egg whites

Preheat the oven to 375 degrees. Spray a 2-quart soufflé dish with non-stick cooking spray.

In a medium saucepan, bring the water to a boil. Reduce the heat to medium-high and whisk in the grits and salt. Reduce the heat to low, cover, and cook, stirring occasionally, until the grits are creamy, about 7 minutes. Pour the grits into a large bowl and let cool, stirring often to prevent a skin from forming.

When the grits are cool, fold in the cheddar cheeses, carrot, scallions, hot sauce, and pepper.

In a large bowl, beat the egg whites until stiff. Mix about one-third of the egg whites into the grits. Then fold in the remaining whites lightly but thoroughly. (Some streaks of white can remain.) Pour into the baking dish and smooth the top.

Bake in the middle rack of the oven for 30 minutes, until well risen and lightly browned on top. Serve immediately.

Calories 272 • Protein 20 gm • Fat 8.1 gm • Percent of calories from fat 26% • Cholesterol 25 mg • Dietary fiber 3 gm • Sodium 832 mg • Calcium 416 mg

Kasha with Bowties

❧

YIELD: 2 TO 4 SERVINGS

Kasha Varniskes—*as kasha with bowties is properly called in Yiddish—is a dish of my youth. It is the perfect combination of nutty buckwheat and pasta lightly flavored with onion.*

1 cup small bowties	1 egg white
1 tablespoon canola oil	2 cups boiling water or vegetable
1 onion, diced	broth
1 cup roasted buckwheat groats	Salt and freshly ground black
or medium-grind kasha	pepper

Cook the bowties in plenty of boiling salted water until al dente. Drain, rinse under tepid running water, and set aside.

Heat the canola oil in a large, heavy saucepan over medium-high heat. Add the onion and sauté for about 5 minutes, until the onion is browned. Set the pan aside.

Combine the buckwheat groats or kasha and egg white in a bowl and mix well. Heat a large, nonstick skillet over medium heat. Add the buckwheat mixture and cook, stirring constantly, until the grains are dry and separated, about 3 minutes.

Return the saucepan with the onion to the heat, add the toasted buckwheat, and mix well. Slowly add the boiling water or broth and salt to taste. Reduce the heat, cover, and cook over very low heat for 15 to 25 minutes, without stirring. When the water has been completely absorbed and the grains are tender, stir in the pasta. Wipe the pot lid dry and cover, placing a crumpled clean kitchen cotton or paper towel between the lid and pot so excess moisture is absorbed. Let stand for 5 minutes. Then fluff with a fork, season generously with salt and pepper, and serve.

Calories 587 • Protein 21 gm • Fat 12 gm • Percent of calories from fat 18% • Cholesterol 58 mg • Dietary fiber 11 gm • Sodium 82 mg • Calcium 37 mg

Kasha with Wild Mushrooms, Leeks, and Dill

YIELD: 3 TO 6 SERVINGS

Buckwheat is probably the most aromatic of grains. This dish, with its mingled earthy aromas of leeks, mushrooms, grains, and dill, is irresistible. It makes a delicious light supper by itself or with steamed broccoli or winter squash. It also can be served as a side dish.

1½ cups medium-grind kasha
 or buckwheat groats
1 large egg
3 cups boiling water or vegetable
 or mushroom broth
Salt and freshly ground black
 pepper
1 tablespoon olive
 or canola oil

2 cups sliced leeks, white part only
 (1 medium-size leek)
2 cups sliced white mushrooms
2 cups sliced wild mushrooms
 (such as shiitakes, chanterelles,
 and oysters)
2 garlic cloves, minced
1½ tablespoons chopped fresh
 dill or 2 teaspoons dried dillweed

Combine the kasha and egg whites in a bowl and mix well. Heat a large, nonstick skillet over medium heat. Add the buckwheat mixture and cook, stirring constantly, until the grains are dry and separated, about 3 minutes. Slowly add the boiling water or broth and salt and pepper to taste. Reduce the heat, cover, and cook over very low heat for 15 to 25 minutes, without stirring, until all of the liquid has been absorbed and the grains are tender.

Meanwhile, heat the oil in a large, heavy skillet over medium-high heat. Add the leeks, white and wild mushrooms, and garlic, and sauté for about 8 minutes, until the mushrooms have given up their juices. Set aside.

When the kasha is tender and all the water has been absorbed, add the mushroom mixture and dill and toss to mix. Taste and add more salt and pepper if needed. Serve hot.

Calories 347 • Protein 12 gm • Fat 8 gm • Percent of calories from fat 20% •
Cholesterol 71 mg • Dietary fiber 9 gm • Sodium 824 mg • Calcium 57 mg

Millet Stir-Fry

YIELD: 4 SERVINGS

Millet is grown and widely eaten in China, so why not a stir-fry such as this?

2 teaspoons sesame oil
1 cup uncooked millet
2¹/₂ cups water
1 tablespoon peanut or
   canola oil
¹/₄ cup finely diced onion
2 garlic cloves, minced
4 cups very thinly sliced green or
   Chinese cabbage

1 large carrot, finely diced
3 teaspoons soy sauce
¹/₄ cup oyster sauce
1 cup bean sprouts
1 cup fresh or frozen peas
3 to 4 scallions, chopped

In a medium saucepan over medium heat, heat the sesame oil. Add the millet and sauté for about 5 minutes, stirring constantly, until the grains are slightly toasted. Add the water. Stir, cover, and bring to a boil. Then reduce the heat and cook over low heat until all of the liquid has been absorbed, 25 to 30 minutes. Uncover and let stand for 10 minutes, then fluff with a fork.

Heat a wok or large skillet over high heat. Add the oil. Then add the onion and garlic and stir-fry for 1 minute. Add the cabbage, carrot, and 1 teaspoon of the soy sauce. Stir-fry until the cabbage is limp, about 2 minutes.

Add the millet, oyster sauce, and remaining 2 teaspoons soy sauce to the wok. Cook over high heat, continuously stirring and tossing, until the millet is heated through. Taste and add more oyster sauce or soy sauce, if needed. Carefully mix in the bean sprouts, peas, and scallions. Cook, carefully tossing and stirring, until heated through, about 2 minutes. Serve hot.

Calories 319 • Protein 10 gm • Fat 8 gm • Percent of calories from fat 23% •
Cholesterol 0 mg • Dietary fiber 9 gm • Sodium 614 mg • Calcium 67 mg

Millet-stuffed Golden Nugget Squash

YIELD: 4 TO 8 SERVINGS

Golden nugget winter squash—small, pumpkin-shaped, and bright orange in color—are perfect for stuffing. The flesh is also colored orange and the flavor is slightly sweet.

4 golden nugget squash (about 10 ounces each)	$^1/_4$ teaspoon crushed saffron
4 teaspoons butter	$^1/_2$ cup raisins
$^3/_4$ cup uncooked millet	$^1/_4$ cup chopped almonds
1$^2/_3$ cups water	$^1/_4$ cup chopped scallions
$^1/_2$ teaspoon salt	Pinch ground cinnamon

Preheat the oven to 375 degrees. To make 8 servings, cut the squash in half crossways. To serve 4, slice off the very top of each squash, exposing the seeds. Remove the seeds and fibers and place upside down in a baking dish with $^1/_4$ inch water. Bake squash halves for about 30 minutes, whole squash for about 40 minutes.

Meanwhile, melt 2 teaspoons of the butter in a medium saucepan over medium heat. Add the millet and sauté, stirring constantly, until the grains are slightly toasted. Add the water, salt, and saffron. Stir, cover, and bring to a boil. Then reduce the heat and cook over low heat until all of the liquid has been absorbed, 25 to 30 minutes. Uncover and let stand for 10 minutes, then fluff with a fork.

Add the remaining 2 teaspoons butter, raisins, almonds, scallions, and cinnamon to the millet. Mound the millet in the squash. At this point, the squash can be held for several hours in the refrigerator. Before serving, return to the oven to heat through, about 15 minutes, allowing extra time if the squash have been refrigerated.

Calories 390 • Protein 11 gm • Fat 11 gm • Percent of calories from fat 23% • Cholesterol 11 mg • Dietary fiber 9 gm • Sodium 353 mg • Calcium 134 mg

Quinoa Pilaf

❧

YIELD: 4 TO 6 SERVINGS

A tasty introduction to this exotic grain.

1 cup uncooked quinoa
2 cups water
1 tablespoon extra-virgin olive oil
4 garlic cloves, minced
2 shallots, finely chopped
2 cups high-quality chicken
   or vegetable broth

1/2 red bell pepper, finely chopped
2 tablespoons finely chopped
   fresh parsley
Salt and freshly ground black
   pepper

To remove the sticky, bitter-tasting saponin that may still cling to the surface of the quinoa, place in a blender with a couple of cups of water. Pulse the motor on and off a few times, until the water becomes cloudy. Strain off the water. Repeat with fresh water until it stays clear. Strain the quinoa through a fine-mesh strainer, discarding the water. Set aside.

Heat the olive oil in a medium saucepan. Add the garlic and shallots and sauté until translucent, about 3 minutes. Add the quinoa and continue to sauté for about 5 minutes, until the grains appear toasted. Add the broth, cover, and bring to a boil. Reduce the heat and simmer slowly for about 12 minutes, until all of the liquid has been absorbed.

Fluff the quinoa with a fork. Stir in the bell pepper, parsley, and salt and pepper to taste. Dry the lid. Crumple a paper or clean kitchen towel and place over the quinoa. Cover and let stand for 5 minutes before serving.

Calories 212 • Protein 7 gm • Fat 7 gm • Percent of calories from fat 27% •
Cholesterol 2 mg • Dietary fiber 3 gm • Sodium 68 mg • Calcium 45 mg

9
The Marriage of Rice and Beans, Beans and Grains

Vegetarian Hoppin' John

Red Bean Gumbo

Quick Louisiana Red Beans and Rice

Slow-cooked Louisiana Red Beans and Rice

Japanese Red Rice and Beans

Jamaican-style Rice and Beans

Back Beans and White Rice

Cuban Yellow Rice and Black Beans

Fiesta Beans and Rice

Saffron Rice with Chickpeas

Mixed Vegetable Curry

Syrian Mujdara (Lentils and Rice)

Brown Rice and Lentils

Lentil Burgers

Khichiri

Spicy Vegetable Couscous

Two-Bean Chili with Bulgur

Black Bean Chili with Wheat Berries

Black Bean and Hominy Stew

Black Bean Tostadas with Cilantro Cream

Black Bean–Corn Bread Casserole

Pinto Bean and Cheese Enchiladas

Nachos Supreme

Mexican Torte

Cowboy Beans 'n' Corn Bread

Vegetable Tamale Pie

Basic Bean Burgers

Wheat Berry Bean Burgers

Roasted Veggie Burgers

The marriage of rice and beans is a union so perfect in terms of flavor and nutrition that divorces rarely occur.

Ever since Frances Moore Lappe wrote her seminal work on complementary proteins, *Diet for a Small Planet*, vegetarians have understood the need to combine plant proteins in such a way as to create complete proteins. Rice and beans or beans and grains were shown to be pairings that made complete proteins. It was understood that in developing countries around the world, this concept of combining proteins was intuitively expressed, and gave the world such brilliant combinations as Syrian rice and lentils and Mexican *frijoles* in corn tortillas.

Unfortunately, not all the rice and bean combinations that we experimented with in those early *Diet for a Small Planet* days tasted good. Does everyone remember baked brown rice and lentil loaves with the same shudders that I do? And those glutinous and ubiquitous mushroom gravies that were supposed to provide the unifying flavor? How did anyone eat that stuff?!

A lion's share of the rice and bean and bean and grain combinations set forth here are classic dishes that are eaten as daily fare around the world. They have stood the test of time, with little intervention and few adaptations. Not all of the recipes in this chapter, however, are ethnic classics. Beans and grains together form the basis of my favorite vegetarian burgers. I add wheat berries to a fairly ordinary black bean chili to get a much heartier, chewier texture. Likewise, bulgur lends substance to another chili recipe. Corn bread and beans are a wonderful combination, and this chapter contains a few different variations on that theme. All of these recipes make hearty one-dish suppers, the kind that fill the belly well, without time-consuming processes or expensive ingredients.

Vegetarian Hoppin' John

YIELD: 4 TO 6 SERVINGS

A Southern classic of black-eyed peas and rice, Hoppin' John was a staple dish among African slaves, particularly in South Carolina. Today it is traditionally served on New Year's Day for luck. No one really knows how the name came to be. Some say that it derives from the way guests were invited to dig in, with a hearty, "Hop in, John." Same say it derives from a New Year's Day ritual in which the children of the house hopped once around the house before eating. Others claim the dish was originally made in the Caribbean with pigeon peas, or pois à pigeon (pronounced ah-pee-jon). Still others say the dish was named after the man who popularized it, a peg-legged Charlestonian named John.

Whatever the origins of the dish, it is one in which vegetarian versions—without the bacon—sometime seem a little lean, a little skimpy. However, here chipotle chiles—smoked-dried jalapeños—do a marvelous job of adding the missing smoke flavor.

1 cup dried black-eyed peas or cowpeas, soaked overnight or using the quick-soak method on page 20
2 dried chipotle chiles
6 cups water
1 tablespoon extra-virgin olive oil

1 onion, diced
1 cup uncooked long-grain rice, rinsed in several changes of water
Salt and freshly ground black pepper

Drain the peas. In a large saucepan, combine the beans, chiles, and the 6 cups fresh water. Bring to a boil, partially covered. Reduce the heat and gently boil until the peas are barely tender, about 20 minutes.

Drain the peas, reserving 2¹/₄ cups of the cooking liquid. Seed and chop the chiles, if desired (leave the seeds in for a spicy flavor).

In a large saucepan, heat the olive oil over medium heat. Add the onion and sauté until limp, about 3 minutes. Add the drained peas, reserved cooking liquid, and rice. Add 1 or more of the chopped chipotle, depending on how hot you want the dish to be. Cover and bring to a boil. Reduce the heat to low and continue to cook until the liquid has been absorbed and the rice and peas are tender, about 15 minutes. Serve hot.

Calories 356 • Protein 14 gm • Fat 4 gm • Percent of calories from fat 11% • Cholesterol 0 mg • Dietary fiber 6 gm • Sodium 54 mg • Calcium 81 mg

VARIATION

Hoppin' John. For more traditional flavor without a lot of fat, replace the chiles with $1/2$ pound diced smoked turkey. Proceed with the recipe as written.

Calories 404 • Protein 24 gm • Fat 4 gm • Percent of calories from fat 10% • Cholesterol 0 mg • Dietary fiber 6 gm • Sodium 730 mg • Calcium 78 mg

Red Bean Gumbo

YIELD: 6 TO 8 SERVINGS

A specialty born of the Creole cooking of New Orleans, gumbo is a thick, stew-like soup, most often made with shellfish, chicken, and sausage. It always begins with a dark roux, a well-cooked paste of flour and oil, which thickens the stew and adds a deep, rich background flavor. I use the roux as a starting point for this bean stew, and add all the traditional gumbo seasonings and vegetables, including tomatoes, peppers, celery, and, of course, okra (or gombo in Bantu), from which the name of this dish is derived.

1 tablespoon extra-virgin olive oil
1 onion, diced
1 green bell pepper, diced
2 celery stalks, thinly sliced
4 garlic cloves, minced
6 cups high-quality chicken
   or vegetable broth
1 pound okra, sliced (about 4 cups)
1½ cups fresh or canned
   diced tomatoes
¼ cup chopped fresh parsley
2 bay leaves
2 teaspoons dried thyme

½ teaspoon freshly ground black
   pepper
½ teaspoon white pepper
½ teaspoon ground red pepper
Salt
¼ cup canola oil
¼ cup unbleached all-purpose
   flour
1½ cups cooked red kidney beans
4 to 6 cups hot, cooked white rice
Filé powder
Louisiana-style hot sauce

In a large soup pot, heat the olive oil. Add the onion, green pepper, celery, and garlic, and sauté until the onion is limp, about 4 minutes. Add the broth, okra, tomatoes, parsley, bay leaves, thyme, black pepper, white pepper, and ground red pepper, and salt to taste. Bring to a boil, then simmer for about 30 minutes. Discard the bay leaves.

Meanwhile, in a separate pot, combine the canola oil and white flour, stirring until you have a smooth paste. Cook over medium-low heat, stirring constantly, until the paste is a rich brown. This will take close to 30 minutes. Do not let the mixture burn. If it does, you must throw it out and start over again. Carefully stir the roux into the gumbo. Add the kidney beans. Taste and adjust the seasonings. Simmer for another 15 minutes.

To serve, ladle the gumbo over the hot rice in large soup bowls. Pass the filé powder and hot sauce at the table.

Calories 421 • Protein 13 gm • Fat 12.6 gm • Percent of calories from fat 26% • Cholesterol 0 mg • Dietary fiber 8 gm • Sodium 475 mg • Calcium 123 mg

Quick Louisiana Red Beans and Rice

YIELD: 4 SERVINGS

In just about the time it takes to cook the rice, you can whip together these delicious beans (as long as you start with cooked or canned beans).

1 tablespoon extra-virgin olive oil
1 onion, diced
1 celery stalk, diced
1 green bell pepper, diced
1 fresh hot green pepper, diced
2 garlic cloves, minced
1 cup water or high-quality chicken or vegetable broth
3 cups cooked red kidney beans
1/4 cup chopped fresh parsley

1 teaspoon dried thyme
1 bay leaf
1 tablespoon Louisiana-style, hot sauce
Salt, white pepper, and freshly ground black pepper
4 cups hot, cooked long-grain white rice

In a medium saucepan, heat the olive oil over medium-high heat. Add the onion, celery, bell and hot peppers, and garlic, and sauté until the onion is limp, about 4 minutes. Add the broth, beans, parsley, thyme, bay leaf, hot sauce, and salt and white and black peppers. Simmer until the beans are hot and the flavors have blended, about 15 minutes. Discard the bay leaf. Serve over the rice, passing more hot sauce at the table.

Calories 469 • Protein 17 gm • Fat 5 gm • Percent of calories from fat 9% • Cholesterol 0 mg • Dietary fiber 11 gm • Sodium 34 mg • Calcium 74 mg

Slow-Cooked Louisiana Red Beans and Rice

YIELD: 4 SERVINGS

This is a slow-cooked vegetarian version of the traditional New Orleans Monday night supper.

1 cup dried red kidney beans,
    soaked overnight or using the
    quick-soak method on
    page 20
6 cups water
2 onions, diced
2 celery stalks, diced
4 garlic cloves, minced
2 bay leaves
1$^1/_2$ teaspoons dried thyme,
    or more to taste
1 tablespoon extra-virgin olive oil
1 green bell pepper, diced

1 fresh hot green pepper, diced
$^1/_4$ cup chopped fresh parsley
$^1/_4$ cup chopped scallions
1 tablespoon Louisiana-style
    hot sauce, or more to taste
Salt, white pepper, and freshly
    ground black pepper
Tabasco sauce
4 cups hot, cooked long-grain
    white rice

Drain the beans. In a large saucepan, combine the beans with the 6 cups fresh water, half of the onion, celery, and garlic, and all of the bay leaves and thyme. Bring to a boil, then reduce the heat and simmer, partially covered, until the beans are tender, about 1 hour. Remove and discard the bay leaves.

In a large skillet, heat the olive oil. Add the remaining onion, celery, and garlic as well as the bell and hot peppers. Sauté until limp, about 3 minutes. Add to the beans, along with the parsley, scallions, and hot sauce. Season with the salt, black pepper, white pepper, and Tabasco sauce to taste. Simmer for about 20 minutes to allow the flavors to blend. Serve hot over the hot rice, passing more Louisiana-style hot sauce at the table.

Calories 442 • Protein 17 gm • Fat 5 gm • Percent of calories from fat 9% • Cholesterol 0 mg • Dietary fiber 10 gm • Sodium 60 mg • Calcium 118 mg

Japanese Red Rice and Beans

YIELD: 4 SERVINGS

The bean cooking water colors the rice red and adds extra flavor.

¹/₃ cup dried adzuki beans	1 teaspoon salt
6 cups water	Sesame seeds, for serving
1¹/₄ cups uncooked short-grain white rice	

Combine the beans and water in a large saucepan. Bring to a boil, then reduce the heat and boil gently, uncovered, for about 2 hours, until the beans are tender. Drain, reserving the cooking liquid for cooking the rice.

Measure the bean cooking water and add water if necessary to make 2¹/₄ cups. Place in a medium saucepan. Rinse the rice and drain. Add to the saucepan along with the salt. Cover and bring to a boil. Then reduce the heat and simmer until the liquid has been absorbed and the rice is tender, about 25 minutes. Mix the beans with the red-colored rice.

To serve, spoon the rice and beans into bowls and top with a sprinkling of sesame seeds.

Calories 277 • Protein 7 gm • Fat .4 gm • Percent of calories from fat 1% • Cholesterol 0 mg • Dietary fiber 4 gm • Sodium 593 mg • Calcium 20 mg

Jamaican-style Rice and Beans

YIELD: 4 SERVINGS

The classic combination of coconut-flavored rice and red beans is surprisingly complex in flavor.

2 cups uncooked long-grain white rice

1 (14-ounce) can light coconut milk

2 cups water

2 teaspoons olive or canola oil

1 fresh hot green pepper, diced

1 green bell pepper, diced

3 cups cooked red kidney beans

4 scallions, chopped

2 teaspoons dried thyme

4 tablespoons chopped fresh cilantro (optional)

Salt and freshly ground black pepper

Wash the rice in several changes of water until the water runs clear. Drain well. Combine the rice with the coconut milk and the 2 cups fresh water in a large saucepan. Cover. Bring to a boil, then reduce the heat and simmer gently until the rice is tender and all of the liquid has been absorbed, 12 to 15 minutes. Fluff with a fork.

Heat the oil in a small frying pan. Add the hot and bell peppers and sauté just until limp, about 3 minutes. Add to the rice, along with the beans, scallions, thyme, and cilantro (if using). Season with salt and pepper to taste. Serve hot.

Calories 595 • Protein 19 gm • Fat 9 gm • Percent of calories from fat 13% • Cholesterol 0 mg • Dietary fiber 10 gm • Sodium 38 mg • Calcium 86 mg

Black Beans and White Rice

YIELD: 4 TO 6 SERVINGS

Black beans and white rice—Moros y Cristianos—is a classic Cuban combination.

Beans

1 cup dried black beans, soaked overnight or using the quick-soak method on page 20

6 cups water
2 dried chipotle chiles
2 bay leaves

Rice

1 tablespoon extra-virgin olive oil
1 onion, finely chopped
2 garlic cloves, minced
1 (15-ounce) can diced tomatoes
1 (3-ounce) jar chopped pimientos, drained

1 cup long-grain white rice, rinsed in several changes of water
1³/₄ cups water
1¹/₂ teaspoons salt

Drain the beans. Combine the beans and the 6 cups fresh water, chiles, and bay leaves in a large saucepan. Bring to a boil, partially covered, then reduce the heat and boil gently until the beans are tender but not mushy, about 1 hour. Drain, discarding the chiles and bay leaves.

Heat the olive oil in a large saucepan. Add the onion and garlic and sauté until the onion is limp, about 3 minutes. Add the tomatoes and pimientos and sauté for 1 minute. Stir in the rice, cooked beans, water, and salt. Cover and bring to a boil, then reduce the heat and simmer until most of the water has been absorbed, about 15 minutes. Remove from the heat and stir with a fork. The rice will be quite moist. Dry the pot lid. Crumple a clean kitchen cotton or paper towel over the rice. Cover and let stand for 5 minutes before serving.

Calories 410 • Protein 16 gm • Fat 5 gm • Percent of calories from fat 10% •
Cholesterol 0 mg • Dietary fiber 11 gm • Sodium 966 mg • Calcium 128 mg

VARIATION

Quick Black Beans and Rice. Omit the dried black beans, 6 cups water, chipotle chiles, and bay leaves. When making the rice, add 2 (15-ounce) cans black beans, drained and rinsed, instead of the home-cooked beans. Reduce the salt to 3/4 teaspoon.

Calories 361 • Protein 14 gm • Fat 6 gm • Percent of calories from fat 12% •
Cholesterol 0 mg • Dietary fiber 15 gm • Sodium 1572 mg • Calcium 127 mg

Cuban Yellow Rice and Black Beans

YIELD: 4 TO 6 SERVINGS

Another classic, this one is often served as a side dish. But the combination is so delicious, I prefer to serve it as the main event, with a green salad to complete the meal. The yellow rice is flavored with annatto (also known as achiote) oil, which is infused with the musky flavor of the seed of the annatto tree. This spice is found in Hispanic and Indian markets. No substitutes are adequate, although saffron is sometimes recommended.

1½ cups long-grain white rice
2 tablespoons annatto oil
    (see Note on page 166)
2 shallots, minced
2 garlic cloves, minced
1 red or green bell
    pepper, diced
3 cups water

1 teaspoon salt, or more to taste
1½ cups cooked black beans
¼ cup chopped scallions
2 tablespoons chopped fresh
    cilantro
Freshly ground black pepper and
Tabasco sauce (optional)

Wash the rice in several changes of water until the rinse water runs clear. Drain well.

In a large skillet, heat the annatto oil over medium heat. Add the rice, shallots, garlic, and bell pepper. Sauté until the rice appears toasted and dry, about 5 minutes. Add the water and 1 teaspoon of the salt, cover, and bring to a boil. Reduce the heat and boil gently until all of the liquid has been absorbed, about 15 minutes.

Remove from the heat. Fluff the rice with a fork. Stir in the black beans, scallions, and cilantro. Dry the pot lid. Crumple a clean kitchen cotton or paper towel over the rice. Replace the lid and allow the heat of the rice to warm the beans. Taste and add additional salt, pepper, and Tabasco sauce, if desired. Serve hot.

Calories 410 • Protein 11 gm • Fat 8 gm • Percent of calories from fat 17% •
Cholesterol 0 mg • Dietary fiber 7 gm • Sodium 594 mg • Calcium 56 mg

Fiesta Beans and Rice

YIELD: 6 SERVINGS

This particular version of rice and beans is a house favorite because it is so tasty with the double spike of flavor from the cumin and cilantro and so colorful with its mix of red tomatoes, green peppers, black and red beans, and white rice. I like it because it is so fast to make—the beans (I use canned) are just about done within the time it takes to cook the rice. Leftover beans (without the rice) can be used as a filling for tacos or burritos.

1 tablespoon canola or olive oil
4 teaspoons ground cumin
1 large onion, finely diced
2 green bell peppers, finely diced
1 to 3 fresh hot red or green
  peppers, finely diced
2 (15-ounce) cans diced tomatoes
1¹/₂ cups cooked black beans

1¹/₂ cups cooked red kidney beans
2 cups fresh or frozen corn kernels
¹/₂ cup chopped fresh cilantro
Salt and freshly ground black
  pepper
4 cups hot, cooked white rice
Salsa, for serving (optional)

Heat the oil in a medium saucepan over medium-high heat. Add the cumin, onion, and bell and hot peppers, and sauté until limp, about 3 minutes. Add the tomatoes, black and red beans, and corn. Simmer for 10 minutes. Just before serving, add the cilantro and salt and pepper to taste.

To serve, spoon the beans on top of a bed of the hot, cooked rice in individual bowls. Pass salsa at the table, if desired.

Calories 378 • Protein 14 gm • Fat 4 gm • Percent of calories from fat 8% • Cholesterol 0 mg • Dietary fiber 11 gm • Sodium 252 mg • Calcium 55 mg

Saffron Rice with Chickpeas

YIELD: 4 SERVINGS

1½ cups uncooked white rice
2 tablespoons olive oil
2 shallots, minced
2 garlic cloves, minced
1 teaspoon ground cumin
1½ cups chopped fresh
   or canned tomatoes
1½ cups cooked chickpeas

¼ teaspoon paprika
1 tablespoon chopped fresh
   cilantro
2¾ cups high-quality chicken
   or vegetable broth
⅛ teaspoon crushed saffron
   threads
Salt

Wash the rice in several changes of water until the rinse water runs clear. Drain well.

In a medium saucepan over medium-high heat, heat the olive oil. Add the shallots, garlic, and cumin, and sauté until fragrant, about 2 minutes. Add the tomatoes, chickpeas, paprika, and cilantro, and reduce the heat to low. Let simmer while you cook the rice.

Combine the rice, broth, saffron, and salt to taste in a saucepan. Cover and bring to a boil, then reduce the heat and boil gently until the rice is tender and the liquid has been absorbed, about 12 minutes. Dry the lid, crumple a clean kitchen cotton or paper towel, and place over the rice. Replace the lid and let stand for 10 minutes. Then fluff with a fork.

To serve, make a bed of the cooked rice on a serving platter. Spoon the chickpeas and cooking liquid onto the center of the rice and serve at once.

Calories 458 • Protein 13 gm • Fat 7 gm • Percent of calories from fat 15% •
Cholesterol 0 mg • Dietary fiber 5 gm • Sodium 322 mg • Calcium 50 mg

✎✎✎

YIELD: 4 TO 6 SERVINGS

A feast of curried vegetables in a rich coconut milk sauce. You can make the flavoring mild or hot, depending on the amount of ground red pepper you add. Some manufacturers of coconut milk offer a light version—it is unadulterated coconut milk, without the coconut cream. I find it perfect for most recipes; the extra fat of the coconut cream is not missed.

3 medium potatoes (about
   1 pound), peeled and diced
1/2 head cauliflower, broken
   into florets
1 stalk broccoli, florets and
   peeled, diced stem
1 carrot, diced
1 cup green beans cut into
   1 1/2-inch lengths
2 tablespoons canola oil
1 onion, minced

3 cloves garlic, minced
1 1/2-inch piece ginger, peeled
   and minced
2 tablespoons curry powder
1/4 teaspoon ground red pepper,
   or more to taste
1 1/2 cups cooked chickpeas
2 cups light coconut milk
1/4 cup chopped fresh cilantro
Salt and freshly ground black
   pepper
Hot, cooked rice, for serving

Parboil the potatoes in salted water to cover until just tender, about 5 minutes. Drain well. Meanwhile, blanch the cauliflower in a large pot of salted boiling water for 1 minute. Then add the broccoli, carrot, and green beans, and continue blanching for 2 minutes. Drain, plunge into cold water to stop the cooking process, then drain again.

Heat the canola oil in a large saucepan over medium-low heat. Add the onion, garlic, ginger, curry powder, and ground red pepper, and sauté until the onion is golden, about 8 minutes. Stir in the blanched vegetables and chickpeas. Toss to coat well with the spice mixture. Stir in the coconut milk and cilantro. Increase the heat to medium and cook just below the boiling point for about 30 minutes, until the vegetables are completely tender. Do not allow the mixture to boil. Taste and adjust the seasonings. Serve hot, over rice.

Calories 390 • Protein 11 gm • Fat 14 gm • Percent of calories from fat 31% •
Cholesterol 0 mg • Dietary fiber 10 gm • Sodium 68 mg • Calcium 112 mg

Syrian Mujdara (Lentils and Rice)

YIELD: 4 SERVINGS

Usually I don't like to dirty three pots for one simple supper—but this is so easy to prepare, so healthful, and so delicious, I have to make an exception. A Syrian friend introduced me to this wonderful comfort dish (pronounced Jud' rah), which is made, with slight variations, in several Middle Eastern countries. Like mashed potatoes, this dish doesn't sound as absolutely wonderful as it tastes; but like mashed potatoes, this is a simple food guaranteed to please the palate, warm the belly, and lift the spirit.

1 cup dried green or
   brown lentils, rinsed
1 teaspoon salt
1 1/2 cups uncooked white
   or brown rice
2 3/4 to 3 1/4 cups water

1 tablespoon extra-virgin olive oil
3 onions, thinly sliced
4 garlic cloves, minced
1 1/4 cups nonfat buttermilk
Salt and freshly ground black
   pepper

In a medium saucepan, cover the lentils with water by about 3 inches and add 1/2 teaspoon of the salt. Bring to a boil, then reduce the heat to a gentle boil and cook until the lentils are tender but still hold their shape, about 25 minutes. Drain and rinse the lentils with hot water.

Meanwhile, combine the rice, the remaining 1/2 teaspoon salt, and the water (about 2 3/4 cups for the white rice and about 3 1/4 cups for brown rice, depending on the variety). Bring to a boil, then reduce the heat to a simmer and cook, covered, until the rice is tender and the water has been absorbed, 15 to 30 minutes, depending on whether you are cooking white or brown rice and the variety of the rice.

While the rice and lentils cook, heat the olive oil over medium-low heat in a large saucepan. Add the onions and cook, stirring constantly, until the onions are golden, about 7 minutes. Add the garlic and cook for 3 minutes more.

Add the cooked lentils and rice to the onions. Add the buttermilk to moisten and bind the mixture. Season with salt and pepper to taste. Serve warm or at room temperature.

Calories 509 • Protein 16 gm • Fat 6 gm • Percent of calories from fat 11% •
Cholesterol 3 mg • Dietary fiber 11 gm • Sodium 391 mg • Calcium 169 mg

Jan '09 - yummy! substituted skim milk & non-fat plain yogurt for buttermilk. Also added curry powder & cardamon & some edamame (soy beans). Tasted like Indian food.

Brown Rice and Lentils

❧❧❧

YIELD: **4** TO **6** SERVINGS

The beauty of this dish—in addition to its flavor and nutrition, of course—is that the rice and lentils cook together in one pot.

2 tablespoons extra-virgin
   olive oil
1 small onion, diced
4 garlic cloves, minced
1 carrot, finely chopped
2 teaspoons ground cumin
1 teaspoon ground coriander

1¼ cups uncooked brown rice
³⁄₄ cup dried brown or
   green lentils, rinsed
4 cups water
1 teaspoon salt
1 scallion, chopped
¼ cup chopped fresh cilantro

In a large skillet, heat the olive oil over medium-high heat. Add the onion, garlic, carrot, cumin, and coriander. Sauté until the onion is limp, about 3 minutes. Add the rice and lentils and sauté for another 2 minutes. Add the water and salt, cover, and bring to a boil. Then reduce the heat and simmer until the rice and lentils are tender, about 40 minutes. Fluff with a fork. Stir in the scallion and cilantro. Dry the lid, place a crumpled clean kitchen cotton or paper towel over the rice, replace the lid, and let stand for 5 minutes before serving.

Calories 401 • Protein 11 gm • Fat 9 gm • Percent of calories from fat 20% •
Cholesterol 0 mg • Dietary fiber 10 gm • Sodium 610 mg • Calcium 92 mg

Lentil Burgers

YIELD: 4 SERVINGS

I like to serve these lentil burgers in pita pockets stuffed with a Greek salad of lettuce, tomatoes, cucumbers, onions, feta cheese, and olives. The moist salad counteracts the slightly dry texture of the burgers.

½ cup dried green or
   brown lentils, rinsed
½ cup uncooked brown rice
1 medium onion, diced
1 carrot, grated

4 garlic cloves, minced
4 teaspoons ground cumin
1 teaspoon ground coriander
1 teaspoon salt
2½ cups water

Combine the lentils, brown rice, onion, carrot, garlic, cumin, coriander, and salt in a medium saucepan. Add the water. Cover and bring to a boil, then reduce the heat and boil gently until the rice and lentils are tender and all of the liquid has been absorbed, about 40 minutes. Drain in a colander to remove any excess liquid. Let cool slightly, then process in a food processor until fairly smooth. Form into 3- to 4-inch patties.

Prepare a medium-hot fire in the grill or preheat the broiler. When you are ready to cook the burgers, mist the burgers with nonstick cooking spray on both sides. Grill or broil the burgers until crisp on both sides, 5 to 10 minutes per side, depending on how hot your fire is. Serve hot.

Calories 186 • Protein 7 gm • Fat 1 gm • Percent of calories from fat 6% •
Cholesterol 0 mg • Dietary fiber 7 gm • Sodium 605 mg • Calcium 72 mg

Khichiri

YIELD: 4 TO 6 SERVINGS

By briefly presoaking the yellow split peas, you can cook the rice and peas together in this classic Indian combination. The spicing is aromatic and fragrant, but not at all hot.

1/2 cup dried yellow split peas
11/2 cups uncooked basmati
   or long-grain rice
2 tablespoons canola oil
1 shallot, minced
2 garlic cloves, minced
2 teaspoons fresh ginger, peeled
   and minced

1/2 teaspoon whole cumin seeds
1/2 teaspoon fenugreek seeds
1/2 teaspoon garam masala
1 teaspoon salt
31/3 cups water
1/4 cup chopped fresh cilantro

Rinse the split peas under running tap water. Combine the split peas with about 2 cups water in a small saucepan. Bring to a boil. Remove from the heat and let sit for at least 1 hour.

Wash the rice in several changes of water until the rinse water runs clear. Drain both the rice and peas.

Heat the canola oil in a medium saucepan over medium heat. Add the shallot, garlic, ginger, cumin, and fenugreek, and sauté for about 3 minutes. Add the drained rice and peas and garam masala and sauté until the rice appears dry and toasted, about 5 minutes. Add the salt and 31/3 cups water, cover, and bring to a boil. Reduce the heat to very low and let cook for about 20 minutes. Turn off the heat and let the pot sit undisturbed for another 10 minutes. Fluff gently with a fork and mix in the cilantro. Serve hot.

Calories 424 • Protein 11 gm • Fat 8 gm • Percent of calories from fat 17% • Cholesterol 0 mg • Dietary fiber 8 gm • Sodium 594 mg • Calcium 35 mg

Spicy Vegetable Couscous

YIELD: 4 TO 6 SERVINGS

The flavors of the Middle East infuse this hearty stew of chickpeas and summer vegetables in a spicy tomato sauce.

2 tablespoons extra-virgin
  olive oil
4 garlic cloves, minced
1 large onion, diced
1 small eggplant, diced
1 small zucchini, diced
1 small yellow summer squash,
  diced
$3/4$ teaspoon ground turmeric
$3/4$ teaspoon ground cumin
$1/2$ teaspoon ground cinnamon

$1/2$ teaspoon ground red pepper
1 (28-ounce) can peeled
  tomatoes with juice
$1^1/2$ cups cooked chickpeas
$1/2$ cup chopped fresh cilantro
Salt and freshly ground black
  pepper
$1^1/2$ cups uncooked couscous
3 cups boiling water

In a large nonstick skillet, heat the olive oil over medium-high heat. Add the garlic, onion, and eggplant, and sauté until the eggplant is almost tender, 5 minutes. Add the zucchini, summer squash, turmeric, cumin, cinnamon, and ground red pepper, and sauté for 3 more minutes, until the eggplant is completely tender. Stir in the tomatoes, chickpeas, and cilantro. Season with salt and pepper to taste. Let simmer for 10 minutes to blend the flavors.

Meanwhile, in a large bowl, combine the couscous with the boiling water. Cover and let steam for about 15 minutes. When all the liquid has been absorbed, fluff with a fork.

To serve, mound the couscous onto a large platter or into individual serving bowls. With a spoon, pat a depression in the center of the mound. Spoon the vegetable mixture on top. Serve hot.

Calories 520 • Protein 18 gm • Fat 9 gm • Percent of calories from fat 16% •
Cholesterol 0 mg • Dietary fiber 12 gm • Sodium 448 mg • Calcium 133 mg

VARIATION

Spicy Chicken and Vegetable Couscous. Replace the eggplant with ³/₄ pound diced boneless, skinless chicken breast. Proceed with the recipe as written.

Calories 643 • Protein 44 gm • Fat 12 gm • Percent of calories from fat 18% • Cholesterol 80 mg • Dietary fiber 10 gm • Sodium 508 mg • Calcium 141 mg

Two-Bean Chili with Bulgur

YIELD: 6 TO 8 SERVINGS

Serve this hearty stew with all the usual chili accompaniments—chopped onions, grated cheese, sour cream, tortilla chips, and sliced avocado.

1 cup dried black beans, soaked overnight or using the quick-soak method on page 20

1 cup dried red kidney beans, soaked overnight or using the quick-soak method on page 20

8 cups water

1 onion, chopped

2 tablespoons chili powder

1 (28-ounce) can peeled tomatoes with juice

1 green bell pepper, chopped

2 tablespoons tomato paste

1 tablespoon ground cumin

2 teaspoons ground coriander

1 teaspoon dried oregano

1 teaspoon dried thyme

1/4 teaspoon ground red pepper, or more to taste

1/4 teaspoon freshly ground black pepper

Salt

1/2 cup uncooked bulgur

2 scallions, chopped

Drain the beans. In a large saucepan, combine the black and red kidney beans with the 8 cups fresh water, the onion, and chili powder. Partially cover, bring to a boil, then reduce the heat and simmer until the beans are tender, about 1 1/2 hours. Add the tomatoes, bell pepper, tomato paste, cumin, coriander, oregano, thyme, ground red and black peppers, and salt to taste. Bring to a boil, add the bulgur and scallions, reduce the heat, and simmer, covered, until the bulgur is tender, about 30 minutes. Taste and adjust seasonings before serving.

Calories 328 • Protein 19 gm • Fat 2 gm • Percent of calories from fat 4% •
Cholesterol 0 mg • Dietary fiber 16 gm • Sodium 232 mg • Calcium 155 mg

Jan '09 - Great Chili! Cook beans for ~1 hour, then add tomatoes, peppers, ect. Cook for another ~45 min. Takes awhile to "cook down". A medium spicyness, omit red pepper if not fond of spicy. No salt necessary. Serve w/ corn bread p.399.

Black Bean Chili with Wheat Berries

YIELD: 8 TO 10 SERVINGS

Wheat berries add texture and heartiness to this spicy party chili. Serve it with grated cheese, chopped sweet onion, chopped tomatoes, and heated flour tortillas or corn chips. Extras can be frozen and served as a burrito filling at a later date.

½ cup uncooked wheat berries, soaked overnight

2 cups dried black beans, soaked overnight or using the quick-soak method on page 20

8 cups water

1 onion, diced

2 dried chipotle chiles

4 garlic cloves, minced

1 (28-ounce) can tomato sauce

2 tablespoons chili powder

1 tablespoon ground cumin

Salt and freshly ground black pepper

½ cup chopped fresh cilantro

Drain the beans and wheat berries, then combine in a large saucepan with the 8 cups fresh water, onion, chiles, and garlic. Bring to a boil, then reduce the heat and simmer, partially covered, until the beans and wheat berries are tender, about 2 hours. Add the tomato sauce, chili powder, cumin, and salt and pepper to taste. Bring to a boil and reduce the liquid to a thick sauce, then reduce the heat and continue simmering, covered, for a total of 30 minutes. Add the cilantro and simmer for 5 minutes more. Serve hot.

Calories 251 • Protein 14 gm • Fat 1 gm • Percent of calories from fat 5% • Cholesterol 0 mg • Dietary fiber 11 gm • Sodium 401 mg • Calcium 102 mg

Black Bean and Hominy Stew

YIELD: 4 TO 5 SERVINGS

You really must plan to serve this as soon as it is ready—when the bright white hominy and peachy orange sweet potatoes stand out against the black beans. After a while, the black beans tend to coat the other ingredients and make the dish look less appealing, though the good flavor remains.

2 sweet potatoes, peeled and diced
2 cups high-quality chicken
    or vegetable broth
3 cups cooked black beans
1 tablespoon extra-virgin olive oil
1 onion, finely chopped
1 red or green bell pepper, diced
2 jalapeño peppers, minced
2 garlic cloves, minced

2 teaspoons ground cumin
1 (15-ounce) can white hominy,
    rinsed and drained
1 tablespoon Worcestershire sauce
Louisiana-style hot sauce
Salt and freshly ground black
    pepper
Flour tortillas

Combine the sweet potatoes and broth in a medium saucepan. Bring to a boil, then boil the potatoes until just tender, about 5 minutes. Drain, reserving the cooking liquid.

Combine the reserved cooking liquid with 1 cup of the black beans in a blender and process until smooth. Set aside.

Heat the oil in a large saucepan over medium heat. Add the onion, bell and jalapeño peppers, garlic, and cumin, and sauté until the onion is limp, about 5 minutes. Add the sweet potatoes, pureed beans, remaining whole beans, hominy, Worcestershire sauce, and hot sauce to taste. Bring just to a boil, then reduce the heat and simmer for 10 minutes. Season with salt and pepper to taste. Serve at once, accompanied by warm flour tortillas.

Calories 358 • Protein 17 gm • Fat 5 gm • Percent of calories from fat 11% • Cholesterol 0 mg • Dietary fiber 17 gm • Sodium 877 mg • Calcium 90 mg

Black Bean Tostadas with Cilantro Cream

YIELD: 4 SERVINGS

Cilantro Cream
1 cup plain nonfat yogurt
3 garlic cloves, minced
2 tablespoons chopped fresh
   cilantro

Salt and freshly ground black
   pepper

Tostadas
8 tostadas
3 cups cooked black beans
1 cup homemade or
   store-bought salsa
1/4 cup chopped scallions

1 cup shredded reduced-fat
   cheddar cheese
1 cup diced tomatoes
2 cups shredded lettuce
1 avocado, diced

To prepare the cilantro cream, combine the yogurt, garlic, cilantro, and salt and pepper to taste. Set aside.

Heat the tostadas according to the package directions.

Combine the beans and salsa in a saucepan or microwave oven. Heat until thoroughly hot. In a food processor, briefly process the bean mixture; the texture should still be somewhat chunky. Stir in the scallions. Set aside in a covered dish to keep warm.

To assemble the tostadas, spread 1/2 cup of the beans on each tostada shell. Top with about 2 tablespoons each of the cheese and tomatoes and about 1/4 cup of the lettuce. Divide the avocado among the 8 tostadas and sprinkle on top. Pass the cilantro cream at the table.

Tostada: Calories 455 • Protein 29 gm • Fat 17 gm • Percent of calories from fat 32% • Cholesterol 47 mg • Dietary fiber 20 gm • Sodium 593 mg • Calcium 391 mg

Cilantro Cream: Calories 36 • Protein 3 gm • Fat .1 gm • Percent of calories from fat 3% • Cholesterol 1 mg • Dietary fiber 0 gm • Sodium 45 mg • Calcium 120 mg

Black Bean—Corn Bread Casserole

YIELD: 9 SERVINGS

Here's a great dish to have in your repertoire when unexpected guests arrive. This tasty one-dish bean-and-corn-bread combination can be made quickly and easily with pantry staples.

Casserole

3 cups cooked black beans
1½ cups homemade or
   store-bought salsa
1 (4-ounce) jar chopped
   pimientos, drained

4 scallions, chopped
¼ cup chopped fresh cilantro
Salt and freshly ground black
   pepper

Corn Bread Topping

1¼ cups stone-ground yellow
   cornmeal
1 cup unbleached all-purpose flour
¼ cup sugar
1 tablespoon baking powder

1 teaspoon baking soda
1 teaspoon salt
1 (15-ounce) can creamed corn
2 large eggs
1 cup nonfat buttermilk

Preheat the oven to 400 degrees. Spray a 9×13-inch baking dish with nonstick cooking spray.

Combine the beans, salsa, pimientos, scallions, cilantro, and salt and pepper to taste in the prepared baking dish.

To make the corn bread topping, in a separate bowl combine the cornmeal, flour, sugar, baking powder, baking soda, and salt. Mix well. In another bowl, beat together the creamed corn, eggs, and buttermilk. Pour into the cornmeal mixture and beat just enough to combine. The batter will be lumpy. Spread over the beans in the baking dish. Use a spatula to smooth the top and bring the batter all the way to the edges of the pan.

Bake for 35 to 40 minutes, until a tester inserted near the center of the baking dish comes out clean. Let stand for 10 minutes before serving. Serve warm.

Calories 254 • Protein 13 gm • Fat 3 gm • Percent of calories from fat 8% •
Cholesterol 48 mg • Dietary fiber 8 gm • Sodium 941 mg • Calcium 136 mg

Mexican Black Bean–Corn Bread Casserole. Substitute 4 cups Mexican Black Beans (page 201) for the black beans and salsa. Proceed with the recipe as written.

Calories 291 • Protein 13 gm • Fat 3 gm • Percent of calories from fat 8% •
Cholesterol 48 mg • Dietary fiber 8 gm • Sodium 640 mg • Calcium 165 mg

Cowboy Corn Bread Casserole. Substitute 4 cups Cowboy Frijoles (page 233) for the black beans and salsa. Proceed with the recipe as written.

Calories 318 • Protein 14 gm • Fat 3 gm • Percent of calories from fat 7% •
Cholesterol 48 mg • Dietary fiber 11 gm • Sodium 637 mg • Calcium 168 mg

Pinto Bean and Cheese Enchiladas

YIELD: 4 TO 6 SERVINGS

The beans and corn tortillas together provide a complete protein, and the protein is further boosted by the cheese. This is one of the classic dishes of the vegetarian repertoire.

Enchiladas

1 cup pinto beans, soaked overnight or using the quick-soak method on page 20
1 onion, diced
1 dried ancho chile
1 bay leaf
6 cups water

1 tablespoon extra-virgin olive oil
Salt and freshly ground black pepper
3 cups grated reduced-fat Cheddar cheese (12 ounces)
12 corn tortillas

Sauce

1 tablespoon olive oil
1 small onion, minced
2 garlic cloves, minced
2 jalapeño peppers, minced (seeded if desired)
2 tablespoons chili powder

1 teaspoon ground cumin
2 cups thick tomato puree
1 1/2 cups water
Salt and freshly ground black pepper

Drain the beans. Combine the beans in a large saucepan with the onion, chile, bay leaf, and 6 cups fresh water. Bring to a boil, then reduce the heat and skim off any foam that has risen to the top. Simmer, partially covered, until tender, about 60 minutes.

While the beans cook, make the sauce. Heat the olive oil in a saucepan over medium heat. Add the onion, garlic, jalapeños, chili powder, and cumin, and sauté until the onion is soft and fragrant, about 5 minutes. Add the tomato puree, 1 1/2 cups water, and salt and pepper to taste. Simmer over a very low heat.

When the beans are tender, drain. Discard the onion and bay leaf. Peel the ancho chile; remove the seeds if desired. Chop the flesh. Combine the chopped ancho and beans with 1 cup of the enchilada sauce in a small saucepan over low heat. Taste, adjust the seasonings, and stir in 2 cups of the Cheddar cheese until melted. Remove from the heat.

Preheat the oven to 350 degrees. Lightly spray a 9×13-inch baking dish with nonstick cooking spray.

To assemble the enchiladas, dip a tortilla, one at a time, in the warm sauce to soften. Place on a plate or other work surface and add about $1/4$ cup of the bean-and-cheese mixture. Roll up and place, seam side down, in the prepared baking dish. Repeat until all of the tortillas and filling are used up. Spread the remaining sauce over the tortillas. Sprinkle with the remaining 1 cup grated cheese. Cover the baking dish with foil and bake for about 15 minutes. Remove the foil and bake for an additional 10 to 15 minutes, until the cheese is melted. Serve hot.

Calories 680 • Protein 48 gm • Fat 18 gm • Percent of calories from fat 24% • Cholesterol 30 mg • Dietary fiber 20 gm • Sodium 444 mg • Calcium 1127 mg

Jan '09 – this tastes like authentic mexican! Used large can of cooked pintos, and only about 3/4 c of cheese total. Also no chile. Next time cook enchiladas w/at sauce on top – then pur sauce on top when on plates. Tartillas fell apart when cooking.

Nachos Supreme

YIELD: 3 TO 4 SERVINGS

Baked tortilla chips and low-fat cheese make it possible to enjoy nachos without guilt. Ladened with refried beans and chopped vegetables, these nachos make a meal for 3 to 4 people with hearty appetites.

4 ounces baked tortilla chips
1$^1/_2$ cups Refried Pinto Beans
   (page 237), Refried Black
   Beans (page 203), or canned
   refried beans
1$^1/_2$ cups chopped canned tomatoes
8 ounces reduced-fat Cheddar
   cheese, shredded (2 cups)

4 ounces ($^1/_4$ cup) chopped canned
   or fresh chile peppers,
   (optional)
2 scallions, finely chopped
1 red or green bell pepper, finely
   chopped
12 black olives, sliced
1 cup homemade or store-bought
   salsa
Nonfat sour cream (optional)

Spread the chips on a baking sheet. Mix together the refried beans and chopped tomatoes. Dab onto the chips. Top with the cheese, then the chiles (if using), scallions, bell pepper, and olives. Spoon the salsa on top. If desired, dab a little sour cream over everything. Place under a broiler and broil until the cheese is melted, about 4 minutes. Serve hot.

Calories 496 • Protein 43 gm • Fat 12 gm • Percent of calories from fat 21% •
Cholesterol 27 mg • Dietary fiber 9 gm • Sodium 1867 mg • Calcium 856 mg

Mexican Torte

YIELD: 6 TO 8 SERVINGS

2 teaspoons canola or olive oil
1/4 cup fresh or canned chopped
  green chiles
2 garlic cloves, minced
1/2 onion, diced
1 red bell pepper, diced
1 green bell pepper, diced
3 cups fresh or canned chopped
  tomatoes
2 teaspoons ground cumin
1 teaspoon chili powder
1/4 cup chopped fresh cilantro

Salt and freshly ground black
  pepper
1 (10-ounce) package corn tortillas,
  cut into wedges
2 cups Refried Pinto Beans
  (page 237), Refried Black
  Beans (page 203), or
  canned refried beans
1 1/4 cups grated low-fat Monterey
  Jack or Cheddar cheese
1 cup sliced black olives

Preheat the oven to 425 degrees.

Heat the oil in a large nonstick skillet over medium-high heat. Add the chiles, garlic, onion, and bell peppers, and sauté until limp, about 3 minutes. Stir in the tomatoes, cumin, and chili powder, and cook until the sauce is slightly thickened. Remove from the heat. Stir in the cilantro and season to taste with salt and pepper.

Spoon about 1/2 cup of the tomato mixture into a 1 1/2-quart casserole dish. Arrange an overlapping layer of tortillas wedges on top (use one-third of the tortillas). Spoon 1 cup of the tomato mixture on top. Spread about half of the refried beans in an even layer on top of the tomato layer. Sprinkle with one-third of the cheese and half the olives. Cover with the another layer of tortillas and tomato mixture. Top with the remaining refried beans, then one-third of the cheese and the remaining olives. Arrange a final layer of tortillas on top. Spoon over the remaining tomato mixture. Top with the remaining cheese.

Bake for about 25 minutes, until the cheese is melted and the filling is heated through. Let stand for 10 minutes before serving.

Calories 400 • Protein 18 gm • Fat 15 gm • Percent of calories from fat 32% •
Cholesterol 17 mg • Dietary fiber 13 gm • Sodium 370 mg • Calcium 154 mg

Cowboy Beans 'n' Corn Bread

YIELD: 4 TO 5 SERVINGS

The chipotle en adobo adds a whiff of campfire smoke to this satisfying one-dish supper. Serve it with plenty of beer—it's spiced to keep you warm on a chilly night.

Bean Filling

1 tablespoon canola or olive oil

1 teaspoon chili powder

1 onion, finely diced

1 green bell pepper, finely diced

2 cups fresh or canned diced tomatoes

1½ cups cooked red kidney or pinto beans

1 tablespoon chipotle en adobo

Salt and freshly ground black pepper

Corn Bread Topping

1 cup yellow cornmeal

¾ cup unbleached all-purpose flour

2 teaspoons baking powder

1 teaspoon salt

1 cup skim milk

2 large egg whites, lightly beaten

2 tablespoons canola or vegetable oil

1 (4-ounce) can roasted chiles, chopped

Preheat the oven to 425 degrees.

To prepare the beans, heat the oil in a large cast-iron or ovenproof skillet over medium-high heat. Stir in the chili powder. Add the onion and bell pepper. Sauté until the onion is translucent, about 3 minutes. Stir in the tomatoes and their juice, beans, and chipotle en adobo. Season with salt and pepper to taste. Cook for 1 minute more. Remove from the heat.

To prepare the corn bread topping, combine the cornmeal, flour, baking powder, and salt in a medium bowl and mix well. In a separate bowl, whisk together the milk, egg whites, oil, and roasted chiles. Pour into the flour mixture and stir just until well moistened. The batter will be lumpy. Spread the batter over the beans in the skillet, taking care to spread the corn bread batter evenly over the surface of the beans so that it touches the edges of the pan.

Place in the oven and bake for about 25 minutes, until the top is golden and firm. Let stand for about 5 minutes before serving. This holds together well and can be served with a pie server or spoon.

Calories 458 • Protein 16 gm • Fat 12 gm • Percent of calories from fat 24% • Cholesterol 1 mg • Dietary fiber 11 gm • Sodium 977 mg • Calcium 219 mg

Vegetable Tamale Pie

YIELD: 4 TO 5 SERVINGS

This tamale pie is similar to the preceding recipe, but milder in flavor and character.

Bean Filling

1 tablespoon canola or olive oil

2 teaspoons ground cumin

1 onion, finely diced

1 green bell pepper, finely diced

2 small zucchini, diced

1 to 3 fresh or roasted hot red or green peppers, finely diced

2 cups fresh or canned diced tomatoes

1½ cups cooked red kidney, pinto, or black beans

2 tablespoons chopped fresh cilantro (optional)

Salt and freshly ground black pepper

Corn Bread Topping

1 cup stone-ground yellow cornmeal

¾ cup unbleached all-purpose flour

2 teaspoons baking powder

1 teaspoon salt

½ red bell pepper, finely diced

½ cup skim or low-fat milk

2 large egg whites, lightly beaten

2 tablespoons canola or vegetable oil

1 (16-ounce) can creamed corn

Preheat the oven to 425 degrees.

Heat the oil in a large cast-iron or ovenproof skillet over medium-high heat. Stir in the cumin. Add the onion, green bell pepper, zucchini, and hot peppers. Sauté until the onion is translucent, about 3 minutes. Stir in the tomatoes and their juice and the beans. Add the cilantro (if using) and salt and pepper to taste. Cook for 1 minute more. Remove from the heat.

To prepare the corn bread topping, combine the cornmeal, flour, baking powder, salt, and red bell pepper in a medium bowl and mix well. In a separate bowl, whisk together the milk, egg whites, oil, and creamed corn. Pour into the flour mixture and stir just until well moistened. The batter will be lumpy. Spread the batter over the beans in the skillet. Use a spatula to smooth the batter over the beans and spread it all the way to the sides of the skillet.

Place in the oven and bake for about 25 minutes, until the top is golden and firm. Let stand for about 5 minutes before serving. This holds together well and can be served with a pie server or spoon.

Calories 473 • Protein 17 gm • Fat 13 gm • Percent of calories from fat 24% • Cholesterol 1 mg • Dietary fiber 14 gm • Sodium 939 mg • Calcium 245 mg

Basic Bean Burgers

YIELD: 8 BURGERS

This very basic bean burger recipe can be whipped together in less than a half an hour, if you have cooked or canned beans on hand. Be sure to serve them with all the traditional burger fixings—ketchup, mustard, pickles, sliced raw onions, etc.

$^2/_3$ cup uncooked bulgur	2 tablespoons tomato paste
$1^1/_3$ cups boiling water	1 tablespoon soy sauce
1 tablespoon extra-virgin olive oil	$^1/_2$ teaspoon dried oregano
1 medium onion, diced	$^1/_2$ teaspoon dried basil
2 cups cooked red kidney beans	1 large egg
$^1/_2$ cup dry bread crumbs	Salt and freshly ground black
$^1/_4$ cup whole-wheat flour	pepper
$^1/_4$ cup chopped fresh parsley	8 burger buns or pita pockets

Combine the bulgur and boiling water in a mixing bowl, cover, and set aside to steam for 10 minutes.

Heat the oil in a medium skillet. Add the onion and sauté until soft and golden, about 5 minutes. Combine with the beans, bread crumbs, flour, parsley, tomato paste, soy sauce, oregano, basil, and egg in a food processor and process until fairly smooth. Drain the bulgur of any excess water and mix into the burger mixture. Salt and pepper to taste. Form into 3-inch burgers.

Prepare a medium-hot fire in the grill or preheat the broiler. Mist the burgers with nonstick cooking spray on both sides. Grill or broil the burgers until browned on both sides, 5 to 10 minutes per side, depending on how hot your fire is. Serve on buns or pita pockets.

Calories 291 • Protein 11 gm • Fat 6 gm • Percent of calories from fat 19% • Cholesterol 27 mg • Dietary fiber 7 gm • Sodium 230 mg • Calcium 60 mg

Wheat Berry Bean Burgers

YIELD: 6 BURGERS

You'll have to plan ahead for these burgers—the wheat berries, which add so much texture, require 1¹/₄ to 1¹/₂ hours to cook. (If soaked overnight, you can reduce that cooking time to 50 to 60 minutes.) The wheat berries do a wonderful job of adding both flavor and a pleasing chewiness to the burgers.

¹/₃ cup uncooked wheat berries
3 cups water
1 tablespoon extra-virgin olive oil
1 medium onion, diced
Leaves from 10 parsley stems
1¹/₂ cups cooked red kidney beans
2 tablespoons tomato-based
   barbecue sauce

1 large egg
1 teaspoon dried thyme
¹/₂ to ³/₄ cup whole-wheat flour
Salt and freshly ground black
   pepper
6 burger buns or pita pockets

Rinse the wheat berries and combine with the water in a medium saucepan. Cover and bring to a boil. Then reduce the heat and simmer until the wheat berries are tender and just begin to split open, 1¹/₄ to 1¹/₂ hours. Drain off any excess water.

Heat the olive oil in a medium skillet. Add the onion and sauté until soft and golden, about 5 minutes. Combine the onion with the parsley leaves in a food processor and process until finely chopped. Add the beans, barbecue sauce, egg, and thyme, and process until fairly smooth. Remove to a bowl. Stir in the wheat berries and mix well. Stir in ¹/₂ cup of the flour. Add more flour if needed to form into burgers. Season with salt and pepper to taste. With wet hands, form into six 3-inch burgers.

Prepare a medium-hot fire in the grill or preheat the broiler. Mist the burgers with nonstick cooking spray on both sides. Grill or broil the burgers until browned on both sides, 5 to 7 minutes per side, depending on how hot your fire is. Serve on buns or pita pockets.

Calories 291 • Protein 11 gm • Fat 7 gm • Percent of calories from fat 20% •
Cholesterol 35 mg • Dietary fiber 6 gm • Sodium 112 mg • Calcium 67 mg

Roasted Veggie Burgers

YIELD: 10 BURGERS

The bean portion of this grain and bean combination is contributed by chickpea flour, which is sold at most natural food stores as well as any store that specializes in Indian foods. If you can't find it, however, you can substitute whole-wheat flour.

4 portobello mushrooms, trimmed
1 onion, quartered
1 red bell pepper, seeded and
  quartered
1 garlic bulb
1 eggplant
1 potato, peeled and grated

1 large egg, slightly beaten
1¼ cups cooked wheat berries
1 cup chickpea flour
¼ cup toasted bread crumbs
1 teaspoon salt
10 burger buns

Preheat the oven to 400 degrees. Coat a large baking dish with nonstick cooking spray. Combine the mushrooms, onion, and bell pepper in the baking dish. Separate the garlic bulb into cloves and peel. Add to the baking dish. Mist with nonstick cooking spray. Roast in the oven until well browned, 30 to 45 minutes.

Meanwhile, prick the eggplant all over with a fork and place in the oven. Roast until completely soft, about 30 minutes. Remove the cooked eggplant from its skin by cutting in half and using a spoon to scrape it out of the shell. Discard the shells.

Combine the roasted eggplant with the roasted vegetables in a food processor and process briefly until finely chopped. Combine in a mixing bowl with the potato, egg, wheat berries, chickpea flour, bread crumbs, and salt. Let stand for at least 5 minutes to allow the mixture to thicken.

Form the mixture into burgers. Coat a nonstick griddle or frying pan with nonstick cooking spray and heat over medium heat. Mist the burgers with nonstick cooking spray on both sides. Cook on both sides until browned, about 4 minutes per side. Serve on buns and pass all of the usual hamburger condiments at the table.

Calories 234 • Protein 9 gm • Fat 4 gm • Percent of calories from fat 15% •
Cholesterol 21 mg • Dietary fiber 4 gm • Sodium 289 mg • Calcium 59 mg

10
Bountiful Breakfasts

Breakfast Corn Cakes

Strawberry-Banana Pancakes

Amaranth Buttermilk Pancakes

Brown Rice Pancakes

Wild Rice Pancakes

Quantity Pancake Mix

Old-fashioned Johnnycakes

Crispy Vanilla Oat Waffles

Banana-Nut Oat Waffles

Hot Barley Cereal

Honey-Orange Barley Porridge

Hot Buckwheat-Pear Cereal

Creamy Sweet Breakfast Grits

Millet Porridge

Creamy Oatmeal

Old-fashioned Steel-cut Oatmeal

Toasted Steel-cut Oatmeal

Hot Rice Cereal

Hot Maple Rice Cereal

Chinese Congee

Hot Wheat Cereal

Cracked Wheat Cereal

Cherry-Almond Granola

Coconut-Almond Granola

Cashew-Honey Granola

Blueberry Morning Granola

Whenever I do more than stick a bowl of granola in front of my children in the morning, I feel a bit like a sit-com mother. They always made such elaborate breakfasts for their families! But this is life in the nineties, and pancakes and waffles are reserved for Sunday breakfasts. My family won't accept pancakes as supper food, though I know many who do—so don't feel you have to enjoy them only at breakfast.

I have a friend who will eat oatmeal by day or night. I can't say I'd look forward to an evening meal of mush, but the wonderful flavors and the sheer variety in hot cereals in this chapter were a revelation even to me. The nice thing about having your pantry stocked with grains is you can have a different hot cereal every morning, with lots of variation in flavor and very little fuss.

I do have a secret, though. When I ready a bowl of hot cereal for myself or my kids, I have a very generous hand with the sweetener, and I often add a little whole milk for extra creaminess. Similarly, the cereals that are cooked in milk can be made with 2-percent milk instead of skim milk. The luxury version may make a convert out of even the most reluctant cereal eater.

If hot cereal requires too much time in the morning, perhaps you will want to take a little weekend time to make your own granola. Homemade granola is fresher and less expensive than the store-bought kind. The recipes included here are all low-fat and rich with plenty of mix-ins. And, of course, with homemade granola you can substitute ingredients according to your own taste.

Every year for Christmas, I make up several batches of granola to give away as gifts. I bundle the granola in plastic bags and label them with colorful stickers (on which I record my ingredients list). Then I wrap the bags in colored cellophane and tie them with ribbon. Simple to make, assembly-line easy to wrap, unbreakable for shipping, and much appreciated.

The breakfasts included in this chapter are hearty and healthy. But don't forget to consider the breads and muffins in Chapter 11. And if you really want some hearty fare, check out the Breakfast Black Bean and Egg Burritos and the Huevos Rancheros in Chapter 6.

Breakfast Corn Cakes

YIELD: 4 TO 6 SERVINGS (ABOUT 22 PANCAKES)

This recipe properly serves six, unless you are serving a gang of big-time corn bread fans. I love these corn cakes dripping with maple syrup.

2 cups skim milk	2 teaspoons baking powder
1 cup stone-ground yellow cornmeal	1/2 teaspoon baking soda
1/4 cup quick-cooking yellow corn grits	1/2 teaspoon salt
	2 large eggs
1 1/4 cups unbleached all-purpose flour	2 tablespoons pure maple syrup or honey
	3 tablespoons canola oil

In a medium saucepan, scald the milk. Remove from the heat and stir in the yellow cornmeal and grits. Set aside to cool for at least 5 minutes.

Preheat the oven to 200 degrees. Place 4 to 6 plates in the oven to keep warm, if desired.

In a large bowl, combine the flour, baking powder, baking soda, and salt.

Add the eggs, maple syrup, and canola oil to the cooled cornmeal mixture. Stir well to combine. Make a well in the flour mixture, add the cornmeal mixture all at once, and stir well to combine.

Spray a well-seasoned cast-iron griddle or nonstick frying pan with nonstick cooking spray and heat over medium heat. Pour the batter onto the griddle to make 4-inch pancakes. Cook until bubbles appear on the tops of the pancakes and the bottoms are lightly browned. Turn and cook on the other side until golden, about 1 minute longer.

Keep the pancakes warm in the preheated oven while you cook the rest of the batter.

Calories 471 • Protein 14 gm • Fat 15 gm • Percent of calories from fat 28% • Cholesterol 108 mg • Dietary fiber 4 gm • Sodium 1045 mg • Calcium 261 mg

Blueberry Corn Cakes. Add 2 cups fresh blueberries to the batter. If using frozen blueberries, thaw and drain before adding to the batter.

Calories 512 • Protein 15 gm • Fat 15 gm • Percent of calories from fat 26% • Cholesterol 108 mg • Dietary fiber 6 gm • Sodium 1049 mg • Calcium 265 mg

Raspberry Corn Cakes. Add 2 cups fresh raspberries to the batter. If using frozen raspberries, thaw and drain before adding to the batter.

Calories 501 • Protein 15 gm • Fat 15 gm • Percent of calories from fat 26% • Cholesterol 108 mg • Dietary fiber 8 gm • Sodium 1045 mg • Calcium 275 mg

Peachy Corn Cakes. Add 2 cups finely diced fresh, canned, or frozen and thawed peaches to the batter.

Calories 518 • Protein 15 gm • Fat 15 gm • Percent of calories from fat 25% • Cholesterol 108 mg • Dietary fiber 6 gm • Sodium 1045 mg • Calcium 267 mg

Pear Corn Cakes. Add 2 cups finely diced fresh or canned pears, well drained, to the batter.

Calories 541 • Protein 15 gm • Fat 15 gm • Percent of calories from fat 24% • Cholesterol 108 mg • Dietary fiber 7 gm • Sodium 1045 mg • Calcium 274 mg

Strawberry-Banana Pancakes

YIELD: 4 GENEROUS SERVINGS (ABOUT 16 PANCAKES)

These light and airy pancakes are a great breakfast treat.

1 cup stone-ground yellow
  cornmeal
1 cup unbleached all-purpose
  flour
1/4 cup toasted wheat germ
3 tablespoons brown sugar
1 1/2 teaspoons baking powder
1/2 teaspoon baking soda
1/2 teaspoon salt

1 cup nonfat vanilla yogurt
3/4 cup skim milk
2 tablespoons canola oil
2 large egg whites
1 ripe banana, quartered lengthwise
  and sliced
1 cup finely chopped fresh
  strawberries

Preheat the oven to 200 degrees. Place 4 serving plates in the oven to keep warm, if desired.

Combine the cornmeal, flour, wheat germ, brown sugar, baking powder, baking soda, and salt. Mix well.

In a separate bowl, combine the yogurt, milk, and canola oil.

In another bowl, beat the egg whites until soft peaks form.

Spray a well-seasoned cast-iron griddle or nonstick frying pan with nonstick cooking spray. Preheat over medium heat. When the griddle is hot, add the yogurt mixture, banana, and strawberries to the dry ingredients. Stir to mix. Fold in the egg whites. Spoon the batter onto the preheated griddle, using about 1/4 cup batter for each pancake. Cook until bubbles cover the surface, then flip and cook until the second side is golden, about 1 minute longer. Keep warm in the oven until all of the pancakes are made. Serve warm, passing maple syrup at the table.

Calories 454 • Protein 14 gm • Fat 9 gm • Percent of calories from fat 18% •
Cholesterol 1 mg • Dietary fiber 6 gm • Sodium 705 mg • Calcium 227 mg

Chocolate-Banana Pancakes. Replace the strawberries with ³/₄ cup mini chocolate chip morsels.

Calories 652 • Protein 17 gm • Fat 21 gm • Percent of calories from fat 28 % •
Cholesterol 1 mg • Dietary fiber 5 gm • Sodium 735 mg • Calcium 282 mg

Amaranth Buttermilk Pancakes

YIELD: 4 SERVINGS (16 TO 18 PANCAKES)

These whole-grain pancakes rise high and taste light and airy. They go down easily and then show surprising stick-to-your ribs ability to get you through a morning of heavy chores or hiking. At my house we like them with the usual pancake fixings—maple syrup and sliced fruit.

1¼ cups unbleached all-purpose flour
½ cup whole-wheat flour
½ cup popped amaranth
3 tablespoons sugar
2 teaspoons baking powder
1 teaspoon baking soda
1 teaspoon salt
2 large egg whites
1 whole large egg
3 tablespoons canola oil
1¾ cups nonfat buttermilk

Preheat the oven to 200 degrees. Place 4 serving plates in the oven to keep warm, if desired.

In a medium mixing bowl, combine the all-purpose and whole-wheat flours, amaranth, sugar, baking powder, baking soda, and salt. Mix well. In a separate bowl, beat together the egg whites, whole egg, canola oil, and buttermilk. Combine with the flour mixture and beat until smooth.

Spray a well-seasoned cast-iron griddle or nonstick frying pan with nonstick cooking spray and heat over medium heat. Pour enough batter onto the griddle to make 4-inch pancakes. Cook until bubbles appear on the tops of the pancakes and the bottoms are lightly browned. Turn and cook on the other side until lightly browned.

Keep the pancakes warm in the preheated oven while you cook the rest of the batter. Serve warm.

Calories 389 • Protein 13 gm • Fat 15 gm • Percent of calories from fat 33% • Cholesterol 57 mg • Dietary fiber 3 gm • Sodium 1253 mg • Calcium 223 mg

Brown Rice Pancakes

❦

YIELD: 4 GENEROUS SERVINGS (ABOUT 16 PANCAKES)

1½ cups unbleached all-purpose
   flour
¼ cup whole-wheat flour
¼ cup stone-ground yellow
   cornmeal
1 tablespoon sugar
2 teaspoons baking powder
1 teaspoon baking soda

½ teaspoon salt
1 cup cooked brown rice
2 large eggs, separated
3 tablespoons melted butter
1 cup skim milk
2 large egg whites
Maple syrup and/or fruit,
   for serving (optional)

Preheat the oven to 200 degrees. Place 4 or 5 serving plates in the oven to warm, if desired.

Combine the all-purpose and whole-wheat flours, cornmeal, sugar, baking powder, and salt in a food processor. Process briefly to mix. Add the rice, egg yolks, melted butter, and milk, and process until the batter is well mixed.

Beat the 4 egg whites until soft peaks form. Fold about a third of the batter into the whites. Then fold in the remaining batter.

Spray a well-seasoned cast-iron griddle or nonstick frying pan with nonstick cooking spray and heat over medium heat. Pour about ⅓ cup batter onto the preheated cooking surface for each pancake. Cook until golden brown on the bottom, then flip and cook the second side. Keep warm in the oven when you cook the remaining batter. Serve warm, passing maple syrup and/or fruit at the table, if desired.

Calories 425 • Protein 14 gm • Fat 13 gm • Percent of calories from fat 27% •
Cholesterol 132 mg • Dietary fiber 4 gm • Sodium 993 mg • Calcium 186 mg

Wild Rice Pancakes

YIELD: 5 TO 8 SERVINGS (18 TO 21 PANCAKES)

Wild rice contributes a nutty flavor to these slightly sweet pancakes. If you like, mix in blueberries or chopped cooked cranberries for a very special New World flavor.

1^1/$_2$ cups cooked wild rice
2 large eggs
1 cup skim milk
3 tablespoons canola oil
1 cup unbleached all-purpose
    flour

^{1}/$_2$ cup whole-wheat flour
1^1/$_2$ teaspoons baking powder
2 tablespoons sugar
1 teaspoon salt

Preheat the oven to 200 degrees. Place 5 to 8 serving plates in the oven to warm, if desired.

Puree ^{3}/$_4$ cup of the wild rice in a blender or food processor. Add the eggs, milk, and canola oil and mix well. In a separate bowl, combine the all-purpose and whole-wheat flours, baking powder, sugar, and salt. Add to the milk mixture along with the remaining ^{3}/$_4$ cup wild rice and mix well.

Spray a well-seasoned cast-iron griddle or nonstick frying pan with nonstick cooking spray. Heat over medium heat. Pour about 3 tablespoons batter for each pancake onto the preheated griddle and cook for about 2 minutes, until bubbles appear on the surface and the edges appear dry. Flip and cook on the other side until golden. Keep warm in the oven while you cook the remaining batter.

Calories 313 • Protein 10 gm • Fat 11 gm • Percent of calories from fat 31% •
Cholesterol 86 mg • Dietary fiber 3 gm • Sodium 638 mg • Calcium 128 mg

Quantity Pancake Mix

❧❧❧

YIELD: **12** CUPS MIX

This is my house mix. I make it every few months and store it in a gallon-size glass jar. Having the mix on hand makes it possible to make pancakes quickly, even on weekdays. The mix makes a hearty yet tender and light pancake. When making the batter, I often throw in a grated apple or a handful of berries. For lighter pancakes, separate the eggs and beat the egg whites.

Dry Mix
5 cups unbleached all-purpose
   flour
2¹/₂ cups whole-wheat flour
2¹/₂ cups stone-ground yellow
   cornmeal

1¹/₂ cups sugar
³/₄ cup baking powder
3 tablespoons salt

To make 1 batch (18 to 20 4-inch pancakes)
2 large eggs
3 tablespoons canola oil
1¹/₄ cups skim milk

1¹/₂ cups Quantity Pancake Mix
   (above)

To make the mix, combine the all-purpose and whole-wheat flours, cornmeal, sugar, baking powder, and salt in a large bowl. Mix well. Store in an airtight jar.

To make a batch of pancakes, preheat the oven to 200 degrees. Place 4 to 6 plates in the oven to warm, if desired.

Combine the eggs, canola oil, and milk in a large glass measuring cup or bowl and beat well. Add the mix and beat until smooth.

Spray a well-seasoned cast-iron griddle or nonstick frying pan with nonstick cooking spray and heat over medium heat. Pour about 3 table-spoons batter for each pancake onto the preheated griddle and cook for about 1¹/₂ minutes, until bubbles appear on the surface and the edges appear dry. Flip and cook on the other side until golden. Keep warm in the oven until all of the batter is cooked.

Per Pancake: Calories 72 • Protein 2 gm • Fat 3 gm • Percent of calories from fat 38% • Cholesterol 24 mg • Dietary fiber 1 gm • Sodium 262 mg • Calcium 65 mg

Old-fashioned Johnnycakes

YIELD: 4 SERVINGS

Johnnycakes hark back to a time when palates were less jaded and simple foods satisfied. I can't say I prefer these little cakes above all others, but my family enjoyed eating these while we were reading The Little House on the Prairie. *In that book, Laura and Mary dipped their johnnycakes in sorghum—and Ma probably fried them in bacon grease. We were happy with maple syrup and butter.*

1 cup white or yellow cornmeal
¹/₂ teaspoon salt
1 cup boiling water

1 tablespoon butter
Maple syrup, for serving (optional)

In a mixing bowl, combine the cornmeal and salt. Stir in the boiling water. Continue stirring until the water is completely absorbed and the mixture is evenly moist. Set aside for at least 5 minutes.

When the mixture is cool enough to handle, form into 10 to 12 small pancakes. Melt the butter in a large, heavy skillet over medium heat. Add the johnnycakes in a single layer and brown on both sides. Serve hot, passing maple syrup at the table, if desired.

Calories 137 • Protein 3 gm • Fat 4 gm • Percent of calories from fat 26% •
Cholesterol 8 mg • Dietary fiber 2 gm • Sodium 334 mg • Calcium 4 mg

Crispy Vanilla Oat Waffles

❧

YIELD: 4 SERVINGS

It's no mistake that these waffles contain no butter or oil. Whereas pancakes need a little oil for tenderizing, the crisp texture of waffles makes the additional fat unnecessary.

2 cups rolled oats (not instant)
1 tablespoon sugar
1¹/₂ teaspoons baking powder
¹/₂ teaspoon baking soda
¹/₂ teaspoon salt
1 cup nonfat vanilla yogurt
¹/₂ cup skim milk, or more if
  necessary to thin batter

2 large eggs
¹/₄ cup toasted wheat germ
  if needed to thicken batter
Fruit and/or maple syrup,
  for serving (optional)

Combine the oats, sugar, baking powder, baking soda, and salt in a food processor. Process for about 1 minute, until the oats are finely ground. Add the yogurt, milk, and eggs, and pulse the machine on and off to mix the batter. Pour the batter into a large glass measuring cup or bowl and let stand for about 5 to 15 minutes to thicken.

Meanwhile, spray the waffle iron with nonstick cooking spray and preheat on medium. Preheat the oven to 200 degrees. Place 4 plates in the oven to warm, if desired.

When you are ready to make the waffles, stir the batter. It should have the consistency of heavy cream. If it is too thin, stir in the wheat germ. If it is too thick, thin with a little more milk. Pour one-quarter of the batter onto the waffle iron. Close and cook until the waffle iron will open easily and the waffles are a golden brown. Keep the waffles warm in the oven, directly on the oven rack, uncovered, to stay crisp. Serve warm, with fruit and/or warmed maple syrup, if desired.

Calories 268 • Protein 13 gm • Fat 5 gm • Percent of calories from fat 17% •
Cholesterol 107 mg • Dietary fiber 4 gm • Sodium 687 mg • Calcium 219 mg

Jan'09 - These were great! Used plain yogurt + vanilla extract — omit salt next time, used only ¹/₄ t, and still too salty. Also try egg whites. Wheat germ not needed.

Banana-Nut Oat Waffles

YIELD: **4** SERVINGS

If you love banana bread, you'll enjoy this wheat-free waffle variation. Maple syrup makes the perfect topping for these crunchy waffles.

2 cups rolled oats (not instant)
1 tablespoon sugar
2 teaspoons baking powder
1 teaspoon baking soda
1/2 teaspoon salt
1 cup nonfat vanilla yogurt
2 large eggs

2 ripe bananas, sliced
1/2 cup chopped nuts (almonds, pecans, walnuts, hazelnuts, etc.)
Milk, if necessary to thin batter
Warmed maple syrup, for serving (optional)

Spray a waffle iron with nonstick cooking spray and preheat on medium. Preheat the oven to 200 degrees. Place 4 plates in the oven to warm, if desired.

Combine the oats, sugar, baking powder, baking soda, and salt in a food processor. Process for about 1 minute, until the oats are finely ground. Add the yogurt, eggs, and bananas, and process until the batter is well mixed. Stir in the nuts.

Pour about 1 cup of the batter onto the waffle iron. Close and cook until the waffle iron will open easily and the waffles are golden brown. Keep the waffles warm in the oven, directly on the oven rack, uncovered, to stay crisp. Continue cooking waffles until all of the batter is used. You will probably need to thin the batter with milk as it will thicken as it stands. Serve warm, with warmed maple syrup, if desired.

Calories 405 • Protein 17 gm • Fat 14 gm • Percent of calories from fat 30% •
Cholesterol 106 mg • Dietary fiber 6 gm • Sodium 879 mg • Calcium 214 mg

Hot Barley Cereal

YIELD: 4 SERVINGS

This porridge benefits from the sweet, nutty flavor and chewy texture of barley. For a smoother porridge, increase the water and cooking time and stir frequently while cooking.

4 cups water
2 cups uncooked rolled barley
   (barley flakes)
¹/₂ teaspoon salt

Sweetener (white or brown sugar,
   honey, or maple syrup)
Milk, for serving

In a medium saucepan, bring the water to a boil. Stir in the barley and salt, reduce the heat, cover, and gently cook, stirring occasionally, until the water has been absorbed and the barley is cooked through, about 15 minutes. Remove from the heat and let stand, covered, for 5 minutes. Serve hot, sprinkled with your favorite sweetener. Pass milk at the table for those who like their cereal creamy.

Calories 165 • Protein 6 gm • Fat 2 gm • Percent of calories from fat 6% •
Cholesterol 0 mg • Dietary fiber 8 gm • Sodium 298 mg • Calcium 5 mg

Honey-Orange Barley Porridge

YIELD: 4 SERVINGS

Fans of hot cereal will appreciate this chewy breakfast cereal as a change of pace from the usual smooth porridge. Whole or 2-percent milk adds a luxurious touch.

1 cup uncooked pearled barley
3/4 cup dried currants or raisins
1 teaspoon finely grated orange
   zest

3/4 teaspoon salt
4 cups water
1/4 cup honey
Milk, for serving

In a heavy-bottomed saucepan, combine the barley, currants, orange zest, salt, and water. Cover and bring to a boil, then reduce the heat and simmer, stirring occasionally, until the barley is tender, about 35 minutes. Stir in the honey. Serve hot. Pass milk at the table.

Calories 338 • Protein 6 gm • Fat 1 gm • Percent of calories from fat 1% • Cholesterol 0 mg • Dietary fiber 9 gm • Sodium 456 mg • Calcium 37 mg

Hot Buckwheat-Pear Cereal

❧❧❧

YIELD: 4 SERVINGS

This is a cereal for serious fans of buckwheat. The sweet pear perfectly pairs with the assertive flavor of roasted buckwheat. It takes about 1 hour to prepare.

**4 cups milk (preferably
    2-percent)**
**1/2 cup uncooked roasted
    buckwheat groats**

3 ripe pears
1/3 cup brown sugar

In the top of a double boiler over boiling water, combine the milk and buckwheat groats and cook for about 45 minutes, until the groats are tender. Peel and core the pears, slice in eighths, then slice thinly. Add the pears and sugar to the cereal and continue to cook for about 15 minutes, until the pears are quite soft. Stir well to break down the pears somewhat. Serve hot.

Calories 334 • Protein 11 gm • Fat 6 gm • Percent of calories from fat 14% • Cholesterol 18 mg • Dietary fiber 5 gm • Sodium 131 mg • Calcium 330 mg

Creamy Sweet Breakfast Grits

YIELD: 4 SERVINGS

This hot cereal is so rich tasting, so perfectly sweetened that it makes the ideal fuel for a hard day's work. I can eat this cereal any time of the day or night.

2^1/$_2$ cups milk (preferably
   2-percent)
^{1}/$_2$ cup quick-cooking grits
3 tablespoons honey

^{1}/$_2$ teaspoon salt
Sliced fresh peaches, nectarines,
   strawberries, or whole berries,
   for serving (optional)

Combine the milk, grits, honey, and salt in a heavy-bottomed saucepan over medium heat. Bring to a boil, stirring frequently. Reduce the heat to low and cook, stirring frequently, until thickened, 8 to 10 minutes. Serve at once, topped with fresh fruit, if desired.

Calories 189 • Protein 7 gm • Fat 3 gm • Percent of calories from fat 14% • Cholesterol 11 mg • Dietary fiber 1 gm • Sodium 368 mg • Calcium 187 mg

Millet Porridge

✿❀✿

YIELD: 4 SERVINGS

4 cups boiling water
1 cup uncooked millet
1 teaspoon salt

½ cup milk (preferably 2-percent),
   plus extra for serving
Sweetener (white or brown sugar,
   honey, or maple syrup)

Bring the water to a boil in a saucepan. Stir in the millet and salt, cover, reduce the heat to very low, and cook slowly, stirring occasionally, until the grain is tender and has absorbed all of the liquid, 30 to 35 minutes. Stir in the milk and continue cooking until the porridge reaches the desired consistency. Sweeten to taste. Serve hot, passing additional milk at the table.

Calories 204 • Protein 7 gm • Fat 3 gm • Percent of calories from fat 12% •
Cholesterol 2 mg • Dietary fiber 4 gm • Sodium 606 mg • Calcium 46 mg

Creamy Oatmeal

YIELD: 4 SERVINGS

There is no one right way to fix oatmeal. This is how we like it at our house.

1¹/₃ cups rolled oats (not instant)
4 cups cold water
¹/₂ teaspoon salt
Milk, for serving

Sweetener (white or brown sugar, honey, or maple syrup), for serving

Combine the oats and water in a saucepan. Bring to a boil, uncovered. Reduce the heat and cook over very low heat, stirring occasionally, until the oatmeal reaches the desired consistency, about 5 minutes. Cover and let stand for 5 minutes. Serve hot, passing milk and a sweetener at the table.

Calories 103 • Protein 4 gm • Fat 2 gm • Percent of calories from fat 14% •
Cholesterol 0 mg • Dietary fiber 3 gm • Sodium 299 mg • Calcium 19 mg

Old-fashioned Steel-cut Oatmeal

YIELD: 4 SERVINGS

Steel-cut oats produce a porridge with a much chewier texture than rolled oats. The only drawback is the cooking time required: about an hour. You must assemble the ingredients the night before you cook this.

4 cups water
1 cup uncooked steel-cut oats

$1/_4$ teaspoon salt

One night ahead, combine the water, oats, and salt in a heavy-bottomed saucepan and set aside. In the morning, bring to a boil, reduce the heat, and cover. Cook gently until the moisture is absorbed and the oats are tender, about 1 hour. The timing will vary depending on the dryness of the oats.

Calories 170 • Protein 6 gm • Fat 3 gm • Percent of calories from fat 16% • Cholesterol 0 mg • Dietary fiber 5 gm • Sodium 152 mg • Calcium 25 mg

Toasted Steel-cut Oatmeal

YIELD: **4** SERVINGS

This is my favorite way to make oatmeal from steel-cut oats. The toasting reduces the cooking time and significantly alters the oats, creating a flavor that is quite wheat-like.

1 cup toasted steel-cut oats
  (see Note)
3^1/$_2$ cups water
^{1}/$_2$ teaspoon salt

Sweetener (white or brown sugar,
  honey, or maple syrup), for
  serving
Milk, for serving

Combine the oats with the water and salt in a saucepan. Stir to mix. Cover and bring to a boil. Reduce the heat and simmer until the liquid is absorbed and the oatmeal is tender, 20 to 25 minutes. It will still be quite chewy. Stir well. Then cover and let stand for 5 minutes before serving. Pass sweetener and milk at the table.

Note: To toast the oats, preheat the oven to 350 degrees. Spread the oats evenly on a baking sheet and toast for about 20 minutes, stirring occasionally. Cool completely before storing in an airtight container for up to 3 months.

Calories 170 • Protein 6 gm • Fat 3 gm • Percent of calories from fat 16% •
Cholesterol 0 mg • Dietary fiber 5 gm • Sodium 297 mg • Calcium 24 mg

Hot Rice Cereal

YIELD: 4 SERVINGS

When I lived in a college dorm I never bothered to get up in time for breakfast except when the cook made this delicious cereal. It took me years to figure out how to recreate it.

1 cup short-grain rice	Approximately 2 cups skim or
1¹/₂ cups water	low-fat milk
¹/₂ teaspoon salt	¹/₂ cups raisins
	¹/₄ cup brown sugar

Combine the rice, water, and salt in a medium saucepan. Cover and bring to a boil, then reduce the heat and simmer until the rice is mostly tender and the water has been absorbed, about 12 minutes. Stir in 2 cups milk, the raisins, and brown sugar. Simmer over low heat until the milk is heated through and the rice is completely tender, 10 minutes. Serve at once. The cereal will thicken on standing, so it may need thinning with additional milk if held for late risers.

Calories 328 • Protein 8 gm • Fat 1 gm • Percent of calories from fat 1% •
Cholesterol 2 mg • Dietary fiber 2 gm • Sodium 364 mg • Calcium 175 mg

Hot Maple Rice Cereal

YIELD: 4 SERVINGS

The next time you are preparing plain rice, make a few extra cups for this delicious hot cereal. It can be made with white or brown rice, but white rice does yield a creamier texture. One especially nice aspect of this cereal is its convenience. Assemble the ingredients one night ahead and cook it on top of the stove while you dress in the morning.

2 cups cooked white or brown rice
$2^1/_2$ cups low-fat or skim milk
$^1/_4$ cup raisins
3 tablespoons pure maple syrup

$^1/_8$ teaspoon ground cinnamon
Sliced fresh fruit, for serving
(optional)

One night ahead, combine the rice, milk, raisins, maple syrup, and cinnamon in a saucepan and leave in the refrigerator. In the morning, cook over medium heat, stirring occasionally, until heated through and slightly thickened, about 15 minutes. Remove from the heat and let stand for 5 minutes to thicken. Top with sliced fresh fruit, if desired.

Calories 242 • Protein 7 gm • Fat 3 gm • Percent of calories from fat 12% •
Cholesterol 11 mg • Dietary fiber 1 gm • Sodium 80 mg • Calcium 214 mg

Chinese Congee

YIELD: 4 SERVINGS

Okay, this breakfast dish is not for everyone, but literally millions of people in Asia start their day with it, so aren't you curious? I love this porridge, but then I don't require the sweet breakfast most Americans prefer. Enjoy it plain with just soy sauce, or top it with pickled vegetables. This takes a little over 2 hours to cook, but it can be made in advance and reheated in the microwave.

³/₄ cup uncooked short-grain rice　　**Soy sauce, for serving**
8 cups water

Rinse the rice in several changes of cold running water until the rinse water runs clean. Drain well. Meanwhile, bring the water to a boil in a medium saucepan. Add the rice, reduce the heat to medium, and simmer, uncovered, for 40 minutes. Then reduce the heat to low, cover, and cook for another 1¹/₄ hours, until the rice is very thick and creamy. Stir in the soy sauce and serve hot.

Calories 134 • Protein 2 gm • Fat .2 gm • Percent of calories from fat 1% •
Cholesterol 0 mg • Dietary fiber 1 gm • Sodium 15 mg • Calcium 11 mg

Hot Wheat Cereal

YIELD: **4** SERVINGS

Why pay for the fancy packaging when wheat flakes (a.k.a. rolled wheat) are available in bulk at your local natural food store and cook up into a cereal that tastes like Ralston? For a creamier version, substitute milk for all or part of the water.

3 cups water
1¹/₂ cups uncooked rolled wheat
   or wheat flakes
¹/₂ teaspoon salt

Sweetener (white or brown sugar,
   honey, or maple syrup), for
   serving
Milk, for serving

In a medium saucepan, bring the water to a boil. Stir in the wheat and salt, reduce the heat, cover, and cook gently, stirring occasionally, until the water has been absorbed and the cereal has a nice smooth consistency, about 10 minutes. Remove from the heat and let stand, covered, for 5 minutes. Serve hot, sprinkled with your favorite sweetener. Pass milk at the table for those who like their cereal creamy.

Calories 124 • Protein 5 gm • Fat 1 gm • Percent of calories from fat 4% • Cholesterol 0 mg • Dietary fiber 6 gm • Sodium 296 mg • Calcium 26 mg

Cracked Wheat Cereal

❧

YIELD: 4 SERVINGS

So you prefer Wheatina to Ralston? Then this is your cereal. Giving the cracked wheat a quick whirl in the blender will bring it closer to the finer texture of Wheatina. Cooking it in milk instead of water will give it a creamier flavor.

1 cup cracked wheat
3 cups hot water
1/2 teaspoon salt

Sweetener (white or brown sugar, honey, or maple syrup)
Milk, for serving

Toast the cracked wheat in a dry saucepan over medium heat for about 7 minutes, until the grains smell fragrant and toasted. Add the salt and hot water carefully (stand back so the hot grain doesn't sputter up onto your arms or face). Cover and bring to a boil. Reduce the heat and boil gently for about 20 minutes, until the liquid has been absorbed and the grains are tender. Stir well. Then cover and let stand for 5 minutes. Sweeten to taste and pass the milk at the table.

Calories 140 • Protein 5 gm • Fat 1 gm • Percent of calories from fat 3% • Cholesterol 0 mg • Dietary fiber 6 gm • Sodium 296 mg • Calcium 9 mg

Cherry-Almond Granola

YIELD: ABOUT 6 CUPS

Granola is a good-for-you food that can pack a lot of fat along with its vitamins, minerals, and fiber. This version, which calls for a minimum of oil and sweetened condensed skim milk, derives only twenty-five percent of its calories from fat. Friends of mine consider this their "all-time favorite granola." When I am inspired to make Christmas food gifts, this is the recipe I turn to most often.

2 cups uncooked rolled oats
   (not instant)
1 cup slivered almonds
1 cup toasted wheat germ
1/2 cup shredded coconut
1 teaspoon salt

1 (14-ounce) can sweetened
   condensed skim milk
2 tablespoons canola oil
1 cup raisins
1 cup sweetened dried cherries

Preheat the oven to 300 degrees. Spray a large shallow roasting pan with nonstick cooking spray.

In a large bowl, combine the oats, almonds, wheat germ, coconut, and salt. Stir in the milk and canola oil and mix well. Spread in the prepared pan and bake, stirring occasionally, until golden, 50 to 60 minutes. Stir frequently during the last 15 minutes to prevent scorching around the edges; do not let the granola get too dark.

Put the baked granola into a large bowl to cool. Let cool completely, then stir in the raisins and cherries. Store in an airtight container.

Calories 522 • Protein 21 gm • Fat 16 gm • Percent of calories from fat 26% •
Cholesterol 2 mg • Dietary fiber 9 gm • Sodium 493 mg • Calcium 303 mg

VARIATION

Apricot-Almond Granola. Replace the cherries with 1 cup finely diced dried apricots.

Calories 509 • Protein 21 gm • Fat 16 gm • Percent of calories from fat 27% •
Cholesterol 3 mg • Dietary fiber 11 gm • Sodium 500 mg • Calcium 313 mg

Coconut-Almond Granola

❧❧❧

YIELD: ABOUT 7 CUPS

Coconut milk is baked into the granola to give a double punch of flavor. For coconut lovers, this granola is a sure hit.

2 cups uncooked rolled oats
  (not instant)
1 cup uncooked rolled barley
  or wheat flakes
1 cup toasted wheat germ
3/4 cup slivered almonds

3/4 cup firmly packed brown sugar
1/2 cup shredded coconut
1 teaspoon salt
3/4 cup light coconut milk
2 teaspoons vanilla extract
1 cup raisins

Preheat the oven to 300 degrees. Spray a large shallow roasting pan with nonstick cooking spray.

In a large bowl, combine the oats, barley flakes, wheat germ, almonds, brown sugar, coconut, and salt. Combine the coconut milk and vanilla. Pour into the oat mixture and combine well. Spread in the prepared pan and bake until golden, about 60 minutes, stirring occasionally during the first 45 minutes and more frequently during the last 15 minutes to prevent scorching around the edges; do not let the granola get too dark.

Transfer to a bowl to cool completely. Stir in the raisins. Store in an airtight container for up to 3 months.

Calories 481 • Protein 14 gm • Fat 14 gm • Percent of calories from fat 25% • Cholesterol 0 mg • Dietary fiber 10 gm • Sodium 370 mg • Calcium 88 mg

Cashew-Honey Granola

YIELD: ABOUT 6 CUPS

Cashew lovers will appreciate the simple flavor of this not-too-sweet granola.

2 cups uncooked rolled oats
  (not instant)
1 cup uncooked rolled barley
  or wheat flakes
1 cup cashew pieces

1 cup toasted wheat germ
1 teaspoon salt
3/4 cup honey
3/4 cup evaporated skim milk
2 teaspoons vanilla extract

Preheat the oven to 300 degrees. Spray a large shallow roasting pan with nonstick cooking spray.

In a large bowl, combine the oats, barley flakes, cashews, wheat germ, and salt.

Heat the honey by placing it in the microwave for about 1 minute on high, or placing it in a jar in a small saucepan filled with hot water, and heating gently for a few minutes. When the honey is warm to the touch and fairly liquid, add the milk and vanilla and mix well. Stir into the oat mixture and mix well. Spread in the prepared pan and bake until golden, 45 to 50 minutes, stirring occasionally during the first 30 minutes and frequently during the final 15 to 20 minutes to avoid scorching at the sides of the pan; do not let the granola get too dark. Turn off the heat and leave the granola in the cooling oven for 1 hour. This helps the granola develop a crisp texture despite the presence of the honey.

Transfer to a large bowl to cool completely before storing in an airtight container for up to 3 months.

Calories 496 • Protein 18 gm • Fat 14 gm • Percent of calories from fat 23% • Cholesterol 1 mg • Dietary fiber 8 gm • Sodium 534 mg • Calcium 116 mg

Fruit-and-Nut Granola. After the granola has cooled, dried fruit can be mixed in, which will make the granola sweeter. Use a total of 2 cups finely chopped dried fruit, including raisins, dried cherries, dried apricots, dried blueberries, and/or dates.

Calories 665 • Protein 19 gm • Fat 13.8 gm • Percent of calories from fat 17% • Cholesterol 1 mg • Dietary fiber 12 gm • Sodium 537 mg • Calcium 139 mg

Blueberry Morning Granola

YIELD: ABOUT 6 CUPS

Dried blueberries are hard to come by in stores, but they are available through the mail. I get mine from the Wooden Spoon, P.O. Box 931, Clinton, CT 06413 (800-431-2207). You can also order them from Timber Crest Farms, 4791 Dry Creek Road, Healdsburg, CA 95448 (707-433-8251). If you prefer, you can substitute another dried fruit.

2 cups uncooked rolled oats
  (not instant)
1 cup uncooked rolled barley
  or wheat flakes
1 cup toasted wheat germ
1 cup slivered almonds
1/2 cup sunflower seeds

1 teaspoon salt
3/4 cup honey
1/4 cup dried nonfat milk
2 tablespoons canola oil
2 teaspoons vanilla extract
11/2 cups dried blueberries

Preheat the oven to 300 degrees. Spray a large shallow roasting pan with nonstick cooking spray.

In a large bowl, combine the oats, barley flakes, wheat germ, almonds, sunflower seeds, and salt.

Heat the honey by placing in the microwave for about 1 minute on high, or by placing it in a glass jar and setting the jar in a small saucepan filled with hot water and heating gently for a few minutes. When the honey is warm to the touch and fairly liquid, combine it with the dry milk powder and canola oil and beat until the milk is dissolved. Stir in the vanilla. Stir into the oat mixture and mix well.

Spread the granola in the prepared pan and bake until golden, 45 to 50 minutes, stirring occasionally during the first 30 minutes and frequently during the final 15 to 20 minutes to avoid scorching at the sides of the pan; do not let the granola get too dark. Turn off the heat and leave the granola in the cooling oven for 1 hour. This allows the granola to develop a crisp texture despite the presence of the honey.

Transfer to a large bowl to cool completely. Stir in the dried blueberries. Store in an airtight container for up to 3 months.

Calories 669 • Protein 21 gm • Fat 26 gm • Percent of calories from fat 34% • Cholesterol 1 mg • Dietary fiber 17 gm • Sodium 407 mg • Calcium 141 mg

11

Whole-Grain Muffins, Biscuits, and Breads

❧

Amaranth Muffins

Buckwheat Corn Muffins

Pineapple Corn Muffins

Orange Marmalade Corn Muffins

Peachy Oat Muffins

Apple-Maple Oat Muffins

Brown Rice–Berry Muffins

Chunky Monkey Muffins

Honey-Orange Scones

Four-Grain Biscuits

Cornmeal Biscuits

Corny Corn Bread

Roasted Pepper Corn Bread

Blueberry Corn Toasties

All-American Pumpkin Bread

Brown Rice Bread

Honey-Oat Soda Bread

Cottage Cheese–Herb Loaf

Wheat Berry Wheat Bread

There's an old Vermont joke in which a backwoods farmer tells a recent immigrant to the state that her kids aren't real Vermonters. "Just 'cause a cat has kittens in the oven, it don't make them muffins." The corollary to that is just because a muffin looks spartan compared to a sugared donut, it doesn't necessarily make it low-fat.

This chapter contains a collection of hearty, healthy muffins and breads—all of them bursting with whole grains, none of them high in fat. The muffins, especially, make quick breakfasts and good snacks for kids' lunch boxes. Some are made with a little butter, which gives the most tender crumb and lightest texture; others are made with oil and contain as little cholesterol as possible.

In these baked goods, much of the flavor comes from the grains themselves. After you've tried the Four-Grain Biscuits, you may never bake bread with just white flour again.

Amaranth Muffins

❧

YIELD: ABOUT 10 MUFFINS

These muffins contain 4 tablespoons butter, just enough to produce superior flavor and texture while maintaining a reasonably low-fat profile. The flavor of these breakfast muffins is plain, making them perfect canvases for jam or marmalade. However, a cup of berries in the batter would do these muffins no harm at all.

2 cups unbleached all-purpose
    flour
³/₄ cup sugar
¹/₂ cup popped amaranth
¹/₄ cup oat bran
2¹/₂ teaspoons baking powder

¹/₂ teaspoon baking soda
¹/₂ teaspoon salt
Pinch nutmeg
4 tablespoons butter
3 large egg whites
1 cup nonfat buttermilk

Preheat the oven to 400 degrees. Spray a muffin tin with nonstick cooking spray.

In a large bowl, combine the flour, sugar, amaranth, oat bran, baking powder, baking soda, salt, and nutmeg; mix well. Cut in the butter until the mixture resembles a coarse meal.

In a medium bowl, beat together the egg whites and buttermilk.

Make a well in the dry ingredients and pour in the buttermilk mixture. Stir just enough to blend. The batter will be stiff.

Divide the batter among the muffin cups. Fill any empty cups with water. Bake for 20 to 25 minutes, until a tester inserted in a muffin comes out clean. Cool the tin on a rack for 5 minutes before removing the muffins.

Calories 211 • Protein 5 gm • Fat 6 gm • Percent of calories from fat 26% •
Cholesterol 14 mg • Dietary fiber 1 gm • Sodium 372 mg • Calcium 76 mg

Buckwheat Corn Muffins

YIELD: ABOUT 10 MUFFINS

Plan to serve these straight out of the oven because the irresistible aroma of the roasted buckwheat groats will call your family to the kitchen. These muffins are not very sweet and should be served as dinner rolls.

1 cup skim milk
¹/₂ cup uncooked roasted
   buckwheat groats
2 large egg whites
¹/₄ cup honey
1¹/₄ cups unbleached all-purpose
   flour

1 cup stone-ground yellow
   cornmeal
1 tablespoon baking powder
¹/₂ teaspoon salt
4 tablespoons butter

Preheat the oven to 425 degrees. Spray a muffin tin with nonstick cooking spray.

Scald the milk in a small saucepan on the stove over low heat or in a microwave for 2 minutes on high. Remove from the heat and stir in the buckwheat. Let stand until lukewarm. Beat in the egg whites and honey.

In a medium bowl, combine the flour with the cornmeal, baking powder, and salt. Cut in the butter until the mixture resembles a coarse meal. Add the buckwheat mixture and stir until just mixed.

Spoon the batter into the muffin cups. Fill any empty cups with water. Bake for about 15 minutes, until the muffins are golden and a tester inserted near the center of one of the muffins comes out clean. Cool the tin on a rack for 5 minutes before removing the muffins. Serve warm.

Calories 210 • Protein 6 gm • Fat 5 gm • Percent of calories from fat 23% •
Cholesterol 13 mg • Dietary fiber 3 gm • Sodium 77 mg • Calcium 93 mg

Pineapple Corn Muffins

❧

YIELD: 12 MUFFINS

The combination of pineapple and cornmeal is surprising and delicious. These make wonderful breakfast muffins—and they go surprisingly well with black bean soup.

1 cup stone-ground yellow
  cornmeal
1¹/₂ cups unbleached all-purpose
  flour
¹/₄ cup sugar
2 teaspoons baking powder
1 teaspoon baking soda

¹/₂ teaspoon salt
2 large egg whites
1 cup nonfat vanilla yogurt
¹/₄ cup canola oil
1 cup well-drained crushed
  pineapple

Preheat the oven to 375 degrees. Spray a muffin tin with nonstick cooking spray.

In a large bowl, combine the cornmeal, flour, sugar, baking powder, baking soda, and salt. Toss to mix well.

In a medium bowl, beat together the egg whites, yogurt, and oil until smooth. Stir in the pineapple and mix until well blended. Make a well in the center of the dry ingredients and pour in the pineapple mixture. Working quickly, stir just enough to moisten the flour. The batter will be lumpy.

Spoon the batter into the prepared muffin tin. Bake for about 18 minutes, until a toothpick inserted into the center of a muffin comes out clean. Cool the tin on a wire rack for 5 minutes before removing the muffins. Serve warm or cooled.

Calories 172 • Protein 4 gm • Fat 5 gm • Percent of calories from fat 27% • Cholesterol 0 mg • Dietary fiber 1 gm • Sodium 295 mg • Calcium 62 mg

Orange Marmalade Corn Muffins

YIELD: ABOUT 12 MUFFINS

1³/₄ cups unbleached all-purpose
flour
1 cup stone-ground yellow
cornmeal
¹/₄ cup sugar
2 teaspoons baking powder
1 teaspoon baking soda

¹/₂ teaspoon salt
¹/₂ teaspoon ground ginger
4 tablespoons butter
2 large egg whites
1 cup nonfat vanilla yogurt
³/₄ cup orange marmalade

Preheat the oven to 375 degrees. Spray a muffin tin with nonstick cooking spray.

In a large bowl, combine the flour, cornmeal, sugar, baking powder, baking soda, salt, and ginger. Toss to mix well. Cut in the butter until the mixture is a coarse meal.

In a medium bowl, beat together the egg whites, yogurt, and orange marmalade. Make a well in the center of the dry ingredients and pour in the yogurt mixture. Working quickly, stir just enough to blend. The batter will be lumpy.

Spoon the batter into the prepared muffin tin. Bake for about 15 minutes, until a toothpick inserted into the center of a muffin comes out clean. Cool the pan on a wire rack for 5 minutes before removing the muffins. These muffins are at their best served warm.

Calories 222 • Protein 4 gm • Fat 5 gm • Percent of calories from fat 18% • Cholesterol 11 mg • Dietary fiber 2 gm • Sodium 339 mg • Calcium 68 mg

Peachy Oat Muffins

❧

YIELD: 12 MUFFINS

You can use fresh, canned, or frozen peaches in these muffins with equally good results.

2 cups unbleached all-purpose flour
1 cup uncooked rolled oats (not instant)
1/4 cup oat bran
1/2 cup sugar
2 1/2 teaspoons baking powder
1/2 teaspoon salt
Pinch nutmeg
4 tablespoons butter
3 large egg whites
1 cup skim milk
1 cup finely chopped well-drained fresh, canned, or frozen peaches

Preheat the oven to 400 degrees. Coat a muffin tin with nonstick cooking spray.

In a large bowl, combine the flour, oats, oat bran, sugar, baking powder, salt, and nutmeg; mix well. Cut in the butter until the mixture resembles a coarse meal.

In a medium bowl, beat together the egg whites and skim milk. Add the peaches.

Make a well in the dry ingredients and pour in the peach mixture. Stir just enough to blend. The batter will be stiff and lumpy.

Spoon the batter into the muffin cups. Bake for about 20 minutes, until a tester inserted into the center of a muffin comes out clean. Cool the tin on a rack for 5 minutes before removing the muffins. Serve warm or cooled.

Calories 187 • Protein 5 gm • Fat 5 gm • Percent of calories from fat 23% • Cholesterol 11 mg • Dietary fiber 2 gm • Sodium 246 mg • Calcium 69 mg

Apple-Maple Oat Muffins

YIELD: 12 MUFFINS

The topping makes these apple muffins delightfully crunchy. A great fall treat.

Muffin Mixture

1 cup finely chopped peeled apple (2 apples)

1/4 cup apple cider plus more as needed

2 large egg whites, slightly beaten

1 cup uncooked rolled oats (not instant)

1/4 cup oat bran

2 1/2 teaspoons baking powder

1/2 teaspoon salt

1/4 teaspoon ground cinnamon

1/8 teaspoon ground nutmeg

4 tablespoons butter

2 cups unbleached all-purpose flour

3/4 cup skim milk

1/2 pure maple syrup

Topping

1 1/2 teaspoons sugar

1 1/2 teaspoons oat bran

1/4 teaspoon ground cinnamon

In a small saucepan, combine the apples and 1/4 cup cider. Simmer over low heat until the apples are soft, about 10 minutes. Watch carefully and add more cider as needed to prevent the apples from becoming too dry. Set aside.

Preheat the oven to 400 degrees. Coat a muffin pan with nonstick cooking spray. To make the topping, combine the sugar, oat bran, and cinnamon in a small bowl and set aside.

In a medium bowl, combine the flour, oats, oat bran, baking powder, salt, cinnamon, and nutmeg; mix well. Cut in the butter until the mixture resembles a coarse meal.

In a separate medium bowl, beat together the egg whites, skim milk, maple syrup, and apple mixture. Make a well in the dry ingredients and pour in the maple syrup mixture. Stir just enough to blend. The batter will be stiff and lumpy.

Spoon the batter into the muffin cups. Sprinkle a little of the topping on each muffin. Bake for about 20 minutes, until a tester inserted into the center of a muffin comes out clean. Cool the tin on a rack for 5 minutes before removing the muffins. Serve warm or cooled.

Calories 196 • Protein 5 gm • Fat 5 gm • Percent of calories from fat 22% • Cholesterol 11 mg • Dietary fiber 2 gm • Sodium 241 mg • Calcium 77 mg

Brown Rice—Berry Muffins

YIELD: ABOUT 12 MUFFINS

The brown rice contributes a sweet nutty flavor and crunchy texture to these simple muffins. Be sure to grind the rice well, or the texture may be too crunchy. White rice can be substituted for the brown and any berry can be used.

1 cup uncooked brown rice
1$^1/_2$ cups unbleached all-purpose
   flour
$^1/_2$ cup sugar
2$^1/_2$ teaspoons baking powder
$^1/_2$ teaspoon baking soda
$^1/_2$ teaspoon salt

$^1/_4$ teaspoon ground cinnamon
4 tablespoons butter
2 large egg whites
1$^1/_2$ cups nonfat buttermilk
1 cup finely chopped strawberries
   or whole berries, such as
   blueberries or raspberries

Preheat the oven to 400 degrees. Spray a muffin tin with nonstick cooking spray. Place the brown rice in a blender and process until you have a fine powder.

In a large bowl, combine the brown rice powder, flour, sugar, baking powder, baking soda, salt, and cinnamon; mix well. Cut in the butter until the mixture resembles a coarse meal.

In a medium bowl, beat together the egg whites and buttermilk.

Make a well in the dry ingredients and pour in the buttermilk mixture. Stir just enough to blend. The batter will be lumpy. Mix in the berries.

Spoon the batter into the muffin cups. Bake for about 25 minutes, until the muffin tops are golden and a tester inserted into the center of a muffin comes out clean. Cool the tin on a rack for 5 minutes before removing the muffins. Serve warm or cooled.

Calories 197 • Protein 4 gm • Fat 5 gm • Percent of calories from fat 22% • Cholesterol 12 mg • Dietary fiber 1 gm • Sodium 316 mg • Calcium 80 mg

Chunky Monkey Muffins

YIELD: ABOUT 12 MUFFINS

These chocolate chip and banana muffins take their inspiration from an ice cream flavor invented by Ben & Jerry's. No muffins disappear more quickly in my house than these, which my son calls "good enough to be cupcakes."

³/₄ cup mashed ripe bananas
(2 bananas)
2 large egg whites
¹/₂ cup nonfat buttermilk
3 tablespoons canola oil
¹/₂ cup firmly packed brown sugar
1¹/₂ teaspoons vanilla extract
1¹/₂ cups unbleached all-purpose
flour
¹/₂ cup toasted wheat germ
¹/₄ cup oat bran
2 teaspoons baking powder
1 teaspoon baking soda
¹/₂ teaspoon salt
¹/₂ teaspoon ground cinnamon
1 cup mini chocolate chips
¹/₂ cup well-drained crushed
pineapple

Preheat the oven to 400 degrees. Spray a muffin tin with nonstick cooking spray.

In a large bowl, combine the bananas, egg whites, buttermilk, canola oil, sugar, and vanilla, and beat well. In a medium bowl, combine the flour, wheat germ, oat bran, baking powder, baking soda, salt, and cinnamon, and mix well. Add to the banana mixture and stir just enough to blend. Stir in the chocolate chips and pineapple. The batter will be lumpy.

Spoon the batter into the muffin cups. Bake for about 20 minutes, until a tester inserted into the center of a muffin comes out clean. Cool the tin on a rack for 5 minutes before removing the muffins. Serve warm or cooled.

Calories 263 • Protein 6 gm • Fat 10 gm • Percent of calories from fat 32% •
Cholesterol 0 mg • Dietary fiber 2 gm • Sodium 306 mg • Calcium 80 mg

Honey-Orange Scones

YIELD: 8 SCONES

What a treat these orange-scented scones are! When I make them for a monthly coffeehouse that is held at the town hall, they disappear in minutes—and I don't even advertise the fact they are low in fat.

2¹/₄ cups unbleached all-purpose flour	¹/₂ cup dried currants
2 teaspoons baking powder	1 tablespoon grated orange zest
¹/₂ teaspoon baking soda	¹/₃ cup honey
¹/₂ teaspoon salt	¹/₂ cup nonfat buttermilk
4 tablespoons butter	1 tablespoon Grand Marnier or other orange-flavored liqueur
1 cup uncooked quick-cooking oats	1 large egg
	1 tablespoon skim milk

Preheat the oven to 425 degrees. Spray a baking sheet with nonstick cooking spray or line with parchment paper.

In a large bowl, combine the flour, baking powder, baking soda, and salt. Cut in the butter until the mixture resembles a coarse meal. Add the oats, currants, and orange zest, and toss to mix well.

In a medium bowl, beat together the honey, buttermilk, Grand Marnier, and egg. Make a well in the dry ingredients and stir in the Grand Marnier mixture until you have a ball. Knead briefly. Do not overwork the dough; it should be slightly sticky.

On a very lightly floured surface, pat the dough into an 8-inch round about ¹/₂ inch thick. Cut into 8 wedges. Use a floured spatula to transfer the scones to the prepared baking sheet. Brush the top of each scone with skim milk for a golden crust.

Bake for about 15 minutes, until the scones are golden and a tester inserted in the center of a scone comes out clean. Transfer to wire racks to cool slightly. These are best served warm on the day they are made, but they can be held for up to 1 day in an airtight tin.

Calories 308 • Protein 7 gm • Fat 8 gm • Percent of calories from fat 23% • Cholesterol 43 mg • Dietary fiber 3 gm • Sodium 415 mg • Calcium 83 mg

Four-Grain Biscuits

YIELD: 8 TO 12 BISCUITS

The mixture of grains is so tasty in these basic baking powder biscuits, it's unlikely you'll ever make white flour biscuits again. These make a great accompaniment to a meal of soup and salad.

1¹/₄ cups unbleached all-purpose flour

¹/₄ cups rolled oats (not instant)

¹/₄ cup stone-ground yellow cornmeal

¹/₄ cup puffed amaranth

2 teaspoons baking powder

1 teaspoon baking soda

¹/₂ teaspoon salt

3 tablespoons cold butter

³/₄ cup nonfat buttermilk

Preheat the oven to 450 degrees. Spray a baking sheet with nonstick cooking spray.

In a large bowl, combine the flour, oats, cornmeal, amaranth, baking powder, baking soda, and salt. Mix well. Cut in the butter until the mixture resembles a coarse meal. Stir in the buttermilk.

Turn the dough out onto a lightly floured work surface. Knead lightly for 30 seconds. Pat out the dough to a thickness of about ¹/₂ inch. Using the rim of a glass or a cookie cutter, cut into 2-inch or 3-inch rounds and place about 1 inch apart on the prepared baking sheet. Bake for 13 to 14 minutes until firm and lightly browned. Serve hot out of the oven.

Calories 141 • Protein 3 gm • Fat 6 gm • Percent of calories from fat 35% •
Cholesterol 13 mg • Dietary fiber 1 gm • Sodium 475 mg • Calcium 72 mg

Cornmeal Biscuits

YIELD: 8 TO 12 BISCUITS

This dough is a little hard to handle; don't be afraid to get rough with it.

1¼ cups unbleached all-purpose flour
¼ cup whole-wheat flour
¾ cup stone-ground yellow cornmeal

2 teaspoons baking powder
1 teaspoon salt
4 tablespoons cold butter
½ cup skim milk

Preheat the oven to 450 degrees. Spray a baking sheet with nonstick cooking spray.

In a large bowl, combine the unbleached and whole-wheat flours, cornmeal, baking powder, and salt. Mix well. Cut the butter into small bits and rub into the mixture using your hands or cut in with a pastry blender. Stir in the milk. Gather the dough into a ball.

Turn the dough out onto a lightly floured work surface. Knead lightly for 30 seconds. Pat out the dough to a thickness of about ½ inch. Using the rim of a glass or a cookie cutter, cut into 2-inch or 3-inch rounds and place about 1 inch apart on the baking sheet. Bake for about 13 minutes, until golden brown. Serve hot out of the oven.

Calories 179 • Protein 4 gm • Fat 6.8 gm • Percent of calories from fat 33% • Cholesterol 17 mg • Dietary fiber 2 gm • Sodium 680 mg • Calcium 26 mg

Corny Corn Bread

❦

YIELD: 9 SERVINGS

This very low-fat version of corn bread is my favorite of all versions—moist, a little sweet, and very corny. The creamed corn is the secret ingredient that allows you to cut the fat while you boost the flavor.

1 cup unbleached all-purpose flour	¹⁄₂ teaspoon baking soda
1 cup stone-ground yellow or white cornmeal	1 teaspoon salt
¹⁄₄ cup sugar	1 (15-ounce) can creamed corn
1 tablespoon baking powder	2 large eggs
	1 cup nonfat buttermilk

Preheat the oven to 400 degrees. Spray an 8-inch square baking pan with nonstick cooking spray.

In a large mixing bowl, combine the flour, cornmeal, sugar, baking powder, baking soda, and salt. In a medium bowl, combine the creamed corn, eggs, and buttermilk. Mix well. Add the wet ingredients to the dry ingredients and stir just enough to thoroughly moisten. The batter will be lumpy. Pour into the prepared pan.

Bake for 25 to 30 minutes, until a tester inserted near the center comes out clean. This is best served warm.

Calories 160 • Protein 6 gm • Fat 2 gm • Percent of calories from fat 11% •
Cholesterol 48 mg • Dietary fiber 2 gm • Sodium 512 mg • Calcium 111 mg

Jan '09 - made whole wheat / low cholesteral version:
- use whole wheat pastry flour in place of all-purpose
- use 3 egg whites in place of eggs
- added 1 T white vinegar to skim milk to make buttermilk

This will completely fill 8-inch square pan - took longer to cook (45-50 min). Try making in cast iron skillet, should be not as thick then, and cook faster. (Dinosaur BBQ style) This is really, really, good cornbread!

Roasted Pepper Corn Bread

YIELD: 9 SERVINGS

1 cup unbleached all-purpose
   flour
1 cup stone-ground yellow
   or white cornmeal
3 tablespoons sugar
1 tablespoon baking powder
1 teaspoon baking soda
1 teaspoon salt

1 cup nonfat buttermilk
1 large egg, slightly beaten
3 tablespoons canola oil
2 red bell peppers, roasted
   (see Note)
1 or 2 fresh green chiles, roasted
   (see Note), optional

Preheat the oven to 400 degrees. Spray an 8-inch square baking pan with nonstick cooking spray.

In a large bowl, combine the flour, cornmeal, sugar, baking powder, baking soda, and salt.

In a medium bowl, combine the buttermilk, egg, and canola oil. Mix well. Chop the bell peppers and green chiles and stir into the buttermilk mixture. Add the wet ingredients to the dry ingredients and stir just enough to thoroughly moisten. The batter will be lumpy.

Pour the batter into the prepared pan. Bake for about 25 minutes, until a tester inserted near the center comes out clean. This is best served warm.

Note: To roast the red peppers and green chiles, hold over a burner or place under a broiler flame until charred all over, turning frequently. Place in a paper bag, close the top tightly, and leave in the freezer for about 10 minutes. Peel off the charred skin and remove the stems, seeds, and ribs.

Calories 176 • Protein 4 gm • Fat 6 gm • Percent of calories from fat 31% •
Cholesterol 25 mg • Dietary fiber 2 gm • Sodium 572 mg • Calcium 92 mg

Blueberry Corn Toasties

❦

YIELD: 6 SERVINGS

Ah! The corn toasties of my youth, which I only enjoyed as a packaged product. Is this a variation of the original johnnycake? Probably. These are tasty enough fresh out of the oven—but extra-special when they are toasted and spread (lightly!) with butter or pure maple syrup.

3/4 cup stone-ground yellow
  cornmeal
1 cup unbleached all-purpose
  flour
1/2 cup sugar
2 teaspoons baking powder
1 teaspoon baking soda
1/2 teaspoon salt

3 tablespoons butter
1/3 cup nonfat buttermilk
2 large eggs, well beaten
1/2 teaspoon vanilla extract
1 cup blueberries
Butter and/or maple syrup,
  for serving

Lightly spray a cast-iron griddle with nonstick cooking spray and place in the oven. Preheat the oven to 425 degrees. Preheat the griddle for at least 15 minutes.

In a food processor, combine the cornmeal, flour, sugar, baking powder, baking soda, and salt. Mix well. Slice the butter into thin bits and add to the food processor. Process until the mixture resembles coarse meal. Add the buttermilk, eggs, and vanilla, and process to combine well. Spoon the batter into a large glass measuring cup for easy pouring. Stir in the blueberries.

Remove the smoking hot griddle from the oven. Using a spatula or large spoon to help regulate the flow of batter, pour the batter onto the griddle in 6 round disks. Bake for about 10 minutes, until a tester inserted near the center of one of the toasties comes out clean. Remove from the griddle and cool on wire racks.

To serve, toast lightly and serve with butter and/or maple syrup.

Calories 289 • Protein 6 gm • Fat 9 gm • Percent of calories from fat 27% •
Cholesterol 87 mg • Dietary fiber 2 gm • Sodium 641 mg • Calcium 85 mg

All-American Pumpkin Bread

YIELD: 1 LOAF

Featuring such native American ingredients as pumpkin, wild rice, cornmeal, and maple syrup, this quick bread deserves a place on every Thanksgiving table.

1½ cups unbleached all-purpose
  flour
½ cup stone-ground yellow
  cornmeal
½ cup sugar
2 teaspoons baking powder
½ teaspoon baking soda
1¼ teaspoons ground cinnamon

1 teaspoon salt
¼ teaspoon ground ginger
1 cup canned or homemade
  pumpkin puree
1 cup cooked wild rice
¼ cup pure maple syrup
1 large egg, slightly beaten
3 tablespoons canola oil

Preheat the oven to 350 degrees. Spray an 8-inch loaf pan with nonstick cooking spray.

In a large bowl, combine the flour, cornmeal, sugar, baking powder, baking soda, cinnamon, salt, and ginger.

In a medium bowl, combine the pumpkin, wild rice, maple syrup, egg, and canola oil. Mix well. Add the wet ingredients to the dry and stir just until combined.

Pour the batter into the prepared pan. Bake for about 55 minutes, until a tester inserted near the center of the loaf comes out clean. Cool in the pan on a wire rack for 10 minutes before turning out of the pan to finish cooling on the rack.

Calories 177 • Protein 3 gm • Fat 4 gm • Percent of calories from fat 22% •
Cholesterol 18 mg • Dietary fiber 2 gm • Sodium 322 mg • Calcium 44 mg

Brown Rice Bread

❧❧❧

YIELD: 9 SERVINGS

The same formula that works for corn bread works for rice bread—just grind the rice in a blender until you have a coarse meal. The bread has a distinctively sweet flavor, and the rice adds a very crunchy texture. Make sure you grind the rice well, or the bread will be a little too crunchy.

2 cups uncooked brown rice
(white rice can be substituted)
1 cup unbleached all-purpose
flour
3 tablespoons sugar
1 tablespoon baking powder

1 teaspoon baking soda
1 teaspoon salt
1 cup nonfat buttermilk
1 large egg, slightly beaten
3 tablespoons canola oil

Preheat the oven to 400 degrees. Spray an 8-inch square baking pan with nonstick cooking spray. Process the brown rice in a blender until you have a fine powder.

In a large bowl, combine the ground rice, flour, sugar, baking powder, baking soda, and salt.

In a medium bowl, combine the buttermilk, egg, and canola oil. Mix well. Add the wet ingredients to the dry ingredients and stir just enough to thoroughly moisten. The batter will be lumpy.

Spoon the batter into the prepared pan. Bake for about 25 minutes, until a tester inserted near the center comes out clean. This bread is best served warm. Leftovers, however, are delicious toasted and served with butter and maple syrup.

Calories 275 • Protein 6 gm • Fat 7 gm • Percent of calories from fat 22% •
Cholesterol 25 mg • Dietary fiber 0 gm • Sodium 569 mg • Calcium 104 mg

Honey-Oat Soda Bread

YIELD: 8 SERVINGS

This bread is similar to an Irish soda bread, but the honey in the dough keeps the bread a little moister and causes the bread to brown more deeply. The flavor is rich, but not too sweet. Although soda bread is traditionally served at tea time, I like it as an accompaniment to a supper of soup or salad—especially when I realize at the last minute that I forgot to pick up bread at the bakery. This bread is quick to make!

1$^1/_2$ cups unbleached all-purpose flour
$^1/_2$ cup whole-wheat flour
1 cup rolled oats (not instant)
2 teaspoons baking soda

$^1/_2$ teaspoon salt
1 cup nonfat buttermilk
2 tablespoons honey
2 tablespoons butter, melted

Preheat the oven to 350 degrees. Spray a baking sheet with nonstick cooking spray.

In a large bowl, combine the all-purpose and whole-wheat flours, oats, baking soda, and salt. Mix well.

In a small bowl, combine the buttermilk, honey, and 1 tablespoon of the butter. Add to the oat mixture and stir until well combined. The dough will be stiff. Turn it out onto a lightly floured board and knead it a few times. Pat the dough into an 8-inch round and place on the baking sheet. Score the top with a cross. Brush the top with the remaining 1 tablespoon butter.

Bake for about 35 minutes, until the loaf is golden brown. Transfer the loaf to a wire rack to cool. Serve warm or cooled.

Calories 198 • Protein 6 gm • Fat 4 gm • Percent of calories from fat 19% • Cholesterol 9 mg • Dietary fiber 3 gm • Sodium 525 mg • Calcium 48 mg

Cottage Cheese—Herb Loaf

❧❧❧

YIELD: 8 SERVINGS

Cottage cheese, pureed in a food processor until smooth, gives bread a rich flavor and a tender crumb. This bread is quick to whip up, and it makes a delicious accompaniment to soups and salads.

1$^1/_2$ cup unbleached all-purpose
   flour
1 cup rolled oats (not instant)
2 teaspoons baking powder
1 teaspoon salt

$^1/_2$ teaspoon dried basil
1 cup cottage cheese
$^1/_4$ cup plus 1 tablespoon
   skim milk

Preheat the oven to 375 degrees. Spray a baking sheet with nonstick cooking spray.

In a medium bowl, combine the flour, oats, baking powder, salt, and basil. Mix well.

In a food processor, combine the cottage cheese and $^1/_4$ cup of the skim milk. Process until smooth. Add the oat mixture and process until the dough comes together in a ball. Turn out onto a lightly floured board and knead a few times. Pat the dough into a 6-inch round and place on the baking sheet. Score the top with a cross and brush with the remaining 1 tablespoon milk.

Bake for about 45 minutes, until the loaf is golden brown and sounds hollow when tapped. Transfer the loaf to a wire rack to cool. Serve warm or cooled.

Calories 148 • Protein 7 gm • Fat 2 gm • Percent of calories from fat 13% •
Cholesterol 4 mg • Dietary fiber 2 gm • Sodium 502 mg • Calcium 76 mg

Wheat Berry Wheat Bread

YIELD: 2 LOAVES

Over the years, this has become our "house bread," light enough to satisfy the kids, chewy and grainy enough to satisfy the grown-ups. This is a great bread for sandwiches and toast.

1 cup uncooked wheat berries	2 large eggs, lightly beaten
3½ cups water	¼ cup canola oil
2½ cups skim milk	2 teaspoons salt
2 tablespoons active dry yeast	Approximately 4 cups unbleached
2 cups whole-wheat flour	all-purpose flour
¼ cup sugar	

Combine the wheat berries with the water in a medium saucepan. Bring to a boil, reduce the heat, cover, and simmer until the berries are tender, 1 to 1½ hours. (If the berries are soaked overnight, you can reduce the cooking time to 50 to 60 minutes.) Drain off any excess water.

Meanwhile, scald the milk, then let cool to 110 degrees. In a large bowl, combine the yeast, whole-wheat flour, and sugar. Stir in the milk. Beat vigorously for 2 minutes. Cover the bowl with a towel and let rise for 30 minutes.

Stir down the dough to deflate it. Then stir in the wheat berries, eggs, oil, salt, and 2 cups of the all-purpose flour. Keep adding flour until the dough is stiff enough to knead. Turn the dough out onto a work surface that has been dusted with flour. Knead, adding more flour as needed, until you have a smooth, elastic dough. Put the dough in an oiled bowl, turning once to coat the entire ball of dough with oil. Cover and let rise until doubled in size, about 40 minutes.

Spray two 8-inch loaf pans with nonstick cooking spray. Turn the dough out onto a work surface and cut in half. Shape each half into a loaf and place in the loaf pans. Cover and let rise for 30 minutes while you pre-heat the oven to 375 degrees.

Bake for 30 to 35 minutes, until the loaves shrink slightly from the sides of the pan and sound hollow when tapped. (The internal temperature of the bread should register 190 degrees on an instant-read thermometer.) Immediately remove from the pans and cool on a wire rack.

Calories 176 • Protein 6 gm • Fat 3 gm • Percent of calories from fat 16% • Cholesterol 18 mg • Dietary fiber 3 gm • Sodium 215 mg • Calcium 44 mg

12
Glorious Desserts

Triple A Oatmeal Cookies

Mixed-Grain Raisin Cookies

Oatmeal Fruit Cookies

Maple-Apple Oatmeal Cookies

Coconut-Oatmeal Chews

Tropical Chews

Peanut Butter–Oatmeal Chocolate Chip Cookies

Peanut Butter–Chocolate Chip Cookies

Whole-Grain Jam Squares

Amaranth Pound Cake

Amaranth Chocolate Spice Cake

Blueberry Corn Cake

Lemon-Berry Couscous Cake

Orange Marmalade–Millet Crunch Cake

Chocolate Chip–Banana Oat Cake

Maple-Apple Oat Cake

Apple Couscous

Fruity Couscous Dessert Timbales

Honey-Apple Crisp

Apple Crunch

Strawberry-Rhubarb Crumble

Crunchy Maple-baked Bananas

Baked Rice Pudding

Almond Rice Pudding

Vanilla Yogurt Rice Pudding

Piña Colada Rice Pudding

Strawberry-Coconut Rice Pudding

Black Rice Pudding

Coconut Cream Rice Dream

Rich Chocolate Rice Pudding

Grand Marnier Rice Torte

Coconut-Almond Rice Torte

This chapter is a favorite of my kids (of course) and provided the most revelations for me. Whole-grain desserts can be lighter and tastier than I had ever imagined possible. Often the trick with baked goods is to use the whole grain as a mix-in, like chopped nuts. As with nuts, the grains provide nutty flavor and crunchy texture—but they do so without the fat.

The chapter begins with a wide-ranging collection of low-fat whole-grain cookie recipes. I find I get the best results using insulated cookie sheets, so that is what I used in testing these recipes. If you are using traditional cookie sheets, you may want to reduce the baking time or oven temperature. In any event, always check cookies frequently during the last five minutes of baking to avoid scorching the bottoms. Low-fat cookies are best eaten on the day they are made, but will keep in airtight containers for several days, becoming quite chewy in texture. Or they can be wrapped individually and stored for a few weeks in the freezer.

I confess to having an obsession with rice pudding and my favorite recipes in this chapter are made with rice—the puddings and Italian rice tortes. The obsession began when I was about eight years old, on my first trip to New York City. My family and I had spent hours at the Metropolitan Museum of Art and even more hours tracking down an army buddy of my father's, all of which culminated in dinner—at well past my bedtime—in a Greek restaurant. By then I was beyond tired and hungry enough to eat a horse—but not the lamb chops smothered in spinach that I had inadvertently ordered. I burst into tears, pushed beyond endurance. A kindly waiter whisked away the offending chops and replaced them with a soup bowl filled with rice pudding. Sweet heavenly comfort! No food has ever tasted so good.

I have spent years trying to replicate that pudding, and finally found it in a version that used heavy cream. None of the recipes here are quite so indulgent, but all are just as wonderful.

Triple A Oatmeal Cookies

YIELD: ABOUT 3 DOZEN

The three A's in the title could refer to apples, applesauce, and amaranth—a great low-fat combination, but they could also be the A's my kids awarded these cookies for crunch, flavor, and goodness.

1 (14-ounce) can sweetened
   condensed skim milk
1/2 cup applesauce
1/4 cup canola oil
2 large egg whites
1 teaspoon vanilla extract
3 cups uncooked rolled oats
   (not instant)
1 1/2 cups unbleached all-purpose
   flour

1 cup popped amaranth
2 teaspoons baking powder
1 teaspoon baking soda
1/2 teaspoon mace
1/2 teaspoon salt
2 apples, peeled and finely chopped
1 cup dried cranberries or cherries

In a large bowl, beat together the condensed milk, applesauce, canola oil, egg whites, and vanilla until smooth.

In a separate large bowl, combine the oats, flour, amaranth, baking powder, baking soda, mace, and salt. Mix well. Add to the applesauce mixture and mix until well combined. Stir in the apples and dried fruit.

Chill in the refrigerator for at least 1 hour. When you are ready to bake, preheat the oven to 350 degrees. Spray baking sheets with nonstick cooking spray.

Drop the batter by rounded tablespoons onto the baking sheets about 1 inch apart. Flatten with the back of a wet spoon. The cookies will not spread during baking but do not overcrowd. Bake for 15 to 18 minutes, until the cookies are lightly browned. Transfer to wire racks to cool thoroughly.

Calories 88 • Protein 3 gm • Fat 3 gm • Percent of calories from fat 24% •
Cholesterol 0 mg • Dietary fiber 1 gm • Sodium 107 mg • Calcium 50 mg

Mixed-Grain Raisin Cookies

❦

YIELD: ABOUT 4 DOZEN

A little butter adds considerably to the flavor and texture of these cookies.

1 (14-ounce) can sweetened
   condensed skim milk
1/2 cup applesauce
1/2 cup canola oil
1/4 cup butter, at room temperature
2 egg whites
1 tablespoon molasses
1 cup rolled oats
1 cup rolled barley

1 cup rolled wheat
1 1/4 cups whole-wheat flour
1/2 cups unbleached all-purpose
   flour
2 teaspoons baking powder
1 teaspoon baking soda
1/2 teaspoon cinnamon
1/2 teaspoon salt
1 1/2 cups raisins

Preheat the oven to 350 degrees. Spray baking sheets with nonstick cooking spray.

In a large bowl, beat together the condensed milk, applesauce, canola oil, butter, egg whites, and molasses until smooth.

In a separate large bowl, combine the oats, barley, rolled wheat, whole-wheat and all-purpose flours, baking powder, baking soda, cinnamon, and salt. Mix well. Add to the applesauce mixture and mix until well combined. Stir in the raisins.

Drop the batter by rounded tablespoons onto the baking sheets about 1 inch apart. Flatten with the back of a wet spoon. The cookies will not spread during baking but do not overcrowd. Bake for about 15 minutes, until the cookies are lightly browned. Transfer to wire racks to cool thoroughly.

Calories 84 • Protein 2 gm • Fat 4 gm • Percent of calories from fat 37% •
Cholesterol 3 mg • Dietary fiber 1 gm • Sodium 101 mg • Calcium 37 mg

Oatmeal Fruit Cookies

YIELD: ABOUT 4 DOZEN

These chewy, fruit-ladened cookies are low in fat, rich in fiber, and incredibly delicious. In fact, there's just one problem with these cookies—they are much too good. The substitution of applesauce for some butter reduces the fat, while the addition of cornstarch eliminates the gummy texture sometimes associated with low-fat cookies.

3 cups uncooked rolled oats
   (not instant)
1½ cups unbleached all-purpose
   flour
¼ cup cornstarch
1 teaspoon baking soda
1 teaspoon ground cinnamon
½ teaspoon salt
½ cup butter, at room temperature

1 cup firmly packed brown sugar
½ cup white sugar
2 large eggs
½ cup unsweetened applesauce
1 teaspoon vanilla extract
1 cup raisins
½ cup chopped dried apricots
1 cup dried cherries, cranberries,
   or blueberries

Preheat the oven to 375 degrees.

In a large bowl, combine the oats, flour, cornstarch, baking soda, cinnamon, and salt. Set aside.

In a separate large bowl, beat together the butter and brown and white sugars until well blended. Add the eggs and beat until creamy. Mix in the applesauce and vanilla, beating until fluffy. Stir in the dry ingredients, blending thoroughly. Add the raisins, apricots, and dried berries, stirring until combined.

Drop the batter by rounded tablespoons 2 inches apart on ungreased cookie sheets. Press with a wet spoon or spatula to flatten.

Bake for about 15 minutes, until golden. Let the cookies cool on the cookie sheets for a few minutes before removing them to wire racks to cool completely.

Calories 105 • Protein 2 gm • Fat 3 gm • Percent of calories from fat 22% • Cholesterol 14 mg • Dietary fiber 1 gm • Sodium 76 mg • Calcium 12 mg

Maple-Apple Oatmeal Cookies

❧❧❧

YIELD: ABOUT 4 DOZEN COOKIES

The maple syrup, apples, and spices add great "apple pie flavor" to these oatmeal cookies.

³/₄ cup pure maple syrup
³/₄ cup unsweetened applesauce
1 large egg
3 tablespoons canola oil
1 tablespoon butter, softened
2 teaspoons vanilla extract
2¹/₄ cups uncooked rolled oats
   (not instant)
1¹/₄ cups unbleached all-purpose
   flour

¹/₄ cup toasted wheat germ
1 teaspoon baking powder
1 teaspoon ground cinnamon
¹/₂ teaspoon salt
¹/₄ teaspoon ground nutmeg
1¹/₂ cups chopped dried apple
¹/₂ cup raisins

Preheat the oven to 350 degrees. Spray cookie sheets with nonstick cooking spray.

In a large bowl, beat together the maple syrup, applesauce, egg, canola oil, butter, and vanilla.

In a separate large bowl, combine the oats, flour, wheat germ, baking powder, cinnamon salt, and nutmeg. Toss to mix. Stir in the apple and raisins. Add to the maple syrup mixture and blend well, but do not overmix.

Drop the batter by the tablespoon about 2 inches apart onto the baking sheets. Bake for 15 minutes, until golden. Transfer to wire racks to cool thoroughly.

Calories 63 • Protein 1 gm • Fat 2 gm • Percent of calories from fat 21% •
Cholesterol 5 mg • Dietary fiber 1 gm • Sodium 40 mg • Calcium 13 mg

Coconut-Oatmeal Chews

YIELD: ABOUT 2½ DOZEN

A cross between macaroons and oatmeal cookies, these cookies are wheat-free. The boost of calcium from the nonfat dry milk puts these cookies into the category of "good-for-you."

4 large egg whites	2 tablespoons cornstarch
½ cup pure maple syrup	2 cups uncooked rolled oats
¼ cup canola oil	(not instant)
1 teaspoon vanilla extract	1 cup shredded coconut
1 cup nonfat dry milk powder	1 cup dried currants

Preheat the oven to 325 degrees. Spray 2 baking sheets with nonstick cooking spray.

In a large mixing bowl, beat the egg whites until foamy. Add the maple syrup, oil, and vanilla, and beat until well mixed. Add the dry milk powder and cornstarch. Beat until well mixed. Stir in the oats, coconut, and currants and mix well.

Drop the cookies by the heaping teaspoon onto the baking sheets about 2 inches apart. Bake for about 20 minutes, until lightly browned. Check after 15 minutes to be sure the cookies are not scorching on their bottoms. Transfer to wire racks to cool thoroughly.

Calories 86 • Protein 2 gm • Fat 3 gm • Percent of calories from fat 34% • Cholesterol 0 mg • Dietary fiber 1 gm • Sodium 21 mg • Calcium 23 mg

Tropical Chews

❦

YIELD: 4 TO 5 DOZEN COOKIES

Dried mango slices that I found at my food co-op inspired these delicious oatmeal cookies, which get a triple taste of the tropics with the addition of coconut and pineapple. You can substitute another dried fruit if dried mango is unavailable.

2 cups uncooked rolled oats
  (not instant)
1½ cups unbleached all-purpose
  flour
1 teaspoon baking soda
1 teaspoon ground cinnamon
½ teaspoon salt
1 cup dried mango, diced

½ cup shredded coconut
1 cup firmly packed brown sugar
3 tablespoons butter, at room
  temperature
3 tablespoons canola oil
½ cup drained crushed pineapple
1 large egg
1 teaspoon vanilla extract

Preheat the oven to 350 degrees. Spray the cookie sheets with nonstick cooking spray.

In a medium bowl, combine the oats, flour, baking soda, cinnamon, and salt. Add the mango and coconut and toss to mix well. Set aside.

In a large bowl, combine the brown sugar, butter, canola oil, pineapple, egg, and vanilla, and whisk to blend or beat well with an electric mixer. Add the dry ingredients and mix with a wooden spoon. Do not overmix.

Drop by the teaspoonful onto the cookie sheets about 1 inch apart. Bake for about 15 minutes, until golden brown. Transfer to wire racks to cool thoroughly.

Calories 74 • Protein 1 gm • Fat 2 gm • Percent of calories from fat 28% •
Cholesterol 6 mg • Dietary fiber 1 gm • Sodium 64 mg • Calcium 9 mg

Peanut Butter—Oatmeal Chocolate Chip Cookies

YIELD: ABOUT 4 DOZEN COOKIES

1 (14-ounce) can sweetened
   condensed skim milk
3/4 cup reduced-fat peanut butter
2 large egg whites
1 teaspoon vanilla extract
1 1/2 cups unbleached all-purpose
   flour

1 1/2 cups uncooked rolled oats
   (not instant)
1 teaspoon baking powder
1/2 teaspoon salt
1 1/2 cups semisweet chocolate
   chips

In a large bowl, beat together the condensed milk and peanut butter until smooth. Beat in the egg whites and vanilla.

In a separate large bowl, combine the flour, oats, baking powder, and salt. Mix well. Add to the peanut butter mixture and beat until well mixed. Stir in the chocolate chips.

Chill in the refrigerator for at least 1 hour. When you are ready to bake, preheat the oven to 350 degrees. Spray baking sheets with nonstick cooking spray.

Drop a rounded tablespoonful of batter for each cookie and flatten the cookie with the back of the spoon. Place about 1 inch apart on the baking sheets; the cookies will not spread during baking, but will bake more slowly if they are overcrowded. Bake for 18 to 20 minutes, until the cookies are lightly browned. Cool on wire racks.

Calories 85 • Protein 3 gm • Fat 4 gm • Percent of calories from fat 35% •
Cholesterol 0 mg • Dietary fiber 1 gm • Sodium 71 mg • Calcium 32 mg

Peanut Butter—Chocolate Chip Cookies

YIELD: ABOUT 60 COOKIES

You will find it hard to believe that these chocolatey, crisp cookies are low in fat. Condensed skim milk replaces the butter usually found in these cookies, while wheat germ and oat bran add crunch and fiber.

1 (14-ounce) can sweetened
   condensed skim milk
3/4 cup reduced-fat peanut butter
2 large egg whites
1 teaspoon vanilla extract
13/4 cups unbleached all-purpose
   flour

3/4 cup toasted wheat germ
1/4 cup oat bran
1 teaspoon baking powder
1/2 teaspoon salt
11/2 cups semisweet chocolate
   chips

In a large bowl, beat together the condensed milk and peanut butter until smooth. Beat in the egg whites and vanilla.

In a separate medium bowl, combine the flour, wheat germ, oat bran, baking powder, and salt. Mix well. Add to the peanut butter mixture and beat until smooth. Stir in the chocolate chips.

Chill in the refrigerator for at least 1 hour. When you are ready to bake, preheat the oven to 350 degrees. Spray baking sheets with nonstick cooking spray.

Drop a rounded tablespoon of batter for each cookie. Place 1 inch apart on the baking sheets; the cookies will not spread during baking, but will bake more slowly if they are overcrowded. Bake for 12 to 15 minutes, until lightly browned. Transfer to wire racks to cool thoroughly.

Calories 68 • Protein 3 gm • Fat 3 gm • Percent of calories from fat 35% •
Cholesterol 0 mg • Dietary fiber 1 gm • Sodium 57 mg • Calcium 25 mg

Whole-Grain Jam Squares

YIELD: 24 SQUARES

1 cup uncooked millet
³/₄ cup butter, at room temperature
1 cup firmly packed brown sugar
1 cup unbleached all-purpose
   flour

1 cup uncooked rolled oats
   (not instant)
¹/₂ teaspoon baking powder
1 teaspoon ground cinnamon
¹/₂ teaspoon salt
1 cup jam or preserves

Preheat the oven to 400 degrees. Spray a 9×13-inch baking pan with nonstick cooking spray. Grind the millet in a blender until it resembles cornmeal.

In a large bowl, cream together the butter and sugar. Stir in the ground millet, flour, oats, baking powder, cinnamon, and salt. Mix well. Press half the mixture into the bottom of the pan. Warm the jam or preserves for a few seconds in a microwave or on top of the stove over low heat until soupy but not completely melted. Spread the jam on top of the pressed cookie mixture. Sprinkle the remaining crumb mixture on top.

Bake for 25 to 30 minutes, until the top is golden brown. Cool on a rack. Then cut into squares. Store in an airtight container. These squares freeze well.

Calories 183 • Protein 2 gm • Fat 7 gm • Percent of calories from fat 32% •
Cholesterol 16 mg • Dietary fiber 1 gm • Sodium 128 mg • Calcium 20 mg

Amaranth Pound Cake

YIELD: 16 SERVINGS

This is the best recipe I know for showing off the distinctive flavor of amaranth. In this cake, I let the butter convey the flavor and richness, while cutting the fat by using egg whites and nonfat buttermilk. It's a delicious indulgence I highly recommend.

2³/₄ cups unbleached all-purpose flour
¹/₂ teaspoon baking soda
¹/₂ teaspoon salt
¹/₂ teaspoon mace
¹/₂ cup popped amaranth

³/₄ cup butter, at room temperature
2¹/₂ cups sugar
1 large egg, at room temperature
4 large egg whites
1 teaspoon vanilla extract
1¹/₃ cups nonfat buttermilk

Preheat the oven to 325 degrees. Grease and flour a 9-inch tube pan.

Into a medium bowl, sift together the flour, baking soda, salt, and mace. Stir in the amaranth. Set aside.

Combine the butter and sugar in a large bowl and beat until light and fluffy. Add the whole egg and egg whites and beat well. Add the vanilla and beat again. Add the flour mixture alternately with the buttermilk and beat until light and smooth.

Spoon the batter into the pan and shake the pan several times to level it. Bake for 1¹/₄ to 1¹/₂ hours, until the top is springy and a cake tester comes out clean.

Cool on a rack for 10 minutes. Then run a knife around the edge of the pan and invert onto a rack. Remove the pan and cool completely before serving.

Calories 294 • Protein 4 gm • Fat 10 gm • Percent of calories from fat 30% • Cholesterol 38 mg • Dietary fiber 1 gm • Sodium 245 mg • Calcium 32 mg

Amaranth Chocolate Spice Cake

YIELD: 8 TO 9 SERVINGS

Amaranth lends a very distinctive flavor and texture to baked goods. In this light cake, the amaranth blends with the spices to give a slightly tropical flavor to the cake.

³/₄ cup cake flour
¹/₃ cup unsweetened cocoa powder
2 teaspoons baking powder
¹/₂ teaspoon ground cinnamon
¹/₄ teaspoon salt
Pinch nutmeg
2 tablespoons butter, at room temperature

1 cup firmly packed light brown sugar
1 large egg
3 large egg whites
2 cups nonfat vanilla yogurt
¹/₄ cup popped amaranth
Confectioners' sugar, for serving

Preheat the oven to 350 degrees. Spray an 8-inch square baking pan with nonstick cooking spray and dust lightly with flour.

In a medium bowl, sift together the flour, cocoa, baking powder, cinnamon, salt, and nutmeg. In a large bowl, cream together the butter and sugar. Add the egg, egg whites, and yogurt. Beat until smooth. Add the flour mixture and beat again until smooth. Stir in the amaranth.

Pour into the prepared pan and bake for 35 to 40 minutes, until a tester inserted near the center comes out clean. Place on a wire rack and let cool.

To serve, dust the top with confectioners' sugar. Cut into 8 or 9 serving pieces.

Calories 252 • Protein 7 gm • Fat 5 gm • Percent of calories from fat 16% • Cholesterol 35 mg • Dietary fiber 1 gm • Sodium 285 mg • Calcium 164 mg

Blueberry Corn Cake

YIELD: 8 TO 9 SERVINGS

Around my house fresh blueberry season is incomplete without this cake. It is also delicious with fresh blackberries.

1 cup stone-ground yellow cornmeal

1½ cups unbleached all-purpose flour

1 tablespoon baking powder

½ teaspoon salt

3 cups blueberries

1 cup sugar

2 teaspoons cornstarch

½ teaspoon ground cinnamon

4 tablespoons butter

2 large eggs

¾ cup skim milk

1 teaspoon vanilla extract

Preheat the oven to 350 degrees. Spray an 8-inch square or 9-inch round baking dish with nonstick cooking spray.

In a medium bowl, combine the cornmeal, flour, baking powder, and salt. Mix well and set aside. In another medium bowl, combine the blueberries with ½ cup of the sugar, the cornstarch, and cinnamon. Mix well and set aside.

In a large bowl, cream together the butter and remaining ½ cup sugar. Add the eggs and beat until light. Beat in the milk and vanilla. Add the flour mixture and beat until smooth. The batter will be stiff.

Spread half the batter in the prepared pan. Spoon the berry mixture over the batter. Top with the remaining batter by spreading the batter with a spatula to the edges of the pan, covering the berries evenly.

Bake on the middle rack of the oven until a tester inserted near the center of the cake comes out clean, about 45 to 50 minutes. Do not underbake. Cool in the pan. Serve warm or completely cooled.

Calories 346 • Protein 6 gm • Fat 8 gm • Percent of calories from fat 21% • Cholesterol 70 mg • Dietary fiber 3 gm • Sodium 394 mg • Calcium 106 mg

Lemon-Berry Couscous Cake

YIELD: 12 TO 16 SERVINGS

Couscous gives a pebbled texture to this simple but flavorful cake.

2$1/4$ cups unbleached all-purpose
    flour
1 teaspoon baking soda
$1/2$ teaspoon salt
$1/4$ teaspoon ground nutmeg
1 cup uncooked couscous
1 teaspoon grated lemon peel
6 tablespoons butter, at room
    temperature

2 cups sugar
1 large egg, at room temperature
4 large egg whites
1 teaspoon vanilla extract
1$1/3$ cups buttermilk
2 cups fresh raspberries,
    blackberries, or blueberries

Preheat the oven to 325 degrees. Grease and flour a 9-inch tube pan.

Into a medium bowl, sift together the flour, baking soda, salt, and nutmeg. Stir in the couscous and lemon peel. Set aside.

In a large bowl, combine the butter and sugar and beat until light and fluffy. Add the egg and egg whites, and beat well. Add the vanilla and beat again. Add the couscous mixture alternately with the buttermilk and beat until light and smooth. Stir in the berries.

Spoon the batter into the prepared pan and shake the pan several times to level it. Bake for about 1$1/4$ hours, until the top is springy and a cake tester comes out clean.

Cool on a rack for 10 minutes. Then run a knife around the edge of the pan and invert onto a rack. Remove the pan and cool the cake completely before serving.

Calories 366 • Protein 7 gm • Fat 7 gm • Percent of calories from fat 17% • Cholesterol 35 mg • Dietary fiber 3 gm • Sodium 317 mg • Calcium 45 mg

Orange Marmalade—Millet Crunch Cake

YIELD: 12 TO 15 SERVINGS

Millet gives this delightfully light cake a nutty flavor, crunchy texture, and golden appearance.

1 cup uncooked millet
1 cup unbleached all-purpose
   flour
2 tablespoons grated orange zest
1½ teaspoons baking powder
½ teaspoon salt
¼ cup canola oil
2 tablespoons butter, at room
   temperature

¾ cup sugar
2 large eggs
2 large egg whites
½ cup nonfat buttermilk
1 tablespoon Cointreau, Grand
   Marnier, or other orange-
   flavored liqueur
3 tablespoons orange marmalade

Preheat the oven to 350 degrees. Spray a 10-inch round cake pan with nonstick cooking spray and dust lightly with flour. Grind the millet in a blender to make a coarse meal (similar to cornmeal).

In a medium bowl, combine the ground millet, flour, orange zest, baking powder, and salt. Mix well.

In a large bowl, cream together the oil, butter, and sugar. Add the eggs and egg whites, one at a time, stirring until just combined. Add the buttermilk and orange liqueur and stir to combine. Fold in the dry ingredients until just combined. Do not overmix.

Pour the batter into the prepared pan. Smooth the top of the batter with a spatula. Bake for about 40 minutes, until the top is firm and golden.

Cool the cake in the pan for 20 minutes on a wire rack, then invert onto the rack and remove the pan. Invert the cake again so that the top side is up. Heat the marmalade in a microwave or on top of the stove over low heat until melted. Brush over the top of the cake. Let cool before serving.

Calories 241 • Protein 5 gm • Fat 8 gm • Percent of calories from fat 31% •
Cholesterol 41 mg • Dietary fiber 2 gm • Sodium 200 mg • Calcium 43 mg

Chocolate Chip—Banana Oat Cake

YIELD: 9 SERVINGS

1¹/₃ cups rolled oats (not instant)
1¹/₂ cups unbleached all-purpose
  flour
2 teaspoons baking powder
1 teaspoon baking soda
1 teaspoon salt
4 tablespoons butter, at room
  temperature

³/₄ cup sugar
3 very ripe bananas
2 large egg whites
¹/₂ cup nonfat vanilla yogurt
1¹/₂ cups chocolate chips

Preheat the oven to 350 degrees. Spray an 8-inch square baking dish with nonstick cooking spray.

Process the oats in a blender until the oats are reduced to a coarse powder; allow some large flakes to remain. Combine this oat flour in a medium bowl with the all-purpose flour, baking powder, baking soda, and salt. Mix well.

In a large bowl, beat together the butter and sugar. Add the bananas, egg whites, and yogurt, and beat until smooth. Add the oat mixture and beat until smooth. Stir in the chocolate chips. Spoon the batter into the prepared baking dish. Bake for about 1 hour, until a knife inserted near the center comes out clean. Cool on a rack.

Calories 439 • Protein 8 gm • Fat 16 gm • Percent of calories from fat 30% •
Cholesterol 15 mg • Dietary fiber 4 gm • Sodium 565 mg • Calcium 69 mg

Maple-Apple Oat Cake

YIELD: 9 SERVINGS

This makes a great snacking cake and packs well into bag lunches. Because it is not overly sweet, I also like to serve it for breakfast on special occasions.

4 medium apples, peeled
  and sliced (about 3 cups)
3 tablespoons sugar
1 teaspoon ground cinnamon
1¼ cups rolled oats (not instant)
1½ cups unbleached all-purpose
  flour
1 teaspoon baking soda

1 teaspoon baking powder
1 teaspoon salt
2 large eggs
1 cup nonfat plain yogurt
¼ cup canola oil
½ cup maple syrup
1 teaspoon vanilla extract

Preheat the oven to 350 degrees. Spray an 8-inch square baking dish with nonstick cooking spray. Arrange the apples in the baking dish. Sprinkle with 2 tablespoons of the sugar and the cinnamon. Set aside.

Process the rolled oats in a blender until the oats are reduced to a coarse powder; allow some large flakes to remain. Combine this oat flour in a large mixing bowl with the all-purpose flour, baking soda, baking powder, and salt. Stir to blend well.

In a medium bowl, beat the eggs. Add the yogurt, canola oil, maple syrup, and vanilla, and blend well. Make a well in the oat mixture, pour in the egg mixture, and stir just to blend. The batter will be lumpy. Spoon over the apples and use a spatula to spread the batter evenly in the pan. Sprinkle the remaining 1 tablespoon sugar over the batter.

Bake for 35 minutes, until a knife inserted near the center comes out clean. This cake is especially good served warm.

Calories 300 • Protein 7 gm • Fat 8 gm • Percent of calories from fat 24% •
Cholesterol 47 mg • Dietary fiber 3 gm • Sodium 477 mg • Calcium 94 mg

Apple Couscous

YIELD: 4 SERVINGS

A delicious dessert, virtually fat-free, with all the flavors of apple pie. Choose a good pie apple for this dessert, such as Granny Smith, Golden Delicious, Jonathan, or Northern Spy. A topping of frozen vanilla yogurt is a wonderful indulgence here.

1³/₄ cups apple juice or cider
3 apples, peeled, quartered,
   and thinly sliced
1 cup uncooked couscous

4 to 6 tablespoons brown sugar
1 teaspoon ground cinnamon
Pinch nutmeg
¹/₂ teaspoon vanilla extract

Heat the apple juice to a simmer in a medium saucepan. Add the apples and simmer until tender, about 10 minutes. Stir in the couscous, 4 tablespoons brown sugar, the cinnamon, nutmeg, and vanilla. Taste and add the additional 2 tablespoons brown sugar, if desired. Remove from the heat, cover, and set aside until the couscous is tender and all of the liquid has been absorbed, about 10 minutes. Serve warm or chilled.

Calories 334 • Protein 6 gm • Fat 1 gm • Percent of calories from fat 2% •
Cholesterol 0 mg • Dietary fiber 5 gm • Sodium 13 mg • Calcium 41 mg

Fruity Couscous Dessert Timbales

※

YIELD: 6 SERVINGS

Here's a very rich, very sweet dessert that is incredibly easy to make and absolutely low in fat. I like the mix of recommended fruits in the recipe, especially with the tropical flavors of the mango or pineapple juice, but other fruits can be substituted.

2 cups mango or pineapple juice
$3/4$ cup uncooked couscous
1 cup dried sweetened tart
   cherries or cranberries
1 cup diced dried sweetened
   pineapple

$1/2$ cup chopped dried mango or
   dried sweetened papaya
$1^1/2$ cups fresh or frozen
   raspberries or sliced strawberries
Sugar and freshly squeezed
   lemon juice (optional)

Heat the fruit juice just until boiling. Combine the couscous and dried fruits in a large bowl. Add the fruit juice, cover, and set aside until the juice has been absorbed, about $1^1/2$ hours.

Make the berry sauce by pureeing the raspberries or strawberries in a blender, adding sugar and/or lemon juice to intensify the flavor as needed.

Spoon the couscous into 6 custard cups and press down on the filling to pack it in. To serve, spoon some berry sauce onto each dessert plate. Unmold each custard cup on top of the sauce, then serve.

Calories 327 • Protein 4 gm • Fat 1 gm • Percent of calories from fat 3% •
Cholesterol 0 mg • Dietary fiber 18 gm • Sodium 6 mg • Calcium 33 mg

Honey–Apple Crisp

YIELD: 6 SERVINGS

The honey, allspice, and orange give this traditional dessert a new twist.

2¹/₂ pounds apples, peeled, cored, and sliced (7 cups)
¹/₃ cup honey
1 teaspoon grated orange zest
¹/₂ teaspoon ground cinnamon
¹/₄ teaspoon ground allspice

³/₄ cup rolled oats (not instant)
¹/₂ cup unbleached all-purpose flour
¹/₃ cup firmly packed brown sugar
5 tablespoons cold butter

Preheat the oven to 425 degrees. Spray an 8-inch square baking pan or 2-quart baking dish with nonstick cooking spray.

In a large bowl, toss the apples with the honey, orange zest, ¹/₄ teaspoon of the cinnamon, and the allspice. Arrange in the baking dish, pressing down on the apples so they are level with the top of the dish.

In a medium bowl, combine the oats, flour, brown sugar, and the remaining ¹/₄ teaspoon cinnamon. Rub the butter into the mixture using your fingers. Sprinkle the topping over the apples, pressing it down and making sure the edges are covered.

Bake for 15 minutes, then reduce the heat to 350 degrees and bake until the top is browned and the apples are tender when tested with a fork, about 30 minutes more. Serve warm or chilled.

Calories 374 • Protein 3 gm • Fat 12 gm • Percent of calories from fat 26% • Cholesterol 27 mg • Dietary fiber 5 gm • Sodium 109 mg • Calcium 32 mg

Apple Crunch

YIELD: 12 SERVINGS

In this variation on the traditional apple crisp, the apple filling is flavored in the traditional way, but the topping of oats and millets is most unusual. The millet makes it very crunchy.

Fruit Filling

4 pounds apples, peeled, cored, and sliced (about 12 cups)

2 tablespoons freshly squeezed lemon juice

$1/2$ cup firmly packed brown sugar

$1^1/2$ teaspoons ground cinnamon

$1/8$ teaspoon nutmeg

Topping

1 cup uncooked millet

1 cup uncooked rolled oats (not instant)

$3/4$ cup brown sugar

$1/2$ cup cold butter

Preheat the oven to 350 degrees. Spray a 9×13-inch baking dish with nonstick cooking spray.

Combine the apples and lemon juice in a large bowl. Add the brown sugar, cinnamon, and nutmeg, and mix well. Spoon into the prepared baking dish, using the back of the spoon to make the surface fairly level.

To make the topping, place the millet in a blender and process until well ground. The millet should look like coarsely ground cornmeal.

In the bowl that held the apples, combine the millet, oats, and brown sugar. Cut the butter into small bits and rub into the grain mixture until it resembles a coarse meal. Sprinkle the topping over the apples, pressing it down and making sure it reaches the edge of the pan.

Bake for about 45 minutes, until the top is browned and the apples are tender when tested with a fork. Serve warm or chilled.

Calories 334 • Protein 3 gm • Fat 10 gm • Percent of calories from fat 25% • Cholesterol 22 mg • Dietary fiber 5 gm • Sodium 93 mg • Calcium 36 mg

Strawberry-Rhubarb Crumble

YIELD: 12 SERVINGS

A delicious salute to spring. Topping this dessert with a little frozen vanilla yogurt brings it over the top.

Fruit Filling

1¼ cups sugar

⅓ cup unbleached all-purpose flour

1 teaspoon grated orange zest

Pinch salt

1 pound fresh rhubarb, cut into 1-inch pieces (4 cups)

4 cups sliced strawberries

Crumble Crust

2 cups uncooked rolled oats (not instant)

1 cup firmly packed brown sugar

½ cup unbleached all-purpose flour

1 teaspoon baking powder

½ teaspoon salt

½ cup cold butter, cut into small bits

1 teaspoon almond extract

Combine the sugar, flour, orange zest, salt, rhubarb, and strawberries in a large bowl. Toss to mix. Set aside.

To make the crust, in a food processor grind 1 cup of the oats to a fine powder. Add the remaining 1 cup oats, brown sugar, flour, baking powder, and salt. Process just long enough to mix. Add the butter and almond extract and process just long enough to combine.

Press half of the crumb mixture into the bottom of a 9×13-inch baking dish. Spoon the strawberry-rhubarb filling over it. Cover the fruit with the remaining crumb mixture.

Bake for about 40 minutes, until the topping is browned. Serve warm or chilled.

Calories 327 • Protein 4 gm • Fat 9 gm • Percent of calories from fat 25% • Cholesterol 22 mg • Dietary fiber 3 gm • Sodium 223 mg • Calcium 80 mg

Crunchy Maple-baked Banana

YIELD: 4 SERVINGS

My son Rory and I dreamed this treat up one hungry afternoon, making it with ingredients we had on hand. I hope your pantry is equally well stocked.

1 orange
1/2 cup toasted wheat germ
4 bananas, peeled
  and halved lengthwise

2 tablespoons maple syrup
1 tablespoon butter

Preheat the oven to 425 degrees. Lightly butter an 8-inch square baking dish.

Grate 1 teaspoon orange zest. Combine with the wheat germ in a shallow bowl. Juice the orange into a medium bowl. Toss the banana halves with orange juice, then roll them in the wheat germ until well coated. Place in the baking dish.

Combine the maple syrup and butter in a small saucepan or microwave-safe container. Heat just until the butter is melted. Drizzle over the bananas.

Bake for 10 to 12 minutes or until golden. Serve warm.

Calories 221 • Protein 6 gm • Fat 5 gm • Percent of calories from fat 18% • Cholesterol 8 mg • Dietary fiber 6 gm • Sodium 33 mg • Calcium 31 mg

Baked Rice Pudding

YIELD: 4 TO 6 SERVINGS

³/₄ cup uncooked Arborio rice
1¹/₂ cups water
2 large egg yolks
¹/₄ cup sugar
1 tablespoon cornstarch
1 teaspoon vanilla extract
¹/₄ teaspoon salt

¹/₄ teaspoon ground cinnamon
¹/₈ teaspoon nutmeg
1 (14-ounce) can sweetened
  condensed skim milk
2 cups warm skim milk
¹/₂ cup raisins
Milk or cream, for serving

Combine the rice and water in a medium saucepan. Cover, bring to a boil, then reduce the heat and boil gently until the water has been absorbed and the rice is tender, about 12 minutes.

Preheat the oven to 325 degrees. Lightly grease a 1¹/₂-quart baking dish or spray with nonstick cooking spray. Set it inside a slightly larger pan that is at least 2 inches deep. Meanwhile, heat water in a kettle to boiling.

In a large bowl, whisk together the egg yolks, sugar, cornstarch, vanilla, salt, cinnamon, and nutmeg. Whisk in the condensed milk, then the warm skim milk. Fold in the rice and raisins. Transfer the rice mixture to the smaller baking dish. Place in the oven, with the smaller of the baking dishes still inside the larger one. Pour boiling water into the larger baking dish so that it rises at least halfway up the sides of the smaller baking dish.

Bake for about 1¹/₂ hours, until set. Remove from the water bath and let cool on a rack. Serve warm or cold with milk or cream.

Calories 422 • Protein 17 gm • Fat 3 gm • Percent of calories from fat 7% •
Cholesterol 112 mg • Dietary fiber 2 gm • Sodium 331 mg • Calcium 462 mg

Almond Rice Pudding

YIELD: 6 TO 8 SERVINGS

Pudding

3/4 cups uncooked short-grain or medium-grain (preferrably Arborio) rice
1 1/2 cups water
4 large eggs

3 cups skim milk
2/3 cup sugar
1 teaspoon vanilla extract
1 teaspoon almond extract

Topping

1/2 cup sliced almonds
1 teaspoon brown sugar

1/4 teaspoon ground cinnamon
Milk or cream, for serving

Combine the rice and water in a medium saucepan. Cover, bring to a boil, then reduce the heat and boil gently until the water has been absorbed and the rice is mostly tender, about 12 minutes.

Preheat the oven to 325 degrees. Lightly grease a 1 1/2-quart baking dish or spray with nonstick spray. Set it inside a slightly larger pan that is at least 2 inches deep. Meanwhile, heat water in a kettle to boiling.

In a large bowl, whisk together the eggs, skim milk, sugar, and vanilla and almond extracts. Fold in the rice. Spoon into the smaller baking dish. Place in the oven, with the smaller of the baking dishes still inside the larger one. Pour boiling water into the larger baking dish so that it rises at least halfway up the sides of the smaller baking dish. Bake for 50 minutes.

Meanwhile, to make the topping, in a small bowl, combine the almonds, brown sugar, and cinnamon. After 50 minutes stir the pudding to lift the rice that has settled to the bottom of the pan, then sprinkle the topping over the pudding. Continue to bake for about 25 minutes or until set.

Remove from the water bath and let cool on a rack. Serve warm or cold with milk or cream.

Calories 359 • Protein 13 gm • Fat 10 gm • Percent of calories from fat 24% • Cholesterol 144 mg • Dietary fiber 2 gm • Sodium 109 mg • Calcium 201 mg

Vanilla Yogurt Rice Pudding

YIELD: 4 TO 6 SERVINGS

Starchy Arborio rice is the secret to making a creamy rice pudding. After simmering the rice in the milk, all that is left to do is stir in the yogurt and flavorings. What could be simpler? This is one of my house standards. I eat it for breakfast, though most people consider it a dessert. Fresh fruit, such as berries or chopped nectarines or peaches, can replace the raisins.

½ cup uncooked Arborio rice
2 cups skim milk
½ cup raisins
2 cups nonfat vanilla yogurt

¼ cup firmly packed brown sugar
¼ teaspoon ground cinnamon
Pinch nutmeg

In the top of a double boiler, combine the rice and milk and simmer for about 1 hour, until the grains are completely tender and most of the milk has been absorbed. Spoon into a bowl and set aside to cool.

Meanwhile, plump the raisins in hot water to cover for about 10 minutes, then drain. When the rice has cooled, mix in the raisins along with the yogurt, brown sugar, cinnamon, and nutmeg. Chill well before serving.

Calories 318 • Protein 13 gm • Fat 1 gm • Percent of calories from fat 1% •
Cholesterol 4 mg • Dietary fiber 1 gm • Sodium 158 mg • Calcium 399 mg

Piña Colada Rice Pudding

YIELD: 6 TO 8 SERVINGS

This is no ordinary rice pudding. Pineapple, coconut milk, and rum transform this dessert into a delicious tropical experience.

1 envelope unflavored gelatin
$^1/_4$ cup light rum
2 large egg yolks
1 (14-ounce) can light coconut milk
$^1/_4$ cup skim milk
2 cups cooked aromatic white rice, preferably jasmine

$^1/_2$ cup sugar
Pinch salt
1 (20-ounce) can crushed pineapple, well drained
1 cup nonfat vanilla yogurt

In a small bowl, sprinkle the gelatin over the rum and let it soften for about 5 minutes. In a separate small bowl, lightly whisk the egg yolks.

Heat the coconut milk and skim milk in a heavy-bottomed, medium saucepan until very hot. Stir a little hot milk into the egg yolks. Then pour the egg mixture into the hot milk, along with the rice, sugar, salt, and gelatin mixture. Stir constantly over medium heat until thickened, about 10 minutes.

Remove from the heat and refrigerate until completely cooled.

When the custard has cooled, fold in the pineapple, then the yogurt. Spoon into serving bowls. Return to the refrigerator for several hours or serve at once.

Calories 298 • Protein 5 gm • Fat 5 gm • Percent of calories from fat 16% • Cholesterol 71 mg • Dietary fiber 1 gm • Sodium 52 mg • Calcium 95 mg

Strawberry-Coconut Rice Pudding

YIELD: 4 TO 6 SERVINGS

A creamy dairy-free rice pudding? Coconut milk is the base for this lovely pudding.

1/2 cup uncooked Arborio rice	1 (14-ounce) can light coconut milk
2 cups water	1 tablespoon cornstarch
3/4 cup sugar	2 large eggs
1 pint fresh strawberries	

In the top of a double boiler, combine the rice, water, and 1/4 cup of the sugar. Simmer until the rice is completely tender and most of the water has been absorbed, about 1 1/2 hours. Set aside to cool.

Meanwhile, wash and hull the berries. Set a few aside for a garnish and slice the remainder. Add 1/4 cup of the sugar to the strawberries, toss to mix, and set aside.

Heat the coconut milk in a heavy-bottomed, medium saucepan over medium-low heat. Combine the remaining 1/4 cup sugar and cornstarch and whisk into the hot coconut milk. Continue whisking until the sugar is completely dissolved. In a medium bowl, whisk the eggs until smooth. Add about 1 cup of the hot coconut milk mixture to the eggs, then slowly pour the eggs into the saucepan, whisking constantly. Cook over medium heat, stirring constantly, until the mixture thickens, 10 minutes. Stir in the cooked rice and strawberries along with any juice that has collected.

Set aside to cool to room temperature, then refrigerate until chilled, at least 2 hours. Serve well chilled.

Calories 375 • Protein 6 gm • Fat 8 gm • Percent of calories from fat 19% • Cholesterol 106 mg • Dietary fiber 2 gm • Sodium 61 mg • Calcium 35 mg

Black Rice Pudding

YIELD: **4** SERVINGS

*B*lack rice can be found in stores that stock Asian ingredients and is worth seeking out as a novelty. It has a distinctively nutty flavor—something of a cross between wild rice and white rice. If you can't find black rice, by all means substitute another kind. The flavor will be different, but pleasing nonetheless. This pudding is also dairy-free; pineapple juice instead of milk acts as the base for the custard.

1 cup uncooked black rice
2$^1/_2$ cups water
1 cup pineapple juice
1$^1/_2$ tablespoons cornstarch

2 large eggs, beaten
$^3/_4$ cup sugar
$^1/_2$ teaspoon salt

Combine the rice and water in a medium saucepan over low heat. Cover and cook for about 35 minutes. Remove from the heat and cool to room temperature.

In a heavy-bottomed, medium saucepan, combine the pineapple juice with the cornstarch and whisk until smooth. Add the eggs, sugar, and salt. Bring to a boil, stirring constantly, until the mixture begins to thicken, about 10 minutes. Mix in the rice and cool to room temperature. Chill for several hours in the refrigerator before serving.

Calories 396 • Protein 8 gm • Fat 4 gm • Percent of calories from fat 8% • Cholesterol 106 mg • Dietary fiber 2 gm • Sodium 329 mg • Calcium 36 mg

Coconut Cream Rice Dream

YIELD: **4** SERVINGS

Plain and creamy, this delicately flavored rice pudding is irresistible. Sometimes I dress it up (and extend the number of servings) by adding tropical fruit, such as sliced banana, diced mango, and/or diced pineapple. Either way this rich-tasting dessert is one of my all-time favorites.

2¹/₂ cups skim milk
1 cup light coconut milk
³/₄ cup uncooked Arborio rice
¹/₂ cup sugar

¹/₄ teaspoon salt
Diced tropical fruit (optional)
Toasted shaved coconut, for
 garnish (optional)

In the top of a double boiler set over hot water, combine the skim milk, coconut milk, rice, ¹/₄ cup of the sugar, and salt. Simmer until the rice is tender and most of the milk is absorbed, about 1¹/₄ to 1¹/₂ hours. Stir in the remaining ¹/₄ cup sugar. Set aside to cool. Just before serving, stir in the fruit and garnish with shaved coconut, if desired.

Calories 343 • Protein 8 gm • Fat 3 gm • Percent of calories from fat 9% •
Cholesterol 3 mg • Dietary fiber 1 gm • Sodium 239 mg • Calcium 204 mg

Rich Chocolate Rice Pudding

YIELD: 4 SERVINGS

A silken smooth, very rich chocolate pudding with the added pebbled texture of rice. You'd never guess that this indulgent dessert has 3 grams of fat per serving. Garnish with fresh raspberries for an especially pretty presentation.

2 tablespoons unsweetened
  cocoa powder
1 tablespoon cornstarch
1 cup skim milk
1 (14-ounce) can sweetened
  condensed skim milk

1 cup cooked white or brown rice
1 ounce semisweet chocolate,
  chopped
1 teaspoon vanilla extract

Combine the cocoa and cornstarch in a heavy-bottomed, medium saucepan. Add 1/4 cup of the skim milk and whisk until smooth. Whisk in the remaining skim milk and the condensed milk and continue whisking until well blended. Stir in the rice. Bring to a boil over medium heat, stirring frequently to prevent scorching. Remove from the heat and stir in the chocolate. Return to medium heat and boil for 2 minutes, stirring constantly. Remove from the heat and stir in the vanilla. Spoon into 4 dessert cups or a serving bowl. Cover with plastic wrap so that the wrap touches the surface of the pudding and prevents a skin from forming. Refrigerate until chilled.

Calories 217 • Protein 12 gm • Fat 3 gm • Percent of calories from fat 12% •
Cholesterol 6 mg • Dietary fiber 1 gm • Sodium 164 mg • Calcium 405 mg

Grand Marnier Rice Torte

YIELD: 16 SERVINGS

A cross between a rice pudding and a cheesecake, this traditional Italian dessert is creamy and rich-tasting. Being a lifelong devotee of rice puddings, I find this an elegantly understated way to serve my favorite dessert.

6$^{1}/_{2}$ cups skim milk
1$^{1}/_{2}$ cups uncooked Arborio rice
1 cup sugar
$^{1}/_{4}$ teaspoon salt
Butter, for greasing the pan
2 tablespoons fine dry bread
   or vanilla cookie crumbs

4 large eggs, separated
1 teaspoon almond extract
$^{1}/_{2}$ teaspoon vanilla extract
1 tablespoon grated orange zest
4 tablespoons Grand Marnier
   or other orange-flavored liqueur
Confectioners' sugar, for serving

In the top of a double boiler set over hot water, combine the milk, rice, $^{1}/_{2}$ cup of the sugar, and the salt. Simmer until the rice is tender and most of the milk has been absorbed, about 1$^{1}/_{2}$ hours. Set aside to cool.

Butter a 10-inch springform pan and coat with the bread or cookie crumbs. Preheat the oven to 350 degrees.

Beat the egg yolks with the remaining $^{1}/_{2}$ cup sugar in a large bowl. Stir in the cooled rice mixture, the almond and vanilla extracts, and the grated orange zest. In a medium bowl, beat the egg whites until stiff but not dry. Fold a third of the whites into the rice mixture to lighten it. Then fold in the remainder. Pour into the prepared pan. Bake for 1$^{1}/_{2}$ hours, until a tester inserted into the cake comes out clean. The cake should feel firm and light and the top should look creamy and golden. Remove from the oven and let cool on a wire rack.

When cool, prick all over with a skewer and pour the Grand Marnier over the top. Leave until the following day, then remove the sides of the pan. Dust the top with confectioners' sugar and serve.

Leftover cake will keep well for several days in the refrigerator if well wrapped.

Calories 198 • Protein 7 gm • Fat 2 gm • Percent of calories from fat 7% •
Cholesterol 55 mg • Dietary fiber 0 gm • Sodium 111 mg • Calcium 132 mg

Coconut-Almond Rice Torte

❧

YIELD: 16 SERVINGS

The traditional Italian rice torte is flavored with orange. This variation is infused with coconut milk and almond-flavored liqueur. When I make this torte I look forward to leftovers, which make a delicious breakfast.

$4^1/_2$ cups skim milk
2 cups light coconut milk
$1^1/_2$ cups uncooked Arborio rice
$1^1/_4$ cups sugar
$1/_4$ teaspoon salt
Butter, for greasing pan

$1/_2$ cup slivered almonds
4 large eggs, separated
1 teaspoon almond extract
$1/_2$ teaspoon vanilla extract
$1/_4$ cup shredded coconut
4 tablespoons amaretto

In the top of a double boiler set over hot water, combine the skim milk, coconut milk, rice, $1/_2$ cup of the sugar, and the salt. Simmer until the rice is tender and most of the milk is absorbed, about $1^1/_2$ hours. Set aside to cool.

Butter a 10-inch springform pan. Combine $1/_4$ cup of the almonds with 1 tablespoon of the sugar in a food processor and grind to a coarse meal. Coat the buttered pan with the almond meal. Preheat the oven to 350 degrees.

Beat the egg yolks with the remaining sugar in a large bowl. Stir in the cooled rice mixture and the almond and vanilla extracts. In a separate bowl, beat the egg whites until stiff but not dry. Fold one-third of the whites into the rice mixture to lighten it. Then fold in the remainder. Pour into the prepared pan. Bake for $1^1/_2$ hours, or until a tester inserted into the cake comes out clean. The cake should feel firm and light and the top should look creamy and golden. Remove from the oven and let cool on a wire rack.

Toast the remaining $1/_4$ cup almonds in a dry skillet over medium heat, stirring constantly, until golden. Immediately remove from the pan. Then toast the coconut in the same dry skillet and immediately remove from the pan. Do not allow the nuts or coconut to overbrown.

When the torte is cool, prick all over with a skewer and pour the amaretto over it. Let stand overnight, then remove the sides of the pan.

Scatter the toasted almonds around the perimeter of the torte and coconut in the center and serve.

Leftover cake will keep well for several days in the refrigerator if well wrapped.

Calories 245 • Protein 6 gm • Fat 6 gm • Percent of calories from fat 21% •
Cholesterol 54 mg • Dietary fiber 1 gm • Sodium 100 mg • Calcium 110 mg

Index

Adzuki beans, 15, 22
  Japanese Red Rice and Beans, 320
All-American Pumpkin Bread, 402
Almond
  Coconut Rice Torte, 443–44
  Granola
    -Cherry, 378
    -Coconut, 379
  Rice Pudding, 435
Almost Mom's Quick Chili, 217
Amaranth, 24
  Basic Cooked, 272
  Biscuits, Four-Grain, 397
  Cake
    Chocolate Spice, 422
    Pound, 421
  Cookies, Triple A Oatmeal, 412
  Muffins, 387
  Pancakes, Buttermilk, 358
Appetizers and Finger Foods
  Black Bean
    Roll-Ups, 47
    Turnovers, 49
    and Goat Cheese Quesadillas, 48
  Chickpea Snacks, Crunchy, 56
  Grape Leaves, Stuffed, 50–51
  Nori Rolls
    Smoked Salmon, 53
    Vegetarian, 52–53
  Pizza-flavored Popcorn, 54

Polenta-Fontina Bites, 55
  Soy Nuts, Garlic-Roasted, 57
  Zucchini Brown Rice Squares, 185
  See also Dips and Spreads
Apple
  Cake, -Maple Oat, 427
  Cookies
    Maple-Oatmeal, 415
    Triple A Oatmeal, 412
  Couscous, 428
  Crisp, Honey-, 430
  Crunch, 431
  Muffins, Maple Oat, 392–93
Apricot
  -Almond Granola, 378
  Oatmeal Fruit Cookies, 414
Arborio rice, 9, 10
Aromatic rice, 8
Artichoke Pasta Salad with Basil
  Vinaigrette, 141
Arugula
  Minestrone with Greens, 94
  Pesto Risotto, 153
  Salad, Tomato, and White Bean,
    with Roasted Garlic Vinaigrette,
    138
Asparagus, Lemon-Thyme Risotto
  with, 158
Avocado, Chunky Black Bean Dip,
  36

Baked Beans
  Honey-Mustard, 230
    Quick Baked Beans, 218
  Maple, 231
  Old-fashioned, 229
  Spicy Barbecued, 234
Banana
  Baked, Crunchy Maple, 433
  Cake, Chocolate Chip–Oat, 426
  Muffins, Chunky Monkey, 395
  Pancakes
    Chocolate, 357
    -Strawberry, 356
  Waffles, -Nut Oat, 364
Barbecued Beans
  15-minute, 235
  Sandwiches with Slaw, 236
  Spicy Slow-baked, 234
Barley, 24–25
  Basic Cooked
    Hulled, 273
    Pearled, 273
  Cereal
    Honey-Orange Porridge, 366
    Hot, 365
  Cookies, Mixed Grain Raisin, 413
  Granola
    Blueberry Morning, 381–82
    Cashew-Honey, 379
    Coconut-Almond, 383
    Fruit-and-Nut, 380
  pearled, 25
  Pilaf
    Baked Barley Pilaf, 286
    Barley-Wild Rice, 287
    Toasted Vermicelli, 285
  Risotto with Wild Mushrooms and
    Peas, 288
  Roasted Fall Vegetables with, 284
  rolled, 25
  Salad, Vegetable with Orange
    Buttermilk Dressing, 102
  Soup
    Hearty Vegetable, 63
    Kale, 66
    Leek, 65
    Mediterranean Vegetable, 62
    Mushroom, 64
    Split Pea-, 87
    Water, 58
Basil
  Cottage Cheese Herb Loaf, 406
  Salad
    Tomato, Green Bean, and White
      Bean with Mint and, 135
    Vinaigrette, Artichoke Pasta with,
      141
  See also Pesto
Basmati rice, 8
Beans, 5–6, 14–15
  buying and storing, 19–20
  cooking, 20–23
  types of, 14–19
  See also Beans and grains recipes;
    Beans and pasta recipes; Beans
    and rice recipes; and specific types
    of beans
Beans and grains recipes, 331–50
  Bean Burger
    Basic, 348
    Wheat Berry, 349
  Chili
    Black Bean, with Wheat Berries,
      335
    Two-Bean, with Bulgur, 334
  Corn Bread Casserole
    Black Bean, 338–39
    Cowboy Beans 'n', 344–45
    Vegetable Tamale Pie, 346–47
  Couscous, Spicy Vegetable, 332–33
  diet, 1–3, 5–32
  Enchiladas, Pinto Bean and Cheese,
    340–41
  Mexican Torte, 343
  Nachos Supreme, 342
  Stew, Black Bean and Hominy, 336
  Tostadas, Black Bean, with Cilantro
    Cream, 337
Beans and pasta recipes (Pasta e
    Fagioli), 247–68
  Black Beans
    Cilantro Pesto Rotini with, 256

Orecchiette with Goat Cheese, Fresh Tomato Sauce, and, 254
in Saffron Tomato Sauce, 253
Tex-Mex, 255
Chickpeas
Cavatelli with Broccoli and, 258
Orecchiette with Broccoli Rabe and, 259
Penne with Spinach and, Baked, 257
Pesto Pasta with Tomatoes and, 262
Rotini with Tomato-Vegetable Sauce and, 260
Ziti with Tomatoes, Feta and, 261
Chili Mac, 268
Cranberry Beans
Fresh, with Pasta, Tomatoes, and Rosemary, 250–51
Pesto Pasta with, 263
Fava Beans, Penne with Fresh, 249
Lentils, Syrian Rishtah, 264
Lima Beans, Summer Vegetables, 252
White Beans
Bow Ties with Fresh Tomato Sauce and, 265
and Fennel Linguine, 266
Penne with Greens and, 267
Beans and rice recipes, 311–31
Black Beans and White Rice, 322
Quick, 323
Brown Rice and Lentils, 329
Burgers, Lentil, 330
Cuban Yellow Rice and Black Beans, 324
Fiesta Beans and Rice, 325
Jamaican-style Rice and Peas, 321
Japanese Red Rice and Beans, 320
Khichiri, 331
Louisiana Red Beans and Rice, 319
Quick, 318
Mixed Vegetable Curry, 327
Red Bean Gumbo, 316–17
Saffron Rice with Chickpeas, 326
Syrian Mujdara (Lentils and Rice), 238

Vegetarian Hoppin' John, 314–15
Beans, rice, and grains, and human diet, 5–6
Berries
Cake, Lemon Couscous, 424
Dessert Timbales, Fruity Couscous, 429
Muffins, Brown Rice, 394
Biscuits
Cornmeal, 398
Four-Grain, 397
See also Muffins; Scones
Black Bean(s), 15, 22
Burritos
Breakfast Egg and, 207
Cheese, 239
Smoky, 206
Cakes
Potato, 208
Sweet Potato, 209
Casserole, Corn Bread, 338
Chili
Two-Bean, with Bulgur, 334
with Wheat Berries, 335
Cuban, 202
Dip
Cheesy, 38
Chunky Avocado, 36
Grilled Tomato Salsa with, 35
Piquant, 37
Huevos Rancheros, 204–5
Mexican, 201
Pasta and
Orecchiette with Goat Cheese, Fresh Tomato Sauce, and, 254
Rotini, Cilantro Pesto with, 256
in Saffron Tomato Sauce, 253
Tex-Mex, 255
Quesadillas, Goat Cheese and, 48
Stew, Hominy and, 336
Tostadas with Cilantro Cream, 337
Rice and
Cuban Yellow, 324
Quick White, 323
White, 322
Refried, 203

448

Index

Black Bean(s) *(cont'd)*
  Roll-Ups, 47
  Salad
    Couscous and, 104
    Chipotle-Honey Vinaigrette with, 122
    Goat Cheese with, 124–25
    New World Quinoa, 107
    Southwestern Corn and, 120
    Southwestern Rice and, 117
    Tomato-Corn with, 123
    Tropical, 126
    Yellow Rice and, 118–19
  Soup
    Butternut Squash with Cilantro and, 77
    Indian Spices with, 76
    Red Peppers and Corn with, 74
    Smoky Tomato and, 75
  10-minute, 200
  Turnovers, 49
Black-eyed peas, 15, 16, 22
  Hoppin' John, Vegetarian, 314–15
  Salad, Summertime, 127
Black rice, 8
  Pudding, 439
  Steamed, 148
Blueberry
  Corn Cake, 423
  Corn Cakes, 355
  Corn Toasties, 401
  Granola, Morning, 382–83
Bow Ties
  Kasha with, 305
  White Beans and Fresh Tomato Sauce with, 265
Bran layer, 23, 24
Bread
    Brown Rice, 403
  Corn Bread
    Black Bean Casserole, 338
    Blueberry Corn Toasties, 401
    Corny, 399
    Roasted Pepper, 400
  Cottage Cheese Herb Loaf, 405
  Honey Oat Soda, 404

Pumpkin, All-American, 402
Spoonbread, Southern, 291
Wheat Berry Wheat, 406–7
See also Biscuits, Muffins
Breakfast Black Bean and Egg Burritos, 207
Breakfast Corn Cakes, 354–55
Breakfasts, 351–83. *See also* Cereal; Granola
Broccoli
  Cavatelli with Chickpeas and, 258
  Pilaf, Curried Rice and, 165
  Ragout, Quick Cannellini and, 242
  Risotto, Cheddar-, 159
  Sautéed Cauliflower and, with Chickpeas, 211
  Salad, Lemony Slaw Rice, 112
  Sesame Stir-Fried, and Brown Rice, 184
Broccoli Rabe, Orecchiette with Chickpeas and, 259
Broth(s), 13, 61
  Chicken, 97
  Mushroom, 96
  Vegetable, 95
Brown rice, 8, 10, 12
  Baked, 151
  Bread, 403
  and Lentils, 329
  Muffins, Berry, 394
  Pancakes, 359
  Pilaf
    Mixed Grain, 172
    Wild Rice and, 171
  Sesame Stir-fried Broccoli and, 184
  Squares, Zucchini, 185
  Steamed, 147
  See also Rice
Buckwheat, 25–26
  Basic Roasted, 275
  Cereal, Hot-Pear, 367
  groats, 25–26
  Kasha
    Basic, 274
    with Bow Ties, 305

with Wild Mushrooms, Leeks, and
Dill, 306
Muffins, Corn, 388
Bulgur wheat, 31
Basic Cooked, 276
Bean Burger, Basic, 348
Pilaf with Creamy Dill Sauce, 289
Tabouli, 103
Two-Bean Chili with, 334
Burgers
Basic Bean, 348
Falafel, 214–15
Lentil, 330
Roasted Veggie, 350
Wheat Berry Bean Burgers, 349
Burritos
Black Bean-Cheese, 239
Breakfast Black Bean and Egg, 207
Grilled Veggie, 240–41
Pinto Chili-Cheese, 238–39
Smoky Black Bean, 206
Buttermilk
Curried Spinach with Chickpeas, 213
Dress, Orange, 102
Pancakes, Amaranth, 358
Butternut Squash
Risotto with, 156
Soup with Black Beans and Cilantro,
77

Cabbage
Rice-Stuffed, in Sweet and Sour
Sauce, 186–87
Fried Rice
Chinese Vegetable, 180
Nasi Goreng (Indonesian), 182–83
Risotto with Caramelized Onions
and, 157
Salad, Kimchee Rice with Tofu, 116
Soup, Tomato-, with Lima Beans, 84
Cake
Amaranth
Chocolate Spice, 422
Pound, 421
Blueberry Corn, 423

Chocolate Chip—Banana Oat, 426
Grand Marnier Rice Torte, 442
Lemon-Berry Couscous, 424
Maple-Apple Oat, 427
Orange Marmalade-Millet Crunch,
425
Whole-Grain Jam Squares, 420
Calmati rice, 8
Cannellini beans, 6, 16, 23
Kale with Garlic and, 243
Ragout, Quick Broccoli and, 242
Salad
Artichoke Pasta, with Basil
Vinaigrette, 141
Tomato, and Arugula with Roasted
Garlic Vinaigrette, 138
Soup
Minestrone alla Genovese, 93
Minestrone with Greens, 94
Tomato, with Fennel and, 92
Quick Garlicky, 89
Quick Roasted Red Pepper and, 90
Spread
Herbed, 44
Roasted Garlic, Red Pepper, and,
45
See also White kidney beans
Caramelized Onion and Kidney Bean
Spread, 42
Caribbean Rice Pilaf, 166–67
Cashew-Honey Granola, 380
Casserole
Black Bean Corn Bread, 338
Cowboy Beans 'n' Corn Bread,
344–45
Vegetable Tamale Pie, 346–47
Cauliflower
Curried Chickpeas with Tomato
and, 212
Sautéed Broccoli and, with
Chickpeas, 211
Cavatelli with Broccoli and Chickpeas,
258
Cereal
Barley
Honey-Orange Porridge, 366

Cereal *(cont'd)*
    Hot, 365
        Buckwheat Pear, Hot, 367
        Chinese Congee, 375
        Cracked Wheat, 377
        Granola
            Blueberry Morning, 382–83
            Cashew-Honey, 380
            Cherry-Almond, 378
            Coconut-Almond, 379
            Fruit-and-Nut, 381
        Grits, Creamy Sweet Breakfast, 368
        Millet Porridge, 369
        Oatmeal
            Creamy, 370
            Old-fashioned Steel-cut, 371
            Toasted Steel-cut, 372
        Rice, Hot, 373
            Maple, 374
        Wheat, Hot, 376
Cheddar cheese
    Burritos
        Grilled Veggie, 240–41
        Black Bean-Cheese, 239
        Pinto Chili-Cheese, 238–39
    Dip, Cheesy Black Bean, 38
    Enchiladas, Pinto Bean and, 340–41
    Grits
        Soufflé, 304
        Spinach, 303
    Mexican Torte, 343
    Nachos Supreme, 342
    Risotto, -Broccoli, 159
Cheese. *See* Cheddar cheese; Feta;
    Fontina; Monterey jack; Mozarella;
    Parmesan
Cherry
    -Almond Granola, 378
    Fruity Couscous Dessert Timbales,
    429
Chicken
    Broth, 97
    Couscous
        Egyptian Slow-simmered Stew on,
        297
        Spicy Vegetable and, 332–33

    Paella with Sausage and, 162
    Pilaf, Caribbean Rice, with, 167
    Risotto with, Golden, 155
Chickpeas, 15, 16, 22
    Burgers, Roasted Veggie, 350
    Couscous, Spicy Vegetable, 332
    Curried
        Cauliflower with Tomato, 212
        Mixed Vegetable, 327
        Spinach with, 213
    Falafel, 214–15
    Hummus, 39
        Curried, 41
        Roasted Red Pepper, 40
    Pasta with
        Cavatelli with Broccoli and, 258
        Orecchiette with Broccoli Rabe
        and, 259
        Penne with Spinach and, Baked,
        257
        Pesto, with Chickpeas and
        Tomatoes, 262
        Rotini with Tomato-Vegetable
        Sauce and, 260
        Ziti with Tomatoes, Feta, and, 261
    Quick Middle Eastern, 210
    Rice with, Saffron, 326
    Salad
        Lemony Couscous, with Feta and,
        105
        with Tomatoes and Feta, 128
    Sautéed Broccoli and Cauliflower
    with, 211
    Snacks, Crunchy, 56
    Soup, Moroccan Rice and, 78
Chili
    Almost Mom's Quick, 217
    Black Bean, with Wheat Berries, 335
    Burritos, Pinto Chili-Cheese, 238–39
    Mac, 268
    Two-Bean, with Bulgur, 334
    Vegetarian, for a Crowd, 220
    White Bean
        Roasted Garlic, 245
        Verde, 244
Chinese Congee, 375

Chinese rice, 9
Chinese Vegetable Fried Rice, 180
Chipotle chiles
  Baked Beans
    Honey-Mustard, 230
    Old-Fashioned, 229
  Dressing
    -Honey Vinaigrette, 122
    -Lime, 129
Chirashi Sushi, 174–75
Chocolate
  Cake
    Amaranth Spice, 422
    Chip–Banana Oat, 426
  Cookies
    Peanut Butter, 419
    Peanut Butter–Oatmeal, 418
  Muffins, Chunky Monkey, 395
  Pancakes, -Banana, 357
  Pudding, Rich Rice, 441
Chunky Monkey Muffins, 395
Cilantro
  Butternut Squash Soup with Black
    Beans and, 77
  Cream, Black Bean Tostadas with,
    337
  Pesto, with Rotini and Black Beans,
    256
Citrus Vinaigrette, 110
Coconut (coconut milk)
  Granola, -Almond, 379
  Chews
    Oatmeal, 416
    Tropical, 417
  Curry, Mixed Vegetable, 327
  Pudding
    Almond Rice Torte, 443–44
    Cream Rice Dream, 440
    Strawberry Rice, 438
    Piña Colada Rice, 437
  Soup
    Black Bean, with Indian Spices, 76
    Butternut Squash, with Black
      Beans and Cilantro, 77
    Curried Red Lentil, 82
Cookies

Coconut-Oatmeal Chews, 416
Maple-Apple Oatmeal, 415
Mixed-Grain Raisin, 413
Oatmeal Fruit, 414
Peanut Butter–Chocolate Chip, 419
Peanut Butter–Oatmeal Chocolate
  Chip, 418
Triple A Oatmeal Cookies, 412
Tropical Chews, 417
Whole-Grain Jam Squares, 420
Corn, 26–27
  Bread, Corny, 399
  Cakes, Red Pepper, 290
  Risotto, Harvest, 160
  Salad
    Smoky, Kidney Bean and, 129
    Southwestern Bean and, 120
    Tomato-, with Black Beans, 123
  Soup
    Black Bean with Red Peppers and,
      74
    Fresh Tomato-Rice, 70
  Succotash, 198
    with Smoked Turkey, 199
  See also Cornmeal; Grits; Hominy
Cornmeal, 26–27
  Biscuits, 398
    Four-Grain Biscuits, 397
  Bread
    All-American Pumpkin, 402
    Black Bean Casserole, 338
    Blueberry Corn Toasties, 401
    Roasted Pepper, 400
    Corny, 399
    Cowboy Beans 'n', 344–45
    Southern Spoonbread, 291
  Cake, Blueberry, 423
  Muffins
    Buckwheat, 388
    Orange Marmalade, 390
    Pineapple, 389
  Pancakes
    Breakfast Corn Cakes, 354–55
    Chocolate-Banana, 358
    Mix, Quantity, 361
    Old-Fashioned Johnnycakes, 362

Corn (cont'd)
  Red Pepper Corn Cakes, 290
  Strawberry-Banana, 356
  Tamale Pie, Vegetable, 346–47
  See also Polenta
Cottage Cheese Herb Loaf, 405
Couscous, 31
  Basic Cooked, 279
  Dessert
    Apple, 428
    Lemon Berry Cake, 424
    Timbales, Fruity, 429
  Egyptian Slow-Simmered
    Vegetables on, 296–97
  Pilaf, 294
  Salad
    and Black Bean, 104
    Lemony, with Chickpeas and Feta,
      105
    -Roasted Vegetables with, 300
  Spicy Vegetable, 332–33
  Stuffed Eggplant, 298–99
  Timbales, 295
Cowboy Beans 'n' Corn Bread, 344–45
Cowboy Corn Bread Casserole, 339
Cowboy Frijoles, 233
Cranberries, Wild Rice Salad with
  Walnuts and Dried, 110
Cranberry Beans, 16–17, 22
  Old Bay, 216
  Pasta
    Pesto with, 263
    Fresh, with Tomatoes, Rosemary,
      and, 250–51
  Soup
    Spinach-Bean, 80
    Ton-o'-Garlic, 79
Creamy Oatmeal, 370
Creamy Sweet Breakfast Grits, 368
Crisp
  Apple Crunch, 431
  Honey Apple, 430
  Strawberry-Rhubarb Crumble, 432
Crispy Vanilla Oat Waffles, 363
Crockpots, 21–22
Cuban Black Beans, 202

Cuban Yellow Rice and Black Beans,
  324
Curried
  Cauliflower and Chickpeas with
    Tomato, 212
  Hummus, 41
  Mixed Vegetable Curry, 327
  Pilaf, Rice and Broccoli, 165
  Salad, Rice and Fruit with Mango
    Chutney Dressing, 114–15
  Soup, Red Lentil, 82
  Spinach with Chickpeas, 213

Desserts, 409–44
Diet for a Small Planet, 2, 312
Dill
  Creamy Sauce, Barley Pilaf with, 289
  Fresh Lima Beans with Lemon and,
    194
  Kasha with Wild Mushrooms, Leeks,
    and, 306
  Mediterranean Fresh Lima Beans
    and Tomatoes and, 196
  Salad
    Mediterranean Tomato-Rice with
      Feta and, 111
    White Bean with Tomatoes, 140
Dips and spreads
  Black Bean
    Cheesy, 38
    Chunky Avocado, 36
    Piquant, 37
  Caramelized Onion and Kidney
    Bean Spread, 42
  Eggplant Caviar, 46
  Hummus, 39
    Curried, 41
    Roasted Red Pepper, 40
  Lima Bean, Egyptian-Style, 43
  Salsa, Grilled Tomato, with Black
    Beans, 35
  White Bean Spread
    Herbed, 44
    Roasted Garlic, Red Pepper, 45
Dressing, Hazelnut Wild Rice, 177

Dressing, Salad
  Chipotle-Lime, 131
  Japanese-Style, 113
  Mango Chutney, 114–15
  Orange Buttermilk, 102
  Southwestern, 120
  Yogurt-Salsa, 142
  Vinaigrette
    Basil, 141
    Chipotle-Honey, 122
    Citrus, 110
    Lemon-Garlic, 134
    Roasted Garlic, 138

Eggplant
  Caviar, 46
  Couscous-Stuffed, 298–99
Eggs
  Burritos, Breakfast Black Bean and, 207
  Huevos Rancheros, 204–5
  Soufflé, Cheese Grits, 304
  Spoonbread, Southern, 291
Egyptian Slow-Simmered Vegetables on Couscous, 296
Egyptian-Style Lima Bean Dip, 43
Enchiladas, Pinto Bean and Cheese, 340–41

Falafel, 214–15
Fava bean, 5, 15, 17
  Fresh, and New Potato Sauté, 193
  Penne with Fresh, 249
  Salad, Marinated, with Roasted Garlic and Onion, 130–31
Fennel
  Soup
    Mediterranean White Bean Vegetable with, 91
    Tomato, with White Beans and, 92
  White Bean Linguine with, 266
Feta cheese
  Salad
    Chickpea with Tomatoes and, 128

Mediterranean Tomato-Rice with Dill and, 111
  Lemony Couscous with Chickpeas and, 105
  Spanakorizzo, 178
  Ziti with Chickpeas, Tomatoes, and, 261
Fiesta Beans and Rice, 325
Fontina-Polenta Bites, 54
Four-Grain Biscuits, 397
French Country White Beans, 227
French green lentils, 17
  with Roasted Onions, 221
  Salad
    with Goat Cheese, 136–37
    with Lemon-Garlic Vinaigrette, 134
  Syrian
    Rishtah, 264
    in Spicy Tomato Sauce, 222
Fried Rice
  Chinese Vegetable, 180
  Nasi Goreng (Indonesian), 182–83
  Pork, 181
  Sesame Stir-Fried Broccoli and Brown Rice, 184
  Shrimp, 181
Frijoles, Cowboy, 233
Fruit
  Corn Cakes, Breakfast, 355
  Cookies
    Oatmeal, 414
    Tropical Chews, 417
  Fruity Couscous Dessert Timbales, 429
  Granola, Nut-and-, 381
  Salad, Curried Rice, with Mango Chutney Dressing, 114–15

Garlic
  Chili, Roasted White Bean, 245
  Kale with White Beans and, 243
  Polenta Squares, Broiled Cheese, 293
  Salad, Marinated Fava Bean, with Roasted Onion and, 130–31

Garlic (*cont'd*)
  Soup
    Cranberry Bean, Ton-o'-, 79
    Quick White Bean, 89–90
  Soy Nuts, Roasted, 57
  Spread, Red Pepper, White Bean,
    and Roasted, 45
  Timbales, Rice, 173
  Vinaigrette
    Lemon-, 134
    Roasted, 138
Gingered Red Lentil Soup with Sweet
    Potatoes, 83
Goat Cheese
  Orecchiette with Black Beans, Fresh
    Tomato Sauce, and, 254
  Quesadillas, Black Bean and, 48
  Salad
    Black Bean with, 124–25
    French Lentil Salad with, 136–37
  Turnovers, Black Bean, 49
Golden Nugget Squash, Millet-Stuffed,
    308
Grains
  breakfast cereals, 365–383
  buying and storing, 32
  cookies and cakes, 411–27
  muffins, biscuits and breads, 387–407
  types of, 23–31
  See also Beans and grains recipes;
    and specific grains
Grand Marnier Rice Torte, 442
Granola
  Apricot-Almond, 378
  Blueberry Morning, 382–83
  Cashew-Honey, 380
  Cherry-Almond, 378
  Coconut-Almond, 379
  Fruit-and-Nut, 381
Grape Leaves, Stuffed (Dolmades),
    50–51
Great Northern beans, 5, 19, 23. *See also*
    White beans
Green beans, 14
  Paella, Vegetarian, 162
  Salad

Three Bean, 133
Tomato, White Bean, and, with
    Basil and Mint, 135
Greens
  growing, 101
  Minestrone with, 94
  Penne with White Beans and, 267
  See also Arugula; Kale
Grits, 26, 27
  Basic, 281
  Breakfast Corn Cakes, 354–55
  Cheese Soufflé, 304
  Creamy Sweet Breakfast, 368
  Spinach Cheese, 303
Groats, 23. *See also* Buckwheat
Gumbo, Red Bean, 316–17

Hazelnut Wild Rice Dressing, 177
Herb
  Cottage Cheese Loaf, 405
  White Bean Spread, 44
Hominy, 26–27
  Salad, Pinto Bean and, 121
  Soup
    QuickPinto Bean-, 67
    Tomato, 68
  Stew, Black Bean and, 336
Honey
  -Apple Crisp, 430
  Baked Beans, Mustard-, 230
    Quick, 218
  Barley Porridge, Orange-, 366
  Granola, Cashew-, 380
  Soda Bread, Oat, 404
  Scones, Orange-, 396
  Vinaigrette, Chipotle-, 122
Hoppin' John, Vegetarian, 314–15
Huevos Rancheros, 204–5
Hummus, 39
  Curried, 41
  Roasted Red Pepper, 40

Indian Spices, Black Bean Soup with,
    76

Jam Squares, Whole-Grain, 420
Jamaican-Style Rice and Peas, 321
Japanese Red Rice and Beans, 320
Japanese rice, 9
Japanese-style Rice Salad, 113
Japanese Thick Rice Soup, 72
Japonica rice, 8
Jasmine rice, 8–9
Johnnycakes, Old-Fashioned, 362

Kale
    Barley Soup, 66
    Penne with White Beans and, 267
    with White Beans and Garlic, 243
Kasha, 25
    Basic, 274
    with Bowties, 305
    with Wild Mushrooms, Leeks, and
        Dill, 306
Khichiri, 331
Kidney beans, 15, 22
    Salad
        Marinated Vegetable, 132
        Smoky, Corn and, 129
    Spread, Caramelized Onion and, 42
    Stew, Sweet Potato and, 219
    See also Cannelini; Red Kidney
        Beans; White Beans
Kimchee Rice Salad with Tofu, 116

Lappe, Francis Moore, 2, 312
Lebanese Navy Beans with Tomatoes
    and Onion, 228
Leek
    Barley Soup, 65
    Kasha with Wild Mushrooms, Dill,
        and, 306
Lemon
    Cake, Berry Couscous, 424
    Fresh Lima Beans with Dill and, 194
    Pilaf, Pistachio, 161
    Risotto, Thyme with Asparagus, 158
    Salad
        Broccoli Slaw Rice, 112

Couscous with Chickpeas and
    Feta, 105
Vinaigrette
    Citrus, 110
    Garlic, 134
Lentils, 14, 15, 17, 18, 22
    Brown, 17
    Brown Rice and, 329
    Burgers, 330
    French Green, with Roasted Onions,
        221
    Red, Vegetable Stew, 223
    Salad
        French, with Goat Cheese, 136–37
        French, with Lemon-Garlic
            Vinaigrette, 134
    Soup
        Curried Red, 82
        Gingered Red, with Sweet
            Potatoes, 83
        Vegetable, 81
    Syrian
        in a Spicy Tomato Sauce, 222
        Mujdara (Lentils and Rice), 239
        Rishtah, 264
Lima bean, 15, 18, 22
    Dip, Egyptian-Style, 43
    Dried, Gratin, 224–25
    Fresh
        Braised with Summer Vegetables,
            197
        with Lemon and Dill, 194
        Mediterranean, and Tomatoes and
            Dill, 196
        Pasta with Summer Vegetables
            and, 252
        Sautéed with Thyme, 195
    Soup, Tomato-Cabbage with, 84
    Succotash, 198
        with Smoked Turkey, 199
    Tomato-Baked, 226
Lime-Chipotle Dressing, 129
Linguine, White Bean and Fennel,
    266
Long-grain rice, 8–10, 11
Louisiana Red Beans and Rice, 319

Macaroni, Chili Mac, 268
Mango
  Chutney Dressing, Curried Rice and
    Fruit Salad with, 114–15
  Fruity Couscous Dessert Timbales,
    429
  Tropical Chews, 417
Maple
  -Baked Banana, Crunchy, 433
  Baked Beans, 231
  Cake, -Apple Oat, 427
  Cereal, Hot Rice, 374
  Cookies, -Apple Oatmeal, 415
  Muffins, Apple-Oat, 392–93
Masa harina, 26, 27
Mediterranean Baked Rice, 179
Mediterranean Fresh Lima Beans and
    Tomatoes and Dill, 196
Mediterranean Tomato-Rice Salad with
    Feta and Dill, 111
Mediterranean Vegetable Soup with
    Barley, 62
Mediterranean White Bean Vegetable
    Soup with Fennel, 91
Medium-grain rice, 9, 11
Mesclun, 101
Mexican Black Bean Corn Bread
    Casserole, 339
Mexican Black Beans, 201
  -Cheese Burritos, 239
Mexican Torte, 343
Mexican Vegetable Sauté with Pink
    Beans, 232
Millet, 28
  Apple Crunch, 431
  Basic Cooked, 282
  Cake, Orange Marmalade Crunch,
    425
  Porridge, 369
  Salad, Sugar Snap, 106
  Squares, Whole-Grain Jam, 420
  Stir-Fry, 307
  -Stuffed Golden Nugget Squash, 308
Minestrone
  alla Genovese, 93
  with Greens, 94

Mint, Tomato, Green Bean, and White
    Bean Salad with Basil and, 135
Mixed Grain Pilaf, 172
Mixed Grain Raisin Cookies, 413
Mixed Vegetable Curry, 327
Monterey jack, Mexican Torte, 343
Moong Dahl Soup, 85
Moroccan Chickpea and Rice Soup, 78
Mozzarella cheese, Broiled Garlic-
    Cheese Polenta Squares, 293
Muffins
  Amaranth, 387
  Apple-Maple Oat, 392–93
  Brown Rice Berry, 394
  Buckwheat corn, 388
  Chunky Monkey, 395
  Honey-Orange Scones, 396
  Orange Marmalade Corn, 390
  Peachy Oat, 391
  Pineapple Corn, 389
Mung beans, 15, 18
  Moong Dahl Soup, 85
Mushroom
  Barley Risotto with Peas and Wild,
    288
  Kasha with Leeks, Dill, and Wild,
    306
  Soup
    Barley, 64
    Broth, 96
    Wild Rice and, 73
Mustard-Honey Baked Beans, 230
  Quick, 218

Nachos Supreme, 342
Nasi Goreng, 182–83
Navy beans, 5, 15, 19, 23
  Honey-Mustard Baked Beans, 230
  Lebanese, with Tomatoes and
    Onion, 228
  Maple Baked Beans, 231
  Old-Fashioned Baked Beans, 229
New World bean, 5–6
New World Quinoa Salad, 107
Nori Rolls

Smoked Salmon, 53
Vegetarian, 52, 53
Nuts
Dressing, Hazelnut Wild Rice, 177
Granola
Almond-Cherry, 378
Almond-Coconut, 379
Cashew-Honey, 380
Granola, Fruit-and-, 381
Pistachio Lemon Pilaf, 161
Rice Pudding, Almond, 435
Salad, Wild Rice with Walnuts and
Dried Cranberries, 110
Torte, Almond Coconut Rice, 443–44
Waffles, Banana Oat, 364

Oats and Oatmeal, 28–29
Bread
Cottage Cheese Herb Loaf, 405
Honey Oat Soda, 404
Biscuits, Four-Grain, 397
bran, 29
Cake
Maple Apple Oat, 427
Chocolate Chip–Banana Oat
Cake, 426
Cereal
Creamy, 370
Old-Fashioned Steel-cut, 371
Toasted Steel-cut, 372
Cookies
Coconut Chews, 416
Fruit, 414
Maple Apple, 415
Mixed Grain Raisin, 413
Peanut Butter–Chocolate Chip, 419
Peanut Butter–Oatmeal Chocolate
Chip, 418
Triple A, 412
Tropical Chews, 417
Whole-Grain Jam Squares, 420
Crisp, Honey Apple, 430
Crumble, Strawberry-Rhubarb, 432
Crunch, Apple, 431
Granola

Blueberry Morning, 382–83
Cashew-Honey, 380
Cherry-Almond, 378
Coconut-Almond, 379
Fruit-and-Nut, 381
Muffins
Apple-Maple, 392–93
Peachy, 391
rolled, 28–29
Scones, Honey-Orange, 396
steel-cut, 29
Waffles
Banana Nut, 364
Crispy Vanilla, 363
Old Bay Cranberry Beans, 216
Onion(s)
Lebanese Navy Beans with
Tomatoes and, 228
French Green Lentils with Roasted,
221
Risotto with Cabbage and
Caramelized, 157
Salad, Marinated Fava Bean, with
Roasted Garlic and, 130–31
Spread, Kidney Bean and
Caramelized, 42
Orange
Barley Porridge, Honey-, 366
Cake, Marmalade Millet Crunch, 425
Dressing
Buttermilk, 102
Citrus Vinaigrette, 110
Muffins, Marmalade Corn, 390
Scones, –Honey, 396
Orecchiette
with Black Beans, Goat Cheese, and
Fresh Tomato Sauce, 254
with Broccoli Rabe and Chickpeas,
259
Orzo–Wild Rice Pilaf, 170

Paella
with Chicken and Sausage, 162
Seafood, 163
Vegetarian, 162

Pancakes
  Amaranth Buttermilk, 358
  Black Bean
    Potato Cakes, 208
    Sweet Potato Cakes, 209
  Corn Cakes
    Breakfast, 354–55
    Red Pepper, 290
  Brown Rice, 359
  Old-fashioned Johnnycakes, 362
  Quantity Mix, 361
  Strawberry-Banana, 356
  Wild Rice, 360
Parmesan, Cheesy Soft Polenta with
  Rich Tomato Sauce, 292
Parsley and Wheat Berry Salad, 109
Pasta
  and Black Beans in Saffron Tomato
    Sauce, 253
  Bowties
    Kasha with, 305
    with White Beans and Fresh
      Tomato Sauce, 265
  Cavatelli with Broccoli and
    Chickpeas, 258
  Cranberry Beans, Fresh, with
    Tomatoes, Rosemary, and, 250–51
  Lima Beans, Fresh, and Summer
    Vegetables with, 252
  Linguine
    Syrian Rishtah, 264
    White Bean and Fennel, 266
  Macaroni, Chili Mac, 268
  Orecchiette
    with Black Beans, Goat Cheese,
      and Fresh Tomato Sauce, 254
    with Broccoli Rabe and Chickpeas,
      259
  Penne
    Baked with Spinach and
      Chickpeas, 257
    with Fresh Fava Beans, 249
    with White Beans and Greens, 267
    Pesto
      with Chickpeas and Tomatoes,
      262
      Cilantro, Rotini with Black
      Beans, 256
    with Cranberry Beans, 263
  Pilaf,
    Pistachio Lemon, 16
    Wild Rice–Orzo, 170
  Rotini
    with Chickpeas and Tomato-
      Vegetable Sauce, 260
    Cilantro Pesto with Black Beans,
      256
  Salad
    Artichoke with Basil Vinaigrette,
      141
    Wagon Train, 142
  Soup
    Minestrone alla Genovese, 93
    Minestrone with Greens, 94
  Tex-Mex Black Bean Pasta, 255
  Ziti with Chickpeas, Tomatoes, and
    Feta, 261
Pea beans, 19, 23
  Maple Baked Beans, 231
  Old-fashioned Baked Beans,
    229
Peachy Corn Cakes, 355
Peachy Oat Muffins, 393
Peanut Butter–Chocolate Chip
  Cookies, 419
  Oatmeal, 418
Pear
  Corn Cakes, 355
  Hot Buckwheat-Cereal, 367
Peas, 15
  Barley Risotto with Wild
    Mushrooms and, 288
  Brown and Wild Rice Pilaf, 171
  Risi e Bisi, 71
  Vegetable Pilau, 164
  See also Split peas
Penne
  with Fresh Fava Beans, 249
  with Spinach and Chickpeas, Baked,
    257
  with White Beans and Greens,
    267

Pesto
Basil, 263
Cilantro, 256
Pasta with Chickpeas and Tomatoes, 262
Pasta with Cranberry Beans, 263
Risotto, 153
Pilaf, 13
Barley
Baked, 286
with Creamy Dill Sauce, 289
-Vermicelli, Toasted, 285
-Wild Rice, 287
Couscous, 294
Cracked Wheat
Simple, 301
Tomato-Vegetable, 302
Mixed Grain, 172
Quinoa, 309
Rice
Brown and Wild, 171
Caribbean, 166–67
Curried Broccoli, 165
Pistachio Lemon Pilaf, 161
Tex-Mex Vermicelli, 169
Vegetable Pilau, 164
Vermicelli, 168
Wild Rice–Orzo, 170
Pineapple
Corn Muffins, 389
Dessert Timbales, Fruity
Couscous, 429
Pudding
Black Rice, 439
Piña Colada Rice, 437
Salad, Tropical Black Bean, 126
Tropical Chews, 417
Pink beans, 18, 22
Mexican Vegetable Sauté with, 232
Pinto beans, 5, 15, 18–19, 23
Barbecued
15-minute, 235
Spicy Slow-baked, 234
Burritos
Chili-Cheese, 238–39
Smoky Burritos, 206

Enchiladas, Pinto Bean and, 340–41
Frijoles, Cowboy, 233
Huevos Rancheros, 204–5
Nachos Supreme, 342
Refried, 237
Salad
Hominy and, 121
Southwestern Corn and, 120
Soup, Quick Hominy-, 67
Pistachio Lemon Rice, 161
Polenta
Basic, 277
Double-Boiler (Foolproof), 278
Cheesy Soft, with Rich Tomato Sauce, 292
defined, 27
-Fontina Bites, 55
Squares, Broiled Garlic-Cheese, 293
Popcorn, 26
Pizza-Flavored, 52
Pork Fried Rice, 181
Posole, 27, 68
Potato
Cakes, Black Bean, 208
Huevos Rancheros, 204–5
Mixed Vegetable Curry, 327
New, and Fresh Fava Bean Sauté, 193
Pudding
Almond Rice, 435
Baked Rice, 434
Black Rice, 439
Coconut Cream Rice Dream, 440
Piña Colada Rice, 437
Rich Chocolate Rice, 441
Strawberry-Coconut Rice, 438
Vanilla Yogurt Rice, 436
Pumpkin Bread, All-American, 402

Quesadillas, Black Bean and Goat Cheese, 48
Quinoa, 29–30
Pilaf, 309
Salad, New World, 107
Tabouli, 108

Raisin
  Mixed Grain Cookies, 413
  Oatmeal Fruit Cookies, 414
Raspberry
  Corn Cakes, 355
  Fruity Couscous Dessert Timbales,
    429
Red kidney beans, 5, 19
  Baked, Quick Honey-Mustard, 218
  Burger
    Basic, 348
    Wheat Berry, 349
  Chili
    Almost Mom's Quick, 217
    Two-Bean, with Bulgur, 334
    Vegetarian, for a Crowd, 220
  Gumbo, 316–17
  and Rice
    Fiesta, 325
    Jamaican-Style, 321
    Louisiana, 319
    Quick Louisiana, 318
  Salad, Three Bean, 133
  Stew, Sweet Potato and, 219
Red lentils, 17–18
  Soup
    Curried, 82
    Gingered, with Sweet Potatoes, 83
  Stew, Vegetable, 223
Red Pepper
  Corn Bread, Roasted, 400
  Corn Cakes, 290
  Soup
    Black Bean, with Corn and, 74
    Quick White Bean and, 90
  Spread
    Garlic, White Bean and, 45
    Hummus, 40
Refried Beans
  Black Beans, 203
  Burritos
    Smoky, 206
    Grilled Veggie, 240–41
  Huevos Rancheros, 204–5
  Mexican Torte, 343
  Nachos Supreme, 342

Pinto Beans, 237
Rhubarb-Strawberry Crumble, 432
Rice, 7–13
  Baked, 12–13
    Brown, 151
    Mediterranean, 179
    White, 150
  Basic Cooked Wild, 152
  Bread, Brown Rice, 403
  Cereal
    Chinese Congee, 375
    Hot, 373
    Hot Maple, 374
  Dressing, Hazelnut Wild, 177
  Fried
    Chinese Vegetable, 180
    Nasi Goreng, 182–83
    Pork, 181
    Shrimp, 181
    Stir-, Broccoli and Brown Rice,
      Sesame, 184
  Muffins, Brown Rice Berry, 394
  Paella
    with Chicken and Sausage, 162
    Seafood, 163
    Vegetarian, 162
  Pancakes, Brown Rice, 359
  Pilaf
    Barley-Wild, 287
    Brown and Wild, 171
    Caribbean, 166–67
    Curried Broccoli, 165
    Mixed Grain, 172
    Orzo—Wild, 170
    Vegetable Pilau, 164
    Vermicelli, 168
    Vermicelli, Tex-Mex, 169
  Pistachio Lemon, 161
  Pudding
    Almond, 435
    Baked, 434
    Black, 439
    Chocolate, Rich, 441
    Coconut Almond Torte, 443–44
    Coconut Cream Dream, 440
    Grand Marnier Torte, 442

Piña Colada, 437
Strawberry Coconut, 438
Vanilla Yogurt, 436
Salad
Curried, with Fruit and Mango
Chutney Dressing, 114–15
Japanese-style, 113
Kimchee, with Tofu, 116
Lemony Broccoli Slaw, 112
Mediterranean Tomato-, with Feta
and Dill, 111
Southwestern Bean and, 117
Yellow, and Black Bean, 118–19
Seasoned, 174–75
Soup
Chickpea and, Moroccan, 78
Japanese Thick, 72
Mushroom and Wild Rice, 73
Risi e Bisi, 71
Tomato-, Fresh, 70
Tomato-, Spanish, 69
Spanakorizzo, 178
Squares, Zucchini Brown Rice,
185
Steamed, 12
Black, 148
Brown, 147
Sticky, 149
White, 146
-Stuffed Cabbage in Sweet and Sour
Sauce, 186–87
Stuffed Grape Leaves, 50–51
Sushi
Chirashi, 174–75
Vegetarian Nori Rolls, 52–53
Timbales, Garlic, 173
Yellow
and Black Bean Salad, 118–19
Cuban, and Black Beans, 324
Festive, 176
See also Risotto
Risotto, 9, 13
alla Milanese, 154–55
Barley, with Wild Mushrooms and
Peas, 288
Butternut Squash with, 156

Caramelized Onions and Cabbage
with, 157
Cheddar-Broccoli, 159
Corn Harvest, 160
Golden
with Chicken, 154
with Shrimp, 154
Lemon-Thyme, with Asparagus, 158
Pesto, 183
Roll-Ups, Black Bean, 47
Rosemary, Fresh Cranberry Beans with
Pasta, Tomatoes, and, 250–51
Rotini with Chickpeas and Tomato-
Vegetable Sauce, 260

Saffron
Rice with Chickpeas, 326
Risotto alla Milanese, 154–55
Tomato Sauce, Pasta and Black
Beans in, 253
Salad, 99–142
Barley Vegetable, with Orange
Buttermilk Dressing, 102
Bean and Corn, Southwestern, 120
Black Bean
with Chipotle-Honey Vinaigrette,
122
and Couscous, 104
with Goat Cheese, 124–25
Tomato-Corn with, 123
Tropical, 126
Black-eyed Pea, Summertime, 127
Chickpea, with Tomatoes and Feta,
128
Couscous
Lemony, with Chickpeas and
Feta, 105
and Black Bean, 104
Fava Bean, Marinated with Roasted
Garlic and Onion, 130–31
French Lentil
with Goat Cheese, 136–37
with Lemon-Garlic Vinaigrette,
134
growing greens for, 101

Saffron (cont'd)
Hominy and Pinto Bean, 121
Kidney Bean
Smoky Corn and, 129
Three Bean, 133
Pasta
Artichoke, with Basil Vinaigrette,
141
Wagon Train, 142
Quinoa
Tabouli, 108
New World, 107
Rice
Curried, and Fruit with Mango
Chutney Dressing, 114–15
Japanese-style, 113
Kimchee, with Tofu, 116
Lemony Broccoli Slaw, 112
Mediterranean Tomato-, with Feta
and Dill, 111
Southwestern Bean and, 117
Yellow, and Black Bean, 118–19
Wild, with Walnuts and Dried
Cranberries, 110
Sugar Snap Millet, 106
Tabouli, 103
Wheat Berry and Parsley, 109
White Bean
with Sun-dried Tomatoes, 139
Tomato, Arugula, and, with Roasted
Garlic Vinaigrette, 138
Tomatoes with Dilled, 140
Tomato, Green Bean, and, with Basil
and Mint, 137
Salsa, Grilled Tomato, with Black
Beans, 35
Sauce
Berry, 429
Creamy Dill, 289
Curried Buttermilk, 213
Enchilada, 340
Tahini-yogurt, 214–15
Tomato
Rich, 292
Fresh, 254, 265
Saffron, 253

Spicy, 222
Sweet and Sour, 186–87
-Vegetable, 260
Sausage
Caribbean Rice Pilaf with, 167
and Couscous-stuffed Eggplant, 299
Paella with Chicken and, 162
Soup, Quick Garlicky White Bean, 90
Scones, Honey–Orange, 396
Seafood Paella, 163
Sesame Stir-Fried Broccoli and Brown
Rice, 184
Shell Beans, Braised Fresh, 192
Short-grain rice, 9, 10, 11
Shrimp
Fried Rice, 181
Golden Risotto with, 155
Nasi Goreng, 183
Seafood Paella, 163
Slaw
Barbecued Bean Sandwiches with,
236
Lemony Broccoli Rice Salad, 112
Smoked Salmon Nori Rolls, 54
Smoky Black Bean and Tomato Soup,
75
Smoky Black Bean Burritos, 206
Smoky Corn and Kidney Bean Salad,
129
Soldier beans, 19, 23
Soufflé, Cheese Grits, 304
Soup, 59–97
Barley-
Kale, 66
Leek, 65
Mushroom, 64
Vegetable, Hearty, 63
Vegetable, Mediterranean, 62
Black Bean
Butternut Squash, with Cilantro
and, 77
with Indian Spices, 76
with Red Peppers and Corn, 74
Smoky, and Tomato, 75
Chickpea and Rice, Moroccan, 78
Cranberry Bean, Ton-o'-Garlic, 79

Hominy
  Pinto Bean, Quick, 67
  Tomato, 68
Lentil-
  Curried Red, 82
  Gingered Red, with Sweet
    Potatoes, 83
  Vegetable, 81
Minestrone
  alla Genovese, 93
  with Greens, 94
Moong Dahl, 85
Rice
  Fresh Tomato-, 70
  Japanese Thick, 72
  Risi e Bisi, 71
  Spanish Tomato-, 69
  Wild, and Mushroom, 73
Spinach-Bean, 80
Split Pea, 86
  Barley, 87
  Vegetable, 88
Tomato
  and Black Bean, Smoky, 75
  -Cabbage with Lima Beans, 84
  Hominy, 68
  -Rice, Fresh, 70
  -Rice, Spanish, 69
  White Bean, with Fennel, 92
White Bean
  Garlicky, Quick, 89
  Roasted Red Pepper and, Quick,
    90
  Tomato, with Fennel, 92
  Vegetable with Fennel,
    Mediterranean, 91
Southern Spoonbread, 291
Southwestern Bean and Corn Salad,
  120
Southwestern Rice and Bean Salad, 117
Soybeans, 15, 19, 23
  Garlic-roasted, 57
Spanakorizzo, 178
Spanish Tomato-Rice Soup, 69
Spinach
  Cheese Grits, 303

Curried, with Chickpeas, 213
Penne Baked with Chickpeas and,
  257
Soup
  -Bean, 80
  Minestrone with, 94
Spanakorizzo, 178
Split peas, 23
  Khichiri, 331
  -Soup, 86
  –Barley, 87
  –Vegetable, 88
Spoonbread, Southern, 291
Stew
  Black Bean and Hominy, 336
  Egyptian Slow-Simmered, on
    Couscous, 297
  Kidney Bean and Sweet Potato, 219
  Red Lentil Vegetable, 223
Sticky rice, 9
  Steamed, 149
Stir-fry
  Millet, 307
  Sesame Broccoli and Brown Rice,
    184
Strawberry
  Crumble, Rhubarb-, 432
  Dessert Timbales, Fruity Couscous,
    429
  Muffins, Brown Rice, 394
  Pancakes, -Banana, 356
  Pudding, Coconut Rice, 438
Succotash, 198
  with Smoked Turkey, 199
Sugar Snap Millet Salad, 106
Sushi
  Chirashi, 174–75
  Nori Rolls, 52–53
Sweet and Sour Sauce, Rice-Stuffed
  Cabbage in, 186–87
Sweet Potatoes
  Cakes, Black Bean, 209
  Soup, Gingered Red Lentil with, 83
Stew
  Black Bean and, 336
  Kidney Bean and, 219

Syrian Lentils in a Spicy Tomato Sauce, 222
Syrian Mujdara, 239
Syrian Rishtah, 264

Tabouli, 103
    Quinoa, 108
Tamale Pie, Vegetable, 346–47
Texmati rice, 8
Tex-Mex Black Bean Pasta, 255
Tex-Mex Vermicelli Rice Pilaf, 169
Thai fragrant rice, 9
Thai sweet black rice, 8
Three Bean Salad, 133
Thyme
    -Lemon Risotto with Asparagus, 158
    Sautéed Fresh Lima Beans with, 195
Timbale
    Couscous, 295
        Fruity Dessert, 429
    Garlic Rice, 173
Tofu
    Kimchee Rice Salad with, 116
    Sesame Stir-fried Broccoli and
        Brown Rice, 184
Tomato
    Cranberry Beans, Fresh, with Pasta,
        Rosemary, and, 250–51
    Curried Cauliflower and Chickpeas
        with, 212
    Lebanese Navy Beans with Onion
        and, 228
    Lima Beans
        -Baked 226
        Mediterranean, with Dill, 196
    Pasta with Fresh Lima Beans and
        Summer Vegetables, 252
    Pesto
        Pasta with Chickpeas and, 262
        Risotto, 155
    Pilaf, -Vegetable Cracked Wheat, 302
    Salad
        Chickpea with Feta, 128
        Corn with Black Beans, 125
        Green Bean, and White Bean, with

        Basil and Mint, 135
        Rice, with Feta and Dill,
            Mediterranean, 111
        White Bean, and Arugula with
            Roasted Garlic Vinaigrette, 138
        White Bean, Dilled, 140
        White Bean, with Sun-dried, 139
Salsa, Grilled, with Black Beans, 35
Sauce
    Fresh, Bow Ties with White Beans
        and, 265
    Fresh, Orecchiette with Black
        Beans, Goat Cheese, and, 254
    Rich, Cheesy Soft Polenta with,
        292
    Saffron, Pasta and Black Beans in,
        253
    Spicy, Syrian Lentils in, 222
    -Vegetable, Rotini with Chickpeas
        and, 260
Soup
    Black Bean, Smoky, 75
    Cabbage with Lima Beans, 84
    Hominy, 68
    Rice, Fresh, 70
    Rice, Spanish, 69
    with White Beans and Fennel, 92
Succotash, 198–99
Syrian Rishtah, 264
Ziti with Chickpeas, Feta, and, 261
Torte
    Coconut Almond Rice, 443–44
    Grand Marnier Rice, 442
    Mexican, 343
Tostados, Black Bean, with Cilantro
    Cream, 337
Triple A Oatmeal Cookies, 412
Tropical Black Bean Salad, 126
Tropical Chews, 417
Turkey
    Hoppin' John, 315
    Split Pea Soup with Smoked, 86
    Succotash with Smoked, 199
    Wild Rice Salad, 111
Turnovers, Black Bean, 49
Two-Bean Chili with Bulgur, 334

Valencia rice, 9
Vanilla
    Oat Waffles, Crispy, 363
    Yogurt Rice Pudding, 436
Vegetable
    Burgers, Roasted Veggie, 350
    Couscous
        Egyptian Slow-simmered, on, 296
            with Roasted, 300
        Spicy, 332–33
    Fall, Barley with Roasted, 284
    Fried Rice, Chinese, 180
    Mixed Curry, 327
    Pilaf, Tomato-cracked Wheat, 302
    Pilau, 164
    Sauce, Tomato, Rotini with
        Chickpeas and, 260
    Sauté with Pink Beans, Mexican, 232
    Stew, Red Lentil, 223
    Summer
        Braised Fresh Lima Beans with,
        197
        Pasta with Fresh Lima Beans and,
        252
    Tamale Pie, 346–47
    Salad
        Marinated, with Kidney Beans,
            132
        Barley, with Orange Buttermilk
            Dressing, 102
    Soup
        Broth, 95
        Hearty Barley-, 63
        Lentil, 81
        Mediterranean White Bean, with
            Fennel, 91
        Mediterranean, with Barley, 62
        Minestrone with Greens, 94
        Minestrone alla Genovese, 93
        Split Pea, 88
Vegetarian
    Chili for a Crowd, 220
    Grilled Burritos, 240–41
    Hoppin' John, 314–15
    Nori Rolls, 52–53
    Paella, 162

Vermicelli Pilaf
    Rice, 168
        Tex-Mex, 169
    Toasted Barley-, 285

Waffles
    Banana-Nut Oat, 364
    Crispy Vanilla Oat, 363
Wagon Train Pasta Salad, 142
Walnuts, Wild Rice Salad with Dried
    Cranberries and, 110
Wehani rice, 9, 11
    Mixed Grain Pilaf, 172
Wheat, 30–31
    berries, 23, 30
        Basic Cooked, 283
        Bean Burgers, 349
        Black Bean Chili with, 335
        Eggplant Caviar, 46
        Parsley Salad, 109
        Roasted Veggie Burgers, 350
        Wheat Bread, 406–7
    Cereal, Hot, 376
    Cookies
        Mixed Grain Raisin, 413
        Peanut Butter–Chocolate Chip, 419
    cracked, 30–31
        Basic, 280
        Cereal, 377
        Mixed Grain Pilaf, 172
        Simple Pilaf, 301
        Tomato-Vegetable Pilaf, 302
    flakes, 31
        Blueberry Granola, 382–83
        Cashew-Honey Granola, 380
        Coconut-Almond Granola, 379
        Fruit-and-Nut Granola, 381
White beans (Haricots), 19, 23
    Bow Ties with Fresh Tomato Sauce
        and, 265
    Chili
        Roasted Garlic, 245
        Verde, 244
    and Fennel Linguine, 266
    French Country, 227

White beans (cont'd)
  Kale with Garlic and, 243
  Penne with Greens and, 267
  Salad
    Artichoke Pasta, with Basil
      Vinaigrette, 141
    Dilled, with Tomatoes, 140
    with Sun-dried Tomatoes, 139
    Tomato, Arugula, and, with
      Roasted Garlic Vinaigrette, 138
    Tomato, Green Bean, and, with
      Basil and Mint, 135
  Soup
    Mediterranean Vegetable with
      Fennel, 91
    Quick Garlicky, 89–90
    Quick Roasted Red Pepper, 90
    Tomato with Fennel, 92
  See also Cannellini
Whole-Grain Jam Squares, 420
Wild rice, 9, 10
  Basic Cooked, 152
  Dressing, Hazelnut, 177
  Pancakes, 360
  Pumpkin Bread, All-American, 402
  Pilaf
    Barley, 287

  Brown Rice and, 171
  Orzo, 170
  Salad
    Turkey, 111
    with Walnuts and Dried
      Cranberries, 110
  Soup, Mushroom, 73

Yellow-eyed peas, 19, 23
Yellow summer squash
  Pasta with Fresh Lima Beans and
    Summer Vegetables, 252
  Pesto Risotto, 153
Yogurt
  Cilantro Cream, Black Bean Tostadas
    with, 337
  Creamy Dill Sauce, 289
  Rice Pudding
    Piña Colada, 437
    Vanilla, 436
  -salsa dressing, 142

Ziti with Chickpeas, Tomatoes, and
  Feta, 261
Zucchini Brown Rice Squares, 185